Professional Learning Communities at Work® and High Reliability Schools™

Cultures of Continuous Learning

Solution Tree | Press

a division of

Solution Tree

555 North Morton Street
Bloomington, IN 47404
800.733.6786 (toll free) / 812.336.7700
FAX: 812.336.7790

email: info@SolutionTree.com
SolutionTree.com

Visit **go.SolutionTree.com/PLCbooks** to download the free reproducibles in this book.

Printed in the United States of America

Library of Congress Cataloging-in-Publication Data

Names: Eaker, Robert E., editor.
Title: Professional learning communities at work and high reliability
    schools : cultures of continuous learning / Editors: Robert Eaker and
    Robert J. Marzano ; Contributors, Mario Acosta, Toby Boss, Robert Eaker,
    William M. Ferriter, Heather Friziellie, Tammy Heflebower, Jan K. Hoegh,
    Marc Johnson, Timothy D. Kanold, Robert J. Marzano, Mike Mattos, Anthony
    Muhammad, Cameron L. Rains, Mike Ruyle, Julie A. Schmidt, Eric Twadell,
    Philip B. Warrick.
Description: Bloomington, IN : Solution Tree Press, [2020] | Series:
    Leading edge | Includes bibliographical references and index.
Identifiers: LCCN 2019036602 (print) | LCCN 2019036603 (ebook) | ISBN
    9781949539639 (hardcover) | ISBN 9781949539646 (ebook)
Subjects: LCSH: Teachers--Professional relationships. |
    Teachers--In-service training. | School improvement programs.
Classification: LCC LB1775 .P764 2020 (print) | LCC LB1775 (ebook) | DDC
    371.1--dc23
LC record available at https://lccn.loc.gov/2019036602
LC ebook record available at https://lccn.loc.gov/2019036603

Solution Tree
Jeffrey C. Jones, CEO
Edmund M. Ackerman, President

Solution Tree Press
President and Publisher: Douglas M. Rife
Associate Publisher: Sarah Payne-Mills
Art Director: Rian Anderson
Managing Production Editor: Kendra Slayton
Senior Production Editor: Suzanne Kraszewski
Content Development Specialist: Amy Rubenstein
Copy Editor: Evie Madsen
Proofreader: Jessi Finn
Text and Cover Designer: Rian Anderson
Editorial Assistant: Sarah Ludwig

Table of Contents

About the Editors

Robert Eaker

Robert Eaker, EdD, is professor emeritus at Middle Tennessee State University, where he also served as dean of the College of Education and later as interim executive vice president and provost. Dr. Eaker is a former fellow with the National Center for Effective Schools Research and Development.

Dr. Eaker has written widely on the issues of effective teaching, effective schools, helping teachers use research findings, and high expectations for student achievement, and has coauthored (with Richard and Rebecca DuFour) numerous books and other resources on the topic of reculturing schools and school districts into professional learning communities (PLCs).

In 1998, Dr. Eaker was recognized by the governor of Tennessee as a recipient of Tennessee's Outstanding Achievement Award. Also, in 1998, the Tennessee House of Representatives passed a proclamation recognizing him for his dedication and commitment to the field of education. In 2003, Dr. Eaker was selected by the Middle Tennessee State University Student Government Association to receive the Womack Distinguished Faculty Award.

For over four decades, Dr. Eaker has served as a consultant to school districts throughout North America and has been a frequent speaker at state, regional, and national meetings.

To learn more about Dr. Eaker, visit AllThingsPLC (www.allthingsplc.info).

Robert J. Marzano

Robert J. Marzano, PhD, is cofounder and chief academic officer of Marzano Resources in Denver, Colorado. During his fifty years in the field of education, he has worked with educators as a speaker and trainer and has authored more than fifty books and two hundred articles on topics such as instruction, assessment, writing and implementing standards, cognition, effective leadership, and school intervention. His books include *The New Art and Science of Teaching*, *Leaders of Learning*, *Making Classroom Assessments Reliable and Valid*, *The Classroom Strategies Series*, *Managing the Inner World of Teaching*, *A Handbook for High Reliability Schools*, *A Handbook for Personalized Competency-Based Education*, and *The Highly Engaged Classroom*. His practical translations of the most current research and theory into classroom strategies are known internationally and are widely practiced by both teachers and administrators.

He received a bachelor's degree from Iona College in New York, a master's degree from Seattle University, and a doctorate from the University of Washington.

To learn more about Dr. Marzano, visit Marzano Resources (https://marzano resources.com).

To book Robert Eaker or Robert J. Marzano for professional development, contact pd@SolutionTree.com.

Introduction

Professional Learning Communities at Work and High Reliability Schools: Merging Best Practices for School Improvement

Robert J. Marzano and Robert Eaker

Many expectations from diverse constituencies drive the complex organizations known as schools. However, there is general agreement that schools should ensure *all* students are physically and psychologically safe, made to feel psychologically confident and mentally healthy, and able to learn at high levels. The question is, How can we create school structures and cultures to support these goals? And, how can we ensure this work is achievable in a reasonable amount of time and in a cost-effective way? The good news is researchers and practitioners alike endorse the concepts and practices that form the Professional Learning Community (PLC) at Work® process and the findings and structures that form the High Reliability Schools™ (HRS) model as our best hope for significant school improvement (Bourrier, 2011; Weick, Sutcliffe, & Obstfeld, 1999).

The PLC process is based on the belief that a highly effective PLC engages in an ongoing process in which educators work collaboratively in recurring cycles of collective inquiry and action research to achieve better results for the students they serve, and PLCs operate under the assumption that the key to improved learning for students is continuous job-embedded learning for educators (DuFour, DuFour, Eaker, Many, & Mattos, 2016). The HRS model's approach to school improvement is similar in that it "involves monitoring the relationship between actions an organization works to enhance its effectiveness" in relation to a set of research-based high reliability indicators "and the extent to which these actions do, in fact, produce the desired effects" (Marzano, Warrick, Rains, & DuFour, 2018, p. 28).

The PLC process and the HRS model *are not competing* approaches to school improvement. Rather, *they are complementary and support and enhance each other.* Together, these approaches to school improvement can be a powerful tool for educational leaders who are serious about ensuring high levels of learning for all students.

> The PLC process and the HRS model are not competing approaches to school improvement. Rather, they are complementary and support and enhance each other.

This book includes information, insights, and practical suggestions from both PLC and HRS researchers and practitioners. The overarching purpose is to demonstrate how these two approaches, taken together, support educators in their efforts to create a culture of continuous improvement.

PLC at Work and HRS

Widespread agreement that the PLC process is a powerful approach for improving student learning raises the questions, What tools are available to educators who are attempting to transform their school or district into a high-performing PLC? How will we know if we are focusing on the things that will have the greatest impact on student learning? and Are there specific research-based factors that collectively provide educators with high reliability indicators of highly effective schools?

Descriptions of effective schools certainly are not new. Fifty years of research, not only from within the educational community but also from organizations outside education, coupled with twenty years of successful implementation of the PLC concept, provide a clear picture of characteristics of highly effective schools. The PLC process is, at its core, an umbrella for best practices. And, the five levels that represent the HRS model, coupled with the accompanying indicators, provide a complementary framework to the PLC umbrella.

The PLC process is built on three big ideas. First is a relentless focus on student learning, skill by skill and student by student. The second is the creation of a collaborative culture through the use of high-performing teams working interdependently to create common goals for which they hold one another mutually accountable. The third big idea is a passionate and persistent focus on results—improved learning of each student (DuFour et al., 2016). The HRS model explicitly and implicitly addresses these same big ideas, organizing the actions one would take to address these ideas into five levels, which we explain later in this introduction.

Importantly, both approaches provide for collaborative processes designed to reflect and improve on the effectiveness of each effort. And both approaches emphasize the necessity of effective leadership. In fact, in the absence of effective leadership, the positive impact of both the PLC process and the HRS model is questionable.

At their core, successful PLCs and HRS depend on effective leadership, just as any successful improvement initiative requires effective leadership. There are no improvement initiatives, including HRS and PLC, strong enough to overcome weak or ineffective leadership.

While researchers recognize the importance of leadership, there is less agreement about what constitutes effective leadership, especially within the educational community. *Effective leadership requires moving beyond the broad recognition that it is essential to success.* Both the PLC process and HRS model are designed to help leaders do the *right work for the right reasons, at the right time, and in the right ways!*

> At their core, successful PLCs and HRS depend on effective leadership, just as any successful improvement initiative requires effective leadership.

In the PLC process, leaders rely on a number of research-based leadership practices. The first is creating a structure and culture of dispersed leadership through the use of high-performing teams. The HRS model also places great emphasis on the importance of an effective collaborative culture. Leaders of a PLC recognize that just organizing schools into teams will do little to improve student learning. Hence, leaders focus teams to engage in the *right work*. In this regard, the leading indicators of the HRS model are valuable guidelines to ensure leaders focus on the right work.

Importantly, effective leaders consistently connect the teams' work back to the *why*—why we are engaging in this specific task or activity. (See Simon Sinek's [2009] *Start With Why* for further insights into the importance of connecting work directly to the *why*.) In both the PLC process and the HRS model, the *why* almost always connects to enhancing the learning of *all* students, either directly or indirectly. Leaders of PLCs seek to create a culture in which the *why*—improving student learning—links to collective inquiry into best practices and action research to test the impact of selected practices. The leading indicators of an HRS, coupled with the high reliability leadership process for addressing lagging indicators, provide leaders of PLCs with power tools for continuous improvement.

Successfully becoming a PLC also requires leaders create a *simultaneous loose-tight* culture in which the entire organization is *tight* about the school's (or district's) core mission, vision, values, and goals, along with a few best practices, but at the same time create a culture that is *loose*—a culture that encourages empowerment, ownership, and creativity. The leading indicators of the HRS model provide clear, concise practices school leaders should be tight about, while at the same time allowing for the creation of a culture of experimentation.

And, leaders of PLCs frequently monitor the learning of students and the work of adults on a timely basis. On the other hand, they balance frequent monitoring and feedback with meaningful and genuine recognition and celebration. Those who successfully implement the processes and practices of the PLC process recognize the power of recognition, appreciation, and celebration.

For leaders who are establishing a PLC school or district or seeking to improve the results of their PLC practices, *specificity* is essential. The HRS model is a powerful tool that enables leaders to ensure they are engaging in the right work by collaboratively examining their school's current reality in relation to research-based best practices (the leading indicators), and a process for monitoring progress toward improvement in key areas of need (the lagging indicators).

Marzano et al. (2018) state, "At its core, a high reliability perspective involves monitoring the relationship between actions an organization takes to enhance its effectiveness and the extent to which these actions do, in fact, produce the desired effects" (p. 29). In short, the HRS model provides leaders with a rational, research-based collaborative approach to closing what Stanford University professors Jeffrey Pfeffer and Robert I. Sutton (2000) refer to as the *knowing-doing gap*—the gap between known best practices and the degree to which organizations fail to engage in actions consistent with those research-based best practices.

Leaders of PLCs emphasize a culture exemplified by *collective inquiry into best practices.* However, effective leaders also recognize that simply implementing *all* practices showing some level of effectiveness is counterproductive. Collectively implementing best practices begins with the *collaborative analysis* of student learning data. Such analysis, when done effectively, results in identifying areas of most need. Leaders generally recognize that high-priority needs require immediate attention, and the results are threefold: (1) creation of a sense of urgency (see John Kotter's [2008] *A Sense of Urgency* for deeper learning into the role a sense of urgency plays in organizational development), (2) development of a few meaningful high-priority goals linked directly to student learning data, and (3) information that enables leaders to monitor and celebrate the right things. Such activities can only be successful to the degree leaders create a fully functioning collaborative culture to capture the power of effective teaming.

HRS and Leadership

Leadership from the PLC perspective inherently overlaps with many aspects of leadership from the HRS perspective. However, the HRS perspective introduces some nuances to leadership uncommon in K–12 education.

The central driving force of leadership in the HRS model involves managing the interaction between two types of indicators, (1) *leading* and (2) *lagging. Leading indicators* are those things a school does to produce specific results to enhance a school's effectiveness. *Lagging indicators* are the concrete results of the leading indicators. For example, a school might establish the leading indicator that all teachers should have growth goals for specific instructional strategies and have support in accomplishing these goals. Concretely, the school would then set up programs and practices to operationalize this leading indicator. The lagging indicator for this leading indicator might be that the school can document 90 percent of the teachers have shown progress relative to their growth goals. For the most part, leading indicators represent the programs and practices schools implement for specific purposes; lagging indicators represent the evidence that these programs and practices are working.

Based on the interaction between leading and lagging indicators, one can articulate distinct levels of school leader effectiveness. These levels appear along with brief descriptions in figure I.1.

Level	Description
Not Using	The school leader does not have programs or practices in place relative to important leading indicators, nor does he or she have any plans to implement such programs or practices.
Beginning	The school leader has programs or practices in place relative to important leading indicators but has not implemented them fully or implements them with significant errors or omissions.
Developing	The school leader has programs and practices in place relative to important leading indicators and implements them without significant errors or omissions.
Applying	The school leader implements programs and practices relative to important leading indicators without significant errors or omissions, and collected data demonstrate they are producing the desired effects.
Sustaining	The school leader regularly and continually collects quick data relative to the programs and practices to monitor their ongoing effectiveness and makes necessary changes when data indicate the need.

Figure I.1: Levels of leadership effectiveness.

At the first level (not using), the leader is unaware that specific programs or practices should be in place for the school to run effectively. For example, the school leader who has no programs or practices in place to help teachers increase their pedagogical skills nor any plans to establish such programs or practices would be at the not-using level for developing teachers' pedagogical skills.

At the second level (beginning), the leader does have programs and practices in place to help teachers increase their pedagogical skills, but not all teachers are actively involved in those programs and practices.

At the third level (developing), the leader not only has programs and practices in place to help teachers increase their pedagogical skills but also can demonstrate that all teachers are involved in those programs and practices.

At the fourth level (applying), the leader has programs and practices in place to help teachers increase their pedagogical skills and can document that 90 percent of teachers are involved and meeting their growth goals.

At the fifth level (sustaining), the leader continually and systematically examines the data regarding teacher development goals and informally interacts with teachers to ensure the programs and practices are maintaining their effects. The leader collects data quickly and efficiently, sometimes using personal observations of teachers, sometimes using informal discussions with teachers, and sometimes using reports that have already been generated. We refer to such data as *quick data* to emphasize the fact that they should impose scant extra work for administrators. If those data indicate a current or potential decline in effectiveness, the leader immediately takes action to alleviate the problem.

The interaction between leading and lagging indicators in the HRS approach implies a straightforward course of action for school leaders relative to these key leading indicators.

1. Identify those factors in the school critical to the school's success.

2. Create leading indicators for those factors in the form of programs and practices.

3. Create lagging indicators for critical programs and practices (leading indicators) by establishing criteria for their success.

4. Collect data on the school's status regarding the lagging indicators.

5. If the school hasn't met lagging indicator minimum requirements, refocus attention on actions inherent in the associated leading indicators.

6. Continually collect data on lagging indicators and respond accordingly.

To a great extent, the chapters in this book provide specific examples of how these actions play out within the context of the PLC process at each of the HRS levels.

PLCs and Cultural Change

Creating a culture of continuous improvement in schools and districts requires leaders to pay attention to changing both school structures and the larger school culture. There is ample evidence that traditional school structures and cultures failed, for the most part, to achieve the goals of both excellence and equity.

Educational leaders often choose to improve by changing the school's *structure* (policies, procedures, schedules, structures, and so on) while ignoring the school's larger *culture* (the beliefs, assumptions,

> Creating a culture of continuous improvement in schools and districts requires leaders to pay attention to changing both school structures and the larger school culture.

values, expectations, and habits that constitute the norm of the school—in short, how people think and behave day in, day out). A school's structure is much easier to change than a school's culture and takes far less time to change. However, unless structural change is anchored in significant and meaningful cultural changes, it is doubtful the structural changes, however well intended, will have a long-term and significant impact on the culture.

Meaningful cultural change is difficult; in fact, it's impossible if leaders are unclear about the kind of culture they are trying to create, and importantly, *why* such cultural shifts are necessary. Viewed together, the PLC process and the HRS model provide leaders with effective concepts and tools for changing school culture—or how things are done day in, day out.

As mentioned earlier, the PLC process is based on three critical cultural shifts—cultural shifts that stand in stark contrast to the cultures of more traditional schools. The first of these shifts, and the basic foundation for virtually all practices in a high-performing PLC, is a shift from a primary focus on *teaching* to a laser-like focus on the *learning* of each student—unit by unit, standard by standard, student by student, skill by skill, name by name. A professional *learning* community is based on the fundamental assumption that the primary purpose of a school—its core mission—is to ensure high levels of learning for all students (DuFour et al., 2016). In short, educators in a PLC accept the fact that they have not been successful simply because they *taught* the right things in the right way. Instead, these educators focus on what students have or have not *learned*. Four critical questions drive schools engaged in the PLC process: (1) What do we want students to learn? (2) How will we know if students are learning? (3) How will we respond when students don't learn? and (4) How will we extend learning for students who are already proficient? (DuFour et al., 2016).

The second shift occurs when schools move from a more traditional culture to a culture reflective of PLCs—or from a culture of teacher isolation to a culture of collaboration. And importantly, that collaborative culture uses high-performing collaborative teams working interdependently to achieve common goals for which members hold one another accountable (DuFour et al., 2016).

Leaders of successful PLCs realize that ultimately *results matter.* The third cultural shift differentiating PLC schools from their more traditional counterparts is a shift from a focus on good intentions to a sharp, consistent, and persistent focus on results, with the collaborative analysis of student learning data primarily measuring those results.

These three cultural shifts drive the work of leaders seeking to reculture their schools into high-performing PLCs. But what would such a school culture look like day in, day out? Authors and PLC at Work experts Richard DuFour, Rebecca DuFour, Robert Eaker,

Thomas W. Many, and Mike Mattos (2016) describe the characteristics that collectively create the foundation for and reflect the culture of a PLC.

- **Shared mission, vision, values, and goals:** The culture of a high-performing PLC is reflected in a cultural foundation built on a PLC's *collaboratively developed* and *interconnected* and, importantly, *frequently used* mission, vision, values, and goals. Taken together, the shared mission, vision, values (collective commitments), and goals drive the work of a PLC.

- **Collective inquiry:** Engaging in meaningful and focused collective inquiry drives improvement efforts, and ultimately growth for both students and adults in a PLC. Importantly, collaborative teams do not seek best practices for every school or learning issue. Instead, collaborative analysis of student learning data drives collective inquiry in a PLC. Collaborative data analysis provides teams with a focus for their collective inquiry into best practices, and because the focus is on the most important things, collective inquiry takes on a sense of urgency.

- **Collaborative teams:** The defining structural and cultural characteristic of a PLC is the use of high-performing collaborative teams—teams of educators who share common work and a common purpose. Collaborative teams are the engine that drives the cultural shift from mere interaction and group decision making that is reflective of more traditional schools to a culture in which teams work interdependently to fulfill the school's core mission of ensuring high levels of learning for all students.

- **Action research and experimentation:** In PLCs, educators recognize that learning best practices does not mean a particular practice will be effective in every unique situation. In a high-performing PLC, various practices—actions—are tried and then members measure the actual impact of each change on student learning. In short, members of a PLC recognize the power of *learning by doing*—learning by experimentation.

- **Continuous improvement:** The culture of a PLC is one of continuous improvement. This commitment to continuous improvement is evident in "an environment in which innovation and experimentation are viewed not as tasks to accomplish or projects to complete, but as ways of conducting day-to-day business, *forever*" (DuFour et al., 2016, p. 13).

- **Results orientation:** Members of a PLC recognize that they must measure their efforts, ultimately, against results rather than their hard work and good intentions. They assess every initiative, every practice within a PLC, on the basis of results. Otherwise, school-improvement activities simply become random acts of hope.

Like the PLC process, the HRS model is based on the foundation of a culture that reflects beliefs and norms regarding school safety, support for both students and adults, and collaboration. And, as in the PLC process, the cultural engine is collaboration (Marzano, Heflebower, Hoegh, Warrick, & Grift, 2016).

A High Reliability Culture

A high reliability culture focuses on key factors. Again, many of these factors are implicit or explicit in a PLC culture. The HRS model organizes its key factors in a hierarchical fashion (Marzano, Warrick, & Simms, 2014).

- **Level 5:** Competency-based education
- **Level 4:** Standards-referenced reporting
- **Level 3:** Guaranteed and viable curriculum
- **Level 2:** Effective teaching in every classroom
- **Level 1:** Safe, supportive, and collaborative culture

These levels represent a hierarchy; so, for one level to work effectively, educators must reliably address the previous levels.

As Marzano et al. (2018) describe, level 1 of the HRS model is foundational because it addresses basic human needs. If students, teachers, and parents do not believe their school is safe, supportive, and collaborative, they will spend their time, energy, and attention trying to get these basic needs met as opposed to focusing on student learning.

Level 2 addresses effective teaching. It appears second in the HRS model because it is one of the hierarchy's most influential, yet alterable variables. Research consistently demonstrates that the quality of teaching students receive is one of the best predictors of their academic success (Nye, Konstantopoulos, & Hedges, 2004). And, with deliberate practice, teachers can dramatically enhance their pedagogical skills over time (Ericsson & Pool, 2016).

Level 3 focuses on a guaranteed and viable curriculum. *Guaranteed* means no matter who teaches a given course or grade level, students will receive the same content. *Viable* means the content is so focused and parsimonious, educators can effectively teach it in the time available.

Level 4 addresses a form of record keeping and reporting that allows schools to monitor the status and growth of each individual student.

Level 5 not only allows educators to monitor individual students but also provides opportunities for each student to move through the curriculum at his or her own pace.

There are twenty-five factors in the HRS model that manifest as leading indicators. In addition to the levels of the model representing a hierarchy, the factors within each level have complex causal relationships. Table I.1 depicts some of these relationships.

Table I.1 shows that at level 1 of the HRS model, schools effectively address the leading indicators for a safe, supportive, and collaborative culture and produce students and teachers who have their basic needs met and parents and guardians who have their concerns for their children met. This creates teachers who are freer to focus their attention on instruction, and students who are freer to focus their attention on learning. Of course, this effect is at the center of the PLC process. By definition, a high-functioning PLC will have a safe, supportive, and collaborative culture.

At level 2 of the HRS model, schools that effectively address the leading indicators for effective teaching produce teachers who develop and maintain high levels of pedagogical expertise, which results in students receiving high-quality instruction. This, in turn, results in a higher probability of students learning the taught curriculum.

Table I.1: Causal Relationships Within HRS Levels

Level 1	Level 2	Level 3	Level 4	Level 5
The school effectively addresses the leading indicators for a safe, supportive, and collaborative culture.	The school effectively addresses the leading indicators for effective teaching in every classroom.	The school effectively addresses the leading indicators for a guaranteed and viable curriculum.	The school effectively addresses the leading indicators for standards-referenced reporting.	The school effectively addresses the leading indicators for competency-based education.
Students have their basic needs met. Teachers have their basic needs met. Parents and guardians have their basic needs for their children met.	Teachers develop and maintain enhanced levels of pedagogical skill.	Teachers are clear about the content to teach and have adequate time and resources to do so. Teachers can design more focused and well-crafted lessons and units.	Teachers track the growth and status of each individual student. Teachers provide specific feedback to each student for each topic in the curriculum.	Teachers take collective responsibility for determining each student's status and growth on specific topics. Teachers take collective responsibility to determine when each student should move to the next level relative to specific topics and subject areas.
Teachers can better focus their attention on instruction. Students can better focus their attention on learning.	Students receive high-quality instruction. Students have a heightened probability of learning the taught curriculum.	Students have increased opportunities to learn the intended curriculum.	Students have a better understanding of what they need to learn or improve relative to specific topics in the curriculum.	Students move through the curriculum at a pace consistent with their development and individual needs. Students do not have gaps in their learning. Students develop an enhanced sense of agency and responsibility.

At level 3 of the HRS model, schools that effectively address the leading indicators for a guaranteed and viable curriculum produce teachers who are clear about what they should teach and have the time and resources to adequately teach that curriculum. This allows them to design and deliver more well-crafted units and lessons. This, in turn, increases students' opportunities to learn the intended curriculum.

At level 4 of the HRS model, schools that effectively address the leading indicators for standards-referenced reporting produce teachers who track the status and growth of each individual student as opposed to only the class as a whole. This allows teachers to provide students with highly specific feedback on each of the topics in the curriculum, which, in turn, produces students who are much more aware of what they must do to enhance their learning for each topic of the curriculum.

At level 5 of the HRS model, schools that effectively address the leading indicators for competency-based education produce teachers who take collective responsibility for determining each student's status and growth on specific topics, and for determining when each student should move to the next level on specific topics and subject areas. These actions create students who move through the curriculum at a pace that is consistent with their development and individual needs. Additionally, students are less likely to have gaps in their learning and are more likely to develop an enhanced sense of agency and responsibility.

It is important to note that the HRS approach, which involves a hierarchical relationship between levels and causal relationships within levels, is different from a relatively common approach in which educators look at the literature on effect size (the increase or decrease in student learning) and use the magnitude of effect sizes to prioritize the factors they will address. The most popular source for such information is the work of John Hattie (2009, 2012, 2015). Hattie's (2009) meta-analytic studies are unprecedented in scope and depth; collectively, these studies span decades of research and synthesize tens of thousands of quantitative relationships expressed as effect sizes (Hattie, 2012, 2015).

Hattie's (2009) book *Visible Learning* identifies 138 factors that have demonstrable correlations with student achievement. In 2012,

Hattie's book *Visible Learning for Teachers* expanded the list of factors to 150, and then in 2015, Hattie updated his body of work in a scholarly article and identified 195 factors. Table I.2 summarizes some of the top-ten findings across these three publications.

Table I.2: Summary of Hattie's Meta-Analytic Studies

Rank	2009 Total Factors = 138	2012 Total Factors = 150	2015 Total Factors = 195
1	Student self-reports grades (1.44)*	Student self-reports grades and expectations (1.44)	Teacher estimates achievement (1.62)
2	Uses Piagetian programs (1.28) (Jordan & Brownlee, 1981)	Uses Piagetian programs (1.28)	Promotes collective teacher efficacy (1.57)
3	Provides formative evaluation (0.90)	Provides response to intervention (RTI; 1.07)	Self-reports grades (1.33)
4	Engages in micro-teaching (0.88)	Establishes teacher credibility (0.90)	Uses Piagetian programs (1.28)
5	Encourages acceleration (0.88)	Provides formative evaluation (0.90)	Employs conceptual change programs (1.16)
6	Improves classroom behavior (0.80)	Engages in micro-teaching (0.88)	Provides RTI (1.07)
7	Adopts comprehensive interventions for students with learning disabilities (0.77)	Utilizes class discussion (0.82)	Establishes teacher credibility (0.90)
8	Delivers teacher clarity (0.75)	Adopts comprehensive interventions for students with learning disabilities (0.77)	Engages in micro-teaching (0.88)
9	Promotes reciprocal teaching (0.74)	Delivers teacher clarity (0.75)	Leverages cognitive task analysis (0.87)
10	Gives feedback (0.73)	Gives feedback (0.75)	Utilizes classroom discussion (0.82)

Note: Effect sizes are in parentheses.
Source: Adapted from Hattie, 2009, 2012, 2015.

At face value, it seems intuitively true that a viable approach to making schools more effective would be to work on the factors Hattie identifies, beginning at the top and working down. Indeed, in our experience, this is the approach many educators take. However, there are at least three reasons why this approach is not optimal and might not even be viable.

Table I.2 (page 15) demonstrates the first and arguably most important reason in its description of the causal relationships within levels of the HRS model. Factors that have a relationship with student learning tend to interact in complex causal ways. Simply addressing factors with large effect sizes and then moving down a rank-ordered list of factors is simplistic and ultimately ineffective. In fact, if educators take this approach, they are likely to never get to or ignore factors that are necessary but not sufficient conditions for effective schooling. For example, consider the factor of decreasing disruptive behavior in the school and classrooms. In the HRS model, this is a component of level 1—providing a safe, supportive, and collaborative culture. While decreasing disruptions is intuitively obvious as foundational for effective schooling, it ranks 103 (Hattie, 2015). The same can be said for the factor of reducing students' levels of anxiety, which he ranks 97, and the factor of enhancing students' motivation, which Hattie (2015) ranks 74. Many of the factors that are central to the PLC process also are found rather low on Hattie's list. Certainly collective efficacy, which is rated second in Hattie's 2015 ranking, is part and parcel of the PLC process. However, other foundational aspects of the PLC process appear much further from the top. These include early intervention (130), school culture (150), and teacher immediacy (160).

A second reason for not starting from the top of a rank-ordered list of effect sizes and progressing down is that educators must be very careful about how much importance they ascribe to the relative magnitude of effect sizes. Some researchers even argue against classifying effect sizes and correlations by size. For example, researchers Gene V. Glass, Barry McGaw, and Mary Lee Smith (1981) explain:

> There is no wisdom whatsoever in attempting to associate regions of the effect size metric with descriptive adjectives such as "small," "moderate," "large," and the like. Dissociated from a context of decision and comparative value, there is little

inherent value to an effect size of 3.5 or .2. Depending on what benefits can be achieved at what cost, an effect size of 2.0 might be "poor" and one of .1 might be "good." (p. 104)

In addressing this issue, research professor at Vanderbilt University Mark W. Lipsey and colleagues (2012) explain those interpreting effect sizes must think in terms of *practical significance*, which involves a comparison with typical expectations, noting:

Practical significance is not an inherent characteristic of the numbers and statistics that result from intervention research—it is something that must be judged in some context of application. To interpret the practical significance of an intervention effect, therefore, it is necessary to invoke an appropriate frame of reference external to its statistical representation. (p. 26)

They note appropriate frames of reference for educational interventions include expectations for normal growth, other similar interventions' results, and the cost and resources associated with the intervention under study (Lipsey et al., 2012).

The third reason is the meta-analytic studies identify factors that change over time. This is not a criticism of Hattie's work or of meta-analytic research in general. Such variation is simply inherent in the approach. But consumers of such research should always keep in mind that as researchers integrate more studies into an existing set of findings, factors change, newly appear, and even disappear. For example, consider the factor of "student self-reports grades," which Hattie ranks first in the 2009 study. In the 2012 study, this factor maintains the number-one position, but changes to "student self-reports grades and expectations." Also, consider the factor of "promotes collective teacher efficacy," which Hattie ranks second in the 2015 study even though it did not appear in either of the two previous studies. Finally, consider the factor of quality of teaching, which Hattie ranks 56 in the 2009 study and 57 in the 2012 study. However, this factor disappears from the list in the 2015 study.

Again, our comments are not designed to impugn Hattie's work or the meta-analytic work of others. Indeed, such studies provide a strong basis with which to identify research-based factors that influence student achievement. However, to be useful, these factors must be organized into coherent cause-and-effect models that apply to specific situations and circumstances.

The HRS Levels Within a PLC at Work Framework

The HRS levels fit quite nicely within the PLC process. Stated differently, the HRS levels and the PLC process are not competing frameworks or frameworks designed to do the same things in differ-

The HRS levels fit quite nicely within the PLC process.

ent ways. Rather, the HRS levels articulate, at a fairly granular level, specific elements to which leaders should attend if they wish to add a high reliability perspective to their PLC work.

Level 1: Safe, Supportive, and Collaborative Culture

Level 1 of the HRS hierarchy is a safe, supportive, and collaborative culture, which the leading indicators in table I.3 operationally define.

Table I.3: Leading Indicators for Level 1

Level 1: Safe, Supportive, and Collaborative Culture	1.1—The faculty and staff perceive the school environment as safe, supportive, and orderly.
	1.2—Students, parents, and community members perceive the school environment as safe, supportive, and orderly.
	1.3—Teachers have formal roles in the decision-making process regarding school initiatives.
	1.4—Collaborative teams regularly interact to address common issues regarding curriculum, assessment, instruction, and the achievement of all students.
	1.5—Teachers and staff have formal ways to provide input regarding the optimal functioning of the school.
	1.6—Students, parents, and community members have formal ways to provide input regarding the optimal functioning of the school.
	1.7—The principal acknowledges the success of the whole school as well as individuals within the school.
	1.8—The principal manages its fiscal, operational, and technological resources in a way that directly supports teachers.

Source: Adapted from Marzano et al., 2018, p. 31.

It would be difficult, if not impossible, to overstate the importance of building a cultural foundation to drive all other aspects of the school-improvement process. Viewed together, the cultural and structural characteristics of a high-performing PLC and the leading indicators of the HRS model, coupled with associated practices, offer educators a valuable tool for developing a culture of continuous improvement.

Level 2: Effective Teaching in Every Classroom

Level 2 of the HRS hierarchy is effective teaching in every classroom, which the leading indicators in table I.4 operationally define.

Table I.4: Leading Indicators for Level 2

Level 2: Effective Teaching in Every Classroom	2.1—The school communicates a clear vision as to how teachers should address instruction.
	2.2—The school supports teachers to continually enhance their pedagogical skills through reflection and professional growth plans.
	2.3—The school is aware of and monitors predominant instructional practices.
	2.4—The school provides teachers with clear, ongoing evaluations of their pedagogical strengths and weaknesses that are based on multiple sources of data and are consistent with student achievement data.
	2.5—The school provides teachers with job-embedded professional development that is directly related to their instructional growth goals.
	2.6—Teachers have opportunities to observe and discuss effective teaching.

Source: Adapted from Marzano et al., 2018, p. 31.

As leaders of PLCs work to embed the cultural shift from a *focus on teaching* to a *focus on learning*, one should not view their efforts as diminishing the importance of effective classroom instruction. In fact, as collaborative teams focus on the learning of each student, skill by skill, the requirement for effective teaching in every classroom becomes even more important. In more traditional schools—as well as in many teacher-accountability initiatives—schools view teaching as an end in itself; in a PLC, schools view teaching as the means to an end—the end being student learning.

PLCs view improving teaching practice through the lens of collaborative teams. Effective teaching begins with clear, appropriate, and focused agreement about what every student needs to learn, and what student work will look like if students are successful. The teams collaboratively develop common formative assessments to monitor the learning of each student on a frequent and timely basis. The team collaboratively analyzes results of these common assessments. The result of this common analysis of student learning data allows team members to address the question of how struggling students receive additional time and support in an effective and timely way. And the team also addresses the question of how to extend the learning of students who demonstrate proficiency.

Importantly, these learning data also provide the team members—both collectively and individually—with information to address their instructional effectiveness in each unit. The questions are, What practices seem to be the most effective? What should we do differently the next time we teach this unit? and What resources can we access to enhance our knowledge of best teaching practices in this subject and grade level? To this end, the team members engage in *collective inquiry* into effective teaching practices, and then test the selected practices in their classrooms through *action research*, with an emphasis on results—the *effect on student learning or behavior.* In short, with the PLC process, collaborative analysis of student learning data and the process of collective inquiry and action research improve teaching. The end result is a culture of continuous improvement of teaching practices.

Level 3: Guaranteed and Viable Curriculum

Level 3 of the HRS hierarchy is a guaranteed and viable curriculum, which the leading indicators in table I.5 operationally define.

Table I.5: Leading Indicators for Level 3

Level 3: Guaranteed and Viable Curriculum	3.1—The school curriculum and accompanying assessments adhere to state (or provincial) and district standards.
	3.2—The school curriculum is focused enough that teachers can adequately address it in the time they have available.
	3.3—All students have the opportunity to learn the critical content of the curriculum.
	3.4—The school establishes clear and measurable goals that are focused on critical needs regarding improving overall student achievement at the school level.
	3.5—The school analyzes, interprets, and uses data to regularly monitor progress toward school achievement goals.
	3.6—The school establishes appropriate school- and classroom-level programs and practices to help students meet individual achievement goals when data indicate interventions are needed.

Source: Adapted from Marzano et al., 2018, p. 31.

In *What Works in Schools*, Marzano (2003) coined the term *guaranteed and viable curriculum*, the recognition that what every student needs to learn must be *guaranteed* regardless of the teacher to whom a student is assigned. A guaranteed curriculum must also be *viable*—schools must provide teachers with adequate time and resources to effectively teach the curriculum (Marzano et al., 2018).

Both the PLC process and the HRS model recognize that embedding a guaranteed and viable curriculum in a school's structure and culture is an essential requirement for improving student achievement. In an effective PLC, teams work from the assumption that if we want all students to learn at high levels, the first question to address is, Learn what?

The PLC process requires a deep understanding on the part of all administrators and teachers regarding what students must know at the end of each unit of instruction (DuFour et al., 2016).

Gaining a deep understanding of what students must learn begins with deep learning within each team. The first step educators in a PLC take when making decisions is to learn together, and developing a guaranteed and viable curriculum begins with collaboratively reviewing high-stakes standards and assessments. Collaborative teams analyze multiple sources of standards beginning with state (or provincial) standards, but also including, for example, standards from professional organizations (such as ACT, SAT, National Assessment of Educational Progress, and advanced placement (AP) standards, and district curriculum guides). Teams literally become "students of the standards" with the ultimate goal of ensuring their students receive not only a guaranteed and viable curriculum but also one aligned with the high-stakes assessments students are likely to encounter.

Simply put, *some standards are more important than others.* This fact alone means teacher teams must engage in the collaborative prioritization of standards, providing more time to the most essential skills and knowledge, and less time to others. In a PLC, this collaborative activity results in a guaranteed and viable curriculum. Importantly, teams use this same approach to "unpack" the standards into learning targets and determine what each target should look like in student work if students demonstrate proficiency.

Implementing a guaranteed and viable curriculum requires both *top-down* and *bottom-up* leadership. On one hand, district- and school-level leaders must provide direction, guidelines, resources (especially high-quality examples), training, and feedback to teacher teams to sharpen their understanding of what is essential. These leaders must also provide an explanation of *why* creating a guaranteed and viable curriculum is the foundation for student success. On the other hand, the actual development of a guaranteed and viable curriculum must be grounded in the work of collaborative teams that bring their collective expertise to the task (Eaker & Keating, 2012). The resulting curriculum is not static or "carved in stone." Teams are constantly examining the efficacy of the agreed-on curriculum as they collaboratively analyze both formative and summative student learning data.

Level 4: Standards-Referenced Reporting

Level 4 of the HRS model is standards-referenced reporting, which the leading indicators in table I.6 operationally define.

Table I.6: Leading Indicators for Level 4

Level 4: Standards-Referenced Reporting	4.1—The school establishes clear and measurable goals focused on critical needs regarding improving achievement of individual students. 4.2—The school analyzes, interprets, and uses data to regularly monitor progress toward achievement goals for individual students.

Source: Adapted from Marzano et al., 2018, p. 32.

It is not uncommon for more traditional schools to focus on these questions: How are our *students* doing? Did they improve over last year? In what areas are our *students* struggling? and In what areas are we showing gains? While such questions are significant and schools should address them, both the PLC process and the HRS model shift the emphasis from a whole-school perspective to a sharp focus on the learning of *each student*, grade by grade, subject by subject, unit by unit, skill by skill, name by name.

Although both concepts reflect this collaborative monitoring of the learning of each student in multiple ways, one of the most important ways is through standards-referenced reporting. In the PLC process, attention to the monitoring and reporting of student learning in relation to a standard begins with the collaborative identification of the skills and concepts *essential for all students* to learn within each standard and unit of instruction (that is, the guaranteed and viable curriculum).

During each unit of instruction, teams monitor the *learning of each student* on a frequent and timely basis through the use of collaboratively developed common formative assessments. Importantly, common formative assessments are not developed to monitor the learning of everything students must learn; the emphasis is on the *most essential skills and concepts that all students must acquire.*

In both the PLC process and the HRS model, the emphasis is on clarity and specificity regarding what students should learn and alignment with national, state, and professional standards and assessments. In PLCs, this means enhancing each student's learning—and reporting it in relation to collaboratively developed standards of proficiency. High-performing PLCs develop an effective, systematic plan for providing each student with additional time, support, or extension of his or her learning within the school day, regardless of the assigned teacher.

The alignment of individual student learning with the reporting of each student's progress in relation to common standards is complete when schools collaboratively develop a standards-referenced reporting system. This system must inform both students and parents of student learning levels in relation to common standards, rather than the more traditional approach of reporting the average learning of students between two fixed points in time.

Level 5: Competency-Based Education

Level 5 of the HRS hierarchy is competency-based education, which the leading indicators in table I.7 operationally define.

Table I.7: Leading Indicators for Level 5

Level 5: Competency-Based Education	5.1—Students move on to the next level of the curriculum for any subject area only after they have demonstrated competence at the previous level.
	5.2—The school schedule accommodates students moving at a pace appropriate to their situation and needs.
	5.3—The school affords students who have demonstrated competency levels greater than those articulated in the system immediate opportunities to begin work on advanced content or career paths of interest.

Source: Adapted from Marzano et al., 2018, p. 32.

In *Leading a High Reliability School* (Marzano et al., 2018), the authors write:

> In level 5, a competency-based system, students progress to the next grade level only after they have demonstrated proficiency in all the priority standards at their current grade level. . . . In a competency-based system, students can work on any level of content for which they are ready. This means some students progress faster than their peers. (p. 153)

As Marzano et al. (2018) also observe, level 5 addresses the same question that PLC critical question four addresses: How will we extend learning for students who are already proficient?

The concepts and practices of a PLC focus on the necessary prerequisites required to successfully create a system of competency-based education. As noted previously in this chapter, in high-performing PLCs, teacher teams collaboratively drill deeply into each standard, identifying the most essential skills and concepts all students must learn, and teams collaboratively agree on what these student outcomes look like in student work.

Such specificity provides the impetus for teams to monitor the learning of each student—skill by skill—through the use of frequent and timely collaboratively developed common formative assessments. Taken together, these two activities allow schools to create systems that provide additional time and support for struggling students on specific competencies, as well as *a systematic plan to extend the learning of students who demonstrate proficiency.*

District Leadership in an HRS and PLC

Consider this progression: Since the 1970s, clear and consistent findings show that an effective teacher is critically important for ensuring high levels of learning for all students. Research findings of the 1980s and 1990s highlight the critically important role principals play in creating effective schools. In more recent years, research focuses on the role of district leadership in impacting student achievement. In short, leadership matters—a lot!

A meta-analysis of research concludes effective district-level leadership has a statistically significant impact on student achievement (Marzano & Waters, 2009). Additional studies continue to confirm these findings. For example, research from author Karin Chenoweth (2015) concludes, "School districts shape the conditions in which schools operate and as such can support or undermine school success and thus student success" (p. 14).

In *Learning by Doing: A Handbook for Professional Learning Communities at Work,* DuFour et al. (2016) address the question of what effective district leaders must do in order to positively impact student achievement:

> Those who hope to lead implementation of the PLC process on a districtwide basis must be prepared to address the following questions:
>
> - What are our priorities?
> - What are the specific conditions we expect to see in every school?
> - What must we do to build the capacity of people throughout the organization to create these conditions?
> - What indicators of progress will we monitor?
> - What attitudes and behaviors will we publicly recognize and celebrate?
> - What current district practices and behaviors and leadership behaviors are not aligned with the purpose and priorities we have articulated?
> - What could we stop doing to provide more time for implementation of the PLC process in all of our schools? (DuFour et al., 2016, p. 235)

The HRS model is a helpful tool for district leaders to address these and other questions. And, in addressing the questions and issues facing district leaders, both the PLC process and the HRS model intentionally work to balance districtwide priorities and goals with building-level staff autonomy.

Leadership practices in PLCs reflect a culture that is simultaneously loose and tight (DuFour et al., 2016; Peters & Waterman, 1982). That is, effective district leadership encourages—in fact, expects—individual creativity, innovation, empowerment, and continuous improvement within a culture of clear priorities and parameters. The HRS model calls this *defined autonomy* (Marzano & Waters, 2009).

The HRS model urges district leaders to do the following.

- Set up collaborative teams for building leaders.
- Focus on critical commitments within the HRS model.

- Establish district roles for each of the five levels of the HRS model.

- Celebrate successes.

About This Book

In his introduction to *Leading a High Reliability School* (Marzano et al., 2018), Richard DuFour observes that the PLC process should be the cornerstone of the creation of an HRS. The PLC process and HRS model are not competing approaches to school improvement. While the PLC process serves as the cornerstone of high reliability schools, the HRS model serves as a valuable tool for educators who are seeking to reculture their schools into high-performing PLCs.

The purpose of this anthology is to drill deeper into this proposition, and the contributors to this tome address the five levels of the HRS model. Each level is discussed in two chapters—the first chapter from an educator with a deep, rich understanding of and experience with the HRS model followed by a companion chapter from an author with successful experiences with the PLC process. We are pleased to present their collective wisdom, insights, and experiences.

> While the PLC process serves as the cornerstone of high reliability schools, the HRS model serves as a valuable tool for educators who are seeking to reculture their schools into high-performing PLCs.

Part I: The Five Levels

The chapters in part I address the five levels in the HRS model and how the PLC process provides the foundation for implementation. In chapter 1, Mario Acosta describes how a safe, supportive, and collaborative culture is the foundation of effective schooling and a necessary condition for the success of any complex school initiative. In chapter 2, Anthony Muhammad argues that the PLC process creates the foundation of success for creating a high reliability school that supports level 1 in the HRS model.

In chapter 3, Toby Boss describes how schools and districts use the leading indicators at level 2 of the HRS model—effective teaching in every classroom—to create a shared language of instruction. In chapter 4, William M. Ferriter provides helpful insights into the role of effective teaching in the PLC process. He discusses how collaborative teams in a PLC use a cycle of inquiry and continuous improvement to analyze and refine their instruction to make effective teaching a reality in their schools.

In chapter 5, Jan K. Hoegh describes the defining features of level 3—a guaranteed and viable curriculum—from the HRS perspective. She lays out the process to design and implement a guaranteed and viable curriculum and describes how schools use such a curriculum to enhance classroom instruction, assessment, intervention, and enrichment. In chapter 6, Heather Friziellie and Julie A. Schmidt drill deeper into the concepts and practices underlying developing, implementing, and improving a guaranteed and viable curriculum within a PLC.

In chapter 7, Tammy Heflebower focuses on the leader's role in making the transformation from traditional grading to standards-referenced reporting, level 4 of the HRS model. In chapter 8, Eric Twadell shares the elements of Adlai E. Stevenson High School's effective standards-referenced reporting system. The United States Department of Education describes Stevenson as one of the most recognized and celebrated schools in America.

In chapter 9, Mike Ruyle describes the HRS perspective on level 5—competency-based education—and provides a solid theoretical and research base for transitioning to the model. In chapter 10, Mike Mattos explores the skills and behaviors students need for college and career readiness, and how PLCs support the acquisition of these skills, and he digs deeper into each of the level 5 HRS indicators, considering how a PLC school would interpret and implement these outcomes.

Part II: Professional Learning Communities, High Reliability Organizations, and School Leadership

The chapters in part II address effective HRS and PLC leadership at the school level. In chapter 11, Philip B. Warrick makes the case that leadership from an HRS perspective requires a fundamental shift from viewing effective leadership as the acquisition of a series of personal traits and skills to having a laser-like focus on specific actions with specific outcomes. In chapter 12, Timothy D. Kanold addresses the issue of effective leadership within a PLC. He provides five coherence-building actions leaders can emphasize in their daily efforts to make the big ideas of a PLC a constant focus.

Part III: Professional Learning Communities, High Reliability Organizations, and Districtwide Leadership

Part III focuses on districtwide leadership of the HRS model and PLC process. In chapter 13, Cameron L. Rains describes how district leaders use the HRS model as the driving force for improvement within each school and classroom. In chapter 14, Marc Johnson offers his insights into districtwide leadership within the PLC context through his journey of transformation as superintendent of Sanger Unified School District, a district the California Department of Education identified as a Program Improvement (PI) district.

It is our hope that after reading this book, you will come to view the merging of these ideas, concepts, and practices as a significant step in the quest to create excellent schools for *all* students.

> It is our hope that after reading this book, you will come to view the merging of these ideas, concepts, and practices as a significant step in the quest to create excellent schools for all students.

References and Resources

Bourrier, M. (2011). *The legacy of the theory of high reliability organizations: An ethnographic endeavor* (Working Paper No. 6). Geneva, Switzerland: Universite de Geneve.

Chenoweth, K. (2015). Teachers matter. Yes. Schools matter. Yes. Districts matter—really? *Phi Delta Kappan, 97*(2), 14–20.

DuFour, R., DuFour, R., & Eaker, R. (2008). *Revisiting Professional Learning Communities at Work: New insights for improving schools.* Bloomington, IN: Solution Tree Press.

DuFour, R., DuFour, R., Eaker, R., Many, T. W., & Mattos, M. (2016). *Learning by doing: A handbook for Professional Learning Communities at Work* (3rd ed.). Bloomington, IN: Solution Tree Press.

DuFour, R., & Eaker, R. (1998). *Professional Learning Communities at Work: Best practices for enhancing student achievement.* Bloomington, IN: Solution Tree Press.

Eaker, R., & Keating, J. (2012). *Every school, every team, every classroom: District leadership for growing Professional Learning Communities at Work.* Bloomington, IN: Solution Tree Press.

Ericsson, K. A., & Pool, R. (2016). *Peak: Secrets from the new science of expertise.* Boston: Houghton Mifflin Harcourt.

Glass, G. V., McGaw, B., & Smith, M. L. (1981). *Meta-analysis in social research.* Beverly Hills, CA: SAGE.

Hattie, J. (2009). *Visible learning: A synthesis of over 800 meta-analyses relating to achievement.* New York: Routledge.

Hattie, J. (2012). *Visible learning for teachers: Maximizing impact on learning.* New York: Routledge.

Hattie, J. (2015). The application of visible learning to higher education. *Scholarship of Teaching and Learning in Psychology, 1*(1), 79–91.

Jordan, V. B., & Brownlee, L. (1981, April 13–17). *Meta-analysis of the relationship between Piagetian and school achievement tests.* Paper presented at the 65th annual meeting of the American Educational Research Association, Los Angeles.

Kotter, J. (2008). *A sense of urgency.* Boston: Harvard Business School Press.

Lipsey, M. W., Puzio, K., Yun, C., Hebert, M. A., Steinka-Fry, K., Cole, M. W., et al. (2012, November). *Translating the statistical representation of the effects of education interventions into more readily interpretable forms.* Washington, DC: Institute for Education Sciences.

Marzano, R. J. (2003). *What works in schools: Translating research into action.* Alexandria, VA: Association for Supervision and Curriculum Development.

Marzano, R. J., Heflebower, T., Hoegh, J. K., Warrick, P. B., & Grift, G. (2016). *Collaborative teams that transform schools: The next step in PLCs.* Bloomington, IN: Marzano Resources.

Marzano, R. J., Warrick, P. B., Rains, C. L., & DuFour, R. (2018). *Leading a high reliability school.* Bloomington, IN: Solution Tree Press.

Marzano, R. J., Warrick, P. B., & Simms, J. A. (2014). *A handbook for high reliability schools: The next step in school reform.* Bloomington, IN: Marzano Resources.

Marzano, R. J., & Waters, T. (2009). *District leadership that works: Striking the right balance.* Bloomington, IN: Solution Tree Press.

Naisbitt, J., & Aburdene, P. (1985). *Re-inventing the corporation: Transforming our job and your company for the new information society.* New York: Little, Brown.

Nye, B., Konstantopoulos, S., & Hedges, L. V. (2004). How large are teacher effects? *Educational Evaluation and Policy Analysis, 26*(3), 237–257.

Peters, T. J., & Waterman, R. H., Jr. (1982). *In search of excellence: Lessons from America's best-run companies.* New York: Warner Books.

Pfeffer, J., & Sutton, R. I. (2000). *The knowing-doing gap: How smart companies turn knowledge into action.* Boston: Harvard Business School Press.

Sinek, S. (2009). *Start with why: How great leaders inspire everyone to take action.* New York: Portfolio.

Weick, K. E., Sutcliffe, K. M., & Obstfeld, D. (1999). Organizing for high reliability: Processes of collective mindfulness. *Research in Organizational Behavior, 1*, 81–123.

PART I

The Five Levels

LEVEL 1:

A Safe, Supportive, and Collaborative Culture

The culture of any organization forms the basis for how people think and act. All organizations, including school districts, schools, teams, and classrooms, have cultures; the issue is what kind of culture drives behavior and attitudes, day in, day out. Leaders attempting to improve their district or school by focusing exclusively on *structural change* (policies, rules, organizational charts, position descriptions, schedules, and so on) rather than *cultural change* (shared beliefs, behaviors, norms, attitudes, habits, and so on) will be disappointed in the fruits of their labor. While structural changes may be necessary, absent the accompanying cultural changes, they are insufficient.

For educational institutions, the primary focus of an effective culture must be linked to the core of the enterprise: *enhancing the learning of both students and adults.* Beyond a persistent and passionate focus on learning, other aspects of an effective district or school culture include areas such as safety, support, and collaboration. And, of these, effective leaders recognize that building *a meaningful and effective collaborative culture* is the central organizing principle that drives high reliability schools and PLCs.

Of course, collaboratively determining the kind of culture faculty and staff seek to develop is one thing; leading an effective process for developing such a culture is another. Effective leaders do not leave culture building to chance. They recognize a huge difference between *planning* and *developing* an effective culture and *hoping* an effective culture will emerge.

In chapters 1 and 2, the authors address what constitutes an effective culture within the HRS model and the PLC process, as well as identify methods for developing an effective school culture.

Mario Acosta

Mario Acosta, EdD, is principal at Westwood High School in Texas, a *Newsweek* top-fifty campus and member of the High Reliability Schools (HRS) network. He has served as a classroom teacher, instructional coach, new teacher professional development specialist, professional development consultant, assistant principal, academic director, and principal. He specializes in campus-level implementation of effective campus culture, professional learning communities (PLCs), instructional improvement, response to intervention, and standards-referenced reporting. As an HRS certifier, Dr. Acosta works with K–12 schools and districts across the United States as they progress through the various levels of certification.

Dr. Acosta holds a doctorate in educational administration from the University of Texas and a superintendent certification in the state of Texas. He earned a bachelor's degree in mathematics from the University of Texas and a master's degree from Lamar University.

To learn more about Dr. Acosta's work, visit marzanoresources.com or follow @marioacosta31 on Twitter.

To book Mario Acosta for professional development, contact pd@SolutionTree.com.

In this chapter, Dr. Acosta describes how a safe, supportive, and collaborative culture is the foundation of effective schooling and a necessary condition for the success of any complex school initiative. He makes the case that school leaders must consider the development of such a culture as their foundational duty.

Chapter 1

Culture Building in a High Reliability School

Mario Acosta

In an era of high-stakes accountability, schools must operate as high-functioning organizations that manage and balance a myriad of complexities to educate an ever-diversifying learner population. As the educational landscape becomes increasingly complex, so, too, does the role of the school leader. School leaders were once looked upon as managers of the operational day-to-day tasks of the school. However, researchers Karen Seashore Louis, Kenneth Leithwood, Kyla L. Wahlstrom, and Stephen E. Anderson (2010) affirm the critical role of today's school leaders by noting, "School leadership, from formal and informal sources, helps to shape school conditions (including, for example, goals, culture, and structures) and classroom conditions (including the content of instruction, the size of classrooms, and the pedagogy used by teachers)" (p. 14).

As school-improvement experts and authors Richard DuFour and Robert J. Marzano (2011) clarify, "Powerful school leadership on the part of the principal has a positive effect on student achievement" (p. 48). Of particular importance is the leader's ability to create a safe, supportive, and collaborative culture in which students, staff, parents, and the community work in tandem to ensure learning thrives. In his definition of *school culture*, Kent D. Peterson, a professor in the Department of Educational Administration at the University of Wisconsin–Madison, states, "The culture of a school consists primarily of the underlying norm values and beliefs that teachers and administrators hold about teaching and learning" (as cited in Education World, n.d.). Peterson adds that culture is composed of "traditions and ceremonies schools hold to build community and reinforce their values" (as cited in Education World, n.d.). The literature has identified school culture as a factor in student achievement for many years. Louis et al. (2010) state, "Collective leadership has a stronger influence on student achievement than individual leadership, likewise, a school's leaders have an impact on student achievement primarily through their influence on teachers' motivation and working conditions" (p. 19). The research suggests by implementing a positive and collaborative school culture, leaders can most directly impact student achievement. Authors Terrence E. Deal and Kent D. Peterson (2016) support this concept regarding school culture:

> In study after study, when cultural patterns did not support and encourage reform, changes did not take place. By contrast, things improved in schools where customs, values, and beliefs reinforced a strong educational mission, a sense of community, social trust among staff members, and a shared commitment to school improvement. (p. 10)

The research suggests by implementing a positive and collaborative school culture, leaders can most directly impact student achievement.

It follows that creating and fostering a healthy school culture is of chief importance for school leaders.

Building Culture Through Leadership

Effective school leaders must have the skills to manage and direct the various functions of school operation. Rubén D. Olivárez (2013), a professor and executive director of the Cooperative Superintendency Doctoral Program at the University of Texas at Austin, identifies the functions and leadership competencies of schools as curriculum and instruction, human resources, safety and security, accountability and technology services, external and internal communications, facilities planning, finance and business operations, and governance. In addition to being effective managers of the various school functions, leaders must also create a healthy school culture. As author and educational consultant Elaine K. McEwan (2003) asserts, "The highly effective principal is a culture builder, an individual who communicates and models a strong and viable vision based on achievement, character, personal responsibility, and accountability" (p. 101). However, often school leaders are not adequately trained or do not have the prerequisite skills to effectively direct each of these school functions.

In their Wallace Foundation study, Louis et al. (2010) exclaim, "Leadership is second only to classroom instruction as an influence on student learning" (p. 9). Researchers have long studied and identified critical school-leadership traits. Author and founder of Creative Leadership Solutions Douglas Reeves (2006) expounds that school leaders must possess visionary, relational, system, reflective, collaborative, analytical, and communicative leadership skills. Furthermore, coauthors Robert J. Marzano, Timothy Walters, and Brian A. McNulty (2005) identify twenty-one responsibilities and day-to-day management duties of a school leader:

1. Establishing an effective monitoring system to provide feedback on the effectiveness of the school's curriculum, instruction, and assessment practices and their effect on student achievement

2. Building and maintaining a culture in which common language is employed, ideas are shared, and staff members operate within the norms of cooperation

3. Operating from a well-articulated and visible set of ideals and beliefs regarding schooling, teaching, and learning

4. Seeking out and keeping abreast of research and theory on effective practices in curriculum, instruction, and assessment

5. Actively helping teachers with issues regarding curriculum, instruction, and assessment in their classrooms

6. Establishing concrete goals relative to student achievement as well as curriculum, instruction, and assessment practices in the school, and keeping these prominent in the day-to-day life of the school

7. Establishing procedures and routines that give staff and students a sense of order and predictability

8. Recognizing and celebrating the legitimate successes of individuals within the school as well as the school as a whole; also recognizing and acknowledging failures when appropriate

9. Fostering knowledge of research and theory on best practices among the staff through reading and discussion

10. Establishing and fostering clear lines of communication to and from the staff as well as within the staff

11. Establishing and fostering procedures that ensure the staff members have input into key decisions and policies

12. Attending to and fostering personal relationships with the staff

13. Providing an optimistic view of what the school is doing and what the school can accomplish in the future

14. Inviting and honoring the expression of a variety of opinions regarding the running of the school and adapting one's leadership style to the demands of the current situation

15. Ensuring that the staff members have the necessary resources, support, and professional development to effectively execute the teaching and learning process

16. Expecting and recognizing superior performance from the staff

17. Being keenly aware of the mechanisms and dynamics that define the day-to-day functioning of the school and using that awareness to forecast potential problems

18. Being an advocate of the school to all relevant constituents and ensuring that the school complies with all important regulations and requirements

19. Being highly visible to teachers, students, and parents through frequent visits to classrooms

20. Protecting staff members from undue interruptions and controversies that might distract them from the teaching and learning process

21. Being willing to challenge school practices that have been in place for a long time and promoting the value of working at the edge of one competence (p. 71)

When examining these twenty-one responsibilities of a school leader, it is evident that effective school leadership is dynamic, intricate, and difficult. Effective school leaders must be talented, growth-minded, and tireless in their pursuit of a high-quality education for all the students they serve.

While the literature is rich with identified traits and skills of effective school leadership, it is also important to note that no one single leader can embody every possible leadership trait and possess each leadership skill at all times. As DuFour and Marzano (2011) underscore, "No one person has the knowledge, skills, or energy to fulfill twenty-one responsibilities simultaneously" (p. 50). According to author and consultant Carol Dweck, "Individuals who believe their talents can be developed (through hard work, good strategies, and input from others) have a growth mindset" (p. 2). The most effective school leaders view themselves with a growth mindset,

Effective school leaders must be talented, growth-minded, and tireless in their pursuit of a high-quality education for all the students they serve.

working continuously to improve their leadership aptitude and effectiveness. Furthermore, school leaders must surround themselves with others who possess complementary talents, activating and empowering others to infuse their talent and expertise for the betterment of the organization and the students. McEwan (2003) addresses how effective leaders manage the complexity and girth of the role, explaining:

Highly effective principals know themselves and that they are works in progress. They have identified their strengths (the behaviors and attitudes that seem easy and natural to them) and use them to complement and enhance their less well-developed traits (the behaviors and attitudes that take practice and discipline to achieve). In addition, successful principals know how to tap and develop the talents and strengths of parents, teachers, and other staff members to compensate for their own less well-developed traits. (p. 165)

While the importance of the leader cannot be overstated, it is important to note that a healthy culture consists of much more than the singular leader.

Focusing on Organizational Culture and School Effectiveness

In *Built to Last*, best-selling coauthors Jim Collins and Jerry I. Porras (2002) dispel the myth that great organizations are the result of the greatness of a single charismatic and extremely skilled leader. Rather, they emphasize organizational success coming from "underlying processes and fundamental dynamics embedded in the organization" (Collins & Porras, 2002, p. 41). As a result of such findings, school leaders should focus intently on implementing the underlying processes and fundamental dynamics to elicit those practices in staff, students, parents, and community members that will result in positive outcomes in student achievement. Furthermore, collaborative teams of professionals (focused on a strategic plan that continuously monitors the effectiveness of specific improvement initiatives) must organize and run schools. DuFour and Marzano (2011) say, "The time principals devote to building the capacity of teachers to work in collaborative teams is more effective than time spent attempting to supervise individual teachers into better performance" (p. 60).

The HRS framework guides and supports school and district leadership with its five levels (safe and collaborative culture, effective teaching in every classroom, guaranteed and viable curriculum, standards-referenced reporting, and competency-based education; Marzano, Warrick, & Simms, 2014). Guiding indicators within the framework guide practitioners to effectively implement and monitor initiatives and actions within each of the school's operating functions. The concepts at level 1 of the framework—safe, supportive, and collaborative culture—guide school leaders in the creation and maintenance of a healthy school culture. Table 1.1 illustrates a comparison between twelve of the school-leadership responsibilities Marzano et al. (2005) offer and specific leading indicators at level 1 of the HRS framework.

Table 1.1: Integration of Leadership Responsibilities Into HRS Level 1

Principal Responsibility	Application to HRS Level 1
Recognizes and celebrates accomplishments and acknowledges failures	*Leading Indicator 1.7:* The principal appropriately acknowledges the success of the whole school, as well as individuals within the school.
Recognizes and rewards individual accomplishments	*Leading Indicator 1.7:* The principal appropriately acknowledges the success of the whole school, as well as individuals within the school.
Establishes strong lines of communication with and among teachers and students	*Leading Indicators 1.5 and 1.6:* Teachers, staff, students, parents, and community members have formal ways to provide input regarding the optimal functioning of the school.
Fosters shared beliefs and a sense of community and cooperation	*Leading Indicator 1.4:* Collaborative teams regularly interact to address common issues regarding curriculum, assessment, instruction, and the achievement of all students.
Protects teachers from issues and influences that would detract from their teaching time or focus	*Leading Indicator 1.8:* The principal manages the fiscal, operational, and technological resources of the school in a way that directly supports teachers.
Adapts his or her leadership behavior to the needs of the current situation and is comfortable with dissent	*Leading Indicators 1.5 and 1.6:* Teachers, staff, students, parents, and community members have formal ways to provide input regarding the optimal functioning of the school.
Communicates and operates from strong ideals and beliefs about schooling	*Leading Indicator 1.4:* Collaborative teams regularly interact to address common issues regarding curriculum, assessment, instruction, and the achievement of all students.
Involves teachers in the design and implementation of important decisions and policies	*Leading Indicator 1.3:* Teachers have formal roles in the decision-making process regarding school initiatives.

Continued →

Is directly involved in the design and implementation of curriculum, instruction, and assessment practices	*Leading Indicator 1.4:* Collaborative teams regularly interact to address common issues regarding curriculum, assessment, instruction, and the achievement of all students.
Monitors the effectiveness of school practices and their impact on student learning	*Leading Indicators 1.5 and 1.6:* Teachers, staff, students, parents, and community members have formal ways to provide input regarding the optimal functioning of the school.
Establishes a set of standard operating procedures and routines	*Leading Indicators 1.1 and 1.2:* The faculty, staff, students, parents, and community members perceive the school environment as safe and orderly.
Is aware of the details and undercurrents in the running of the school and uses this information to address current and potential problems	*Leading Indicators 1.5 and 1.6:* Teachers, staff, students, parents, and community members have formal ways to provide input regarding the optimal functioning of the school.

Source: Adapted from Marzano et al., 2005, 2014.

According to researchers and coauthors Robert J. Marzano, Philip B. Warrick, Cameron L. Rains, and Richard DuFour (2018):

A high reliability school does not leave culture up to chance or happenstance. Rather, leaders in an HRS strive to ensure the organization fosters shared beliefs, behaviors, and norms relative to at least three areas: (1) safety, (2) support, and (3) collaboration. (p. 37)

This chapter will focus on the importance of installing a safe, supportive, and collaborative culture and how school leaders can use the HRS framework to guide the creation of short-term strategic initiatives and monitoring systems to ensure successful long-term sustainability of a healthy school culture.

Creating a Vision to Inspire a Supportive and Collaborative Culture

Any organization's culture has a direct and substantial impact on performance because its culture drives its beliefs and practices.

Therefore, the effectiveness of the organization's culture will impact its overall effectiveness. For this reason, it is important for schools to use a calculated focus to develop their cultures. School leaders should focus efforts to intentionally define and foster a healthy school culture. School culture experts Anthony Muhammad and Luis F. Cruz (2019) offer an example of a healthy school culture by asserting that "educators in a healthy school culture believe that all students can excel, and they willingly challenge and change their own practices to meet that end" (p. 14). School leaders must ensure clarity of purpose and action regarding school culture. Research on successful organizations in both the educational and corporate sectors identifies the importance and complexity of establishing healthy cultures. As D. D. Warrick (2017), an author who specializes in developing and coaching leaders, teams, and organizations, asserts, "Culture significantly affects how an organization is run and organizational practices significantly affect organizational culture" (p. 397). Global leadership director of New Pedagogies for Deep Learning and a worldwide authority on educational reform, Michael Fullan (1991) makes clear to leaders they should "assume that changing the culture of institutions is the real agenda, not implementing single innovations" (p. 107).

According to Louis et al. (2010), there is perhaps no more important function of school leadership than to establish a school vision centered on high student achievement, develop an atmosphere of care and trust, and empower educators to learn and grow according to the school-created vision. It is not enough, however, for a school to have written vision and mission statements. Organizational cultures define the *clarity of both purpose and action* for the members of the organization. Coauthors Richard DuFour, Rebecca DuFour, Robert Eaker, Thomas W. Many, and Mike Mattos (2016) proclaim, "We have found no correlation between the presence of a written mission statement, or even the wording of a mission statement, and a school's effectiveness" (p. 19). Often, schools' written vision or mission statements fall short of declaring or identifying the school's actionable ideology (expected behaviors) and beliefs. These statements are frequently broad and do not clearly define the expectations for the campus. For educators to truly believe in and adopt practices in alignment with a school's

School leaders should focus efforts to intentionally define and foster a healthy school culture.

vision, mission, values, and goals, they must first understand what ideological expectations have been set.

A critical first step in the process of defining and fostering a healthy school culture is identifying and clarifying core ideology. Much has been written about organizational vision, mission, and values in business since the 1950s. The Disney Institute (2011) discusses vision, mission, and values, asserting, "Management thinkers have identified these statements of organizational intent as highly effective workplace unifiers and have shown in studies that companies with well-defined ideologies are successful in the long-term" (p. 39). DuFour et al. (2016) identify the four core pillars that form the foundation of the PLC process.

> *A critical first step in the process of defining and fostering a healthy school culture is identifying and clarifying core ideology.*

1. **Mission (purpose):** Why does a school exist?

2. **Vision:** What must a school become in order to fulfill its fundamental purpose?

3. **Collective commitments (values):** How must the members of the school behave?

4. **Goals:** Which steps will the school take and when?

It is critical that school leaders ensure clarity regarding the organization's purpose and core values. Marzano et al. (2018) explain:

> Above all else, leaders of any effective organization must know the importance of clarity. Having clarity means communicating consistently in words and actions the organization's purpose, the future the organization will attempt to create, the specific actions members can immediately take to achieve its goals, and the progress indicators it will track. (pp. 4–5)

Schools are advised against skipping this foundational first step. Schools can be tempted to bypass identifying their core ideology and move straight to defining operational procedures, policies, and practices. While dealing in the concrete work of procedures, policies, and practices may be more palatable for staff than identifying core purpose and values, failing to clearly set or identify their core ideology will cause the school to struggle with the implementation of conditions set forth within the HRS framework.

Schools are, therefore, well served to take the time to identify and address their core ideology to construct their schools' culture. This core ideology will become the cornerstone of the organization's beliefs. In their research regarding visionary companies, which the authors define as premier institutions that prosper over long periods of time, Collins and Porras (2002) remark, "Core values need no rational or external justification. Nor do they sway with the trends and fads of the day. Nor even do they shift in response to changing market conditions" (p. 75).

A school cannot simply declare its core ideology, consisting of its vision, mission, values, and goals. Instead, the school must either reflect existing truths about the organization or create new ideals to pursue until they become inherent truths (Collins & Porras, 2002).

For organizations to remain successful in the long term, they must be willing to change and adapt their practices as their situation changes with time. Indeed, this is true for schools as well. Notions of traditional schooling practices have begun to fall flat as today's schools struggle to educate new learners in a digital and global era. Educators face the challenge of serving an ever-diversifying student population, increasingly rigorous state and federal standards, and heightened accountability measures. American society has raised its expectation of schools. Schools must now rise to the challenge of ensuring that all students learn essential knowledge and obtain skills that will prepare them for postsecondary opportunities in college, a career, or the military. Despite all of the changes in the educational landscape, effective leaders and schools with healthy school cultures ensure their core ideology (mission, vision, values, goals) does not change, despite the fact that their practices, policies, and procedures must.

Collins and Porras (2002) clarify that a visionary company carefully preserves and protects its core ideology while relentlessly driving for progress that propels change and forward movement in all that is not part of the core ideology. School leaders should take note of this important distinction and work to ensure the school identifies its mission, vision, values, and goals and then entrenches them in the school's belief system. Likewise, school leaders should instill a ceaseless drive to improve and inspect all of the organization's practices, policies, and procedures in their quest to ensure all students acquire the knowledge and skills to prepare them for postsecondary opportunities.

Building Consensus

For the school's core ideology to become a pervasive belief system throughout the organization, the staff must relate to and believe in the ideology. A critical first step in the identification of a school's core ideology is consensus building. According to DuFour et al. (2016), "The creation of a guiding coalition or leadership team is a critical first step in the complex task of leading a school" (p. 15). The authors proceed to advise school leaders to move quickly to action, build shared knowledge among the organization's members, use the core ideology to guide day-to-day decisions, use the ideology to identify existing practices to eliminate, translate the school vision into a succinct explanation of the fundamental purpose, write value statements as behaviors (not beliefs), focus on what each person must do and not do, recognize that the process of solidifying core ideology is nonlinear, and model the way (DuFour et al., 2016). Marzano et al. (2005) expand on this notion, stating:

For the school's core ideology to become a pervasive belief system throughout the organization, the staff must relate to and believe in the ideology.

> We attempt to . . . organize our findings and conclusions into a plan of action that will help any school leader articulate and realize a powerful vision for enhanced achievement of students. Our proposed plan involves five steps:
>
> 1. Develop a strong school leadership team.
>
> 2. Distribute some responsibilities throughout the leadership team.
>
> 3. Select the right work.
>
> 4. Identify the order of magnitude implied by the selected work.
>
> 5. Match the magnitude style to the order of magnitude of the change initiative. (p. 98)

When school leaders have effectively built consensus and clarity regarding the school's purpose, a supportive and collaborative culture will take root. All beliefs, actions, and initiatives will align, and misalignments of former actions and beliefs will be eliminated. "In order to highlight, preserve the core, and stimulate progress, leaders would be well served to impose a tight ideology, indoctrinate new people into the ideology, eject those who do not fit, and give those who remain the tremendous sense of responsibility and belonging that comes with membership in an elite organization" (Collins & Porras, 2002, pp. 138–139).

Ultimately, school leaders have the potential to have a significant positive impact on student achievement by identifying, clarifying, and fostering a healthy school culture in which members produce high levels of student success and staff satisfaction.

Identifying, Clarifying, and Fostering a Core Ideology

I am principal of Westwood High School, a large suburban school in Texas serving a diverse population with a history of successful student performance. To ensure sustainability of this success, my staff engaged in a yearlong process to identify and clarify the school's core ideology. Along with a small group of interested teachers, I (as principal) formed the *visioning committee* to initiate the process. These committee members represented different departments with varying levels of experience in both years of experience and years served on the campus. I selected committee members. These selected staff members were profiled as having a growth mindset and a desire to identify and implement practices and beliefs to help the school on its journey of continuous improvement.

This committee of volunteers began by participating in a book study of *Built to Last: Successful Habits of Visionary Companies* (Collins & Porras, 2002). Upon completion of the book study, the group set out to gain input from all staff members to catalog the school's core ideology in the form of a vision document. This document contains the school's identified core purpose, core values, and big goals. At multiple faculty meetings throughout the year, members of the visioning committee presented information to and solicited input from the entire faculty and staff regarding their opinions on the core purpose, values, and big goals of the school. After presenting three drafts to the staff for feedback, the committee finalized the school's core ideology by creating a vision document. Figure 1.1 (page 48) shows the final version of the Westwood High School vision document.

Vision Document

Core Purpose: To transform lives for the benefit of society

Core Values:

- Respect all in a welcoming and accepting environment.
- Uphold a learning culture built on perseverance and continuous growth.
- Value both inquiry and experience.
- Encourage innovative and creative thinking.
- Foster excellence and balance.
- Embrace professional autonomy and collaboration.
- Practice, promote, and support honesty.

Big Goals:

- To have 100 percent of students graduate from Westwood High School what the state of Texas defines as college, career, and military ready.*
- To be rated the number-one public school in the United States by any of the major publications.
- To earn a top-ten state ranking in all extracurricular and cocurricular clubs and organizations.

---

*College, career, and military readiness is defined by the Texas Education Agency (2019).
Source: Westwood High School, Austin, Texas, 2017. Reprinted with permission.

Figure 1.1: Westwood High School vision document consisting of the school's collaboratively created core purpose, values, and goals.

School leaders use this document to ensure alignment of all beliefs, practices, and initiatives. Westwood High School is an HRS network school. Schools in the HRS network are connected globally through a digital platform. They form a network of educators who share best practices in the pursuit of ensuring effective education for all learners. Campus leadership uses the school's core ideology to guide implementation of leading indicators at levels 1, 2, and 3 of the HRS framework (safe and collaborative culture, effective teaching in every classroom, and guaranteed and viable curriculum). Likewise, the ideology guides the development and support of existing staff. The school's vision document was used to create a hiring profile and new staff induction program. Finally, the document also aided in the removal of personnel and practices not aligned with our school ideology.

Monitoring and Providing Feedback to Collaborative Teams

Earlier in this chapter, the importance of the school leader and his or her ability to foster and maintain a healthy school culture was discussed. Marzano et al. (2005) also identified the twenty-one responsibilities of school leaders. As school leaders entertain the use of the HRS framework to guide their ability to identify, cultivate, and sustain a healthy school culture, parallels can be made between the leading indicators of the HRS framework and the twenty-one responsibilities of school leaders. Of significant importance is the responsibility of school leaders to foster shared beliefs and a sense of community and cooperation, and to be directly involved in the design and implementation of curriculum, instruction, and assessment practices. Similarly, the HRS framework supposes the creation of the leading indicator for putting a PLC process in place as collaborative teams regularly interact to address common issues regarding curriculum, assessment, instruction, and the achievement of all students.

PLC transformation is critical to the successful installation of a safe, supportive, and collaborative culture. Marzano et al. (2014) identify using the PLC process as "critical to high reliability status at level 1" (p. 27). Ensuring the PLC process is in place is of utmost importance for a high reliability school and of particular importance when working to achieve high reliability status at level 1. School leaders intending to install, foster, or maintain a safe, supportive, and collaborative culture should prioritize the implementation of an effective PLC process. As Marzano et al. (2018) point out, "Collaboration through the PLC process is central not only to this level [level 1] of the HRS model but to all the model's levels" (p. 55). DuFour and Marzano (2011) elaborate on the PLC process by explaining that leaders must do the following.

> PLC transformation is critical to the successful installation of a safe, supportive, and collaborative culture.

1. Organize staff into meaningful teams.

2. Give teams time to collaborate.

3. Provide support structures to help groups become teams.

4. Clarify the work teams must accomplish.

5. Monitor the work of teams and provide direction and support as needed.

6. Avoid shortcuts in the collaborative team process.

7. Celebrate short-term wins, and confront those who do not contribute to their teams.

School leaders working to create a collaborative culture need to ensure teachers and staff members have the time, resources, and support they require to cultivate an effective PLC process. School leaders can directly participate in the cultivation of the PLC process and, therefore, have a direct impact on student achievement. According to DuFour and Marzano (2011), the PLC process allows principals to execute a number of the responsibilities of school leadership in an integrated and focused fashion while creating the structure for shared leadership (see figure 1.2).

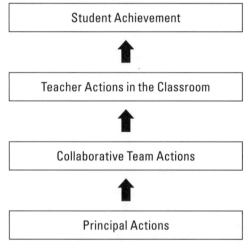

Source: Adapted from DuFour & Marzano, 2011.

Figure 1.2: Relationship between principal behavior and student achievement with collaborative teams in a PLC.

While a specific strength of the PLC process is that teachers engage in a cycle of collective inquiry and collaboratively develop their knowledge and skills (increasing their capacity as individual instructors), it is also an opportunity for the school leader to become directly involved with design and implementation of curriculum, instruction, and assessment practices. One of the seven areas essential for building the collective capacity of collaborative teams is monitoring their work and providing direction and support as needed. DuFour and Marzano (2011) point out:

Establishing expectations for creating and presenting specific products is an important step in building capacity of educators to work as members of a collaborative team. When educators understand the tangible work products that must be created as a result of their collaboration, they develop greater clarity regarding the nature of their work. (p. 84)

School leaders should, therefore, work collaboratively with staff to understand the specificity of required work products, as well as the time line and format for submission. Once they are submitted, school leaders can provide specific, timely feedback to teacher teams. Teamwork products can also provide school leaders with a sense of the functionality and effectiveness of the collaborative teams so leaders can provide supports as needed.

School leaders and teacher teams may use the statements in figure 1.3 as a self-reflection guide to determine the effectiveness of their collaborative teams and the status of each team's PLC process implementation.

1: Strongly Disagree 2: Disagree 3: Neutral 4: Agree 5: Strongly Agree							
1.4 Collaborative teams regularly interact to address common issues regarding curriculum, assessment, instruction, and the achievement of all students.	A professional learning community (PLC) process is in place in our school.	1	2	3	4	5	N/A
	Our school's PLC collaborative teams have written goals.	1	2	3	4	5	N/A
	School leaders regularly examine PLC collaborative teams' progress toward their goals.	1	2	3	4	5	N/A
	Our school's PLC collaborative teams create common assessments.	1	2	3	4	5	N/A
	Our school's PLC collaborative teams analyze student achievement and growth.	1	2	3	4	5	N/A
	Data teams are in place in our school.	1	2	3	4	5	N/A
	Our school's data teams have written goals.	1	2	3	4	5	N/A
	School leaders regularly examine data teams' progress toward their goals.	1	2	3	4	5	N/A
	School leaders collect and review minutes and notes from PLC collaborative team and data team meetings to ensure that teams are focusing on student achievement.	1	2	3	4	5	N/A

Source: Adapted from Marzano et al., 2014, p. 18.

Figure 1.3: Level 1 leading indicator 1.4 survey for teachers and staff.

Figure 1.4, a PLC planning cycle, shows lagging indicators (monitoring systems) leaders use to address reciprocal accountability to their collaborative teams (by monitoring team work products and providing timely feedback and support). At Westwood High School, collaborative teams must complete a PLC work product submission form (see figure 1.5) each time they convene to collaborate. The log asks them to list the participants, areas of the PLC planning cycle they addressed during the meeting, and notes or artifacts of practice.

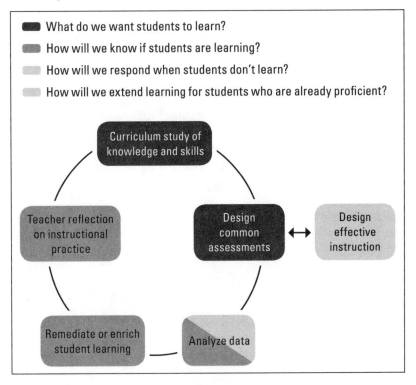

Source: Westwood High School, Austin, Texas, 2017. Reprinted with permission.

Figure 1.4: Westwood High School PLC planning cycle clarifying the work collaborative teams must accomplish.

Westwood High School's campus administration meets weekly to review, discuss, and provide written feedback to each collaborative team. Trained in what to look for in effective PLC work products, the administrative team shares the responsibility of giving feedback to each of the teams using an artifact log feedback form (figure 1.6, page 54). To provide face-to-face feedback, campus administrators systematically visit each weekly team meeting and log their observations in a spreadsheet. They use these observations in conjunction with the work products to determine each team's operational autonomy. Teams with greater need for support and guidance score lower on the operational autonomy rubric (see figure 1.7, page 55). The administration uses these data to help allocate time, resources, and support.

PLC Log		
Work Cycle:		
1. Curriculum study of knowledge and skills 2. Design common assessments 3. Design effective instruction 4. Analyze data 5. Remediate or enrich student learning 6. Teacher reflection on instructional practice		
Directions: In column two, note the stages of the work cycle the team addressed (list more than one number if applicable). Use the notes column to log minutes or include a link to an artifact. For example, if your artifact is a test or assignment the team collaborated on, please provide context and information in this column in addition to the document link so your principal can better understand your team's work. Your artifact could also be a link to an agenda with embedded notes or minutes.		
Attendees	**Work Cycle Number**	**Notes**
Sandy, Kerry, April, Chris	1, 3	Reviewed calendar dates for fourth six weeks and *Odyssey* unit, discussed the need to find more advanced placement multiple-choice passages for the upcoming APMC. (Sandy will find them. Kerry will merge and format the documents.) April showed us how to use an escape room activity to teach background for the *Odyssey*. https://sites.google.com/a/teachnouvelle.com/telemachus-quest/home
Jane, Chris, Sandy, Kerry	2	Jane's email to Chris: I have a passage for us. I am attaching the 2017 language test. I think we should use passage three, "Walk for walking's sake," questions 30–37. It's an older passage and British, but I did not find passage four, "An old photograph," questions 42–50. It's more recent but slightly harder. Pair "Walk for walking's sake" with "Washington" and "Photo" with "Touchwood."

Figure 1.5: Westwood High School PLC work product submission form.

Continued →

Jane, Sara, Sandy, Kerry	3	Sara merged low APMC documents in order to have A-day and B-day versions. Jane created a practice assignment focusing on a few strategies.
Cheryl, Mike, Sara, Jane	4	Shared APMC scores: Looked at high and low scores of orange-day APMC. Mike is creating debrief for B-day; need debrief for A-day. Cheryl will take one passage from orange day and Sara will take the other. A day = 3 points each. Waiting on B scores. Reading district common assessment scheduled 2/4–5 (located in third six weeks on district curriculum pacing guide). Revising and editing DCA scheduled February 26 (located in second six weeks on ARRC).

Source: Westwood High School, Austin, Texas, 2017. Reprinted with permission.

PLC Artifact Log Feedback Form

DATE:

Date
mm/dd/yyyy

TEAM:

Your answer

Members of the team:

Your answer

Praise:

Your answer

Probing questions:

Your answer

Action steps:

Your answer

Source: Westwood High School, Austin, Texas, 2017. Reprinted with permission.

Figure 1.6: Westwood High School PLC artifact feedback form.

Autonomy Rating Guide

1	**No Autonomy**
	The team has not established norms.
	Collaboration is not evident.
2	**Partial Autonomy**
	Individual ownership of student achievement is the predominant practice.
	Collaboration is occurring on specific issues.
	PLC norms exist and individuals hold themselves accountable to the norms.
3	**Developing Autonomy**
	Collective ownership of student achievement is emerging in some practices and artifacts.
	A collaborative culture is emerging, but not constant in practices and artifacts.
	Teacher reflective practice is emerging, but not constant in practices and artifacts.
	PLC norms exist and members hold themselves and each other accountable to them.
	Two or three of the critical questions of a PLC are the focus of meetings and agenda items.
4	**Operational Autonomy**
	Collective ownership of student achievement is evident in practice and artifacts.
	A productive culture of collaboration is evident in practice and artifacts.
	Teacher reflective practices (using a growth mindset) are evident in practice and artifacts.
	Team norms exist and guide all practice, and the team evaluates their effectiveness.
	The four critical questions of a PLC are the focus of meetings and agenda items.

Source: Westwood High School, Austin, Texas, 2017. Reprinted with permission.

Figure 1.7: Westwood High School PLC operational autonomy rubric.

Since 2000, the PLC process has been one of the most prevalent and effective school-improvement strategies deployed in schools. Given the importance of the PLC process, school leaders would do well to develop, coach, and grow their teacher teams and collaborative groups. In fact, Marzano et al. (2014) assert that in order for schools to effectively implement level 1 of the HRS framework, leading indicator 1.4, in which teacher teams and collaborative groups interact regularly to address common issues regarding curriculum, assessment, instruction, and the achievement of all students, must be in place and healthy. Therefore, school leaders must train, develop, and build feedback systems for their collaborative teams in order to ensure their effectiveness. School leaders cannot leave to chance that groups of teachers will come together to produce high-quality work. As with any endeavor in education, proficiency requires deliberate practice with a quality feedback loop. Ultimately, collaborative teams, using an effective PLC process, become the vehicle for improvement strategies found within subsequent levels of the HRS framework and therefore must be prioritized by schools and school leaders.

> School leaders cannot leave to chance that groups of teachers will come together to produce high-quality work. As with any endeavor in education, proficiency requires deliberate practice with a quality feedback loop.

Conclusion

A safe, supportive, and collaborative culture is the foundation of a high reliability school, and creating it is also the first order of business for an effective leader. This chapter linked the actions and indicators for level 1 of the HRS model with the literature on leadership to provide a blueprint for school leaders regarding what should be at the top of their list in terms of necessary actions to take and conditions to foster.

References and Resources

Collins, J., & Porras, J. I. (2002). *Built to last: Successful habits of visionary companies.* New York: HarperCollins.

Deal, T. E., & Peterson, K. D. (2016). *Shaping school culture* (3rd ed.). San Francisco: Jossey-Bass.

Disney Institute. (2011). *Be our guest: Perfecting the art of customer service* (Rev. ed.). New York: Disney Editions.

DuFour, R., DuFour, R., Eaker, R., Many, T. W., & Mattos, M. (2016). *Learning by doing: A handbook for Professional Learning Communities at Work* (3rd ed.). Bloomington, IN: Solution Tree Press.

DuFour, R., & Marzano, R. J. (2011). *Leaders of learning: How district, school, and classroom leaders improve student achievement*. Bloomington, IN: Solution Tree Press.

Dweck, C. (2016, January 13). What having a "growth mindset" actually means. *Harvard Business Review*, 2–4.

Education World. (n.d.). *Is your school's culture toxic or positive?* Accessed at https://education world.com/a_admin/admin/admin275.shtml on June 21, 2019.

Fullan, M. (1991). *The new meaning of educational change* (2nd ed.). New York: Teachers College Press.

Hechanova, R. M., & Cementina-Olpoc, R. (2013). Transformational leadership, change management, and commitment to change: A comparison of academic and business organizations. *Asia-Pacific Education Researcher, 22*(1), 11–19.

Louis, K. S., Leithwood, K., Wahlstrom, K. L., & Anderson, S. E. (2010, July). *Learning from leadership: Investigating the links to improved student learning*. New York: Wallace Foundation. Accessed at https://wallacefoundation.org/knowledge-center/pages /investigating-the-links-to-improved-student-learning.aspx on June 21, 2019.

Marzano, R. J., Warrick, P. B., Rains, C. L., & DuFour, R. (2018). *Leading a high reliability school*. Bloomington, IN: Solution Tree Press.

Marzano, R. J., Warrick, P. B., & Simms, J. A. (2014). *A handbook for high reliability schools: The next step in school reform*. Bloomington, IN: Marzano Resources.

Marzano, R. J., Waters, T., & McNulty, B. A. (2005). *School leadership that works: From research to results*. Alexandria, VA: Association for Supervision and Curriculum Development.

McEwan, E. K. (2003). *10 traits of highly effective principals: From good to great performance*. Thousand Oaks, CA: Corwin Press.

Muhammad, A. (2018). *Transforming school culture: How to overcome staff division* (2nd ed.). Bloomington, IN: Solution Tree Press.

Muhammad, A., & Cruz, L. F. (2019). *Time for change: 4 essential skills for transformational school and district leaders*. Bloomington, IN: Solution Tree Press.

Olivárez, R. D. (2013). *Framework of district functions and leadership competencies of school superintendents*. Austin, TX: The Cooperative Superintendency Program Field Experience Guidebook.

Reeves, D. (2006). *The learning leader: How to focus school improvement for better results*. Alexandria, VA: Association for Supervision and Curriculum Development.

Schmoker, M. (2011). *Focus: Elevating the essentials to radically improve student learning*. Alexandria, VA: Association for Supervision and Curriculum Development.

Texas Education Agency. (2019). *Texas Education Agency academic accountability system framework*. Accessed at https://tea.texas.gov/sites/default/files/2019%20Accountability %20Framework_final.pdf on November 11, 2019.

Warrick, D. D. (2017). What leaders need to know about organizational culture. *Business Horizons, 60*(3), 395–404.

Whitaker, T. (2003). *What great principals do differently: Fifteen things that matter most*. Larchmont, NY: Eye on Education.

Anthony Muhammad

Anthony Muhammad, PhD, is an international consultant and speaker on topics such as the Professional Learning Community (PLC) at Work process and the importance of organizational culture. As principal of Levey Middle School in Southfield, Michigan, he led the school to being recognized as a National School of Excellence, having doubled students' proficiency rate within five years. He is a prolific writer. His book *Transforming School Culture: How to Overcome Staff Division* is widely used by school leaders who seek to develop a powerful and effective culture. He is also the coauthor of *Time for Change: Essential Skills for Transformational School and District Leaders*, and *Overcoming the Achievement Gap Trap: Liberating Mindsets to Effect Change*.

To learn more about Dr. Muhammad's work, visit New Frontier 21 (www.newfrontier 21.com) or follow @newfrontier21 on Twitter.

To book Anthony Muhammad for professional development, contact pd@Solution Tree.com.

In this chapter, Dr. Muhammad combines a strong research base with his own practical experience leading a highly regarded middle school. He argues that the PLC process creates the foundation of success for creating a high reliability school that supports level 1 (a safe, supportive, and collaborative culture) in the High Reliability Schools (HRS) model. He believes schools must examine the collective beliefs, values, and mindset of collaborative team members to build such a culture.

Chapter 2

Frames of Mind and Tools for Success: Organizational Culture in a PLC

Anthony Muhammad

The culture of any organization is an important factor—if not the *most important* factor—in progress toward fulfilling its purpose. What is the purpose of a school in the contemporary context? PLC at Work process architect Richard DuFour notes, "Schools that strive for excellence must take steps to ensure that all students not only have equal access to but also acquire the knowledge, skills, and dispositions that will prepare them for their future" (as cited in Marzano, Warrick, Rains, & DuFour, 2018, p. 1). In essence, a school is charged with both *access* (equity) and *excellence* (achievement).

Are schools equitable? Do all students have access to the knowledge, skills, and dispositions necessary to prepare them for their future? The evidence affirms that schools have not been equitable. A *Civil Rights Data Collection* brief includes findings from every public school in the United States, comprising about forty-nine million students (U.S. Department of Education, 2014). The purpose of this brief is to give insight into disparities in educational opportunities in the United States that most citizens don't have the access or resources to collect and analyze. Some of the U.S. Department of Education's (2014) findings include the following.

- Impoverished students attend schools with higher concentrations of first-year teachers than students in higher-income communities.

- Among high schools serving the highest populations of African American and Latino students, one in three do not offer a single chemistry course, and one in four do not offer a course more advanced than algebra 1.

- In schools that offer gifted and talented programs, African American and Latino students represent 40 percent of students, but only 26 percent of those enrolled in such programs.

These data provide some insight into a systemic problem with access to rigorous opportunities for some American students. It is very difficult to ensure excellence for all if there is no access for all.

It is very difficult to ensure excellence for all if there is no access for all.

Is there evidence of universal excellence for students attending American schools? Like with equity, there are some glaring disparities in student academic outcomes. The National Assessment of Educational Progress (NAEP), also called the *Nation's Report Card*, is a national academic assessment of an equitable sample of American students to gather evidence on national trends in both mathematics and reading. The collected data give the best snapshot of academic trends in the United States. The assessment is of twelfth-grade students and reveals a shocking disparity in mathematics and reading called the *four-year gap* (as cited in Lee, 2014). The test reveals the average African American or Latino high school senior operates at proficiency levels in mathematics and reading equal to those of an average white eighth grader (as cited in Lee, 2014). Successfully completing a postsecondary course is difficult even for the most prepared student, but it is nearly impossible if a student enters a postsecondary course with skills equivalent to those required to enter the ninth grade.

The HRS model ensures schools monitor, analyze, and strategically implement systems that produce student success. If schools can systemically monitor their high-impact behaviors and systems, the likelihood of gaps in access and excellence decreases. "A high reliability school, by definition, monitors the effectiveness of critical factors within the system and immediately takes action to contain the negative effects of any errors that occur" (Marzano, Warrick, & Simms, 2014, p. 1). The HRS model contains five levels that schools should monitor, analyze, and assess to ensure excellence. Success at level 1 (safe, supportive, and collaborative culture) provides the context or foundation for success at the other four levels, and a healthy school culture with high-functioning collaborative teams is imperative. Failure at level 1 almost certainly guarantees trouble at the higher levels. Using the HRS model and PLC process is strongly linked in producing cultures of student success.

HRS level 1 contains eight leading indicators; I would like to explore four of those indicators.

> *Using the HRS model and PLC process is strongly linked in producing cultures of student success.*

1.1: The faculty and staff perceive the school environment as safe, supportive, and orderly.

1.2: Students, parents, and community members perceive the school environment as safe, supportive, and orderly.

1.3: Teachers have formal roles in the decision-making process regarding school initiatives.

1.4: Collaborative teams regularly interact to address common issues regarding curriculum, assessment, instruction, and the achievement of all students.

In this chapter, I argue that the foundation for success with the first three leading indicators of level 1 is the collaborative team. We must examine the collective beliefs, values, and mindset of those collaborative team members. I'll address leading indicator 1.4 later in this chapter.

The Value of Culture and Collaborative Teams

The lexicon of school professionals includes the term *school culture* quite frequently. What is school culture and why is it vital to ensuring equity and excellence for all students? According to University of Madison–Wisconsin professor Kent D. Peterson, "School culture is the set of norms, values and beliefs, rituals and ceremonies, symbols and stories that make up the 'persona' of a school" (as cited in

Education World, n.d.). A positive or healthy school culture exists when "educators have an unwavering belief in the ability of all their students to achieve success, and they pass that belief on to others in overt and covert ways" and "create policies and procedures and adopt practices that support their belief in every student's ability" (Muhammad, 2018, p. 20). In essence, school culture represents a set of beliefs and values that translate into the desire to adopt practices that drive those beliefs. If the school culture is positive and healthy, it is fair to assume the faculty members embrace practices that support their student-centered goals and objectives.

The PLC process requires some shifts in educators' thinking and assumptions in order to achieve the goal of high levels of learning for all students (DuFour, DuFour, Eaker, Many, & Mattos, 2016; see table 2.1).

Table 2.1: A Shift in Fundamental Purpose

From a focus on teaching . . .	to a focus on learning
From emphasis on what was taught . . .	to a fixation on what students learned
From coverage of content . . .	to demonstration of proficiency
From providing individual teachers with curriculum documents such as state standards and curriculum guides . . .	to engaging collaborative teams in building shared knowledge regarding essential curriculum

Source: Adapted from DuFour et al., 2016, p. 258.

These shifts in beliefs and collective purpose represent the transition from viewing student learning as an offering to students to having teachers embrace their own efficacy to ensure students learn. In a PLC, teams view their own practices (not students' backgrounds or interests) as the catalyst for student success. This is very nontraditional, and teams often struggle with this shift in mindset.

Should we assume all educational professionals are naturally prepared to make these shifts in their assumptions? Should we assume that all educators automatically view students as highly capable and that educators will organically seek out the best practices to support this egalitarian idealism? I would advise against embracing these general assumptions. You, as the leader, must nurture your culture, like any other aspect of an organization. There are several challenges in the pursuit of nurturing positive collective beliefs and achieving the shifts in fundamental purpose, including the following two.

1. All members of the school community join our profession with different ways of viewing the world and the people in it. Our own individual worldviews sometimes conflict with the school's, and ultimately the collaborative team's, stated goals and objectives.

2. Educators were raised, socialized, and indoctrinated using the old model (offering content as opposed to guaranteeing learning) and assumptions of the traditional educational system. Breaking from those norms and assumptions can be challenging as a practitioner, not because it is impossible, but because it does not jibe with some of our default behaviors and general assumptions.

A *team* is a collection of individuals who decide to work together interdependently and hold each other mutually accountable for accomplishing goals and objectives they collectively view as valuable. Each team member brings his or her own perceptions, background, and ideas to this endeavor. As with the persistent gaps in educational equity noted earlier in this chapter, it is important to note that students' backgrounds have always been the best predictor of each student's success or failure in school (Lareau & Goyette, 2014). Factors like race, family income, disability, English mastery, and gender have been made synonymous with student expectations of school performance. One of the goals of the HRS framework is to reduce these persistent inequities. Examining the beliefs of the educators who participate in this process is an important step in reaching that end.

Educators and educational institutions are a microcosm of issues of bias and discrimination that are prevalent in the greater society but that duplicate themselves within the school reality (for example, racism, sexism, and xenophobia). I call these issues *predeterminations*. One critical predetermination is *perceptual predetermination*, which I define as "an educator's own socialization and the impact of that socialization on his or her practice in the classroom, including expectations for student performance" (Muhammad, 2018, p. 31). Author Robert Green (2005) defines *teacher expectations* as "inferences that teachers make about the present and future academic achievement and general classroom behavior of their students" (p. 29). In American society, the prevailing ideology is that citizens who are white (of European origin), are native English speakers, and earn a middle- or upper-class income are more capable and naturally more gifted than people from other backgrounds. This is often referred to as *unconscious bias* (Singleton & Linton, 2006). This bias can be detected through what I call *dangerous synonyms*.

- *Changing demographics* means, "More non-white students are populating our schools and we anticipate trouble."

- *Title I* means, "Our students come from poor backgrounds and we anticipate that they will not have the academic skills or home support to succeed in school."

- *EL* is an acronym typically associated with students of Latino or Hispanic origin who speak Spanish as their first language, and is typically associated with a lack of language, cultural, and academic skills necessary to succeed in school.

If staff use any of these terms to describe your students or school community, there is a breach in creating a strong level 1 foundation for your HRS journey. These assumptions collectively validate perceived flaws in students and assume their lack of capacity, rather than affirming positive intentions. In author John Hattie's (2012) visible learning research, he finds the teacher's estimate of student learning has an effect size of 1.29, making it one of the strongest factors impacting student learning. When a school leader places teachers in collaborative teams to engage in important work and then buries his or her head in the sand, pretending some of these counterproductive ideologies don't exist in the school, the leader is dooming the teams' HRS efforts to failure.

The other important philosophical obstacles to success at HRS level 1 are the default behaviors that produce a clash between the motivators of the old system of schooling (access to learning) and the promise of the HRS model (ensure learning). The mere fact that educators are striving to ensure all students are successful is revolutionary. The traditional premise of schooling was based on an unwritten, informal contract: *it is the teacher's job to teach and the student's responsibility to learn.* Schools traditionally operated to sort and select students for ability groups based on the staff's perception of student compliance to expectations, background knowledge, and self-motivation, using tools like letter grades and academic tracking to institutionalize this mentality (DuFour & Marzano, 2011). Most educators were nurtured in this traditional environment, and most also found personal success. This experience creates an interesting dilemma. Dan C. Lortie (1975), professor emeritus of education at the University of Chicago, finds that because most educators found their own success within the traditional system of schooling, innovation is difficult. He concludes those who benefit from a traditional system are less likely to reform that same system; in fact, you should expect them to subconsciously protect the system because innovation generates cognitive dissonance (Lortie, 1975). This mindset makes it difficult to address overtly and obviously flawed practices (such as grading compliance and zero credit for late assignments), not because evidence shows these practices are working, but because teachers experienced and thrived under these conditions as students. Lortie (1975) concludes their experiences lead most teachers to believe that when a student underperforms, it is because of his or her unwillingness to comply with the school's demands. This conclusion also leads to some educators' unwillingness to examine their own personal practices, especially if the student is the architect of his or her own demise.

The Mindset of the Collaborative Team

The collaborative team is the platform for the HRS work within the larger PLC model. The team is a collection of people who have their own individual beliefs and norms. To become a high-performing team, those individual beliefs must form a set of collective beliefs to provide a solid foundation for the team's work. The team should operate with a collective mindset to provide a healthy context for its collective work. Lewis and Virginia Eaton professor of psychology at Stanford University Carol S. Dweck (2006) defines *mindset* as a set of beliefs held by a person (or group of people).

The collaborative team is the platform for the HRS work within the larger PLC model.

The collective beliefs of a team whose members understand their behavior is the difference between student success and failure must be a *student-centered* mindset. The successful collaborative team understands members are on a mission much bigger than themselves. The members understand their practice might be the difference between life success and failure for some of their most vulnerable students. A concept that captures this mission is *moral egalitarianism*, which is a belief that equality is central to the concept of justice (Gordon, n.d.). In short, these team members believe every student is valuable, no exceptions.

In *Overcoming the Achievement Gap Trap: Liberating Mindsets to Effect Change*, I call this highly efficacious set of beliefs the *liberation mindset* (Muhammad, 2015). "The *liberation mindset* is an unwavering set of collective beliefs and actions rooted in the goal of achieving high levels of academic and social success for all students despite internal or external barriers" (Muhammad, 2015, p. 92). This mindset consists of three critical beliefs (Muhammad, 2015).

1. **Equality:** We believe all men and women are created equal. Human potential is not a function of personal characteristics like race, gender, economic status, home language, national origin, or disability.

2. **Responsibility:** We accept the responsibility to develop the professional knowledge, embrace the practice, and incorporate the systems to best meet the needs of all learners.

3. **Advocacy:** We believe people and entities outside our school have an obligation to play a role in supporting students' growth, and we will advocate and lobby (in- and outside our team) to procure the resources and conditions necessary for all students to thrive.

At face value, these beliefs may seem simple and obvious, but what is obvious is not always easy to actualize. Every school openly claims that its purpose is *learning for all*, but the indicators of student success do not confirm this value. To ensure these beliefs are central to the mindset of your collaborative teams, the following set of surveys (see figures 2.1, 2.2, and 2.3, pages 67, 68, and 70) will provide evidence of alignment with the liberation mindset for each member of a collaborative team.

1: Strongly Disagree 2: Disagree 3: Neutral 4: Agree 5: Strongly Agree						
1.1: We carefully monitor our student achievement data to ensure equity across all student groups, and we make adjustments to policies, practices, and procedures in response to those results to achieve greater levels of equity.	We are alarmed when our student achievement data are not equitable.	1	2	3	4	5
	Our collaborative meetings are student centered and focused on equity.	1	2	3	4	5
	We make changes to our practice when our data are disproportionate.	1	2	3	4	5
1.2: We carefully monitor our course offerings and academic programs to ensure we do not create a culturally or socioeconomically based caste system in relation to student enrollment in advanced or remedial coursework, and we adjust our policies, practices, and procedures to produce more equitable representation.	We have created a fair process that allows all students to pursue advanced coursework.	1	2	3	4	5
	It bothers us when advanced or remedial courses have skewed student representation.	1	2	3	4	5
	Our assessment system is fair and free of cultural or socioeconomic bias.	1	2	3	4	5
	We believe that students have a fair opportunity to achieve in our school.	1	2	3	4	5
1.3: We carefully monitor our student engagement data to ensure equitable representation and to guard against bias. Some of the areas of monitoring include discipline data, attendance, extracurricular activity participation, and academic honor roll. We make adjustments to policies, practices, and procedures to achieve greater levels of equity.	Our discipline procedures are fair and do not reflect cultural or economic bias.	1	2	3	4	5
	We are alarmed when inequitable discipline data are identified.	1	2	3	4	5
	Our attendance procedures are fair and do not reflect cultural or economic bias.	1	2	3	4	5
	We are alarmed when student recognition is not equitable.	1	2	3	4	5
	We make adjustments to our student engagement policies when they are disproportionate.	1	2	3	4	5

Figure 2.1: Survey for assessing perceptions about equality. Continued →

1.4: We carefully monitor our school environment and learning material to ensure fair and equitable representation of cultural heritage, language, and economic background. We make adjustments to policies, practices, and resources to achieve greater levels of equity.	Our teaching material is culturally and economically diverse.	1	2	3	4	5
	We use methods that respect all cultural and economic backgrounds.	1	2	3	4	5
	We seek professional development opportunities that help us become more culturally responsive in our practice.	1	2	3	4	5
1.5: We carefully monitor parental involvement data to ensure equitable representation, especially in the area of ethnic background and socioeconomic status. We make adjustments to our policies, practices, and procedures to achieve greater levels of equity.	We reach out to all parents and make an honest attempt to involve all parents in school decisions and activities.	1	2	3	4	5
	We build systems that make the process of parent engagement easy and inviting.	1	2	3	4	5
	We make adjustments to our behavior when our data inform us that parent involvement is disproportionate.	1	2	3	4	5

Source: Adapted from Muhammad, 2015, pp. 110–111.

*Visit **go.SolutionTree.com/PLCbooks** for a free reproducible version of this figure.*

1: Strongly Disagree 2: Disagree 3: Neutral 4: Agree 5: Strongly Agree						
2.1: We have an unwavering focus on and commitment to universal student achievement, and we will not stop experimenting and innovating until we achieve that goal.	Our collaborative conversations are egalitarian, and we focus on student achievement.	1	2	3	4	5
	We use data and feedback as tools for growth, and they strengthen our commitment to student achievement.	1	2	3	4	5
	We make adjustments to our practice when necessary to achieve greater levels of achievement.	1	2	3	4	5

2.2: We develop an unwavering focus on and commitment to high achievement for our students and parents, and we will not stop experimenting and innovating until we achieve that goal.	We have high expectations of achievement for all our students.	1	2	3	4	5
	We demand that students continue to practice until they accomplish mastery.	1	2	3	4	5
	We develop perseverance and grit in our students.	1	2	3	4	5
2.3: We monitor and disaggregate student achievement and engagement data, and strategically use our professional development resources and time to address professional skill development in the high-needs areas.	We believe it is our responsibility to be responsive to student needs.	1	2	3	4	5
	We believe developing student responsibility for mastery of their own learning is partially our responsibility.	1	2	3	4	5
	We seek opportunities to help us grow professionally when we cannot meet a student need.	1	2	3	4	5
2.4: We monitor and disaggregate student achievement and engagement data to strategically develop policies and systems to support and develop struggling students.	We believe student content mastery is our responsibility.	1	2	3	4	5
	We believe developing student confidence and character is partially our responsibility.	1	2	3	4	5
	We develop systems that respond to specific student needs.	1	2	3	4	5
2.5: We refrain from using negative and pessimistic language when collaborating about high-needs students and families.	We refrain from using negative or defamatory language in our informal and formal interactions.	1	2	3	4	5
	We are willing to confront our colleagues' negative attitudes.	1	2	3	4	5
2.6: Our physical school environment reflects and displays the best qualities of our students and community, and we use it to encourage our students and families to strive for excellence.	We believe we are responsible for displaying symbols and artifacts that positively reinforce our values and build student confidence.	1	2	3	4	5
	We recognize (and have evidence of) student strengths both formally and informally in our practices and environment.	1	2	3	4	5

Source: Adapted from Muhammad, 2015, pp. 112–113.

Figure 2.2: Survey for assessing perceptions about responsibility.

*Visit **go.SolutionTree.com/PLCbooks** for a free reproducible version of this figure.*

1: Strongly Disagree 2: Disagree 3: Neutral 4: Agree 5: Strongly Agree						
3.1: We empower students and parents with information about resources available to them both inside and outside school that promote academic and personal development.	We view students as powerful advocates for their own success, and we provide opportunities for them to do that advocating.	1	2	3	4	5
	We view parents as powerful advocates for their child's success, and we provide opportunities for them to do that advocating.	1	2	3	4	5
	We communicate with parents about political, economic, and educational issues that affect their child, and we view them as a powerful lobby.	1	2	3	4	5
3.2: We are politically involved as a school unit or in cooperation with an agency or organization to lobby our board of education, state legislature, and federal legislature to pass policies and laws that benefit our students.	We actively lobby and influence local, state, and federal officials to secure the resources and conditions necessary for optimal student growth.	1	2	3	4	5
	We believe we are powerful and influential, and we have the efficacy necessary to change systems.	1	2	3	4	5
	We support causes and agencies that advance our collective purpose.	1	2	3	4	5
3.3: We educate parents and the community about opportunities and resources available to them to influence local, state, and federal policies that impact our students.	We communicate with parents with the intent of empowering them.	1	2	3	4	5
	We encourage parents to be active advocates for their child in the area of resource allocation and favorable policy.	1	2	3	4	5

3.4: We organize to create partnerships with outside agencies to provide additional resources and opportunities for our students' academic and personal development.	We actively seek resources and opportunities for our students through partnering with outside agencies.	1	2	3	4	5
	We believe we share in the responsibility to create powerful life experiences for students.	1	2	3	4	5
	We are resourceful and we do not let limitations stop our drive for universal student achievement.	1	2	3	4	5
3.5: We actively publicize and highlight the achievements of our students, staff, and parents to create a sense of pride and goodwill for our school.	We believe it is our responsibility to inform the public about the great things happening in our school.	1	2	3	4	5
	We communicate regularly with the local media to create positive press for our school.	1	2	3	4	5
	We prominently display positive press or student accomplishments around our school.	1	2	3	4	5

Source: Adapted from Muhammad, 2015, pp. 114–115.

Figure 2.3: Survey for assessing perceptions about advocacy.

Visit *go.SolutionTree.com/PLCbooks* for a free reproducible version of this figure.

A collaborative team's work focuses on improving team members' instructional methods, thus improving the learning of the students the team impacts. These surveys will assist the team to meet those ends in two different ways. First, they provide safe vulnerability; collecting evidence and analyzing the anonymous surveys gives the team a safe way to examine and discuss general beliefs about students and their potential without the fear of personal vilification. Sharing data and creating collective goals are two important characteristics of a strong team. Reviewing this evidence is a good way to improve those team characteristics. Second, they provide instructional enhancement; a sincere reflection of

A collaborative team's work focuses on improving team members' instructional methods, thus improving the learning of the students the team impacts.

personal beliefs and expectations about student performance will allow the team to examine important instructional elements like rigor, vocabulary, and cultural responsiveness. The team might discover that members' beliefs about students might be affecting what they teach and how they teach.

The Work of the Collaborative Team

Once teams address issues of beliefs and bias and liberate the school culture, educators are ready to move forward with the work of improving student achievement. The best platform for that work is the collaborative team. This is stressed in HRS indicator 1.4: collaborative teams regularly interact to address common issues regarding curriculum, assessment, instruction, and the achievement of all students. Although there have always been great and effective individual teachers, for schools to become highly reliable organizations, that excellence cannot be limited to a few members of the faculty; those great practices must be readily available to *all students in every classroom*. The best way to accomplish this end is through ensuring each school has a collection of highly effective teacher teams. The degree to which people are working together in a coordinated, focused effort is a major determinant of the effectiveness of any organization (Patterson, Grenny, Maxfield, McMillan, & Switzler, 2008). Collaboration is a true reflection of the school's authentic culture. If people truly believe their fundamental purpose is to ensure equity and excellence, they will engage with like-minded people working toward that end. When people work together to achieve something more profound than what they could achieve on their own, they are truly a part of a healthy school culture.

Although there have always been great and effective individual teachers, for schools to become highly reliable organizations, that excellence cannot be limited to a few members of the faculty; those great practices must be readily available to all students in every classroom.

Desires and *beliefs* provide a foundation for a highly productive team, but the team must also do the *right work*. "Simply organizing people into teams does not improve a school. Steps must be taken to ensure that those team members engage in collaboration on the issues that most impact student learning" (DuFour et al., 2016, p. 75). Student learning can be greatly improved when strong teams focus on four areas: (1) curriculum (guaranteed and viable), (2) assessment, (3) intervention, and (4) extension (for students who are ready to investigate a concept at a deeper level). The PLC process organizes the work of teams with the following four questions (DuFour et al., 2016).

1. What do we want students to learn? (curriculum)

2. How do we know if students are learning? (assessment)

3. How will we respond when students don't learn? (intervention)

4. How will we extend learning for students who are already proficient? (extension)

The focus on these essential questions within the context of a healthy culture allows any school access to the other four levels of the HRS framework. Educators collectively can meet the challenge of *access* and *excellence*, but only with the right culture, structures, and practices.

Conclusion

The process of schooling is critical to the future of students, and ultimately to the future of a progressive society. The HRS model and PLC process are important innovations in our effort to improve the schooling process and make a greater impact on student learning. The common thread of both processes is the effectiveness of the professional educator. Educators' beliefs, attitudes, expectations, and dispositions ultimately determine the depth of their engagement with these frameworks. When teachers believe that all students can learn at high levels and they are not compromised by stereotypes and negative preconceived notions, they become better professionals and stronger team members, consequently producing strong teams, strong schools, and highly educated students.

The common thread of both processes is the effectiveness of the professional educator.

References and Resources

DuFour, R., DuFour, R., Eaker, R., Many, T. W., & Mattos, M. (2016). *Learning by doing: A handbook for Professional Learning Communities at Work* (3rd ed.). Bloomington, IN: Solution Tree Press.

DuFour, R., & Marzano, R. J. (2011). *Leaders of learning: How district, school, and classroom leaders improve student achievement.* Bloomington, IN: Solution Tree Press.

Dweck, C. (2006). *Mindset: The new psychology of success.* New York: Random House.

Education World. (n.d.). *Is your school's culture toxic or positive?* Accessed at https://educationworld.com/a_admin/admin/admin275.shtml on June 21, 2019.

Gordon, J.-S. (n.d.). Moral egalitarianism. *Internet Encyclopedia of Philosophy.* Accessed at https://iep.utm.edu/moral-eg/#SH4a on June 24, 2019.

Green, R. (2005). *ExpectA+ions: How teacher expectations can increase student achievement and assist in closing the achievement gap.* Columbus, OH: McGraw-Hill SRA.

Hattie, J. (2012). *Visible learning for teachers: Maximizing impact on learning.* New York: Routledge.

Lareau, A., & Goyette, K. (Eds.). (2014). *Choosing homes, choosing schools.* New York: SAGE.

Lee, T. (2014, May 7). Education racial gap wide as ever according to NAEP. *MSNBC.* Accessed at www.msnbc.com/msnbc/student-proficiency-stagnant-race-gap-wide on June 24, 2019.

Lortie, D. C. (1975). *Schoolteacher: A sociological study.* Chicago: University of Chicago Press.

Marzano, R. J., Warrick, P. B., Rains, C. L., & DuFour, R. (2018). *Leading a high reliability school.* Bloomington, IN: Solution Tree Press.

Marzano, R. J., Warrick, P. B., & Simms, J. A. (2014). *A handbook for high reliability schools: The next step in school reform.* Bloomington, IN: Marzano Resources.

Muhammad, A. (2015). *Overcoming the achievement gap trap: Liberating mindsets to effect change.* Bloomington, IN: Solution Tree Press.

Muhammad, A. (2018). *Transforming school culture: How to overcome staff division* (2nd ed.). Bloomington, IN: Solution Tree Press.

Patterson, K., Grenny, J., Maxfield, D., McMillan, R., & Switzler, A. (2008). *Influencer: The power to change anything.* New York: McGraw-Hill.

Singleton, G. E., & Linton, C. P. (2006). *Courageous conversations about race: A field guide for achieving equity in schools.* Thousand Oaks, CA: Corwin Press.

U.S. Department of Education. (2014). *Civil rights data collection.* Washington, DC: Author. Accessed at https://search.usa.gov/search?utf8=%E2%9C%93&affiliate=ed.gov&query=2004+civil+rights+data+collection on November 20, 2019.

LEVEL 2:
Effective Teaching in Every Classroom

The concepts and practices that collectively reflect the PLC process are based on one overarching idea or organizing principle: the fundamental purpose of schools is to ensure high levels of learning for all students. In other words, the fundamental purpose of schools is not to simply *teach*, but to ensure students, in fact, *learn*. Put another way, *teaching is viewed as a means to an end, not an end unto itself.* Further, the use of high-performing collaborative teams positively impacts the power of effective teaching. Teams of teachers enhance instructional effectiveness when members collaboratively plan together, share instructional strategies and materials, review the impact of their instructional practices through the frequent monitoring and analysis of student learning data, and continually seek ways to improve their instructional effectiveness.

This is not to say teaching is unimportant. In fact, effective teaching is the most important tool educators have at their disposal to positively affect student learning. Hence, both the HRS model and the PLC process place heavy emphasis on effective teaching in every classroom, and by inference, a continuous, research-based, data-driven focus on improving instructional practice.

In chapters 3 and 4, the authors address what constitutes effective teaching within the HRS model and the PLC process, as well as identify methods for developing practices for effective teaching.

Toby Boss

Toby Boss, EdD, is director of professional development at a regional service agency in Nebraska. He has experience as a classroom teacher, district administrator, and professional development consultant. Dr. Boss has worked directly with schools to provide training on topics such as implementing an instructional model, goal setting and reflective practice, and supervision of instruction. He also serves as a High Reliability Schools (HRS) associate and has certified more than thirty-five schools in the HRS framework. Dr. Boss earned a bachelor of science in secondary education, a master of arts in economics, and a doctoral degree from the University of Nebraska–Lincoln.

To learn more about Dr. Boss's work, follow @tobyboss on Twitter.

To book Toby Boss for professional development, contact pd@SolutionTree.com.

In this chapter, Dr. Boss describes how schools and districts use the leading indicators at level 2 of the HRS model—effective teaching in every classroom—to create a shared language of instruction. He provides examples of how to use that common language to not only raise the level of pedagogical skill within a building but also create a culture continually striving for improved instructional expertise at both the individual and collective levels.

Chapter 3

Six Steps for Effective Teaching in Every Classroom

Toby Boss

An architect overseeing the remodeling of an elementary school was asked, "What do you keep in mind during construction?" He responded, "Students only get to experience each grade one time; I'm not going to ruin it by interrupting their learning." Think about how profound those words are: *students only get to experience each grade one time.* No matter how long any of us are in the education business, for students, each year is their one chance to fully experience learning at that grade or course level.

Instruction is the heart of education. It is "the energy that drives the classroom journey" (Knight, 2011, p. 62). High-quality instruction in every classroom is one of the important characteristics of effective schools. The direct link between a teacher's quality and his or her effect on student achievement is clear: student achievement in classes with highly skilled teachers is better than achievement with less-skilled teachers (Marzano, Frontier, & Livingston, 2011). Let's put it this way: of the millions of students attending school, how many of them deserve effective instruction? The answer is simple—*all of them.*

Therefore, school leaders are obliged to ensure teachers are providing high-quality instruction that reaches all students. To ensure this, successful schools provide a framework with intentional processes

School leaders are obliged to ensure teachers are providing high-quality instruction that reaches all students. to improve teacher expertise and subsequently improve student learning. So this begs the question, How many teachers deserve a system that allows them to improve their skills for their students? Again, the answer is simple—*all of them.*

The HRS model provides a framework of leading indicators schools can use to help meet the promise of effective instruction (Marzano, Warrick, & Simms, 2014). The leading indicators for level 2 are as follows.

2.1: The school communicates a clear vision as to how teachers should address instruction.

2.2: The school supports teachers to continually enhance their pedagogical skills through reflection and professional growth plans.

2.3: The school is aware of and monitors predominant instructional practices.

2.4: The school provides teachers with clear, ongoing evaluations of their pedagogical strengths and weaknesses that are based on multiple sources of data and are consistent with student achievement data.

2.5: The school provides teachers with job-embedded professional development that is directly related to their instructional growth goals.

2.6: Teachers have opportunities to observe and discuss effective teaching.

Schools should consider these six indicators a system of instructional improvement, each informing and building on the work of the whole. Educators can use this approach schoolwide or within collaborative teams working to improve instructional competence (Marzano et al., 2014), such as those using the PLC process. Coauthors and researchers Robert J. Marzano, Tammy Heflebower, Jan K. Hoegh, Philip B. Warrick, and Gavin Grift (2016) write in *Collaborative Teams That Transform Schools* how teachers and administrators work together as learners: "They also work together, sharing resources and knowledge to help one another improve teaching practices" (p. 6).

Collaborative teams working in a PLC ask themselves these four critical questions (DuFour, DuFour, Eaker, Many, & Mattos, 2016).

1. "What do we want students to learn?"

2. "How will we know if students are learning?"

3. "How will we respond when students don't learn?"

4. "How will we extend learning for students who are already proficient?"

Marzano et al. (2016) add the following critical questions.

5. "How will we increase our instructional competence?"

6. "How will we coordinate our efforts as a school?"

Questions five and six are at the core of an effective teaching system. Increasing instructional competence is critical to the ongoing PLC process and the driver behind improved student learning.

Building a System of Instruction

This chapter describes a system of effective teaching with three distinct themes.

1. **Growth:** The goal is improved individual and collective teacher expertise.

2. **Collective wisdom:** The system leverages the talents of staff to build, monitor, and adjust practice.

3. **Monitoring:** Staff collect and analyze formative data to correct and improve practice.

I explore each of the six leading indicators for level 2 (the six steps) in the sections that follow, providing tips for campus leaders and collaborative teams, along with examples of practice from real schools.

Step One: Communicate a Clear Vision of Instruction

The first step in building the system is to be clear about your school's vision of instruction and consider these questions.

- What is good teaching?

- What does it mean to teach in our school?

- What instructional standards will we hold ourselves to achieving?

In *The New Art and Science of Teaching*, Marzano (2017) provides a framework for a common language to define elements of instruction. (See Marzano [2017] for a list of all forty-three elements in the framework.) This common language becomes the structure for the system of improved teacher expertise. The common language or *model of instruction* (*MOI*) becomes the foundation for teacher goal setting, monitoring and evaluating instruction, providing job-embedded professional development, and observing quality teaching. The MOI is the *theory of action* regarding improved student achievement. The MOI also makes expectations of quality teaching transparent across the school. This transparency allows leaders and others in the school to use the MOI for all discussions involving teaching, learning, and improvement. In this way, both campus leaders and collaborative team members use the school's vision for instruction to continually communicate and leverage sustained growth. The Examples of Practice section shows this use in action.

> The MOI is the theory of action *regarding improved student achievement. The MOI also makes expectations of quality teaching transparent across the school.*

Campus Leaders

The campus leader is critical to developing the school's vision for instruction, communicating the vision, and ensuring implementation of the vision. The system of improvement relies on leadership to provide the support necessary to improve the school as a whole. If the MOI is based on elements of high-quality instruction, and the school continually executes the model at increased levels of proficiency, the result should be increased levels of student achievement. Effective campus leaders continually focus discussions about improving pedagogy through a system of improvement. A vision for instruction sets the stage for the system of improvement campus leadership leads and supports.

Collaborative Teams

The MOI provides the structure to focus teams' efforts for instructional improvement. Teams can leverage the MOI as it applies to specific areas of student need and follow the same process as the school: develop a set of practices to serve as the team theory of action. Relying on the wisdom of teams to focus improvement provides authenticity when addressing the unique needs of both teachers and students.

Examples of Practice

The following examples show how schools communicate and support their clear vision of instruction using an MOI along with other related strategies.

The Playbook

The Educational Service Unit 9 (ESU 9) professional development staff serve fourteen school districts in Nebraska, facilitating K–12 teams of teachers and administrators to each develop a playbook for instruction. The playbook includes the elements of instruction, associated strategies, snapshots of instruction, and related resources (Schultz & Slechta, 2017).

The ESU 9 staff work with teachers to develop playbooks through their collaborative journey, ensuring each teacher has a voice about the content. Each teacher receives a working copy of the playbook, which is based on the model in *The Art and Science of Teaching* (Marzano, 2007). The ESU 9 staff work with teams of teachers from the whole school to identify important elements and encourage teachers to develop a deeper understanding of the MOI. The playbook is designed to be reviewed and updated as necessary. The final playbook features the non-negotiables for instruction and builds the evaluation system with walkthrough tools and reflective practices. Developing the playbook in this way utilizes the teachers' collective wisdom. The following list is an example of an ESU 9 playbook's table of contents.

1. **Professional practice—What?:** In this section, you will find our instructional model—our comprehensive framework of effective teaching practices. The framework offers you a common language of instruction.

2. **Professional practice—Why?:** You can use the framework for many purposes, but its full value is in the foundation it creates for professional conversations among you and your colleagues as you seek to enhance your skill in the complex task of teaching.

3. **District alignment practice:** Aligning all district work to the instructional model is critical. The alignment includes a self-assessment about the extent to which the school district engages in activities such as establishing goals, supporting professional development, establishing a culture for learning, and allowing for professional reflection, as well as providing peer feedback regarding teaching and learning.

4. **Year one implementation plan:** The implementation plan outlines the dates and training sessions organized around *The Art and Science of Teaching* (Marzano, 2007) design questions.

5. **Instructional leadership:** This includes administrator responsibilities such as actively supporting the implementation of the instructional model and committing time and resources. This section also includes an administrator checklist with items such as meeting informally to collect snapshots, looking for goal posters, and setting a goal along with teachers.

6. **Snapshots:** The snapshots, based on the implementation plan, include What You Will See, What You Might See, and What You Won't See examples of practice for each of the design questions. The snapshots are built throughout the implementation process.

7. **Progress plotting:** You will chart progress on a scatter diagram to show growth over time. This shows the staff's collective improvement in implementing instructional strategies based on a simple scale (0 = Have not tried it yet; 1 = Attempted; 2 = Improving; 3 = Part of my practice; and 4 = Ready for another strategy).

8. **Goal setting:** This section refers to the goal posters to display in your classroom.

9. **Anecdotal evidence:** This section includes samples of anecdotal evidence, including pictures, teachers can use as evidence of improvement.

10. **Existing district initiatives:** This section features a narrative of district goals, objectives, and other initiatives the district is undertaking to show that the work is part of a system of improvement and is linked to overall district plans.

11. *The Art and Science of Teaching* **model:** This section includes a visual of *The Art and Science of Teaching* model (Marzano, 2007) with the model's elements organized into three lesson segments.

12. **Notes:** This section includes space for you to take notes.

Reviewing, Revising, and Recommitting

Once the MOI is in place, schools can develop activities to continually review and revise work around instruction in a logical manner. For example, schools could use in-service days at the beginning of the year to review the MOI with the entire staff. Also at the beginning of the year, teachers new to the school might meet with mentors to develop an action plan based on the MOI. During the first month of school, mentors might focus strategies for new teachers on one or two elements of the MOI to help them implement the model with intention.

At the end of the year, a school might provide the opportunity for teachers to revisit the MOI and reflect on the elements. Once the teachers have a chance to reflect, a school could revise the MOI as appropriate and recommit to the implementation during the ensuing school year.

Snapshots

Particularly illuminating parts of the playbook are the instructional *snapshots*. Teacher teams develop these snapshots (based on the MOI) to answer the questions, "What should we see and hear daily in the classroom?" "What might we see and hear, but not daily?" and "What should we never see or hear?" The answers become part of the playbook that teams and individual teachers use as a reference for examples and non-examples of best practice. Schools often organize an instructional model team made up of teachers and administrators to collaborate around the schoolwide MOI. The instructional model team reviews the snapshots to draft a final version for approval by administration. Figure 3.1 (page 84) shows an example of an instructional snapshot.

What You *Should* See	What You *Might* See	What You *Should Never* See
Teacher using a transition procedure (bell, countdown, clapper, music, and so on) Students using "taught" routines on a regular basis	Students following attention signals quickly and consistently Teacher awarding and celebrating student success with intrinsic motivators (ten-finger woo, silent scream, and so on)	Teacher assigning students to groups on a daily basis Students receiving prizes for personal or group successes Students excessively calling out

Source: © 2015 by Norris High School, Firth, Nebraska. Reprinted with permission.

Figure 3.1: Example of an instructional snapshot.

The Coach's Corner

At Wilmeth Elementary School in McKinney, Texas, the instructional coaches provide a monthly MOI newsletter to staff. The newsletter highlights elements of the MOI, examples of practice, and new strategies. The newsletter also celebrates staff when they achieve successful MOI implementation. Figure 3.2 is an example of the *Coach's Corner* newsletter Michelle McHugh, the former instructional coach at Wilmeth Elementary School, developed.

Step Two: Provide Support to Teachers

Once the MOI is in place, teachers can then use the framework for goal setting and reflective practice for improvement. In *Becoming a Reflective Teacher*, Marzano (2012) outlines a process for teachers to set instructional goals, determine a plan for improvement, reflect on progress, and collect data about student achievement gains. In applying this step in the MOI system, teachers become adept at determining areas of need and plans to improve their expertise (Frontier & Mielke, 2016).

Making teacher growth part of the entire staff's routine (not just that of the teachers you identify as needing improvement) is key.

Making teacher growth part of the entire staff's routine (not just that of the teachers you identify as needing improvement) is key. This also requires a shift in staff thinking; teaching is not static, but dynamic. It is the school leader's responsibility to create systems for improvement through reflective

Setting Up for a Successful Year

Establishing solid routines and procedures is one of (if not THE) most important things you will teach all year. I saw so many teachers working hard on this last week that it seemed like the students had been with you for months already. What a wonderful start to the year already with setting those expectations high from the start. #BestTeachersEver #week1DONE

THE BEST THING ABOUT BEING A TEACHER IS THAT **IT MATTERS.**

THE HARDEST THING ABOUT BEING A TEACHER IS THAT **IT MATTERS EVERY DAY.**

—Todd Whitaker

One of my favorite rules of thumb is that if something with your students' behavior doesn't feel "right" or "good" to you, stop and have a "reset." Don't go on with your lesson if you don't feel good about what students are doing. (I saw this several times in Robin Keating's room!) YOU are their leader and they look to you for guidance on what they should be doing. Here are some resources that might help!

♡ *Michelle*

For a child to learn something new, you need to repeat it on the average eight times.

For a child to unlearn an old behavior and replace it with a new behavior, you need to repeat the new behavior on the average of twenty-eight times.

—Harry Wong
The First Days of School: How to Be an Effective Teacher

Figure 3.2: *Coach's Corner* newsletter.

practice. Reflective practice allows teachers to not only set instructional goals but also reflect about what worked well, what didn't work, and what they might do next. The system should include methods for teachers to routinely track their progress and plan for their next steps.

Campus Leaders

The MOI provides the foundation for improved teacher expertise. The leader's role is to design and support the systems necessary. Principal actions to drive this step include the following.

- Provide a written record of all teacher growth goals.
- Monitor growth goals individually and collectively.
- Have formal and informal discussions with teachers about their goals and progress.
- Deploy time and resources to ensure teachers have the opportunity to engage in reflective practice.
- Utilize instructional coaches as a resource for developing and supporting the instructional goals.

Collaborative Teams

Teams provide a natural structure for developing and setting professional development goals and reflective practice. Developing common instructional goals within the PLC process creates a shared improvement vision for the team. Embedding goals in collaborative teams addresses the fifth critical question Marzano et al. (2016) pose: How will we increase our instructional competence? Specifically, schools must consider what systems are in place to help teachers improve their pedagogical skills. Developing teacher skills, monitoring those skills, collecting data, and implementing professional development regarding team goals is an example of such a system.

> Teams provide a natural structure for developing and setting professional development goals and reflective practice.

However, collaborative team goals need not exclude individual teacher goals the team can support. Many schools allow teachers to have both levels of goals. For example, leadership at Milford Public Schools in Nebraska requires all teachers to have a goal aligned with the element of the MOI *well-defined expectations with timely feedback*, which becomes the focus of team goals. Leadership organizes teachers into seven teams to work on their goals, develop practices, and engage in reflective practice for the semester. These leaders also encourage teachers to set individual goals about other elements, such as *motivating and inspiring students*. In this way, the power of collaboration is evident as teacher teams work toward improvement on collective goals to move the school forward, and to support goal setting for individual teachers' unique areas for improvement.

Examples of Practice

The following examples are teacher strategies for setting goals, making those goals visible, and celebrating achievement of goals.

Setting the Goal

At the beginning of the year, teachers perform a self-audit on the MOI, identifying their strengths and areas for growth. The teachers review their self-audit and draft professional growth goals based on the elements of the MOI. The teachers then gather data from other sources, such as a video for self-observation, student surveys, and student achievement goals. Each teacher then works with instructional coaches, team leaders, and administrative staff to develop a professional growth goal and plan.

Focusing on New Teachers

During the first month of school, mentors have all new teachers set goals on two elements of the MOI: (1) initiating classroom procedures and (2) building relationships with students. The mentors provide support and resources to ensure these teachers focus on these two elements before setting goals for other elements of the MOI.

Posting the Goals

Teachers post their goals inside and outside classrooms. The goal posters include the MOI elements for improvement and a brief description of the plan. The posters make the teachers' goals visible to students and staff; the posters also help keep teachers accountable for their progress. All staff, including administrators, should set their own goals and display their posters in a conspicuous location. Figure 3.3 (page 88) is an example of a template for a poster developed at Milford Public Schools.

My goal is . . .

Recording and Representing Knowledge

The plan to meet my goal includes the following:

- Using interactive notes
- Creating one-word summaries
- Finding the main idea
- Using reflective writing
- Providing rubrics when giving feedback

NAME: _____*Haley*_____

Figure 3.3: Sample teacher goal poster.

Goal Setting and Celebration

The Educational Service Unit 6 (ESU 6) professional development team in Milford, Nebraska, developed a process for reflective practice based on *Becoming a Reflective Teacher* (Marzano, 2012). Teachers use a *Becoming a Reflective Teacher* (BART) packet to keep their self-audit, goals, reflections, progress, and results for the year. This way, teachers have an ongoing record of their work and progress toward their defined goal.

The following steps are in a protocol included in the BART packet that individuals or teams can adapt.

1. Complete a self-audit on the elements from *The Art and Science of Teaching* (Marzano, 2007), using the teacher-reflective scales.

2. Determine one element from the self-audit for your goal. There are three zones to consider for a goal: (1) the comfort zone, (2) the stretch zone, and (3) the panic zone. Goals in the stretch zone offer the ideal opportunity for development (Marzano, Warrick, Rains, & DuFour, 2018). This element should be something in your stretch zone that will help your students.

3. Write a plan of specific strategies and behaviors that will help you reach your goal. Refer to *The New Art and Science of Teaching* (Marzano, 2017) for strategies for your element.

4. Consider this: What tools or support will you need to accomplish your goal?

5. Consider this: How will you know your strategies are working? This could include student surveys, video observations, peer observations, and student achievement data.

After the goals and plans are set (and shared with the principal), the teacher team (or individual teacher) should perform a check-in about goal progress. These check-ins could occur during team meetings or professional development opportunities. At these check-ins, teacher teams (or individual teachers) reflect on their actions, share their successes and challenges, and chart their progress. Figure 3.4 is a summary of this protocol—a "five-minute write"—teachers engage in to reflect on a goal, the actions they have taken, and their successes and challenges.

Name: _____

Five-Minute Write and Reflection Notes

In the left column, write the date and your current level, 0–4, on your goal progress. In the right column, write about your goal progress. What did you do to implement your goal? What worked? What were your successes and challenges? What would you do differently? Be ready to share with your team.

4: Innovating—I adapt behaviors and create new strategies for unique student needs and situations.

3: Applying—I use the strategies and behaviors associated with this element, and I monitor the extent to which my actions affect students.

2: Developing—I use the strategies and behaviors associated with this element, but do not monitor the effect on students.

1: Beginning—I use the strategies and behaviors associated with this element, incorrectly or with missing parts.

0: Not Using—I am unaware of the strategies and behaviors associated with this element.

Figure 3.4: Five-minute writing prompt.   Continued →

Date and Level	I tried new methods to improve response rates among my students. I chose random student names from cards after I asked student questions. This worked pretty well, but it took more time than I thought it might, and I had some students still respond with incorrect answers.
October 17, 2020	
Level 2	Next time I'm going to try pairing the students to get an answer first, and then call on them using random name cards.

Source: © 2015 by ESU 6. Reprinted with permission.

During each check-in, teachers track their progress individually in the BART packet and post their progress on a chart recording the school's progress to date. A scatter diagram example (see figure 3.5) provides a tangible record of the entire staff's progress.

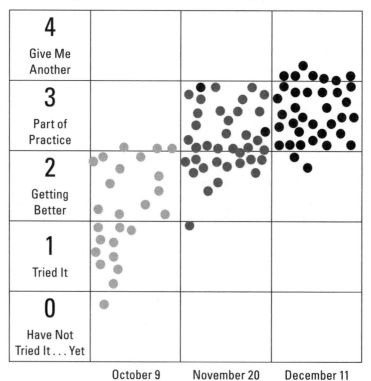

Source: © 2015 by ESU 6. Reprinted with permission.

Figure 3.5: Sample staff goal-progress scatter diagram.

The leader's final step in the goal-setting cycle is to hold a celebration at the end of the year to highlight teachers' goals and progress. At these celebrations, each teacher provides a short presentation to staff that includes his or her goal, plan, successes, challenges, and data. The leader encourages teachers to provide a description of their activities and pictures as part of their showcase.

Such celebrations are beneficial not only for the teachers reporting their progress but also for all staff, as they collect new ideas to implement in their classroom. Teachers record their reflections in their BART packet using the following guiding questions.

- What is an idea I would like to pursue?
- What is being done in another classroom that may benefit my students?
- What is something new I learned?
- What is something I used to do, but haven't done recently?

Schools can also host *instructional fairs*, where teachers provide poster sessions about their goals and progress. Teachers set up their sessions in a common space, and staff visit posters of interest to get new ideas and to see the great work of their colleagues.

Step Three: Monitor Instructional Practices

The third step to achieving level 2 of the HRS model (Marzano et al., 2014) is to implement systems to continually monitor the school's operations. The MOI provides expectations for practices. Monitoring what is happening in classrooms is the precursor to developing an intentional method of continuous improvement.

Monitoring instruction provides the data for a cycle of inquiry informing actions throughout the school. Transparency is crucial so leaders and teachers understand their current reality. The school's monitoring system also informs leaders on decisions about using professional development, allocating resources to improve instructional practice, using instructional coaching, and observing master teachers.

Monitoring what is happening in classrooms is the precursor to developing an intentional method of continuous improvement.

Campus Leaders

The quality of the system to monitor instruction determines the quality of data leaders can use to move the school to improved levels of performance. The monitoring system should include frequent data collection, a display of the results, methods to analyze the data, a plan for short-term improvement, and the implementation of action steps. Using this continuous cycle allows the school to move the collective needle on important instructional practices. School leaders use this method of inquiry and action to position school improvement toward improved instruction.

Collaborative Teams

Monitoring instructional practices should be done at the team level to inform the team's theory of action. Teams should intentionally track data about classroom practice and utilize those data to develop plans and action steps. This is at the heart of what collaborative teams in PLCs do—conduct a cycle of continuous inquiry and action (DuFour et al., 2016). Collaborative teams can take the same approach as leaders—regularly monitoring practice, sharing the results, and developing actions to improve. High-functioning teams can conduct classroom observations and provide data back to the team in aggregate form.

Consider these guiding questions for teams.

- What do we expect to see in our classrooms?
- To what extent is our team implementing the instruction we expect?
- Based on student data, what are some exemplary practices we would like to replicate?
- What do we need to improve?

Examples of Practice

The following examples show strategies for monitoring instructional practices, including collecting data and using instructional coaching.

Collecting Data

The administrative team of principals develops a walkthrough form and system to collect data based on the MOI. The team then develops a plan to monitor instructional practices and observe teachers as part of a weekly school leadership team meeting. At each weekly meeting, this team shares the results of the observations, looking for strengths and areas to improve. Figure 3.6 shows how to display this team's walkthrough data.

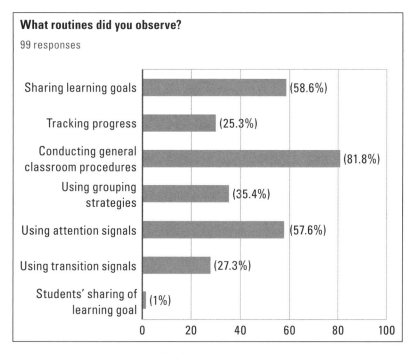

Source: © 2017 by ESU 6. Reprinted with permission.

Figure 3.6: Sample walkthrough data.

The administrative team now has the opportunity to theorize why the practices are in evidence and what actions might improve the results. Leaders should also share the results with staff so everyone can see the school's current reality and engage in improvement practices. Schools should display the results in either physical or digital spaces that all staff frequent.

Instructional Coaching

Schools can also use instructional coaches to monitor instructional practices. Instructional coaches using the same walkthrough tool as the administrative team provide another set of eyes to gather formative data about how teachers realize the MOI in their classrooms.

Step Four: Give Teachers Clear, Ongoing Evaluations of Their Pedagogical Strengths and Weaknesses

Evaluation is a summation of the school-improvement system. If the parts of this system are working together for improved teacher efficacy, then the resulting evaluation data will be improving as well. While evaluation is important, it is just one step in achieving level 2 (indicator 2.4) of the HRS model. Leaders should consider evaluation an equal part of the school-improvement system, not the driving force. Schools successful in developing an evaluation system begin with the MOI and embed goal setting, professional development, and reflective practice. This process changes the evaluation dynamic from the opinions of a single evaluator to a collaborative conversation about improvement.

Campus Leaders

Leaders need to ensure their evaluations of teachers' strengths and weaknesses are based on accurate data. Leaders can use the school-improvement system to gauge teachers' effectiveness through multiple points of data. The MOI provides the theory of action for student improvement; therefore, evaluation data should be consistent with student achievement data (Marzano et al., 2014). This means the evaluation data will correlate with student achievement data; if the aggregate scores on evaluations are improving, then student scores will be improving as well. This correlation serves as an important check on the ratings leaders assign and informs the evaluation system.

> Leaders need to ensure their evaluations of teachers' strengths and weaknesses are based on accurate data.

Collaborative Teams

Teams should consider a formative approach to summative evaluations. Teams should formatively use the same scales and rubrics for the evaluation process. Collaboration about evidence ratings allows teams to align their conversations and actions with the MOI and evaluation process. The regular sharing of self-ratings and discussions as a team provides transparency and focus.

Examples of Practice

The following examples show strategies that provide teachers with clear, ongoing evaluations of their pedagogical strengths and weaknesses.

Scheduling Observations

Principals schedule observations to protect time for teacher evaluation. Time is a scarce resource, and if principals do not schedule evaluations, they can lose time to other issues (Marzano et al., 2018). By simply blocking off times and dates for observations, principals can help ensure they have the opportunity to gather multiple data sources for teacher evaluation. Many principals set goals for the number of weekly observations and strive to meet the goal through intentional planning of observations.

Gathering Artifacts of Practice

Principals gather artifacts of teacher practice in addition to observing teacher behaviors. When conducting a classroom observation, principals can gather authentic artifacts used in the classroom. A learning goal tracking sheet used by a student might indicate the teacher is having the students actively track and reflect on progress. Principals can take pictures of the artifacts and use them as examples during postobservation conferences with the teacher.

Including Teachers

Teachers self-rate using the MOI as part of the formal observation process. The formal observation process then becomes a conversation about the level of agreement between the evaluator and the teacher. Did they see the same things? If not, why not? What are the agreed-on next steps? When teachers are actively engaged in the process, the results are more accurate ratings and a focus on development rather than measurement (Marzano & Toth, 2013).

Consider actions of the teacher and evaluator during three segments of the observation process: (1) preobservation, (2) observation, and (3) postobservation (see figure 3.7, page 96).

Preobservation	Teacher identifies the MOI elements for the lesson.
	Teacher shares his or her improvement goals for the year.
Observation	Evaluator provides a narrative and ratings on the MOI elements from the lesson.
	Teacher self-rates on MOI elements from the lesson.
Postobservation Reflection	Teacher and evaluator share their ratings.
	Teacher provides a reflection for the MOI elements from the lesson.
	Teacher provides ratings and reflection on improvement goals for the year.
	Evaluator and teacher agree to a plan of action for continued improvement.

Figure 3.7: Observation process.

Principals who embrace evaluation as part of a system for teacher growth find that conversations become about teacher efforts to improve on agreed-on goals. Discussing successes, challenges, and ideas becomes the norm, rather than rating just to complete the evaluation. The formative collecting of data, giving of feedback, and engaging in conversations between the evaluator and teacher creates a condition where evaluation is done no longer *to* teachers, but *with* them.

> Principals who embrace evaluation as part of a system for teacher growth find that conversations become about teacher efforts to improve on agreed-on goals.

Step Five: Furnish Job-Embedded Professional Development

Job-embedded professional development aligned with teacher professional goals is critical to improving instructional practice. Learning Forward defines *job-embedded professional development* as focusing on teaching the assigned students and occurring in three settings (as cited in Croft, Coggshall, Dolan, & Powers, 2010).

1. In the classroom, in real time, with current students, and centering on issues of actual practice

2. In the classroom, in nearly real time, away from students, and centering on issues of actual practice

3. In school, shortly before or after instruction, away from students, and centering on issues of actual practice

Directly relating teacher growth goals to job-embedded professional development aligns the system of instruction. Professional development is the component that supports teacher goals. Implementing new learning in the classroom is more likely when it is relevant to the needs of the teacher and the students.

Campus Leaders

Jim Knight (2011) writes, "Principals as designers are the primary creators of opportunities that enable professional learning to flourish" (p. 55). The system principals design, support, and monitor provides the foundation for learning among the teaching staff. Leadership is critical to building an intentional professional development program, rather than providing a random menu of activities. Leaders should be thoughtful about the content, delivery, and implementation of professional development.

The least effective professional development programs might be interesting or even include valuable information, but they fail when staff members don't implement them. A one-size-fits-all professional development program has little chance of schoolwide implementation, as adult learners are continually building an array of unique skills to apply in their unique classrooms. Leaders should make a practice of vetting professional development requests based on how teachers perceive the learning will help them meet their goals. A caveat to this would include professional development designed as awareness, because sometimes teachers need to scout for new ideas.

Leaders who dedicate time and resources to professional development have an obligation to monitor the *implementation* of new classroom strategies. Leaders can use formal and informal methods to periodically check on the progress of implementation. Leaders should continually follow up and reach out to staff about their professional development. Communicating through emails and informal conversations is important and demonstrates both support and accountability.

> Leaders who dedicate time and resources to professional development have an obligation to monitor the implementation *of new classroom strategies.*

Collaborative Teams

The PLC process provides collaborative teacher teams an effective method of professional learning (Marzano et al., 2016), and is a natural fit for embedding this learning into the classroom. Defining new learning to reach common instructional goals allows the team to engage in collective inquiry. Teams can monitor the professional development as well, tracking data about the strategies and their impact on student learning. Putting teachers into teams for this kind of inquiry provides support and processes for focusing on goals and the opportunity to learn from peers.

Examples of Practice

The following examples show strategies for providing job-embedded professional development.

Teachers Choose

In *Unmistakable Impact*, Knight (2011), a research associate at the University of Kansas Center for Research on Learning and president of the Instructional Coaching Group (www.instructionalcoaching .com), sums up the power of choice:

> Everyone in the school must be actively engaged in professional growth and development, with the principal as the first learner. My experience has been that most people are interested in, even excited about learning. But as adults, they just want to have some say in what and how they learn. (p. 93)

Many schools allow for *teacher choice* by providing breakout sessions during professional development. Teachers choose which sessions to attend. During presentations, individual teachers can demonstrate authentic practice, inviting attendees to visit their classrooms later for more content and guidance. As a follow-up activity, the principal can require attendees submit a written summary of the sessions they attended, including the strategies they are planning to try.

Choice boards are a great way for teachers to select learning activities that align with goals and embed ongoing training. Figure 3.8 (page 100) is a sample choice board from Wilmeth Elementary School in McKinney, Texas. The board provides interactive links to resources, written content, and videos all related to the team goal of student goal setting and progress tracking. The choice board allows for flexible professional learning and collaboration among team members.

Teachers Lead

Teacher-led professional development allows a school to tap into teachers' collective wisdom, leveraging their existing knowledge base of best practice. Including just a few teacher-led breakout sessions during professional development time can be of great benefit. First, it honors the excellent work staff are already doing. Second, it provides ongoing support and extension opportunities, as teachers can go to presenters with questions and observe how strategies might work in the classrooms. It is not uncommon for teachers to make follow-up visits to presenters to gain more insight. Third, it promotes a positive culture of support and school pride. Excellent teacher-led professional development sessions celebrate the great work of staff and highlight the school's commitment to students.

Step Six: Supply Teachers With Opportunities to Observe and Discuss Effective Teaching

Making expertise visible is a powerful practice schools should intentionally and consistently implement as part of a coordinated system of improvement. The collective wisdom of the teaching staff is a fundamental resource schools should continuously leverage. Marzano et al. (2011) identify instructional rounds and video as methods schools can use for this purpose.

The collective wisdom of the teaching staff is a fundamental resource schools should continuously leverage.

Campus Leaders

Campus leaders play a critical role in the implementation of instructional rounds (Marzano et al., 2018). The logistical support for instructional rounds campus leaders provide includes developing a schedule, identifying the teachers to be observed, and helping ensure the instructional rounds protocols are in place and followed.

Resource	Resource	Reading	Reading
Look at the MOI—Marzano table the lesson-design team created to pick some elements to implement in your upcoming instruction that aligns with your goals.	Check out some of these examples of student goal setting and progress monitoring: Student Texas Essential Knowledge and Skills (TEKS, the K–12 state standards) monitoring page—Mathematics Student TEKS monitoring page—English language arts Jennifer Serravallo: Reading goal sheet Grade 4 mathematics reflection	Click this link to access journal articles that relate to student goal setting and instructional feedback. Choose one article you want to read and reflect on it today. These are fantastic, research-driven articles that will give you some ideas and things to think about!	Browse through the books and resources from the student progress basket (a collection of books for teachers about tracking student progress). If you choose to check out a book to take with you for further learning, please fill out one of these Google forms: Wilmeth library form Michelle's books form Feel free to browse through some of the other baskets!

Video	Student Progress	Video
60-Second Strategy: Closing the Loop 60-Second Strategy: Fishbowl Discussion 60-Second Strategy: Interview Assessments 60-Second Strategy: Appreciation Apology, Aha!	As you work your way through the tasks that follow, be thinking about these questions: • What type of data am I using to guide student goals? • How much of the student goal do students themselves choose? • How often do we check our progress? • Are my students able to self-assess their progress? Two tasks for today: 1. Choose a **Video** or a **Reading** activity to explore and post your reflection at Article/Video Reflection on Google Classroom. 2. Look at the **Resource** activities to find something you will commit to implementing. Then, post your commitment at Resource Commitment on Google Classroom. If you have extra time, continue your learning by choosing another activity. **Don't forget to take time and document your learning today as Texas Teacher Evaluation and Support System (T-TESS) evidence!**	Teach Student Goal-Setting and Reflection Student Mathematics Notebook Conferences Jennifer Serravallo Reading Conferences: Research-Decide-Teach Coaching Conference Compliment Conference

Source: © 2018 by Wilmeth Elementary School, McKinney, Texas. Reprinted with permission.

Figure 3.8: Choice board example.

Collaborative Teams

Collaborative teams can embed the instructional rounds process as part of their team meetings. The team can work out the schedule for teachers on the team to observe each other. Teachers on the team might observe teachers not on the team as well. An important part of the instructional rounds process is to debrief the experience, which can be done within the collaborative team process.

Examples of Practice

The following examples show strategies for supplying teachers with opportunities to observe and discuss effective teaching.

Instructional Rounds

Instructional rounds (or *learning walks*) allow teachers to observe expert teachers to gain new ideas about how they might approach instruction. This activity provides ideas for the observer, not feedback to the presenter. The purpose of instructional rounds for teachers is to learn from colleagues, reflect on teaching practices, and ultimately apply new strategies in the classroom.

The following are some ground rules for instructional rounds.

- Rounds are not for evaluation.
- Rounds are for the collaboration and professional reflection of observers.
- Observe, reflect, and consider teacher behaviors with emphasis on effectiveness.
- Show mutual respect, sensitivity, and kindness.
- Share observed practices that would be of benefit to other teachers.
- Do not offer suggestions to the observed (expert) teachers unless they explicitly ask for feedback.
- Thank and acknowledge observed (expert) teachers for their willingness to open their classrooms to others.

Consider the following logistical protocol (see figure 3.9) for implementing instructional rounds.

Team Size	• Three to five teachers, plus lead teachers
Rounds Leaders	• Leaders should be respected colleagues. • Leaders can be administrators, but remember that rounds are not for formal evaluation. • Leaders should receive training in the process.
Observed (Expert) Teachers	• School leaders recruit and vet the teachers to observe. • Ideally, these teachers should be the strongest teachers.
Scheduling	• Use planning time, rotating subs, administrator subs, and so forth to schedule rounds. • Ideally, debriefing should occur immediately after an observation. • Teams may require ten minutes prior to observation to review the purpose, norms, needed forms, and so on.
Observation	• Classroom observation should take fifteen to twenty minutes. • Team members should record affirmations, questions, and applications to their own professional practice. • If teams use a note-taking form, it should emphasize district foci and use the common language of instruction.
Debriefing	• Include five to ten minutes for debriefing immediately or soon after each observation. • Team members share affirmations, questions, and applications. • Rounds leaders should ensure respectful dialogue and take note of affirmations for observed teachers (if requested). • Team members have the option to pass.
Frequency	• At least once per semester

Source: © 2015 by ESU 6. Reprinted with permission.

Figure 3.9: Instructional rounds protocol.

During instructional rounds, teachers address reflective prompts and share their answers during the debriefing session following their observation. There are three types of prompts: (1) affirmations, (2) questions, and (3) applications.

1. **Affirmations:** How did this experience validate what I do?

2. **Questions:** What questions did this experience generate about what I'm doing in my own classroom?

3. **Applications:** What's one thing I might try in my classroom?

Schools committed to engaging in instructional rounds will find creative methods to schedule teachers into peer classrooms.

Instructional rounds serve as a method to breaking down isolated silos of practice and sharing expertise (Marzano et al., 2018). Schools committed to engaging in instructional rounds will find creative methods to schedule teachers into peer classrooms, such as administrators' covering classes, using rotating substitutes, implementing common planning time, and using video rounds.

Video Rounds

Video is a powerful tool schools can use to curate exceptional practices. Videos featuring their colleagues provide an authentic experience for teachers, as the content and context are familiar. The videos need not be of an entire class period, but rather examples of strategies that align with the MOI. Schools that create a video library of best practices have a treasure trove of resources for professional development, team discussion, and new teacher induction. Figure 3.10 is an example of how Laura Kroll, the K–12 principal in Exeter-Milligan Public Schools in Nebraska, organizes videos in a catalog on a shared digital space.

Putting It All Together

Consider this hypothetical account of one school's journey to building a system of instruction during the course of a school year.

During planning for the upcoming school year, the school leadership team of administrators, teachers, and instructional coaches meet to determine the plan for back-to-school in-service days. They consider the continued use of the school MOI an important step to improving both teacher practice and student achievement. They decide they need to remind teachers of the MOI and set some goals for improvement. The team also puts together a plan to monitor the model and provide support for the staff to do this work. It is the consensus of the team to communicate two things to teachers: (1) "The

Design Question 1: Communicating Learning Goals and Feedback (Instructional Elements 1–3)	Design Question 2: Helping Students Interact With New Knowledge (Instructional Elements 6–13)	Design Question 3: Helping Students Practice and Deepen New Knowledge (Instructional Elements 14–20)
2, 3—Assessing and celebrating learning	7—Using hook stations (in which students discover information for themselves)	14—Using alphaboxes as a strategy for previewing and reviewing content
3—Creating a positive classroom culture	13—Getting instant student feedback	15, 19—Streamlining classroom procedures
3—Positively reinforcing class participation	13—Using talk moves such as questioning and response strategies	15—Assigning independent and group work
4—Making smooth transitions in the classroom	13—Using teacher assessment strategies	18—Making teacher backup plans
2—Tracking student progress	10—Using hint cards as supports to help students work independently	
2—Texting to assess student learning	13—Making daily lesson assessments	

Source: © 2017 by Exeter-Milligan Public Schools, Exeter, Nebraska. Reprinted with permission.

Figure 3.10: Digital video catalog example.

goal is improved instruction for our students," and (2) "The work is done for and by all of us; everyone will have a role and a voice."

The school leadership team organizes teachers into MOI teams for doing this work and designates teacher leaders to guide the work of the school and the teams. The team also decides that regular team leader meetings will be essential to ensuring the success of the process. The MOI team leaders are responsible for the following.

- Facilitating the work of their MOI team, including:

    + Setting goals, reflecting, and charting progress

    + Reflecting on instructional and video rounds

- Meeting with the school leadership team to provide input
- Assisting in the planning of instructional model professional development sessions

The MOI teams meet during one of the first in-service days of the year to examine and refamiliarize themselves with the school's MOI. Teams conduct a team-bonding activity during which they come up with a team name and take a team selfie to post on the school's shared digital space, which also holds all their resources and reflections.

These MOI teams then conduct a short self-audit of the MOI elements to determine two team goals: (1) one goal about an element all members work on together, and (2) one individualized goal based on something each teacher wants to improve in his or her particular classroom. The MOI teams review and discuss implementation strategies. The day concludes with each teacher completing a short online survey to report his or her goals and plans to the building principals and creating a goal poster.

The building principals review the teachers' goals from the online survey and commit to touch base with each teacher during the first two weeks of school about his or her goals. They also meet with MOI team leaders to discuss the process and make any needed adjustments.

The building principals develop a plan to visit each teacher's classroom at least four times each semester to monitor his or her MOI implementation, verify that his or her goals are posted in the classroom, and provide feedback. The building principals decide to use five-minute walkthroughs or fifteen-minute sit-down observations to collect teacher data. The building principals include an agenda item to share observation data at their weekly principal meetings. The building principals develop a formal and informal observations schedule for each member to conduct with a deadline for all summative evaluations due April 15.

During one school in-service day, teachers share their goal progress with their MOI team, including what they have done and their successes and challenges. Teachers chart their progress individually and on a scatter diagram that shows schoolwide progress to date. They repeat this procedure during short goal check-ins during MOI team meetings and at monthly staff meetings.

Training about instructional rounds also occurs during this in-service day. The entire staff receives training on the process, and the school leadership team shares a rounds protocol. Each staff member will go on rounds during individual planning periods once each semester. The school leadership team organizes rounds teams, with one teacher serving as the instructional rounds leader. The rounds team members then determine a date to go on classroom visits based on their individual calendars. The school leadership team later recruits teachers for these teams to observe based on the rounds teams' schedules.

The school leadership team creates an MOI *strategy board* in a designated teacher workroom to track the frequency of strategies the teachers observe during walkthroughs and other observations. Instructional coaches add data to the strategy board based on their observations and interactions. The school leadership team encourages collaborative teams to add data from any of their peer observations. Teachers record the elements they observe during instructional rounds and add data to the strategy board as part of the rounds debriefing.

The MOI teams next come together to reflect on their goals and instructional rounds observations, and then plan to discuss the data they have collected for the MOI strategy board. The MOI team leaders lead their members through the check-in, again charting progress and discussing successes and challenges. The instructional coaches facilitate an MOI strategy board data discussion, with each MOI team suggesting one or two action items.

During the monthly MOI team leader meeting, a member suggests teachers use video self-observation data for improvement. The group believes the form for teacher video self-observation should be the same walkthrough form the school leadership team uses. The MOI team leaders plan some activities for the next staff meeting they can use within their teams to become familiar with the form, and to plan the video logistics. The MOI team leaders' meeting concludes with planning for the upcoming professional development day with a decision to offer teacher-led breakout sessions on topics that align with the goals teachers set in the fall.

Finally, the school holds a celebration to showcase the progress teachers have made on their journey of improvement. Each MOI team presents to one or more other teams, highlighting its goals, data, successes, and challenges. The school leadership team meets with the MOI team leaders to debrief about the celebrations, data, and activities for the year. The school leadership team also drafts an action plan for summer professional development activities and ideas for the next school year.

Conclusion

Every school has the resources to do this work, but it requires commitment. Goals without plans and implementation are like New Year's resolutions; they often go unfulfilled. When schools commit to the process of improving instruction through the six steps in level 2 of the HRS model, they can make amazing things happen for staff and ultimately students. Teachers can fulfill the promise of providing effective instruction through each step of a student's journey if they rely on their collective wisdom.

Goals without plans and implementation are like New Year's resolutions; they often go unfulfilled.

References and Resources

Boogren, T. H. (2017). *The beginning teacher's field guide: Embarking on your first years.* Bloomington, IN: Solution Tree Press.

Croft, A., Coggshall, J. G., Dolan, M., & Powers, E. (2010, April). *Job-embedded professional development: What it is, who is responsible, and how to get it done well* [Issue brief]. Washington, DC: National Comprehensive Center for Teacher Quality.

DuFour, R., DuFour, R., Eaker, R., Many, T. W., & Mattos, M. (2016). *Learning by doing: A handbook for Professional Learning Communities at Work* (3rd ed.). Bloomington, IN: Solution Tree Press.

Frontier, T., & Mielke, P. (2016). *Making teachers better, not bitter: Balancing evaluation, supervision, and reflection for professional growth.* Alexandria, VA: Association for Supervision and Curriculum Development.

Hirsh, S. (2009). A new definition. *Journal of Staff Development, 30*(4), 10–14.

Knight, J. (2011). *Unmistakable impact: A partnership approach for dramatically improving instruction.* Thousand Oaks, CA: Corwin Press.

Marzano, R. J. (2007). *The art and science of teaching: A comprehensive framework for effective instruction.* Alexandria, VA: Association for Supervision and Curriculum Development.

Marzano, R. J. (2012). *Becoming a reflective teacher.* Bloomington, IN: Marzano Resources.

Marzano, R. J. (2017). *The new art and science of teaching.* Bloomington, IN: Solution Tree Press.

Marzano, R. J., Frontier, T., & Livingston, D. (2011). *Effective supervision: Supporting the art and science of teaching*. Alexandria VA: Association for Supervision and Curriculum Development.

Marzano, R. J., Heflebower, T., Hoegh, J. K., Warrick, P. B., & Grift, G. (2016). *Collaborative teams that transform schools: The next step in PLCs*. Bloomington, IN: Marzano Resources.

Marzano, R. J., & Toth, M. D. (2013). *Teacher evaluation that makes a difference: A new model for teacher growth and student achievement*. Alexandria, VA: Association for Supervision and Curriculum Development.

Marzano, R. J., Warrick, P. B., Rains, C. L., & DuFour, R. (2018). *Leading a high reliability school*. Bloomington, IN: Solution Tree Press.

Marzano, R. J., Warrick, P. B., & Simms, J. A. (2014). *A handbook for high reliability schools: The next step in school reform*. Bloomington, IN: Marzano Resources.

Schultz, A., & Slechta, K. (2017). *Effective instruction playbook*. Hastings, NE: Educational Service Unit 9.

Serravallo, J. (n.d.). *Free resources*. Accessed at www.heinemann.com/jenniferserravallo /resources on November 1, 2019.

Serravallo, J. (2014a, October 30). *Coaching conference* [Video file]. Accessed at www.youtube .com/watch?v=o6M4pR7iZdE on November 1, 2019.

Serravallo, J. (2014b, October 30). *Compliment conferences* [Video file]. Accessed at www .youtube.com/watch?v=7GKTU2PsKEc on November 1, 2019.

Serravallo, J. (2014c, October 30). *Research-decide-teach conference* [Video file]. Accessed at www.youtube.com/watch?v=3g9vk07JkFs on November 1, 2019.

Wong, H. K., & Wong, R. T. (2009). *The first days of school: How to be an effective teacher* (4th ed.). Mountain View, CA: Author.

William M. Ferriter

William M. Ferriter is a National Board Certified classroom teacher in Wake County, North Carolina. He is a frequent speaker at Professional Learning Community at Work institutes and conferences. He is an accomplished author, having numerous articles published in *Journal of Staff Development*, *Educational Leadership*, *Phi Delta Kappan*, and *Threshold Magazine*.

Ferriter is a contributing author to two assessment anthologies, *The Teacher as Assessment Leader* and *The Principal as Assessment Leader*. He is also coauthor of several books, including *Teaching the iGeneration*, *Building a Professional Learning Community at Work*, *Making Teamwork Meaningful*, and *Creating a Culture of Feedback*. Ferriter maintains a popular blog, *The Tempered Radical* (http://blog.williamferriter.com), where he writes regularly about teaching in today's world.

Ferriter earned a bachelor of science and master of science in elementary education from the State University of New York at Genesco.

To learn more about Ferriter's work, follow @plugusin on Twitter.

To book William M. Ferriter for professional development, contact pd@Solution Tree.com.

In this chapter, Ferriter provides helpful insights into the role of effective teaching in the PLC process. He discusses how collaborative teams in a PLC use a cycle of inquiry and continuous improvement to analyze and refine their instruction in order to make effective teaching a reality in their schools.

Chapter 4

Effective Teaching in a Professional Learning Community

William M. Ferriter

Let's start with a simple, research-based truth: nothing has a greater impact on student learning than organizing teachers into collaborative teams and convincing them that if they work together, they can have a positive impact on the learning of all students in their classroom, including those who come from disadvantaged backgrounds and those who have traditionally struggled in schools (Hattie, 2017). Teams with high confidence in their shared ability to move learning forward are more persistent, more likely to set challenging goals for themselves, and more willing to experiment with their practices. What's more, teams with high confidence in their shared ability to move learning forward tend to foster higher confidence in their learners, leaving *students* convinced that they can do well in school too (Donihoo, 2017).

Author John Hattie (2017) calls this *collective teacher efficacy*, and in his summary of research on teachers' practices, it is first in a list of 252 strategies ranked from "likely to have a negative impact on student achievement" to "potential

> Nothing has a greater impact on student learning than organizing teachers into collaborative teams.

to considerably accelerate student achievement." But Hattie (2018) would be quick to remind you that collective teacher efficacy isn't just about making teachers feel good about themselves or their practice. In fact, the potential of collective teacher efficacy is only unlocked when teams support their belief in their own ability to drive change with tangible evidence of improvement. "It isn't just growth mindset," Hattie (2018) argues. He continues:

> It's not just rah-rah thinking; it's not just, "Oh—we can make a difference!" But it is the combined belief that it is us that causes learning. It is not the students. It's not the students from particular social backgrounds. It's not all the barriers out there. Because when you fundamentally believe that you can make the difference, and then you feed it with the evidence that you are, that is dramatically powerful. (Hattie, 2018)

To realize the promise and potential of collective teacher efficacy as a tool for school improvement depends on something more than assigning teachers to groups and providing them with encouragement. It depends on restructuring schools as PLCs and helping collaborative teams develop the skills necessary to engage in ongoing cycles of inquiry about the impact their professional choices have on student learning. These cycles of inquiry provide the evidence necessary to build teachers' confidence in their capacity to be agents of change.

To realize the promise and potential of collective teacher efficacy as a tool for school improvement depends on something more than assigning teachers to groups and providing them with encouragement. It depends on restructuring schools as PLCs.

Student Learning Data and Urgency for Inquiry About Instruction

What does a cycle of inquiry look like in a PLC? It starts by asking collaborative teams to answer the first critical question of a PLC: What do we want students to learn? (DuFour, DuFour, Eaker, Many, & Mattos, 2016). Educational researcher Robert J. Marzano (2003) calls this creating a guaranteed and viable curriculum, and it can be a powerful tool for encouraging effective teaching.

To develop a guaranteed and viable curriculum, collaborative teams work together to identify *need to knows* and *nice to knows* for every unit they teach during a school year. *Need to knows* are small sets of concepts and skills every student must master to be successful. *Nice to knows* are concepts and skills that are important, but not essential for students to master before moving to the next grade level. Students benefit from a guaranteed and viable curriculum because it ensures every student—regardless of the teacher—learns the same content (Marzano, Warrick, Rains, & DuFour, 2018). Collaborative teams benefit from a guaranteed and viable curriculum because it focuses their work. Studying the impact of professional practice for *every* concept and skill in state (or provincial) and district curriculum materials is simply impossible given the limited amount of collaborative time available to teachers in most districts. The solution is to use the knowledge and expertise of teachers—combined with evidence gleaned from data sources documenting student performance—to prioritize inquiry on the concepts and skills that matter most.

After a collaborative team identifies a handful of essential learning outcomes for each unit in the required curriculum, members tackle the second critical question of a PLC: How will we know if students are learning? Teams develop common assessments to track student progress on the standards to answer this question. Teams collect common assessment data and then use the data to answer the third and fourth critical questions of a PLC: How will we respond when students don't learn? and How will we extend learning for students who are already proficient? (DuFour et al., 2016). Teachers generate lists of students in need of remediation, extra practice, and extension for each of the essential outcomes on their guaranteed and viable curriculum, and then act together, planning and providing interventions to meet the unique needs of every learner.

Collaborative teams benefit from a guaranteed and viable curriculum because it focuses their work.

But here's the critical point: in a PLC, the common assessment data that teams collect *also* provide practitioners with tangible evidence of the impact their teaching is having on learners. Sometimes, data indicate an individual teacher has discovered an instructional strategy that helps more students learn at higher levels. In this case, collaborative team members amplify the strategy, integrating it into the work happening in every classroom to ensure all students have access to the highest-quality learning experiences. On the other hand, when teachers discover that strategies they embrace are ineffective, they borrow an idea from American educator John Holt (1964) and flunk their unsuccessful methods—not their students. "The question that drives *inquiry into effective teaching* for collaborative teams, then," argues architect of the PLC at Work process Robert Eaker, "is, Are the kids learning—skill by skill—and how do we know?" (personal communication, February 8, 2019).

In a PLC, the common assessment data that teams collect also provide practitioners with tangible evidence of the impact their teaching is having on learners.

Does this make sense to you? In PLCs, team-developed common assessments generate student learning data on the agreed-on essential standards, and then this creates urgency for inquiry about instruction. Teams are driven to study their practice because they know the quickest way to improve learning is to constantly rethink the way they teach. And, as teacher teams develop the shared capacity to use data to inform and improve their practice, they build the kind of collective teacher efficacy— the belief in their own ability to have a positive impact on students as learners—with the potential to considerably accelerate student achievement (Hattie, 2017).

For careful pupils of the PLC process, the notion that the student learning data teams generate create the urgency for inquiry about instruction isn't surprising. In fact, those behaviors are found in many of the definitions of collaboration detailed in the core texts of the PLC process. Here's how PLC at Work architects Richard DuFour, Rebecca DuFour, and Robert Eaker (n.d.) describe collaboration in the brochure *A Big Picture Look at Professional Learning Communities*:

> Teams in a PLC relentlessly question the status quo, seek new methods of teaching and learning, test the methods, and then reflect on the results. Building shared knowledge of both current reality and best practice is an essential part of each team's decision-making process.

And here's how DuFour et al. (2016) describe collaboration in *Learning by Doing: A Handbook for Professional Learning Communities at Work*:

In a PLC, *collaboration* represents a systematic process in which teachers work together interdependently in order to *impact* their classroom practice in ways that will lead to better results for their students, for their team, and for their school. (p. 12)

It is worth noting that the systematic study of practices in a PLC is *the process by which collaborative teams achieve better results for students.* That subtle shift in thinking can move collaborative teams away from general statements of good intentions ("Our goal is to improve student learning") and toward tangible action ("Our goal is to improve student learning *by studying our teaching together*").

The Systematic Study of Practices in a PLC

My first experience with the systematic study of practice in a PLC came as a member of a sixth-grade language arts and social studies team. As a team, we decided to focus our instructional efforts on helping students effectively participate in collaborative conversations. Not only did this outcome appear prominently in the speaking and listening portions of our required curriculum, but we also knew from informal observations that collaborative conversations were rarely productive in our classrooms. Our students struggled to listen to and learn from one another, instead slipping into conversational patterns like talking over or ignoring one another. We were also surprised that so many of our students would sit silently during classroom discussions, allowing their more vocal classmates to control the direction of the conversation.

As a group, we answered the first critical question of a PLC by selecting three conversation behaviors we felt were essential for students to master.

1. Using questions—instead of comments—to encourage participation in the conversation

2. Building on the thoughts and ideas peers share

3. Monitoring personal contributions to the conversation to create space for others to speak

Next, we researched several different strategies for teaching these skills to our students. We settled on two to test: (1) *Paideia seminars* (facilitating collaborative intellectual dialogue with open-ended questions about a text) and (2) *Put Yourself on the Line* (asking students to rate their level of agreement with controversial statements and then develop evidence-based arguments to defend their personal point of view). Finally, we created a performance-tracking tool (see figure 4.1) so we could collect observational data during classroom conversations, select the strategy we wanted to test in our own classrooms, develop a few lessons to introduce students to the discussion behaviors we wanted them to master, and bring data from two classroom conversations to a data-review meeting scheduled later that month.

Essential Conversation Behaviors: (Tally each time you observe one of these behaviors during your classroom conversations.)	Period One	Period Two	Period Three	Period Four
Using questions (instead of comments) to encourage peer participation				
Building on the thoughts and ideas peers share				
Weaknesses We Are Trying to Address: (Tally each time you observe one of these behaviors during your classroom conversations.)	Period One	Period Two	Period Three	Period Four
Dominating the conversation				
Forgetting to respond to one another				
Failing to encourage participation from all group members				

Figure 4.1: Performance-tracking template—conversational behaviors.

Visit go.SolutionTree.com/PLCbooks for a free reproducible version of this figure.

On the date of our data-review meeting, we compiled our initial results into a shared table to see if there was any evidence to indicate that one of our researched instructional strategies—Paideia seminars or Put Yourself on the Line—helped students master the essential skills we had identified as more important than the others. What we found (see figure 4.2) was that students exposed to Paideia seminars demonstrated higher levels of mastery of the discussion behaviors we monitored. In fact, the students exposed to our Put Yourself on the Line strategy became even *more* competitive in their interactions with one another than they had been originally, turning conversations into debates with clear winners and losers.

Essential Conversation Behaviors: (Record the total number of times these conversation behaviors appear during conversations you observe.)	Put Yourself on the Line		Paideia Seminars	
	Teacher One	Teacher Two	Teacher Three	Teacher Four
Using questions (instead of comments) to encourage peer participation	6	4	23	14
Building on the thoughts and ideas peers share	2	4	14	10
Weaknesses We Are Trying to Address: (Record the total number of times you observe these conversation behaviors.)	Teacher One	Teacher Two	Teacher Three	Teacher Four
Dominating the conversation	12	15	2	6
Forgetting to respond to one another	11	9	1	7
Failing to encourage participation from all group members	10	13	1	5

Figure 4.2: Initial data table—conversational behaviors.

Our initial data also revealed another interesting trend: students in class with teacher three consistently demonstrated more positive and fewer negative conversation behaviors than any other students. As we debriefed about the ways we were teaching our students to engage in collaborative conversations, we learned that teacher three was using three different strategies during his Paideia seminars none of the rest of us had considered. First, to encourage students to use questions to spark conversations, he scribed interesting questions on the classroom whiteboard during his discussions. Those questions became an "idea bank" students could draw from whenever their conversation stalled. Second, he borrowed an idea from Matt Copeland (2005), author of *Socratic Circles: Fostering Critical and Creative Thinking in Middle and High School*, and started making participation maps (see figure 4.3) on the whiteboard to help students monitor their own involvement in each discussion. Finally, he had students observe the conversation from an outer circle and rate the participation patterns of their peers at the end of each discussion. All three steps, he argued, provided students with the scaffolding necessary to begin successfully experimenting with the conversation behaviors we had identified as essential at the beginning of our cycle of collective inquiry.

Participation Map: Is bullfighting animal cruelty or an important part of culture?

Initials indicate the students participating in this conversation. Lines indicate individual contributions to the conversation. What does this tell us about our patterns of participation?

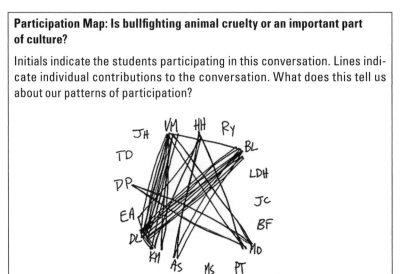

Figure 4.3: Sample collaborative conversation participation map.

At that point, we drew on another powerful tool for studying effective teaching in a PLC and arranged a time when we could observe teacher three lead his class through a Paideia seminar. Our goal was to learn more about how he integrated question scribing, participation mapping, and systematic reflection on participation patterns into his seminars, and to see how students responded to each of those teacher moves. This observation left us convinced that the teaching strategies teacher three embraced were worth integrating into our own attempts at facilitating collaborative student conversations, and we promised again to return at the end of the month with data from two additional discussions we would review together. We also revised our data collection plan (see figure 4.4), asking teachers to record the initials of students who were meeting—and those who were struggling with—our grade-level expectations for effective participation. Doing so would allow us to use the data to provide targeted remediation and extension to individual students.

Essential Conversation Behaviors: (Record the initials of students you observe demonstrating these behaviors during your classroom conversations.)	Period One	Period Two	Period Three	Period Four
Using questions (instead of comments) to encourage peer participation	VS, LJ, SP, JLL, BM, CM, LL, SL	RA, DJP, AV	EA, SN, OT, AM	EB, MP
Building on the thoughts and ideas peers share	VS, LJ, CM, LL, SK, CL, DT	RA, DJP, NV, MQ	LB, CS, SN, OT	SP, DP, PD
Weaknesses We Are Trying to Address: (Record the initials of students you observe demonstrating these behaviors during your classroom conversations.)	Period One	Period Two	Period Three	Period Four
Dominating the conversation			KM, BL, DL, VM	AP, SM
Forgetting to respond to one another	MO	ZA, DMS, SG, SK	JP	AP, SM, KB, KQ, AT
Failing to encourage participation from all group members			KM, VM, DL	AP, SM, ZS

Figure 4.4: Performance-tracking template—conversational behaviors with student initials.

After implementing the strategies teacher three modeled in two additional classroom conversations, we scheduled a second data-review meeting to determine if our efforts to improve our teaching were having a positive effect on student learning. Again, our data (see figure 4.5) told an interesting story: we were seeing increasing numbers of students demonstrating mastery of the discussion skills we had identified as essential, and fewer students demonstrating the kinds of discussion behaviors we were trying to correct. Our team determined the improvement was a result of our decision to incorporate question scribing, participation mapping, and systematic reflection on participation patterns into our instruction. So we added each of those instructional strategies to a team list of promising practices (see figure 4.6). While we did not require teachers to use these promising practices, we did highly recommend them because we had tangible evidence of their effectiveness with our students.

	Paideia Seminars With Question Scribing, Participation Mapping, and Systematic Reflection on Participation Patterns			
Essential Conversation Behaviors: (Record the total number of times you observe these conversation behaviors.)	Teacher One	Teacher Two	Teacher Three	Teacher Four
Using questions (instead of comments) to encourage peer participation	21	23	27	24
Building on the thoughts and ideas peers share	18	18	21	19
Weaknesses We Are Trying to Address: (Record the total number of times you observe these conversation behaviors.)	Teacher One	Teacher Two	Teacher Three	Teacher Four
Dominating the conversation	4	3	0	3
Forgetting to respond to one another	7	5	1	7
Failing to encourage participation from all group members	2	2	3	1

Figure 4.5: Secondary data table—conversational behaviors.

Promising Practices: Sixth-Grade Language Arts and Social Studies

Our team has researched these practices and activities. Our common assessments data show each of these practices and activities has a positive impact on helping more students learn at higher levels. We do not require teachers use them in instruction; however, we believe in these practices and activities and highly recommend teachers use them.

Practices and Activities for Teaching . . .			
Critical Thinking	**Figurative Language**	**Collaborative Dialogue**	**Elaboration**
Metaphorical Thinking With the Curiosity Box	Metaphorical Thinking With the Curiosity Box	Participation Mapping	Claim, Evidence, Reasoning Organizers
Gap Thinking Activities		Question Scribing	"Glue Boy" Assignment
Pacific Northwest Tree Octopus Activity		Systematic Reflection on Participation Patterns	

Figure 4.6: Team promising practices list.

Let's look at this cycle of inquiry again: it started when our team determined students lacked the skills to effectively participate in classroom conversations with one another. We then defined what effective participation in collaborative conversations looks like by detailing three specific behaviors we wanted to see students using in discussions with peers. Next, we developed a simple tool for collecting observational data to help us evaluate the effectiveness of the instructional strategies we were using to teach students about classroom conversation participation, and we used the collected data to both inform and improve our professional practice. Finally, we added three new teacher moves to our team's promising practices list, a collection of instructional strategies (based on the tangible evidence from our own action research) that helped more students learn at higher levels.

That's what studying effective teaching looks like in a PLC. Evidence of gaps in mastery create the urgency for inquiry about instruction, and then teams work to research and test new strategies together to discover what works best to help more

Evidence of gaps in mastery create the urgency for inquiry about instruction, and then teams work to research and test new strategies together to discover what works best to help more students learn at higher levels.

students learn at higher levels. Teachers in a PLC aren't just turning to outside experts' lists of effective teaching practices. Instead, these teachers use team-developed common assessment evidence in *their own* schools to generate *their own* lists of high-leverage instructional practices. The result is teachers develop new instructional skills and teams gain new confidence in their collective ability to positively impact student learning.

Conclusion

The most accomplished teachers in any school are passionate students of *their own instruction.* They stay up to date on the research detailing what works in schools, they tune into emergent strategies other accomplished practitioners are experimenting with, and they constantly tinker with their own lessons to help more students learn. Accomplished teachers are also passionate students of *the learners in their classrooms.* They can detail the common misconceptions their students hold about the content, they account for students' developmental readiness when planning instruction, and they constantly create learning experiences to address the unique needs of contemporary learners. Finally, accomplished teachers are passionate students of *themselves*—they are aware of their own instructional strengths and weaknesses and determined to address gaps in their own skill sets.

In traditional schools, this professional reflection almost always happens in isolation. Some teachers develop their abilities while others stagnate or struggle. This means that in traditional schools, some students are in classrooms with highly effective teachers while others are with teachers unlikely to have the pedagogical know-how to move them forward. As a result, and as research consistently shows, the variability in learning experiences students have access to is far greater *within* schools than *between* schools (Hattie, 2015; Organisation for Economic Co-operation and Development, 2010). The well-documented impact of this instructional variability across classrooms is that students with highly effective teachers significantly outperform their peers with ineffective teachers on every measure of academic performance (Haycock, 1998; Nye, Konstantopoulos, & Hedges, 2004; Wright, Horn, & Sanders, 1997).

The variability in learning experiences students have access to is far greater within *schools than* between *schools.*

And in traditional schools, addressing instructional variability across classrooms has almost always been a function of teacher supervision and evaluation practices. Principals and assistant principals work with individual teachers to identify areas for improvement. Leaders write professional development plans and complete observations to drive improvement and to monitor progress. These leaders pair new teachers or struggling veteran teachers with instructional coaches or mentors who offer additional support—that is, teaching sample lessons, offering feedback on materials, pointing to promising strategies worth considering, and so on.

The challenge, however, is there is simply not enough time for these administrators to evaluate teachers to improve their pedagogical capacity across an entire building. While researchers Robert J. Marzano and Michael Toth (2013) estimate it can take up to ten observations for a principal to accurately assess a teacher's pedagogical capacity, administrators typically only have time for two or three observations of each teacher per year. Complicating matters, research shows when administrators feel like they haven't had enough time to accurately assess a teacher's pedagogical capacity, they tend to give the teacher higher observation scores than warranted (Kraft & Gilmour, 2017). The result? Even in schools state ranking systems deem failing, less than 1 percent of teachers receive unsatisfactory ratings on yearly evaluations (Weisberg, Sexton, Mulhern, & Keeling, 2009).

That's why educators need to restructure schools as PLCs. When administrators empower teacher teams to study their own practices, the administrators can leverage the power of shared knowledge to improve the quality of all teaching in their buildings. Pedagogical capacity grows as members share their expertise and gather evidence about the impact their instructional choices have on student learning. No longer is it the job of a single administrator to improve the abilities of each teacher he or she supervises, and no longer is feedback on practice limited to a handful of formal observations each year. Instead, regular exposure to the strategies, practices, and results of colleagues working in the same context and content area drives the improvement of individual teachers. DuFour (2004) explains:

> Collaborative conversations call on team members to make
> public what has traditionally been private—goals, strategies,

materials, pacing, questions, concerns, and results. These discussions give every teacher someone to turn to and talk to, and they are explicitly structured to improve the classroom practice of teachers—individually and collectively. (p. 10)

The most important step you, as a school leader, can take to increase the instructional capacity of teachers in your building is to make the shared study of practices a collaborative priority.

Stated more simply, in a PLC, meaningful collaboration *about*—instead of comprehensive evaluation *of*—effective teaching is the engine driving school improvement. The most important step you, as a school leader, can take to increase the instructional capacity of teachers in your building is to make the shared study of practices a collaborative priority.

References and Resources

Copeland, M. (2005). *Socratic circles: Fostering critical and creative thinking in middle and high school*. Portland, ME: Stenhouse.

Donihoo, J. (2017, January 9). *Collective teacher efficacy: The effect size and six enabling conditions* [Blog post]. Accessed at https://thelearningexchange.ca/collective-teacher-efficacy on June 24, 2019.

DuFour, R. (2004). What is a professional learning community? *Educational Leadership, 61*(8), 6–11.

DuFour, R., DuFour, R., & Eaker, R. (n.d.). *A big picture look at professional learning communities* [Brochure]. Accessed at www.allthingsplc.info/files/uploads/brochure.pdf on August 21, 2019.

DuFour, R., DuFour, R., Eaker, R., Many, T. W., & Mattos, M. (2016). *Learning by doing: A handbook for Professional Learning Communities at Work* (3rd ed.). Bloomington, IN: Solution Tree Press.

Hattie, J. (2015). *What doesn't work in education: The politics of distraction*. London: Pearson.

Hattie, J. (2017). *Visible learning plus: 250+ influences on student achievement*. Accessed at https://visible-learning.org/wp-content/uploads/2018/03/VLPLUS-252-Influences-Hattie-ranking-DEC-2017.pdf on June 24, 2019.

Hattie, J. (2018, May 1). *What is "collective teacher efficacy?"* [Video file]. Accessed at https://vimeo.com/267382804 on June 24, 2019.

Haycock, K. (1998). Good teaching matters: How well-qualified teachers can close the gap. *Thinking K–16, 3*(2), 1–14.

Holt, J. (1964). *How children fail*. New York: Pitman.

Kraft, M. A., & Gilmour, A. F. (2017). Revisiting the widget effect: Teacher evaluation reforms and the distribution of teacher effectiveness. *Educational Researcher, 46*(5), 234–249.

Marzano, R. J. (2003). *What works in schools: Translating research into action.* Alexandria, VA: Association for Supervision and Curriculum Development.

Marzano, R. J., & Toth, M. D. (2013). *Teacher evaluation that makes a difference: A new model for teacher growth and student achievement.* Alexandria, VA: Association for Supervision and Curriculum Development.

Marzano, R. J., Warrick, P. B., Rains, C. L., & DuFour, R. (2018). *Leading a high reliability school.* Bloomington, IN: Solution Tree Press.

Nye, B., Konstantopoulos, S., & Hedges, L. V. (2004). How large are teacher effects? *Educational Evaluation and Policy Analysis, 26*(3), 237–257.

Organisation for Economic Co-operation and Development. (2010). *PISA 2009 results: What students know and can do—Student performance in reading, mathematics and science* (Vol. I). Accessed at http://dx.doi.org/10.1787/9789264091450-en on February 3, 2019.

Weisberg, D., Sexton, S., Mulhern, J., & Keeling, D. (2009). *The widget effect: Our national failure to acknowledge and act on differences in teacher effectiveness* (2nd ed.). New York: New Teacher Project.

Wright, S. P., Horn, S. P., & Sanders, W. L. (1997). Teacher and classroom context effects on student achievement: Implications for teacher evaluation. *Journal of Personnel Evaluation in Education, 11*(1), 57–67.

LEVEL 3:
A Guaranteed and Viable Curriculum

Ensuring high levels of learning for all students is the driving force behind the concepts and practices inherent in both the HRS model and the PLC process. And ensuring high levels of student learning requires schools and districts engage in developing a sharp focus on these fundamental questions: Learn what? What is essential for every student to learn in every grade, every subject, every course, and every unit—regardless of the teacher to whom he or she is assigned? In other words, what curricula are *guaranteed*? And, how can leaders ensure teachers have adequate time and resources to effectively teach a *guaranteed* curriculum? Is the curriculum *viable*? One of the first, and most important, tasks for leaders is to create a collaborative process that results in a *guaranteed* and *viable* curriculum.

Such a process must be more than a simple averaging of opinions. Rather, the outcome of collaboration at this level should be concrete answers to questions like, What are the elements of a guaranteed and viable curriculum? What essential learning does a guaranteed and viable curriculum address? or What *indicators* would be reflective of a research-based curriculum? And how can leaders engage in a developmental process that results in an effective guaranteed and viable curriculum? Chapters 5 and 6 address these questions.

Jan K. Hoegh

Jan K. Hoegh has an extensive background with guaranteed and viable curricula, first as a district K–12 curriculum coordinator, then with a state department of education, and now as a consultant for Marzano Resources. Hoegh supports numerous schools and districts in designing and implementing processes and products related to developing and implementing a guaranteed and viable curriculum. She is the author of *A Handbook for Developing and Using Proficiency Scales in the Classroom* and a coauthor of numerous books about collaboration, assessment, and grading.

She holds a bachelor of arts in elementary education and a master of arts in educational administration, both from the University of Nebraska at Kearney. She also earned a specialization in assessment from the University of Nebraska–Lincoln.

To learn more about Hoegh's work, visit www.marzanoresources.com.

To book Jan K. Hoegh for professional development, contact pd@SolutionTree.com.

In this chapter, Hoegh describes the defining features of a guaranteed and viable curriculum from the HRS perspective. She not only lays out the process to design and implement a guaranteed and viable curriculum but also describes how schools use such a curriculum to enhance classroom instruction, classroom assessment, intervention, and enrichment.

Chapter 5

Six Action Steps for a Guaranteed and Viable Curriculum

Jan K. Hoegh

Everything in a school begins with the curriculum. Author and researcher Robert J. Marzano (2003) affirms this idea with his identification of five levels of high reliability schools that impact student achievement. Of the five, Marzano (2003) concludes a guaranteed and viable curriculum is the most powerful level. It is easy to see why Marzano (2003) reaches this conclusion when studying a guaranteed and viable curriculum. A *guaranteed and viable curriculum* is a combination of *opportunity* to learn and *time* to learn.

It is also an assurance that the curriculum educators teach is the curriculum they assess. This means individual teachers do not have the option to disregard or replace the content. In short, the big idea here is the written, taught, and learned curricula align, and teachers organize the curriculum to provide sufficient time for student learning to occur. This chapter provides insight into the answer to a very important question inherent within level 3 of the HRS model: How can school and district leaders make sure curriculum alignment occurs?

> *The big idea here is the written, taught, and learned curricula align, and teachers organize the curriculum to provide sufficient time for student learning to occur. . . . How can school and district leaders make sure curriculum alignment occurs?*

There are six leading indicators within HRS level 3.

3.1   The school curriculum and accompanying assessments adhere to state and district standards.

3.2   The school curriculum is focused enough that teachers can adequately address it in the time they have available.

3.3   All students have the opportunity to learn the critical content of the curriculum.

3.4   The school establishes clear and measurable goals that are focused on critical needs regarding improving overall student achievement at the school level.

3.5   The school analyzes, interprets, and uses data to regularly monitor progress toward school achievement goals.

3.6   The school establishes appropriate school- and classroom-level programs and practices to help students meet individual achievement goals when data indicate interventions are needed.

This collection of leading indicators requires school and district leaders ensure a standards-based learning environment, as indicator 3.1 states (*adhere to state and district standards*). In other words, district, state, or national standards are at the heart of curriculum, instruction, and assessment practices. School and district leaders must be knowledgeable about processes and products that ensure a guaranteed and viable curriculum. While there are certainly a plethora of ways a leader can foster a guaranteed and viable curriculum, the following action steps are worthy of consideration.

> *School and district leaders must be knowledgeable about processes and products that ensure a guaranteed and viable curriculum.*

1. Ensure teachers identify the essential standards or content for the subject areas and grade levels they teach.

2. Provide time for school teams to articulate the knowledge and skills the essential content or standards encompass.

3. Give an opportunity for school teams to examine the amount of time needed to adequately teach the essential standards or content.

4. Determine protocols for ensuring the quality of assessments related to the essential content.

5. Establish protocols for analyzing data related to classroom assessments.

6. Make certain appropriate school- and classroom-level programs are in place to help all students achieve at optimum levels.

When schools implement these action steps and the resulting products and processes are an integral part of the school culture, they have the potential to accomplish HRS level 3.

Action Step One: Ensure Teachers Identify the Essential Standards or Content for the Subject Areas and Grade Levels They Teach

The first action step requires teacher teams to work together and decide which standards (or content) have the highest importance within the total set of standards. The first critical question educators in a PLC address aligns with this action step: What do we want students to learn? (DuFour, DuFour, Eaker, Many, & Mattos, 2016). Since the onset of the standards era in the mid-1990s, teachers have faced the challenge of providing students with adequate opportunities to learn the content the standards encompass in the instructional time available. In fact, coauthors Robert J. Marzano, John S. Kendall, and Barbara B. Gaddy (1999) actually quantify the amount of instructional time teachers need to teach the standards content. The conclusion of their study is that teachers have far less instructional time available than teaching the standards demands.

To attain success with HRS level 3, an effective school leader must think this quandary through carefully and determine a plausible process for identifying standards with a higher degree of importance than the others. One such process is to use a set of criteria for making these decisions. Figure 5.1 (page 132) presents five criteria and questions for consideration. See also *A School Leader's Guide to Standards-Based Grading* (Heflebower, Hoegh, & Warrick, 2014) for more information about using these criteria for making these important decisions.

An effective school leader must . . . determine a plausible process for identifying standards with a higher degree of importance than the others.

Criteria for Priority
Teacher judgment: Includes knowledge and skills the teacher or content expert considers very important (non-negotiable)
Assessment connection: Includes content likely to appear on a classroom, district, or large-scale assessment
Endurance: Includes knowledge and skills that will last beyond a grade level or course
Leverage: Includes knowledge and skills that cross over into multiple domains
Readiness: Includes knowledge and skills important to success in a subsequent course

Additional Questions for Consideration
Does the standard meet numerous criteria for priority? How many?
Is mastery of the standard necessary for mastering another standard in the course or in a subsequent course?
Is the standard so important the teacher gives it significant instructional time *and* then assesses it formally?
Is the standard so important it requires articulation in a learning progression on a proficiency scale?
Is the prioritized standard tested on the high-stakes assessment?

Figure 5.1: Process for identifying standards with a higher degree of importance than others.

Visit *go.SolutionTree.com/PLCbooks* for a free reproducible version of this figure.

Of equal importance to the process for identifying the most important standards or content is the amount of time available for this work. There are multiple ways a leader can ensure adequate allocation of time. In some schools, leaders develop a schedule so teachers of the same grade level or content area have a common planning period. When this is the case, curriculum work can occur on a regular basis, leading to gradual and consistent progress. Some leaders might choose to bring teacher teams together during the summer months for two or three consecutive work days. While this method tends to be intellectually exhausting, the result is often the completion of significant work and a high level of satisfaction among participants. Finally, it is becoming a more common practice in schools to integrate a weekly late start or early dismissal time into the school calendar to provide teachers time to work on identifying essential content.

There are multiple ways a leader can ensure adequate allocation of time.

Regardless of the method, a school leader must be clear about how teachers use time and then hold them accountable to ensure they optimize their time. School leaders can and should participate in work sessions not only to support teachers but also to communicate their own commitment to this work. When school leaders identify a clear process and provide adequate time, teacher teams have the capacity to produce a meaningful product, such as figure 5.2 shows.

What is so important in this grade level, content area, or course that teachers identify it as a priority?				
Topic	Priority Standard	Quarter Introduced	Quarter Reinforced	Quarter Assessed
Central Idea	Determine a central idea of a text and analyze its development over the course of the text, including its relationship to supporting ideas; provide an objective summary of the text (RI.8.2).	First	Second, third, fourth	First
Author's Point of View	Determine an author's point of view or purpose in a text and analyze how the author acknowledges and responds to conflicting evidence or viewpoints (RI.8.6).	First	Second, third, fourth	First

Figure 5.2: Middle school guidance for teaching and assessing priority standards. Continued →

Comparing Multiple Texts	Analyze a case in which two or more texts provide conflicting information on the same topic and identify where the texts disagree on matters of fact or interpretation (RI.8.9).	Second	Third, fourth	Second
Elements of Literary Text	Analyze how particular lines of dialogue or incidents in a story or drama propel the action, reveal aspects of a character, or provoke a decision (RL.8.3).	First	Second, third, fourth	Second
Cite Textual Evidence	Make claims about what a text says explicitly and use relevant textual evidence to support those claims (CTTS, p. 52).	First	Second, third, fourth	First
Word Meaning	Determine the meaning of words and phrases as they are used in a text, including figurative and connotative meanings; analyze the impact of specific word choices on meaning and tone, including analogies or allusions to other texts (RL.8.4).	First	Second, third, fourth	Second
Argumentative Writing	Write arguments to support claims with clear reasons and relevant evidence (W.6.1).	First	Second, third, fourth	Third

Informative Writing	Write informative or explanatory texts to examine a topic and convey ideas, concepts, and information through the selection, organization, and analysis of relevant content (W.6.2).	Second	Third, fourth	Third
Speaking and Listening	Analyze the purpose of information presented in diverse media and formats (such as visually, quantitatively, orally) and evaluate the motives (for example, social, commercial, political) behind its presentation (SL.8.2).	Third	Fourth	Third
Research	Gather relevant information from multiple print and digital sources, using search terms effectively; assess the credibility and accuracy of each source; and quote or paraphrase the data and conclusions of others while avoiding plagiarism and following a standard format for citation (WHST.6–8.8).	First	Second, third, fourth	Third

Source for standards: Adapted from National Governors Association Center for Best Practices & Council of Chief State School Officers (NGA & CCSSO), 2010.

This product (see figure 5.2) provides valuable information to teachers of middle-level English language arts content. It not only displays the most important grade-level standards but also identifies when the standard will receive significant instructional focus, as well as when teachers will formally assess it.

Action Step Two: Provide Time for School Teams to Articulate the Knowledge and Skills the Essential Content or Standards Encompass

This second action step helps foster consistent understanding among all teachers of a grade level or course regarding the knowledge and skills the essential content or standards encompass. Many standards teachers expect students to master are comprehensive statements of intended knowledge gain. In fact, when thoroughly examining standards, it is quite easy to discern they are often multidimensional (contain multiple ideas). For example, consider the following grade 3 social studies standard: "The student will explain that governments provide certain types of goods and services in a market economy, and pay for these through taxes; describe services such as schools, libraries, roads, police and fire protection, and military" (Hoegh, 2019, p. 32). This standard clearly encompasses multiple ideas.

To ensure consistent understanding among teachers of what students need to learn, the school leader should encourage teachers to work collaboratively to identify the knowledge and skills they must teach and students must learn.

To ensure consistent understanding among teachers of what students need to learn, the school leader should encourage teachers to work collaboratively to identify the knowledge and skills they must teach and students must learn. In essence, this action step requires teacher teams "unpack" the essential standards. In the case of the previous social studies standard, figure 5.3 displays the specific knowledge and skills a third-grade teacher team might identify.

Standard: The student will explain that governments provide certain types of goods and services in a market economy, and pay for these through taxes; describe services such as schools, libraries, roads, police and fire protection, and military.

1. Explain the certain types of goods and services the government provides in a market economy.

2. Describe how people support the services (such as schools, libraries, roads, police and fire protection, military) through their tax payment.

3. Define *economy*, *good*, *service*, and *taxes*.

4. Distinguish between *a good* and *a service* by categorizing examples of each.

Source for standard: Georgia Department of Education, 2016.

Figure 5.3: Knowledge and skills for grade 3 social studies.

This action step ensures clear understanding among teachers, which increases the likelihood for students to also have clarity about what they need to learn.

Action Step Three: Give an Opportunity for School Teams to Examine the Amount of Time Needed to Adequately Teach the Essential Standards or Content

This action step addresses curriculum viability with respect to the amount of time available for instruction. A school leader certainly wants to be confident teachers have time to provide students adequate opportunity to learn the essential content. Additionally, it is important teachers believe the written curriculum is the basis of what they teach. Some schools implement a two-phase process for ensuring curriculum viability.

Marzano (2003) addresses the first phase of this action step in *What Works in Schools* when he suggests asking teachers to estimate the number of hours or class periods it would take to address the essential content. Following this estimation process, teachers compare their estimates with the total number of hours or class periods available for instruction. In conjunction with this process, it is helpful if leaders determine (or ask teachers to generate) a template for recording the results. Figure 5.4 (page 138) is an example of such a template.

The second phase of the curriculum viability process entails teachers providing students an opportunity to learn the content and then determining the accuracy of their previous estimates based on the actual amount of time required for students to learn the content. In the far-right column on the template (see figure 5.4), individual teachers record the actual time spent teaching the essential standard and any relevant notes. Adjustments to the original estimates are based on the notes teachers record throughout the academic year.

A leader can organize an end-of-the-school-year session specifically for teacher teams to consider what each teacher records in this final column. As teachers discuss the curriculum viability based on their experiences, they can adjust the needed number of hours or class periods. It is important that this process occur annually, as numerous factors can impact the amount of time needed to teach the guaranteed curriculum, such as a new instructional resource, a scheduling

Viability of Curriculum: Phase I and Phase II Results

Topic	Essential Standard	Quarter Taught	Duration of Time	Quarter Reinforced	Actual Time Spent Teaching and Notes
Equations and Inequalities	Solve linear and absolute value equations and inequalities (MA 11.2.2.g).	First	Fifteen to eighteen class periods	Second, third, fourth	Eighteen class periods
Functions	Analyze a relation to determine if it is a function given graphs, tables, or algebraic notation (MA 11.2.1.b).	First, second	Nine to eleven class periods	Second, third, fourth	Fifteen class periods Definitely need to increase number of class periods for teaching this standard; students lack background knowledge at the beginning of the unit.
Graphing	Analyze and graph linear functions and inequalities (point-slope form, slope-intercept form, standard form, intercepts, rate of change, parallel and perpendicular lines, vertical and horizontal lines, and inequalities) (MA 11.2.1.e).	Second	Twelve to fifteen class periods	Second, third, fourth	Thirteen class periods

Source for standards: Adapted from Nebraska Department of Education, 2015b.

Figure 5.4: Template for recording the results of teacher instruction time estimates.

Visit go.SolutionTree.com/PLCbooks for a free reproducible version of this figure.

change, or the amount of background knowledge students bring to the learning opportunity.

Action Step Four: Determine Protocols for Ensuring the Quality of Assessments Related to the Essential Content

When educators identify standards or content as non-negotiable (essential), it makes sense that monitoring progress must occur to know whether or not students are learning. This idea corresponds with the second critical PLC question: How will we know if students are learning? (DuFour et al., 2016). It also makes sense for teachers to use high-quality assessment processes in their classrooms. A school leader must develop his or her expertise about classroom assessment to ensure teachers have adequate knowledge about this important topic. School and district leaders can't assume teachers come to the profession with the necessary knowledge about assessment. In fact, a National Council on Teacher Quality publication discloses that 80 percent of teachers feel inadequately prepared as a result of teacher preparation programs regarding assessment literacy (as cited in Greenberg & Walsh, 2012). This implies that the school leader must possess assessment knowledge to overcome the potential need for assessment knowledge among teachers in the school.

> A school leader must develop his or her expertise about classroom assessment to ensure teachers have adequate knowledge about this important topic. School and district leaders can't assume teachers come to the profession with the necessary knowledge about assessment.

An important first step is for a school leader to convey to teachers that assessment and tests are *not* synonymous. Instead, assessment is *anything* a teacher does to gather information about what a student knows or is able to do about a specific topic. A *test* is just one type of assessment. In *The New Art and Science of Teaching*, Marzano (2017) discusses formal and informal assessment:

> At its core, assessment is a feedback mechanism for students and teachers. Assessments should provide students with information about how to advance their understanding of content and teachers with information about how to help students do so. (p. 21)

Consider this second-grade English language arts standard: "The student will use text features to locate information and gain meaning from print and digital grade-level text" (LA 2.1.6.f; Nebraska Department of Education, 2015a). A teacher might determine some informal assessment processes for monitoring progress on this essential standard. These include probing conversations with students, exit slips, or discussion structures (for example, inside-outside circle, think-pair-share, or learner line-ups), as coauthors Tammy Heflebower, Jan K. Hoegh, Philip B. Warrick, and Jeff Flygare (2019) suggest in *A Teacher's Guide to Standards-Based Learning*.

There will be times, though, when a teacher determines formal assessment is appropriate. When this is the case, it is important for the teacher-identified knowledge and skills (which the teacher determines during the standards-unpacking process) to be the primary focus of the assessment. For example, for the previous text-features standard, a formal assessment might include items like those in figure 5.5.

Score 4.0	Make a suggestion for an additional text feature to a grade-appropriate text and provide a rationale for this decision.	What additional text feature would you add to the passage "All About Martin Luther King"? Why would you add this text feature?
Score 3.0	Use text features to locate information and gain meaning from print and digital grade-level text.	Explain why the caption under the picture is important for a reader. *A scientist from the Environmental Protection Agency tests water quality after an oil spill.*
Score 2.0	Identify text features (for example, illustration, diagram, glossary, headings, bold print, captions, graphs).	Write the name of the text feature.

Source: Hoegh, 2019, p. 48.

Figure 5.5: Formal assessment items example.

Regardless of whether teachers use informal or formal assessment to monitor progress, a leader must impress upon them the importance of assessment quality. In some schools, leaders provide (or facilitate the development of) an assessment review checklist for ensuring the quality of individual assessments, particularly formal assessments. The checklist may include criteria such as the following.

- The assessment measures the knowledge and skills the standard describes.
- The assessment is free from bias.
- The assessment includes clear and concise directions.
- The assessment includes high-quality assessment items.
- The format of the assessment is friendly to students.

When schools determine, communicate, and use criteria in relation to assessments, the potential for quality tools increases.

Action Step Five: Establish Protocols for Analyzing Data Related to Classroom Assessments

To attain the full benefit of high-quality classroom assessments, school and district leaders should consider how to support teachers in using the results. Three uses can and should be expected of teachers: (1) for monitoring the degree of student achievement, (2) for adjusting instruction, and (3) for improving the assessments teachers administer.

Consider a classroom where a teacher has spent considerable time teaching the knowledge and skills necessary for achieving an important standard. The teacher chooses to administer a formal assessment for determining the current level of student understanding. After scoring the assessment, the teacher learns she has three levels of learning among students, as figure 5.6 depicts.

> To attain the full benefit of high-quality classroom assessments, school and district leaders should consider how to support teachers in using the results.

Low Level of Knowledge	Moderate Level of Knowledge	High Level of Knowledge
Six students	Nine students	Eight students

Figure 5.6: Classroom assessment results example.

A significant benefit of the teacher using such information is that she can more easily determine the next steps for instruction. The six students in the left column will likely require some reteaching of the content, as they may lack some foundational skills they can acquire through an additional opportunity to learn. The nine students with a moderate level of knowledge may just need some additional practice or a bit more time to solidify their understanding of the content. The eight students in the right column will likely benefit from some enrichment related to the content. It is through analyzing this classroom assessment information that the teacher is better able to determine the needs of much smaller groups of students. In the end, this practice typically leads to better understanding of the academic content because the follow-up instruction closely aligns with the students' current levels of knowledge.

When multiple teachers administer a common assessment, it is paramount for them to analyze the data carefully and thoroughly for the sake of planning appropriate next steps for instruction. In *Collaborative Teams That Transform Schools*, assessment experts Robert J. Marzano, Tammy Heflebower, Jan K. Hoegh, Philip B. Warrick, and Gavin Grift (2016) state, "After giving and scoring an assessment, teachers should discuss the results in a collaborative team meeting" (p. 58). A school leader might provide a set of questions for the teacher teams to ask themselves during this data discussion, including the following (Marzano et al., 2016).

- "On which parts of the assessment did our students have success?"

- "On which parts of the assessment did our students struggle? Why do we think this is the case?"

- "Were there any patterns evident in the student responses that require us to discuss them as a team?"

- "Does the assessment need revision? Which items? Why?"

- "Which students are in need of special attention?"

Once the team answers these questions, members then begin the process of collaboratively planning for next instructional steps. Because the data give team members such detailed information, it is easier for them to plan instruction that closely aligns with each learner's individual needs, therefore increasing the potential for improving overall student achievement.

It is important to note the questions related to the assessment itself: Does the assessment need revision? Which items? Why? Through data analysis, teams can examine and revise individual assessment items based on student performance. For example, suppose a teacher team discovers that no fewer than five students in each of four classrooms respond inaccurately on a particular item. This should trigger the teachers' desire to examine the item carefully to determine how to improve it. It may be that the language of the item is unclear, or maybe the teachers haven't adequately taught the content of the item. Regardless of the reason for less-than-ideal student performance on the item, it is vital for the teacher team to revise it (or the instruction related to it) for another, future assessment.

Action Step Six: Make Certain Appropriate School- and Classroom-Level Programs Are in Place to Help All Students Achieve at Optimum Levels

Once teachers identify the essential standards or content for each grade level or course, have clarity about the necessary knowledge and skills students need to master the content, determine which aligned assessment practices to use, and use the assessment data to determine each student's needs, the school is in a position to attain optimum levels of student learning. The sixth action step demands that leaders examine what additional existing school programs and practices could support student learning even further, including after-school, tutorial, or enrichment programs. While these programs can indeed support individual students, the school leader should consider how he or she could provide all students with support during a block of time on any given day. This is where a leader's expertise on response to intervention (RTI) becomes necessary.

RTI is a model of support available for *all* students, not just those in need of intervention (Heflebower et al., 2019). At any time, a teacher may face the challenge of instructing students who have and have not learned the important academic content. For this reason, the PLC process

The school leader should consider how he or she could provide all students with support during a block of time on any given day.

includes questions 3 and 4: What will we do when students have not learned? and What will we do when they have learned? These two questions suggest that overcoming challenges related to learning is best addressed through collaboration. The RTI process is a means for teachers to work together at optimum levels to support all students. This model provides intervention options at three different tiers specifically designed to provide support for struggling students. To review the three tiers of intervention, consider what RTI experts Austin Buffum, Mike Mattos, and Janet Malone (2018) state:

> The pyramid is commonly separated into tiers: Tier 1 represents core instruction, Tier 2 represents supplemental interventions, and Tier 3 represents intensive student supports. The pyramid is wide at the bottom to represent the instruction that all students receive. As students demonstrate the need for additional support, they receive increasingly more targeted and intensive help. Because timely supplemental interventions should address most student needs when they are first emerging, fewer students fall significantly below grade level and require the intensive services Tier 3 offers, creating the tapered shape of a pyramid. (p. 2)

Clearly, RTI is a valuable model of support that ensures all students, especially those who struggle to learn the essential content, achieve at high levels.

To provide even more support than RTI, some schools include an intervention block of time during each school day. This idea is grounded in the belief that *all* students need support on a consistent basis, not just struggling learners. While this block of time may not be beyond about thirty minutes, leaders allocate it for the sake of meeting the goal of all students learning at high levels. The following is a sample *purpose statement* a teacher team might develop in a school with a daily intervention block (South Sioux City Community Schools, n.d.):

RTI is a valuable model of support that ensures all students, especially those who struggle to learn the essential content, achieve at high levels.

> Our goal is for all students to learn at high levels. We know students do not always learn at the same rate. WIN (What I Need) provides time in our school's schedule for reteaching, homework assistance, and enrichment. In the past, students

have had to retake assessments or get help from a teacher before school, during lunch time, or after school. WIN time allows teachers to give students what they need on a daily basis.

In this school, the WIN structure potentially provides support to individual teachers when they face the challenge of some students learning the content and others struggling to learn it. It also provides ongoing and meaningful support to all learners for increasing their understanding of the essential content.

Conclusion

HRS level 3 is about ensuring teachers have clarity about what students need to learn. It also requires teachers use quality assessments for making important decisions about whether or not students have learned the essential content. The use of data is prominent within this level, as is examining existing programs that support all learners and planning additional structures to improve student achievement. The action steps this chapter addresses imply a leader must understand the importance of his or her role in moving through this important work with a high level of success. Ensuring a guaranteed and viable curriculum requires collaboration and significant time to ensure student learning. Effective leadership will ensure the presence of both in a school or district.

> *Ensuring a guaranteed and viable curriculum requires collaboration and significant time to ensure student learning.*

References and Resources

Buffum, A., Mattos, M., & Malone, J. (2018). *Taking action: A handbook for RTI at Work*. Bloomington, IN: Solution Tree Press.

DuFour, R., DuFour, R., Eaker, R., Many, T. W., & Mattos, M. (2016). *Learning by doing: A handbook for Professional Learning Communities at Work* (3rd ed.). Bloomington, IN: Solution Tree Press.

Georgia Department of Education. (2016). *Georgia standards of excellence*. Accessed at www .georgiastandards.org/Georgia-Standards/Documents/Social-Studies-K-5-Georgia -Standards.pdf on March 25, 2019.

Greenberg, J., & Walsh, K. (2012, May). *What teacher preparation programs teach about K–12 assessment: A review*. Washington, DC: National Council on Teacher Quality. Accessed at https://files.eric.ed.gov/fulltext/ED532766.pdf on June 25, 2019.

Heflebower, T., Hoegh, J. K., & Warrick, P. B. (2014). *A school leader's guide to standards-based grading*. Bloomington, IN: Marzano Resources.

Heflebower, T., Hoegh, J. K., Warrick, P. B., & Flygare, J. (2019). *A teacher's guide to standards-based learning*. Bloomington, IN: Marzano Resources.

Hoegh, J. K. (2019). *A handbook for developing and using proficiency scales in the classroom*. Bloomington, IN: Marzano Resources.

Marzano, R. J. (2003). *What works in schools: Translating research into action*. Alexandria, VA: Association for Supervision and Curriculum Development.

Marzano, R. J. (2010). *Formative assessment and standards-based grading*. Bloomington, IN: Marzano Resources.

Marzano, R. J. (2017). *The new art and science of teaching*. Bloomington, IN: Solution Tree Press.

Marzano, R. J., Heflebower, T., Hoegh, J. K., Warrick, P. B., & Grift, G. (2016). *Collaborative teams that transform schools: The next step in PLCs*. Bloomington, IN: Marzano Resources.

Marzano, R. J., Kendall, J. S., & Gaddy, B. B. (1999). *Essential knowledge: The debate over what American students should know*. Aurora, CO: Mid-continent Research for Education and Learning.

Marzano, R. J., Warrick, P. B., & Simms, J. A. (2014). *A handbook for high reliability schools: The next step in school reform*. Bloomington, IN: Marzano Resources.

National Governors Association Center for Best Practices & Council of Chief State School Officers. (2010). *Common Core State Standards for English language arts and literacy in history/social studies, science, and technical subjects*. Washington, DC: Authors. Accessed at www.corestandards.org/assets/CCSSI_ELA%20Standards.pdf on August 27, 2019.

Nebraska Department of Education. (2015a). *Nebraska K–12 language arts standards*. Accessed at www.education.ne.gov/wp-content/uploads/2017/07/2014_Updated_ELA_Standards_Vertical_Version_k_12.pdf on March 25, 2019.

Nebraska Department of Education. (2015b). *Nebraska K–12 mathematics standards*. Accessed at www.education.ne.gov/wp-content/uploads/2017/07/2015_Nebraska_College_and_Career_Standards_for_Mathematics_Vertical.pdf on March 25, 2019.

South Sioux City Community Schools. (n.d.). *What I need (WIN)*. Accessed at www.ssccardinals.org/assets/files/High_School/WIN-TIME-(What-I-Need)-on-Website.pdf on December 20, 2019.

Heather Friziellie

Heather Friziellie is superintendent of schools for Fox Lake School District 114 in Fox Lake, Illinois. She previously served as a director overseeing special education as well as an elementary and middle school principal. As a leader, she is involved in response to intervention (RTI), closing the gap for special education–entitled students, professional learning communities, literacy curriculum development, data analysis, and staff development. With experience as a building- and district-level administrator, curriculum specialist, and classroom teacher, Friziellie has consulted with districts throughout the United States and presented at national conferences. She received a Those Who Excel award in Illinois in the School Administrator category. She is coauthor of *Yes We Can! General and Special Educators Collaborating in a Professional Learning Community*.

To learn more about Friziellie's work, follow @FGLSD114 on Twitter.

Julie A. Schmidt

Julie A. Schmidt is superintendent of schools for Kildeer Countryside Community Consolidated School District 96 in Buffalo Grove, Illinois. During more than thirty years in education, Schmidt has been a superintendent, an associate superintendent, a high school director of student services, a school psychologist, an assistant to the superintendent, and an assistant director of special education spanning early childhood through high school. She continues to work with elementary and secondary schools across the United States as a speaker and facilitator on RTI, closing the gap for special education students, leadership and change, and the implementation of PLC practices at all levels of an organization. She has served on the national PLC advisory board for Solution Tree. Julie received the Principals' Award of Excellence during her service at the high school level, where she also earned the Administrative Award of Excellence. She was recognized as the Lake County Superintendent of the Year by her colleagues for 2016 and a Superintendent of Distinction in the state of Illinois in 2017. She serves on the Executive Board for the Exceptional Learners Collaborative and on the Board of Directors for the Illinois Association of School Administrators, where she serves as the state professional development chairperson.

To learn more about Schmidt's work, follow @kildeer on Twitter.

To book Heather Friziellie or Julie A. Schmidt for professional development, contact pd@SolutionTree.com.

In this chapter, Friziellie and Schmidt drill deeper into the concepts and practices underlying developing, implementing, and improving a guaranteed and viable curriculum. The authors are well qualified for this undertaking, having led the development and implementation of a guaranteed and viable curriculum within their respective districtwide PLCs.

148

Chapter 6

PLC, HRS, and a Guaranteed and Viable Curriculum

Heather Friziellie and Julie A. Schmidt

As leaders of two different districts both on the journey to build and sustain high-performing PLCs, we view this chapter as both a reflection on the specific steps we have taken to build a guaranteed and viable curriculum for all learners in our systems, and an opportunity to self-assess our current reality in relation to alignment with the HRS model. What has become clear is the PLC process is the cornerstone to being highly reliable. The PLC process, when deeply implemented, forces schools to focus constantly on answering the four critical questions (DuFour, DuFour, Eaker, Many, & Mattos, 2016), and, by doing so, align with the six leading indicators of a guaranteed and viable curriculum (Marzano, Warrick, Rains, & DuFour, 2018).

3.1 The school curriculum and accompanying assessments adhere to state (or provincial) and district standards.

3.2 The school curriculum is focused enough that teachers can adequately address it in the time they have available.

3.3 All students have the opportunity to learn the critical content of the curriculum.

3.4 The school establishes clear and measurable goals that are focused on critical needs regarding improving overall student achievement at the school level.

3.5   The school analyzes, interprets, and uses data to regularly monitor progress toward school achievement goals.

3.6   The school establishes appropriate school- and classroom-level programs and practices to help students meet individual achievement goals when data indicate interventions are needed.

In this chapter, we tell our stories through the lens of the six indicators of level 3 while illustrating how the work of collaborative teams in a PLC naturally aligns with HRS model indicators. Please note, the tools we share are simply examples of protocols and processes we and our teams developed and implemented to achieve higher levels of learning for our students. We do not present them as "the way"; rather, they serve as examples of a way two different districts have brought PLC and HRS into action on a daily basis.

> *We tell our stories through the lens of the six indicators of level 3 while illustrating how the work of collaborative teams in a PLC naturally aligns with HRS model indicators.*

Curriculum and Assessments Adhere to State and District Standards

In a PLC, critical question number one—What do we expect all learners to learn?—drives the work (DuFour et al., 2016). Effective schools' main focus is, at all times, in all ways, across grade levels and specialties, on this essential question. Determining the answer cannot, however, be based on the perspectives, experiences, or beliefs related to mastery. Rather, teacher and curriculum teams first focus on the state (or provincial) standards. In our districts, this means using the Common Core standards for literacy and mathematics (National Governors Association Center for Best Practices & Council of Chief State School Officers [NGA & CCSSO], 2010a, 2010b), the Next Generation Science Standards (NGSS Lead States, 2013), the C3 standards for social studies (National Council for the Social Studies, 2013), and national and state standards in the fine arts and physical education as the foundation of teaching and learning. These documents guide the work of teams much like a GPS guides people when driving to a new destination. Achieving the outcomes of the broad standards is our goal for learners to ensure they are future ready.

When considering any of the standards documents that guide this work, our teacher teams received training and regularly applied the skill of deconstructing the standards to ensure deep and shared understanding. As in all states or regions, standards are complex animals, oftentimes written in complex terms encompassing many different concepts, targets, or skills. No matter what this process is called—*unwrapping, unpacking, deconstructing,* or *dissecting*—the purpose remains the same: ensuring clarity of what mastery of the standard means. All teachers of a grade level or course must agree to ensure teaching and learning in each classroom aim for the same end goal, or, continuing the GPS analogy, the same end location.

Over time, this process had gotten quite a bad rap in many districts and systems because teacher teams weren't clear on *why* they should truly break down a standard to ensure consensus on its meaning and rigor, and *how* powerful their conversations are for learning. Doing this work often became a compliance task, eliciting eye rolls and under-the-breath statements like, "I can't believe we have to do this *again*. What a waste of time."

Let's look at what can happen if teams skip the step of focusing on and creating shared understanding of standards. Consider this standard from the sixth-grade Common Core State Standards for mathematics (NGA & CCSSO, 2010b): "Interpret and compute quotients of fractions, and solve word problems involving division of fractions by fractions, e.g., by using visual fraction models and equations to represent the problem" (CCSS.Math.Content.6.NS.A.1).

If left to independent interpretation, teachers may identify, teach to, assess, and report on the following destinations.

- Division of fractions with like denominators
- Division of fractions with unlike denominators
- Application of division of fractions to word problems
- Determination of which operation to use when solving a word problem
- Or all of the above, with or without visual models!

Within the same school or district, the issue with this scenario is if all sixth-grade mathematics teachers have not agreed on what mastery of the standard looks like, then they—with the very best intentions—will teach to their own interpretation of the standard. This can lead to student mastery of sixth grade and readiness for seventh grade depending solely on the decisions of the mathematics teacher. This puts students—and the seventh-grade mathematics teachers who will have to determine who had which teacher—in a difficult and unfair position. In the absence of collaborative clarity on standards, educators regularly send students to the next grade level or course with differing levels of proficiency, creating an inequitable path for students to be successful.

A key fundamental responsibility for all schools is to ensure that, no matter which teacher, the expectation of mastery does not vary. We cannot leave students' learning to the single teacher to whom they are assigned.

A key fundamental responsibility for all schools is to ensure that, no matter which teacher, the expectation of mastery does not vary.

We can efficiently and effectively move past independent interpretation of standards to a consistent, aligned instructional plan that leads to standard mastery with three action steps for teams. Teacher teams apply the following action steps to make sure everyone has the same understanding of the standard.

1. Pick an upcoming unit or topic of instruction and clarify what students should know and be able to do.

2. Prioritize the list using a simple process, such as ABC prioritizing (three steps; Friziellie, Schmidt, & Spiller, 2016).

   a. Make initial choices individually based on criteria.

   b. Develop an initial list of priority standards using the following criteria for developing priority standards (Reeves, 2002).

      • *Endurance.* Does the standard have knowledge and skills valued beyond a single test date (like point of view and place value)?

      • *Leverage.* Are the knowledge and skills valued in multiple disciplines (like reading informational text in different subject areas and doing mathematics unit rate problems in science)?

      • *Readiness.* Are the knowledge and skills necessary for success in the next grade level or next unit of instruction (like letter-sound recognition and logarithms)?

   c. Review other sources of information to make a final decision.

3. Unpack the priority standards using, for example, a seven-step unpacking process (Friziellie et al., 2016).

   a. Identify the priority standards for a particular unit or topic of instruction.

   b. Circle or highlight the verbs and underline the knowledge or concepts.

   c. Identify learning targets.

   d. Determine the level of rigor for each learning target and consider the type of assessment that matches the rigor expectations.

   e. Identify key vocabulary.

   f. Determine a logical learning progression.

   g. Determine potential scaffolds or supports.

Grade- and course-level teams then create curriculum maps and pacing guides to indicate which standards they will teach in what sequence and at what pace to ensure students move from their initial level of understanding to mastery. Teams then collaborate to create assessments aligned with standard mastery. Beginning with the end in mind, teams develop the end-of-unit assessment to define mastery of each learning target and also to reflect mastery of the standard itself. Teams then use these assessments to preassess student learning on the learning targets, allowing teachers to prioritize their time based on student understanding before instruction even begins.

This is a major shift in practice! Rather than traditional methods, when teachers might proclaim, "We will spend four weeks on the fractions unit and start with lesson one," teacher conversations sound like, "We now have data before we even begin to teach to help us prioritize instructional time." Additional collaboratively created common assessments check student mastery of the standard's target, and with laser-like focus, teachers plan instruction as well as identify specific students who need intervention and those who are ready to extend their understanding by learning more deeply about the target. When teachers use assessments for formative learning and feedback, they help themselves make midcourse adjustments, just like a car GPS may reroute you when traffic issues arise. This just-in-time course adjustment supports students in moving to mastery.

> When teachers use assessments for formative learning and feedback, they help themselves make midcourse adjustments.

Our staffs specifically indicate for each assessment which standard or targets within a standard are the focus in the task. This serves the following two purposes.

1. Students who are completing the assessment task are clear on the skills of focus.

2. Assessment validity dramatically increases because the goal of the focused check-in is crystal clear.

When teams create and then pace instruction using a backward method with mastery as the goal, using preassessment data—likely built as examples that mirror the final summative assessment of standard mastery—to determine where instruction needs to begin and a clear plan to check in formatively along the way, teachers then plan instruction targeting the standards (or even more specific learning targets). Teaching becomes not about the task first; instead, it focuses on the learning target and the best ideas for making sure students reach the end goal. Having teacher collaborative teams focus on this dialogue is powerful and key for answering PLC critical question one: What do we want all students to learn? (DuFour et al., 2016).

The Curriculum Is Focused

The reality is teacher teams find there are simply too many standards to teach within the time available and with intensity. Author Robert J. Marzano (2003) in his book *What Works in Schools* states to truly teach to mastery all the standards in a typical K–12 curriculum, we would need up to ten years of additional instructional time. Students do not have this kind of time!

As educators, we are then left with the following two distinct choices.

1. Allotting time equally to make sure each standard is covered, knowing it is mathematically impossible to ensure all students master all the standards within the course of a school year

2. Prioritizing standards to determine which ones get us more "bang for the buck" (that is, teams allocate time purposefully to give the most essential standards the most instructional time and focus)

The choice seems to be common sense: if we know we want all students to demonstrate mastery, then we must be critical consumers of the standards to ensure we allocate time and resources to the standards with the most long-term benefits for students.

How this is determined cannot be left to individual teachers. Just as teams work together to ensure all members deeply understand what each standard means, members must also agree on which standards will get the most time or take priority over others. This does not imply the other standards are not taught; rather, it means that teams allocate more time, focus their assessments, and implement systems of intervention and extension for the team-identified priority standards.

> Just as teams work together to ensure all members deeply understand what each standard means, members must also agree on which standards will get the most time or take priority over others.

Additionally, teams cannot determine priorities without criteria. Without clear metrics to identify what standards are priorities, teams can—even with the best intentions—rely on the following to identify the priority standards.

- What they are most comfortable teaching

- What they have done in the past

- Already developed units

- The easiest standards for students to manage and master

When working to identify priority standards, we turned to Douglas B. Reeves (2002) to guide our decision making. Teams in both districts used the following four clear descriptors to guide discussions and decisions in our districts.

1. **Readiness:** Does a learner need to master this standard to be ready for the next grade level or course?

2. **Endurance:** Will the content of the standard matter over time? Is it important for learners to know the standard and apply it for years to come?

3. **Assessment:** Does the standard align with external accountability assessment expectations?

4. **Leverage:** Does mastery of the standard in one content area help students be more successful in other content areas?

A specific example teams studied together is the following standard, identified in the Common Core (NGA & CCSSO, 2010a): "By the end of the year, read and comprehend literature, including stories, dramas, and poems, at the high end of grades 6–8 text complexity band independently and proficiently" (CCSS.ELA-Literacy.RI.8.10).

Full staffs discussed the standard using Reeves's (2002) criteria and came to consensus on the following.

- **Readiness:** Yes—students entering high school must be able to read grade-level text.

- **Endurance:** Yes—reading rigorous text is a life skill.

- **Assessment:** Yes—student ability to read grade-level text is assessed on multiple metrics.

- **Leverage:** Yes—being able to read and comprehend grade-level text is important in all content areas.

Thus, teams identified this standard as a priority for teaching and learning in grade 8. Teams also came to agreement that, since this same standard is a component of each grade level, the standard of reading at grade level would be a priority at all grade levels.

Once they had this shared learning experience, they were then ready to work as content- and grade-level teams to determine priorities at each level. A key to making these determinations for standards is having completed the unwrapping process. Our teams were absolutely clear on the meaning and learning targets of the standards they were considering. This allowed them to consider the four criteria with deeper understanding; they were truly able to look at each standard and have robust conversations to determine if they would identify the standards as priorities.

Teams hit a stumbling block along the way, however. When considering standards and their priority level, conversations began to indicate that, if a standard wasn't identified as a priority, then it would not be taught. This was clearly *not* the intent, so they needed to reframe the work. They did so using the following analogy.

In Fox Lake District 114 in Illinois, we found a metaphor helped us cooperatively attack this. Consider student learning as a living, breathing entity to protect and nurture. To do so, build a "fence" to keep learning in and keep out any distractions that may get in the way. When thinking about a fence, there are two primary components: fence posts and rails. The fence posts are sturdy. They go deep into the ground and, in general, last far longer than rails. They are put in place first. After all, how effective is a fence if it is made of rails only? Gravity takes over, leaving you with a pile of rails.

The fence posts are the *priority standards*—what must get the most time and attention. The rails, then, are the supports that connect the posts and keep, in this case, learning in and distractors out. They are not as sturdy, and they likely will not take as much time to build, nor will they last as long. However, they are essential to the fence serving its purpose. A fence is not going to work if only built as a series of posts in the ground. The rails—the supports—must be in place to complete the fence. The rails, then, are the *supporting standards*. Teachers expose learners to them, and provide instruction on them, but these supporting standards do not get the same time and focus as the priority standards or fence posts.

In our stories, we also see a fence with no scrap pile. There is no discarded wood, nothing to throw out. We do not ignore any standards; rather, we purposefully prioritize time and then commit to instruction, assessment, intervention, and extension aligned with the standards teams have identified as the most important—the fence posts.

A fence is not going to work if only built as a series of posts in the ground. The rails—the supports—must be in place to complete the fence.

This creates the perfect opportunity for meaningful vertical articulation across teams and cross-content dialogue as well. At the middle school level, all teachers in grades 5–8 who taught English language arts, social studies, and science were asked to work together to identify the essential Common Core Reading standards. This included special educators who worked with each team. Since reading—especially reading informational text—is critical in all three content domains, teachers were asked to engage in the work in order to build bridges and make connections across the different content areas. To begin, each teacher was provided a copy of the CCSS for literacy and informational text. Teams then received three dot stickers to identify the standards they felt were the most essential. This individual think time was key to making sure each team member had time to consider and prioritize on his or her own without unintentionally engaging in group think.

Next, each standard was put on its own chart paper. Teachers then added dots to these charts to match their own thinking. Using a gallery walk format, grade-level teams considered the charts and collaborated to identify trends in priorities. They then came together as a whole group to share their thinking based on the "dot data." In addition to this list, all agreed that CCSS RL/RI 10—reading text at grade level—was a priority standard across grade levels and to be focused on in all content areas.

Next, grade-level teams identified student proficiency expectations at each grade to then vertically articulate to ensure they were increasing rigor at each subsequent grade level, to discuss commonalities for focus across grades, and to describe student work tasks. Figure 6.1 shows a sample standard outcome.

Teams completed this dialogue for each of the essential standards. They then compiled the work into an anchor document to help guide the work in all three content areas and to help ensure instruction was connected across content to truly enhance student learning.

All Students Have the Opportunity to Learn the Critical Content

Researchers and authors Richard DuFour and Robert J. Marzano (2011) note:

> The only way the curriculum in a school can truly be guaranteed is if the teachers themselves, those who are called upon to deliver the curriculum, have worked collaboratively to do the following:

Determine central ideas or themes of a text and analyze their development; summarize the key supporting details and ideas (RI.2).		
Grade 5: Determine two or more main ideas of a text and explain how they are supported by key details; summarize the text (RI.5.2).	Grade 6: Determine a central idea of a text and how it is conveyed through particular details; provide a summary of the text distinct from personal opinions or judgments (RI.6.2).	Grade 7: Determine two or more central ideas in a text and analyze their development over the course of the text; provide an objective summary of the text (RI.7.2).
		Grade 8: Determine a central idea of a text and analyze its development over the course of the text, including its relationship to supporting ideas; provide an objective summary of the text (RI.8.2).
Commonalities • Students avoid making personal opinions and judgments. • The complexity of text increases from one grade level to the next. • The standards support a bridge between main idea and central idea.		
Student work will look like . . .		
Students identify two main ideas; each main idea has two pieces of support found within the text. Student gives a summary for each main idea.	Students give a summary of the text (oral or written) that includes the central idea and at least two details throughout the text. Student does not use personal opinion.	Students identify two or more central ideas in the text that develop over the course of the text. Student writes an objective summary using only information from the text (two or more main ideas; close examination of the parts to understand the whole; no opinion, background knowledge, or bias).
		Student determines the main idea of a passage. Students analyze the development of the central idea throughout the text (identify the main idea of each paragraph and explain its relationship to the overall central idea—for example, compare and contrast). Student writes an objective summary using who, what, why, where, when, and how without personal opinion or prior knowledge.

Source for standards: NGA & CCSSO, 2010a.
Source: Fox Lake School District 114, Illinois. Reprinted with permission.

Figure 6.1: Identifying student proficiency expectations at each grade.

- Study the intended curriculum.

- Agree on priorities within the curriculum.

- Clarify how the curriculum translates into student knowledge and skills.

- Establish general pacing guidelines for delivering the curriculum.

- Commit to one another that they will, in fact, teach the agreed-upon curriculum. (p. 91)

The challenge then becomes taking curriculum documents and putting the pieces together with best practice to design instruction. In District 114, teams implemented Maria Nielsen's (n.d.) 15-Day Challenge construct to guide the work. The concept is for teacher teams to work in fifteen-day cycles of instruction, focusing on a standard or components of a standard. Within this cycle, all teacher teams that teach students content (including special educators, bilingual educators, and so on) lay out instructional plans and identify specifically when they will use formative assessments to tailor instruction based on short-cycle assessment data. Our staff created a common planning template using the following information for this work.

The challenge then becomes taking curriculum documents and putting the pieces together with best practice to design instruction.

- The essential standard of focus

- Learning targets of focus within the fifteen-day cycle

- Essential vocabulary within the standard and targets

- Specific tasks in progression to reach proficiency

- Formative assessment stopping points and targets

- A space to capture to-dos along the way

In this example, pink notes describe instructional plans and tasks for a given day, and yellow notes signal assessments teams will use formatively to drive instruction and intervention. Teams specifically built the 15-Day Challenge protocol with three days in each row to signal the intent is not to do instructional planning throughout a five-day week, but to build increased flexibility and break the habit of assessments always happening—in all content areas—on Fridays.

These planning guides can be found in the hallway of each grade-level team and are constantly the focus during collaborative team time. Students are seen frequently checking the plans to see where they are heading in a class, which has led to higher levels of student engagement in their own learning. Also, because students can see where each class is going at all times, they have increased clarity around what teachers expect and what they will be working to master.

In District 114 elementary classrooms, a focus on mathematics has been the unifying content area across our preK through fourth-grade classrooms, as mathematics has historically been our district's greatest area of need. Teams worked to identify essential standards in mathematics, and they consistently use the same 15-Day Challenge (Nielsen, n.d.) to construct a plan in their collaborative teams. Again, special educators are always included in this work to ensure even our most challenging learners receive support in reaching grade-level expectations.

The beauty of the 15-Day Challenge construct is that, when applied to agreed-on essential standards and implemented with fidelity, a true guaranteed and viable curriculum with embedded assessments built into the plans is created. Teams write these assessments with standard mastery in mind before instruction even begins. The assessments also drive systematic intervention and enrichment supports, with time in the schedule each school day.

Clear and Measurable Goals Focus on Critical Needs for Improving Student Achievement

Aligned goals at all levels drive a systemwide, deeply embedded PLC in Kildeer Countryside Community Consolidated School District 96 in Buffalo Grove, Illinois. This means district, school, and team goals must align and be specific at each level. As DuFour et al. (2016) note, "There is *nothing* more important in determining the effectiveness of a team than each member's understanding of and commitment to the achievement of results-oriented goals to which the group holds itself mutually accountable" (p. 103).

District, school, and team goals must align and be specific at each level.

In 2001, a new visionary board of education at District 96, in collaboration with the district superintendent, set two board-adopted goals. The work of author Jim Collins (2001) in *Good to Great* drove these goals; specifically, he notes, "Simplify a complex world into a single organizing idea, a basic principle, or concept that unifies and guides everything" (p. 91). The first goal the board adopted was 90 percent of all students will reach proficiency in reading, and the second was 90 percent of all students will reach proficiency in mathematics. All school and team goals stemmed from those two very specific priorities. This began District 96's commitment to specific and aligned goals to support a laser-like focus on what is most important—student learning.

The districtwide goal-setting process has evolved over the years as access to and organization of data has improved simultaneously with the ability of teacher teams to analyze and plan using those data. Goal setting is a multitiered process that begins each April with teacher feedback sessions. During those sessions, Schmidt (as superintendent) spends a day in each of the seven schools soliciting feedback on the year's work and potential next steps in the improvement process. This kicks off multiple rounds of feedback and brainstorming, which results in the process figure 6.2 (page 164) outlines.

District Goals

The superintendent, in collaboration with District 96 staff and administration, develops district goals and then presents them to the board of education for consideration. The district uses these goals to guide decision making related to allocation of time and resources, and to drive continuous school improvement. The district administrative team that includes all building-level and district-level leaders reviews the goals following fall, winter, and spring data updates, and principals review them with full faculties at least twice per year. Ongoing connections made to school and team goals are highlighted. The board of education receives updates regarding progress periodically through goal updates during public board of education meetings.

School Goals

Principals propose school goals based on current school-improvement data and data projections to identify students not projected to meet grade-level expectations by the end of the year. The principals then use the data to develop an action plan and to meet the needs of individual students through multitiered systems of support. Principals discuss and monitor these goals with the superintendent at goal meetings three times per year. The entire district administrative team reviews data and discusses school-based progress at its meetings as well. This provides principals with the support and assistance from district-level leaders, as well as the opportunity to discuss the data and collaborate with their peers around best practices for improvement.

Grade-Level Team Goals

Grade-level and content-area teams develop, implement, and monitor goals using numerous data points, including the Northwest Evaluation Association Measures of Academic Progress (NWEA MAP), student growth and proficiency projections, and results of the yearly accountability assessment. These are typically yearlong goals. All teams develop goals, including physical education teams, which use fitness data. Teams discuss and adjust the goals regularly at team meetings using fall, winter, and spring data.

Teams also develop short-term or short-cycle goals using common formative assessment and end-of-unit assessment data. The problem-solving (or intervention) team uses tiered intervention data to set appropriate short-term goals. These goals are set in short cycles in order to tailor and differentiate instruction and instructional decision making. Teams discuss and adjust the goals at collaborative team meetings that align with assessment windows using the data described in the preceding process.

Individual Goals

As part of the professional growth and evaluation system, individuals set goals for personal and professional growth. Individual teachers develop these goals with guidance from principals and assistant principals. They use the goals to guide their own professional growth and improvement. The teacher or staff member and the principal, assistant principal, or district-level leaders discuss and monitor individual goals throughout the school year.

District 96 Goals Structure

District Goals (Superintendent and District 96 staff and administrator developed)

Development, Purpose, and Use	Goal-Monitoring Process
• Administrative team developed using feedback from teachers • For the purpose of continuous improvement • Used to guide district decision making	• Reviewed at all district administrative meetings following fall, winter, and spring data updates • Superintendent reviews with full faculty two times per year. • Superintendent gives updates to the board of education in the fall, winter, and spring.

School Goals (School-improvement goals, principal completed)

Development, Purpose, and Use	Goal-Monitoring Process
• Principal developed using NWEA MAP (K–1) data or PARCC (state accountability assessment; 3–8) projections • For the purpose of school improvement and to identify students projected not to meet grade-level expectations • Used to determine an action plan for school improvement and to meet the needs of identified students • Used to guide school decision making	• Principal and superintendent discuss and adjust at goal meetings three times per year using projections in the fall, winter, and spring. • Principal and superintendent discuss at administrative council meetings.

Grade-Level Team Goals		Team Data Wall Goals (Unit differentiated instructional plan process and team SMART goals; grade-level teams engaged in this process)	
Development, Purpose, and Use	**Goal-Monitoring Process**	**Development, Purpose, and Use**	**Goal-Monitoring Process**
• Team (grade-level, coaches, low-incidence) developed using NWEA MAP (K–1) or PARCC (3–8) projections (Physical education uses fitness data.) • For the purpose of school, grade-level, fitness-level, and individual student improvement • Used to guide team decision making	• Teams discuss and adjust regularly at team meetings using fall, winter, and spring data and fitness data.	• Team developed using data from common formative assessments and end-of-unit assessments; problem-solving team uses tiered intervention data. • For the purposes of tailoring and differentiating instruction • Used to guide decision making for students	• Teams discuss and adjust at scheduled meetings that align with assessment windows using data from ongoing common formative assessments and end-of-unit assessments. Problem-solving team uses progress-monitoring and other intervention data.

Personal and Professional Goals (Individual goals for personal and professional growth)	
Development, Purpose, and Use	**Goal-Monitoring Process**
• Individual teacher developed with guidance from the school (principals and assistant principals) • For the purpose of continued personal and professional growth • Used to guide individual decision making and improvement	• Staff member and principal or assistant principal discuss and adjust at the beginning, middle, and end of the school year.

Student Goals (Student goals using Northwest Evaluation Association Measures of Academic Progress data)	
Development, Purpose, and Use	**Goal-Monitoring Process**
• Student developed with guidance from school principals and assistant principals • For the purpose of student understanding of strengths and areas for improvement • Used to guide student decision making and improvement	• Student and teacher meet to discuss and adjust in the fall, winter, and spring using NWEA MAP data.

Source: Kildeer Countryside Community Consolidated School District 96, Buffalo Grove, Illinois. Reprinted with permission.

Figure 6.2: District 96 goals structure for feedback and brainstorming.

Student Goals

During the 2017–2018 school year, pilot classrooms engaged in yearlong student goal setting using NWEA MAP data with the goal for 100 percent of classrooms participating in the process during the 2018–2019 school year. Results show classrooms that participated in the 2017–2018 pilot program had higher overall student growth than classrooms that did not participate. Thus, each student in the system now engages in student goal setting. With guidance from the teacher, all K–12 students set growth goals for the purpose of understanding their strengths and areas for improvement. Students engage in the process of understanding their current achievement level and where they want to be and how they will get there. This process also helps ensure teachers have a better understanding of what the MAP data tell them about their students and how they can utilize the data to effectively differentiate instruction. Through individual conferences, teachers and students monitor the goals throughout the school year using fall, winter, and spring data. Students share their goals and outcomes with their parents during family and educator conferences in the spring.

Relating and aligning goals at all levels of the organization will yield powerful results. A hard-learned lesson was when we, as leaders, realized misaligning goals really translated to "throwing everything against a wall in order to see what might stick." In other words, it was not a good use of anyone's time, energy, and resources. Only when the system became more cognizant of careful alignment did the district see improved learning outcomes for students.

> *Relating and aligning goals at all levels of the organization will yield powerful results.*

Regularly Monitor Progress Toward School Achievement Goals

The previously described multilayered goal-setting process for a district, a school, and teams provides goals in response to data in a well-organized way that gives everyone in the system a clear picture of student learning and progress. Multiple sources of data provide a robust picture that includes summative accountability data and growth data annually. This time line allows teachers to be able to project which students may struggle over the course of a given year and intervene when the data indicate the need for intervention. Once district- and school-level goals are set, teams then align their goals to the greatest areas of need for their particular grade level or subject matter.

School-based teams' analyzing and interpreting data regularly to monitor student learning and growth only becomes feasible if the school or system ensures the data are easily accessible, purposefully arranged, and publicly discussed. Consultant and author Thomas W. Many (2009) concisely lays out the case for using these *rules of data.* Many (2009) notes the importance of organizing the data in simple—not simplistic—ways. Over the years, we have found that first providing well-organized district- and schoolwide data supports the meaningful and efficient use of the data and allows teams to drill down to create team-level goals.

School-based teams' analyzing and interpreting data regularly to monitor student learning and growth only becomes feasible if the school or system ensures the data are easily accessible, purposefully arranged, and publicly discussed.

Once well-organized systems provide team members, adults supporting the team, and the principal easy access to the data, teams then commit to efficient data entry to prepare for team-level discussion. When data are presented in a complete, accurate, and straightforward manner, team members can spend more time publicly discussing the data to make timely instructional decisions. As data discussions become deeply embedded in the culture of a school and teams, the public discussions focus on data, and this has led to deeper content knowledge and sharper pedagogy based on collective experience and wisdom.

At the team level, a results orientation continues with a high level of specificity. The cycle of instruction includes planning for instruction and analyzing formative data to differentiate and intervene at Tier 1 (first best instruction within the response to intervention model; Buffum, Mattos, & Malone, 2018). This cycle evolves continually over the years. Each year, we all learn more about what is effective and efficient and what is not. And while the district provides and presents data in various ways (and as tools become available), teacher teams become more and more proficient at organizing and analyzing team-level data with the use of data-protocol templates.

The assessment continuum and a data-analysis protocol (see figure 6.3, page 168) use repeating cycles for units of instruction.

PLC Critical Question One:
What is it we want all students to learn?

District 96 Assessment Continuum and Data Analysis
Repeating Cycle for Units of Instruction

PLC Critical Question Two:
How will we know if students are learning?

Before the Unit Begins Team Deep Dive: Unpack unit priority standards, review unit calendars for *what* and *when* assessments and data conversations will occur, give the assessments, review the rubrics, review *how* to give the assessment (anticipating errors, confusion, and so on).

Optional Preassessment With Data Conversation

Data-Driven Instruction

Formative Classroom Assessments

Data-Driven Instruction

During-Unit Common Formative Assessments With Data Conversation

Data-Driven Instruction

End-of-Unit Common Formative Assessment With Data Conversation

KCSD96

Preassessment
- Administer at least one to two weeks in advance of instruction.
- Use preassessment data to determine what students already know and tailor the instructional unit plan to differentiate and meet specific student needs.
- May or may not be a common assessment.

Formative Classroom Assessments
- Administer daily.
- Use to make decisions in the moment or day to day (checklists, observations, conferencing, and so on).
- May or may not be a common assessment.

During-Unit Common Formative Assessments
- Administer during the unit of instruction within a defined window.
- Use to check in on student *progress toward* mastery of essential learning outcomes.
- Are common assessments at the team and district levels.

End-of-Unit Common Formative Assessment
- Administer at the end of a unit of instruction within a defined window.
- Use to assess *current level* of mastery after a significant amount of instruction.
- Is a common assessment at the district level.

PLC Critical Question Three:
How will we respond when students don't learn?

PLC Critical Question Four:
How will we extend learning for students who are already proficient?

Source: Kildeer Countryside Community Consolidated School District 96, Buffalo Grove, Illinois. Reprinted with permission.

Figure 6.3: Assessment continuum and a data-analysis protocol.

One or two weeks before the unit begins, teams take a deep dive to prepare for the upcoming instruction. District 96 assistant superintendent of teaching and learning Jeanne Spiller developed a pre-unit module and planning protocol for this purpose. Spiller created the protocol as a next step for providing clarity and consistency on instructional planning and using data to drive instruction. She titled the process the *CLEAR protocol* and included guidance for teams during each of the following steps.

C   **Create collective understanding** when teams ask what the purpose and priorities of the upcoming unit are, whether or not there is agreement or clarity on what the target looks like instructionally, and how to use instructional resources effectively.

L   **Look at the calendar and devise an initial instructional plan** during which teams determine what common formative assessments to develop, how those assessments align with learning goals, and when to review the data and plan differentiated instruction. Figure 6.4 (page 170) shows an example of this planning for sixth-grade English language arts.

E   **Examine assessment administration and attitude** so teams can ensure consistency in administering assessments, portray positivity about the assessments to support students, and communicate high expectations for all students.

A   **Anticipate instructional planning, student needs, and student involvement** so teams consider where students might struggle and plan necessary scaffolding to meet individual student needs and involve students through goal setting and feedback loops.

R   **Review unit rubrics**, which requires teams to consider consistency of rubric interpretation, collaboratively score to calibrate rubric application, and consider any rubric revisions.

Teams may or may not administer a preassessment before providing instruction. Teachers provide data-driven instruction and ongoing formative assessments to make decisions in the moment. Data-driven instruction continues, leading to common formative assessments

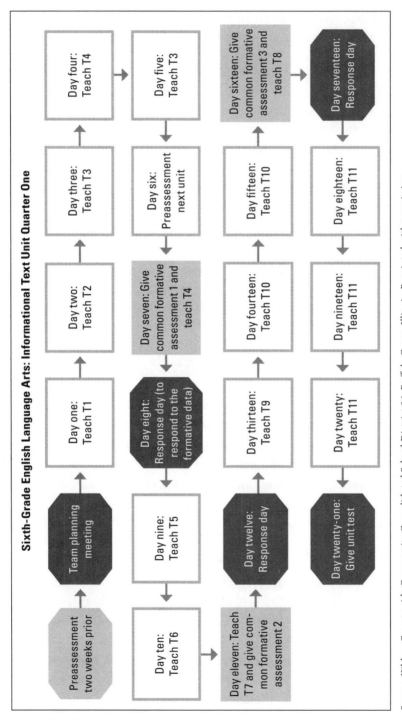

Sixth-Grade English Language Arts: Informational Text Unit Quarter One

Figure 6.4: Initial team instructional plan continuum example.

teachers administer during an identified window of time. Teachers then use these data to check on student progress toward mastery of essential learning outcomes. Team members discuss the data and use them to drive Tier 1 intervention and differentiation. Teachers enter the data into a template like the example in figure 6.5 (page 172).

Teacher teams may then use a protocol similar to the one in figure 6.6 (page 174) to guide their conversations and instructional planning.

Finally, teacher teams administer an end-of-unit common formative assessment within an identified window and use it to assess each student's current level of mastery after a significant amount of instruction. These data also inform progress toward team goals.

Periodically, the principal and coaches incorporate progress on team-level goals into leadership team and staff meeting agendas, and students use the data to track their progress toward individually set goals.

Establish Programs and Practices to Help Students Meet Achievement Goals

All educators must work together to decide how they will respond when students don't learn and share responsibility for every student's learning to function as an effective intervention system (Friziellie et al., 2016). In addition, educators must decide how they will respond when students demonstrate readiness for extension, enrichment, or acceleration.

In high-functioning PLCs, intervention structures are embedded in the schedule, intervention and extension criteria are clear, and monitoring of student data is more systematic.

In *Learning by Doing*, DuFour et al. (2016) stress the importance of providing the extra time and support students need during the school day to ensure their participation is not optional. All educators recognize some students and families could not or would not access additional time and support if only offered before or after the school day. Thus, the school schedule must accommodate this need. While master schedules, whether at the elementary or secondary level, can be sacred, leaders must examine them so they meet the needs of students.

All educators must work together to decide how they will respond when students don't learn and share responsibility for every student's learning to function as an effective intervention system.

Teacher A

Data Point and Date of Meeting	Extends: 4.0	Mastery: 3.0	Partial Mastery: 2.5	Developing: 2.0	Not Mastering: 1.0
Data Point 1					
Data Point 2					
Data Point 3					
Data Point 4					
Data Point 5					

Teacher B

	Extends: 4.0	Mastery: 3.0	Partial Mastery: 2.5	Developing: 2.0	Not Mastering: 1.0
Data Point 1					
Data Point 2					
Data Point 3					
Data Point 4					
Data Point 5					

Teacher C				
	Extends: 4.0	Mastery: 3.0	Partial Mastery: 2.5	Developing: 2.0	Not Mastering: 1.0
Data Point 1				
Data Point 2				
Data Point 3				
Data Point 4				
Data Point 5				

Teacher D				
	Extends: 4.0	Mastery: 3.0	Partial Mastery: 2.5	Developing: 2.0	Not Mastering: 1.0
Data Point 1				
Data Point 2				
Data Point 3				
Data Point 4				
Data Point 5				

Source: Kildeer Countryside Community Consolidated School District 96, Buffalo Grove, Illinois. Reprinted with permission.

Figure 6.5: Sample teacher team data template.

1. Celebrate strengths in the data. Did a particular classroom do extremely well? Find out what happened instructionally in that classroom. Look at samples of student work. What skills did the proficient students demonstrate in their work that set their work apart? Which instructional strategies helped students learn?

Data Point 1	Data Point 2	Data Point 3	Data Point 4	Data Point 5

Using a standards-based gradebook and samples of student work, determine areas of student struggle. What may be the cause?

ADD 2.5 to 3.0 and 4.0 and beyond

TARGET A

Data Point 1: 1.0 to 2.0	Data Point 2: 1.0 to 2.0	Data Point 3: 1.0 to 2.0	Data Point 4: 1.0 to 2.0	Data Point 5: 1.0 to 2.0
Growth Areas	Growth Areas	Growth Areas	Growth Areas	Growth Areas
Instructional Plan	Instructional Plan	Instructional Plan	Instructional Plan	Instructional Plan
Student Names (For middle schools, full names in these boxes are unnecessary, but discuss who the students are and the specific plans for each.)	Student Names	Student Names	Student Names	Student Names
Data Point 1: 2.0 to 3.0	Data Point 2: 2.0 to 3.0	Data Point 3: 2.0 to 3.0	Data Point 4: 2.0 to 3.0	Data Point 5: 2.0 to 3.0
Growth Areas	Growth Areas	Growth Areas	Growth Areas	Growth Areas
Instructional Plan	Instructional Plan	Instructional Plan	Instructional Plan	Instructional Plan

Source: Kildeer Countryside Community Consolidated School District 96, Buffalo Grove, Illinois. Reprinted with permission.

Figure 6.6: Protocol to guide team conversations and instructional planning.

About ten years ago, District 96 began the examination at the elementary level. First, the elementary level moved to a master schedule so all first-grade teachers teach the literacy block, mathematics, and so on at the same time. So, when first-grade students went to lunch, recess, physical education, and other electives, first-grade teachers had time to collaborate. Shortly thereafter, we created a thirty-minute daily block at each grade level when all new instruction stops and teachers provide intervention or extension and enrichment. During the first year of implementation, school leaders asked each grade-level team to begin to use data to drive planning for this block of time. The master schedule allowed grade-level teachers to intervene collectively if appropriate, which was new! However, this planning time created an initial sense of unease; teachers would have preferred to have a clear "answer" for what would work best. However, this process allowed team members to begin to own their data and increase levels of collective responsibility for student learning.

The elementary schedule in figure 6.7 (page 176) is one example of how this process might work. Note the embedded intervention (or extension and enrichment) time does not happen at the same time across grade levels, allowing additional personnel (interventionists, specialists, special educators, and other adults) to provide additional support, which allows for deeper differentiation at each grade level.

The middle school schedule came next. A working group made up of various stakeholders studied best practices on current middle school and secondary school schedules and then developed recommendations over a two-year period before reallocating instructional time and adding a daily flex period at each grade level. The flex periods are for supporting and extending academic and social-emotional learning for all students while building relationships and interconnected learning across content areas. The new schedule was implemented at the beginning of the 2017–2018 school year. The flex period structure continues to evolve through an ongoing committee structure of teachers and leaders. Teams utilize the flex periods for real-time Tier 1 intervention (based on formative data), Tiers 2 and 3 intervention, extension and enrichment, Genius Hour projects, and other student-choice options. These options have expanded to include more student choice and independence, such as with topics that include conversational world languages, virtual reality, architecture, and so on. The schedule that appears in figure 6.8 (page 178) provides an example of how to organize students' day.

Time	Grade 1	Grade 2	Grade 3	Grade 4	Grade 5
7:45–8:25 a.m.				Literature	Literature
8:25–8:30 a.m.					
8:30–8:45 a.m.	Intervention 8:30–9:00 a.m.	Specials	Science or Social Studies		
8:45–9:00 a.m.			Specials		
9:00–9:15 a.m.	Literature				
9:15–9:30 a.m.					
9:30–9:45 a.m.			Literature	Intervention 9:30–10:00 a.m.	
9:45–10:00 a.m.					
10:00–10:15 a.m.		Science or Social Studies		Literature	
10:15–10:30 a.m.					
10:30–10:45 a.m.		Mathematics 10:30–11:30 a.m.			Intervention 10:30–11:00 a.m.
10:45–11:00 a.m.	Science or Social Studies (continued)	(continued)	(continued)	(continued)	

Time slots (row labels):

- 11:00–11:15 a.m.
- 11:15–11:30 a.m.
- 11:30–11:45 a.m.
- 11:45 a.m.–12:00 p.m.
- 12:00–12:15 p.m.
- 12:15–12:30 p.m.
- 12:30–12:45 p.m.
- 12:45–1:00 p.m.
- 1:00–1:15 p.m.
- 1:15–1:30 p.m.
- 1:30–1:45 p.m.
- 1:45–2:00 p.m.
- 2:00–2:15 p.m.
- 2:15–2:30 p.m.
- 2:30–2:45 p.m.

Schedule (grade-level groups):

Group 1
- Science or Social Studies
- Recess 11:30 a.m.–12:10 p.m. / Lunch
- Mathematics 12:15–1:15 p.m.
- Specials
- Literature
- Intervention 2:15–2:45 p.m.

Group 2
- Mathematics 10:30–11:30 a.m.
- Recess 11:30 a.m.–12:10 p.m. / Lunch
- Literature

Group 3
- Mathematics 11:10 a.m.–12:10 p.m.
- Recess 12:10–12:50 p.m. / Lunch
- Intervention 12:55–1:25 p.m.
- Literature

Group 4
- Literature
- Specials
- Recess 12:10–12:50 p.m. / Lunch
- Mathematics 12:55–1:55 p.m.
- Science or Social Studies

Group 5
- Recess 11:00–11:40 a.m. / Lunch
- Specials
- Science or Social Studies
- Mathematics 1:45–2:45 p.m.

Source: Kildeer Countryside Community Consolidated School District 96, Buffalo Grove, Illinois. Reprinted with permission.

Figure 6.7: Sample elementary schedule with embedded intervention time.

Day in the Life . . .

Grade 6	Grade 7	Grade 8
Exploratory (A day)	Core (Daily)	Core (Daily)
Spanish (B day)	Core (Daily)	Core (Daily)
Core (Daily)	Exploratory With Band or Orchestra Option (A day)	Flex (Daily)
Core (Daily)	Spanish (B day)	Core (Daily)
Flex (Daily)	Physical Education or Health (Daily)	Core (Daily)
Physical Education or Health (Daily)	Twenty-Five-Minute Lunch (Daily)	Twenty-Five-Minute Lunch (Daily)
Twenty-Five-Minute Lunch (Daily)	Flex (Daily, Independent Study Option)	Exploratory With Band or Orchestra Option (A day)
Core (Daily)	Core (Daily)	Spanish (B day)
Core (Daily)	Core (Daily)	Physical Education or Health (Daily)
*After School: Band or Orchestra Full Rehearsals	*After School: Band or Orchestra Full Rehearsals	*After School: Band or Orchestra Full Rehearsals

Source: Kildeer Countryside Community Consolidated School District 96, Buffalo Grove, Illinois. Reprinted with permission.

Figure 6.8: Sample middle school schedule with flex period options.

With deeply embedded structures, processes become more and more systematic. The first level of intervention focus is at Tier 1 through a robust instruction cycle in the classroom. (We find that as Tier 1 instruction becomes more and more effective, the need for Tiers 2 and 3 intervention decreases, as do referrals for special education.) Over a four to five-year period, District 96 went from 16.6 percent of students qualifying for special education services to 9.9 percent. The percentage of students eligible for special education fluctuates slightly from year to year but remains significantly lower in District 96 due to a robust, tiered system of intervention.

Leaders review the intervention system at the end of each school year to determine potential areas for improvement. Figure 6.9 (page 180) memorializes this process graphically to ensure all staff are familiar with and can clearly articulate the process. The intervention team establishes and uses very clear criteria to monitor progress through a problem-solving process.

With deeply embedded structures, processes become more and more systematic.

Over time, the problem-solving team in collaboration with district leadership hones the best practice–aligned criteria for students to enter intervention (or extension and enrichment). The example in figure 6.10 (page 182) outlines the criteria for second-grade literacy intervention with specific questions for teachers and support personnel to consider when making eligibility decisions. An additional data point for teachers and support personnel to consider is the state-required accountability assessment, which could support proactively providing interventions at the beginning of the school year based on results the previous spring. The purpose of the example (see figure 6.10) is not to advocate for these criteria specifically, as teachers and support personnel should establish criteria at the local level based on local data, but to demonstrate the importance of establishing clear guidelines for entry and exit.

Multitiered System of Supports Flowchart: Academics

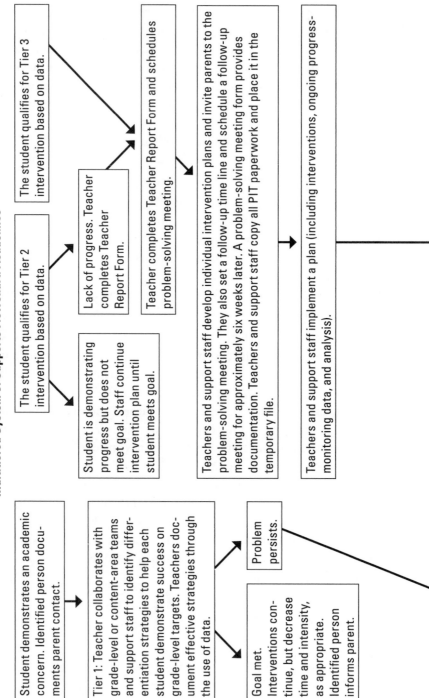

Student demonstrates an academic concern. Identified person documents parent contact.

Tier 1: Teacher collaborates with grade-level or content-area teams and support staff to identify differentiation strategies to help each student demonstrate success on grade-level targets. Teachers document effective strategies through the use of data.

Problem persists.

Goal met. Interventions continue, but decrease time and intensity, as appropriate. Identified person informs parent.

The student qualifies for Tier 2 intervention based on data.

The student qualifies for Tier 3 intervention based on data.

Student is demonstrating progress but does not meet goal. Staff continue intervention plan until student meets goal.

Lack of progress. Teacher completes Teacher Report Form.

Teacher completes Teacher Report Form and schedules problem-solving meeting.

Teachers and support staff develop individual intervention plans and invite parents to the problem-solving meeting. They also set a follow-up time line and schedule a follow-up meeting for approximately six weeks later. A problem-solving meeting form provides documentation. Teachers and support staff copy all PIT paperwork and place it in the temporary file.

Teachers and support staff implement a plan (including interventions, ongoing progress-monitoring data, and analysis).

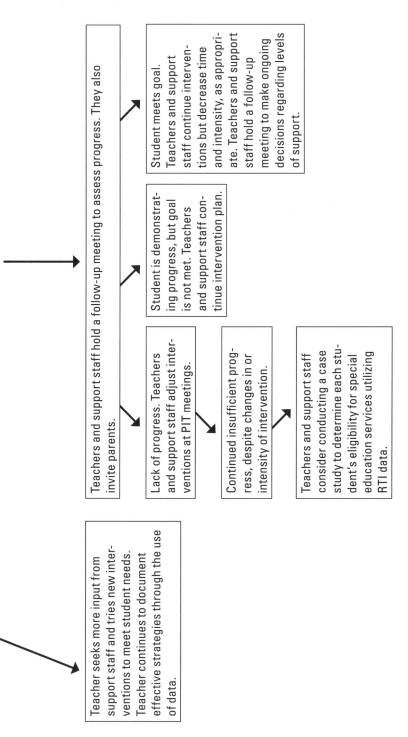

Teacher seeks more input from support staff and tries new interventions to meet student needs. Teacher continues to document effective strategies through the use of data.

Teachers and support staff hold a follow-up meeting to assess progress. They also invite parents.

Lack of progress. Teachers and support staff adjust interventions at PIT meetings.

Student is demonstrating progress, but goal is not met. Teachers and support staff continue intervention plan.

Student meets goal. Teachers and support staff continue interventions but decrease time and intensity, as appropriate. Teachers and support staff hold a follow-up meeting to make ongoing decisions regarding levels of support.

Continued insufficient progress, despite changes in or intensity of intervention.

Teachers and support staff consider conducting a case study to determine each student's eligibility for special education services utilizing RTI data.

Source: Kildeer Countryside Community Consolidated School District 96, Buffalo Grove, Illinois. Reprinted with permission.

Figure 6.9: Intervention criteria.

Grade 2			
Measure One	**Measure Two**	**Tier**	**Considerations**
11th–25th percentile on MAP	11th–25th percentile on Curriculum-Based Measurement reading (fluency) and comprehension efficiency	2	• Is the student culturally and linguistically diverse?
< 11th percentile on MAP	11th–25th percentile on Curriculum-Based Measurement reading (fluency) and comprehension efficiency	2	• What were the most recent ACCESS (English language proficiency assessment) scores, if available, for this student in each subscore (not just the language domain)?
11th–25th percentile on MAP	< 11th percentile on Curriculum-Based Measurement reading (fluency) and comprehension efficiency	3	• How long has the student been in District 96?
< 11th percentile on MAP	< 11th percentile on Curriculum-Based Measurement reading (fluency) and comprehension efficiency	3	• What is the student's data history? • What level of interventions has the student had in the past? • What is the background of the student—culture, home, previous schooling, and so on? Think about the student's story.

Source: Kildeer Countryside Community Consolidated School District 96, Buffalo Grove, Illinois. Reprinted with permission.

Figure 6.10: Sample criteria for second-grade literacy intervention.

The middle school example (figure 6.11) includes an accountability assessment predictor as part of the criteria for tiered reading intervention.

Along with establishing the criteria, a problem-solving team implements a process; this is a way of monitoring not only implementation fidelity but also the individual progress of each student receiving intervention. Referrals to the problem-solving team should

Grade	MAP	PARCC (State Accountability Assessment) Predictor	Curriculum-Based Measure Reading (Fluency)	Curriculum-Based Measure (Comprehension) Administer only to students who score below the 25th percentile on MAP.
6–8	Tier 2: 11th to 25th percentile	Below 750	Tier 2: 11th to 25th percentile	Tier 2: 11th to 25th percentile
	Tier 3: 1st to 10th percentile	Below 750	Tier 3: 1st to 10th percentile	Tier 3: 1st to 10th percentile

Source: Kildeer Countryside Community Consolidated School District 96, Buffalo Grove, Illinois. Reprinted with permission.

Figure 6.11: Example criteria for tiered middle school reading intervention.

include information about the student's strengths and weaknesses (with supporting data), plus information on other relevant characteristics as well as all previous and current interventions and outcomes.

Once the problem-solving team receives a referral, members engage in problem analysis, which includes identifying any additional needed data to collect. The team develops and implements a plan that identifies a schedule for data collection to monitor progress and determine the effectiveness of the intervention. The team also sets a time line to review the collected data.

Finally, it is important to note that while schools across the United States have been working to implement multitiered intervention systems for students who need more time and intensity to master grade-level expectations, significantly fewer schools are discussing and implementing a systematic way to extend, enrich, and accelerate students who show readiness.

Significantly fewer schools are discussing and implementing a systematic way to extend, enrich, and accelerate students who show readiness.

In 2010, Illinois adopted the Common Core State Standards (NGA & CCSSO, 2010a, 2010b). At the same time, District 96 began the process of unpacking and prioritizing the newly adopted standards side-by-side with Adlai E. Stevenson High School, where all District 96 students attend high school. This presented the opportunity for both staffs to make a deeper commitment to extension for *all* students as they showed readiness. Targets were scaled to provide a 4.0 extension for every target the teams deemed extendable in their grade level or course. District 96's goal was not to provide extension for a small group of students who met static criteria, but rather to provide extension for every student as he or she showed readiness on every target in the curriculum. This, of course, led to a complete transition to standards-based reporting and the elimination of letter grades through grade 8—a topic for another book. Figure 6.12 is an example of what the extensions might look like.

This was an important step in District 96's commitment to providing rigor for all students. During the 2017–2018 school year, the District 96 curriculum leadership team developed an extension and acceleration plan to provide yet another pathway for students.

At the elementary level, the plan provides three tiers of acceleration. Students who qualify at Tier 1 receive an individualized learning plan (ILP). Students with an ILP remain in their grade level but receive a high level of differentiation and possible acceleration aligned to their needs. The principal, district curriculum coordinator, classroom teacher, and instructional coach in the qualifying content area monitor the plan. Parents meet with the team to develop the plan.

Students who qualify for Tier 2 acceleration move to the next grade level in their area of high proficiency. If a student qualifies in both literacy and mathematics, the principal, district curriculum coordinator, classroom teacher, parent, and instructional coach as a team may consider a full grade-level acceleration.

And students who qualify for Tier 3 acceleration can be considered for acceleration to two grade levels above in the areas of qualification.

Note that, as figure 6.13 (page 186) illustrates, teams consider performance tasks and social-emotional development when making acceleration decisions.

Grade 5 Bridges Mathematics Pacing Guide 2018–2019			
4.0 Target	3.0 Target	2.0 Target	Trimester and Unit
Operations and Algebraic Thinking			
Evaluate complex expressions or inequalities that include parentheses, brackets, or variables.	**Use parentheses, brackets, or braces in numerical expressions, and evaluate expressions with these symbols (5.OA.A.1).**	Use parentheses, brackets, or braces, in simple numerical expressions, and evaluate expressions with these symbols.	Trimester 1 Unit 1
Write a simple expression, and create a real-world situation that matches it.	**Write simple expressions that record calculations with numbers, and interpret numerical expressions without evaluating them (5.OA.A.2).**	Inconsistently write simple expressions to record calculations with numbers, and interpret numerical expressions without evaluating them.	Trimester 1 Unit 1
Use the relationship between *x* and *y* coordinates to generate a multiple-operation expression that represents the rule for the coordinate pairs.	**Generate two numerical patterns using two given rules. Identify apparent relationships between corresponding terms. Form ordered pairs consisting of corresponding terms from the two patterns, and graph the ordered pairs on a coordinate plane (5.OA.B.3).**	Generate two numerical patterns using two given rules. Form ordered pairs of corresponding terms. Form ordered pairs consisting of corresponding terms from the two patterns, and graph the ordered pairs on a coordinate plane.	Trimester 3 Unit 6

Source for standards: NGA & CCSSO, 2010b.
Source: Kildeer Countryside Community Consolidated School District 96, Buffalo Grove, Illinois. Reprinted with permission.

Figure 6.12: Extension and acceleration plan.

Elementary Grade-Level Acceleration Process Flow Map
Initial Screening (All Students) NWEA MAP
Curriculum coordinator notifies parent. Why NWEA MAP? • MAP provides initial information about what students know and informs teams of what they're ready to learn next. • High MAP RIT scores help us identify students who demonstrate high ability and who may be ready for more rigorous curriculum.
Secondary Assessment or Performance Tasks and Review of Student Performance
Why include a secondary assessment? • Ensures academic readiness of students for more rigorous content and accelerated placement through content-specific standards-based performance tasks • Provides in-depth understanding of content-specific standards, which is critical to student success
Social-Emotional and Developmental Screening—Teacher Input and Feedback
Why social-emotional and developmental screening? • Ensures developmental readiness for potential acceleration to a higher grade level
Parent Meeting to Discuss Results and Gather Parental and Other Input
Why have a parent meeting? • The partnership between parents and the school is a critical component for student success. • The school district will share student data regarding acceleration testing with parents. • When a student meets the criteria, parents will work with the school district to determine placement.

Source: Kildeer Countryside Community Consolidated School District 96, Buffalo Grove, Illinois. Reprinted with permission.

Figure 6.13: Sample elementary grade-level acceleration process flow map.

Acceleration of students in middle school involves the same flow-chart process but is focused on course acceleration by subject area.

In District 96, data indicate students who qualify for acceleration are performing at high levels. The team will, however, continue to analyze the data to improve the process each year. But overall, it is safe to say this plan is impactful when it comes to deeper and more specific differentiation.

Conclusion

In leading the journey in two different districts over time, we, as leaders, have both realized that there is a strong relationship between the PLC journey and the levels of the HRS model, specifically when considering the importance of and implementation strategies for establishing and ensuring a guaranteed and viable curriculum for *all* learners in a team, department, grade, school, or district. As illustrated in this chapter, the PLC process provides a foundation for HRS. In a complementary way, the levels of HRS provide the blueprint for leaders working to move their system to even greater levels of student learning through the PLC process.

> There is a strong relationship between the PLC journey and the levels of the HRS model.

References and Resources

Buffum, A., Mattos, M., & Malone, J. (2018). *Taking action: A handbook for RTI at Work.* Bloomington, IN: Solution Tree Press.

Collins, J. (2001). *Good to great: Why some companies make the leap—and others don't.* New York: HarperBusiness.

DuFour, R., DuFour, R., Eaker, R., Many, T. W., & Mattos, M. (2016). *Learning by doing: A handbook for Professional Learning Communities at Work* (3rd ed.). Bloomington, IN: Solution Tree Press.

DuFour, R., & Marzano, R. J. (2011). *Leaders of learning: How district, school, and classroom leaders improve student achievement.* Bloomington, IN: Solution Tree Press.

Friziellie, H., Schmidt, J. A., & Spiller, J. (2016). *Yes we can! General and special educators collaborating in a professional learning community.* Bloomington, IN: Solution Tree Press.

Hattie, J. (2012). *Visible learning for teachers: Maximizing impact on learning.* New York: Routledge.

Lezotte, L. W. (n.d.). *Revolutionary and evolutionary: The effective schools movement.* Accessed at www.brjonesphd.com/uploads/1/6/9/4/16946150/revolutionary_and _evolutionary-_the_effective_schools_movement_-_dr._lawrence_w._lezotte.pdf on November 1, 2019.

Many, T. W. (2009). Three rules help manage assessment data. *TEPSA News, 66*(2), 7, 9.

Marzano, R. J. (2003). *What works in schools: Translating research into action.* Alexandria, VA: Association for Supervision and Curriculum Development.

Marzano, R. J., Warrick, P. B., Rains, C. L., & DuFour, R. (2018). *Leading a high reliability school.* Bloomington, IN: Solution Tree Press.

National Council for the Social Studies. (2013). *College, career and civic life: C3 framework for social studies state standards—Guidance for enhancing the rigor of K–12 civics, economics, geography, and history.* Silver Spring, MD: Author. Accessed at www.socialstudies .org/sites/default/files/2017/Jun/c3-framework-for-social-studies-rev0617.pdf on January 13, 2020.

National Governors Association Center for Best Practices & Council of Chief State School Officers. (2010a). *Common Core State Standards for English language arts and literacy in history/social studies, science, and technical subjects.* Washington, DC: Authors. Accessed at www.corestandards.org/assets/CCSSI_ELA%20Standards.pdf on June 26, 2019.

National Governors Association Center for Best Practices & Council of Chief State School Officers. (2010b). *Common Core State Standards for mathematics.* Washington, DC: Authors. Accessed at www.corestandards.org/assets/CCSSI_Math%20Standards.pdf on June 26, 2019.

NGSS Lead States. (2013). *Next Generation Science Standards: For states, by states.* Washington, DC: The National Academies Press.

Reeves, D. (2002). *The leader's guide to standards: A blueprint for educational equity and excellence.* San Francisco: Jossey-Bass.

Spiller, J. (2018). *Get CLEAR protocol.* Kildeer Countryside Community Consolidated School District 96, Buffalo Grove, Illinois.

LEVEL 4:
Standards-Referenced Reporting

Few things are done as poorly in America's schools as reporting students' progress. Ask a group of principals to describe how teachers generate student grades (for example, Are grades based on how students compare to each other? On the averaging of test scores? On improvement? Do such things as effort, homework, or behavior impact grades?"), and the response will likely be, "We leave that up to the individual teacher." The implication of such an approach to grading is that luck is the defining feature; in effect, the teacher assigned to the student primarily determines his or her grade.

Thinking about grading from the perspective of a parent can be helpful. What do parents want from grades? Mainly, parents want grades to reflect how much their child has learned in relation to what he or she is supposed to learn. They want grades to be fair, and they want consistency between teachers. Effective standards-referenced reporting provides a way to achieve these goals.

Standards-referenced reporting identifies student progress on a collaboratively developed, predetermined standard. But it does more than provide an effective and meaningful way to report students' progress. The process of developing a standards-referenced reporting system becomes an excellent staff development exercise. What better way to sharpen a guaranteed and viable curriculum than to engage teachers in a process to develop a reporting system that reflects how well individual students are learning that curriculum? It is impossible to develop an effective standards-referenced reporting system absent clarity regarding the question, Learn what?

Collaboration is key to answering this question. Whereas chapters 5 and 6 highlighted the need for collaboration when designing a guaranteed and viable curriculum, chapters 7 and 8 address collaboration in the context of designing a reporting system that focuses on both status and growth for individual students. This can be a difficult process since grading has traditionally been an idiosyncratic process, with individual teachers having great latitude in the components they include in a grade and how they weight those components. The collaborative effort required to change this historical precedent is worth the requisite expenditure of time and energy because once a school agrees on a common standards-referenced format, scores on classroom assessments have common points of reference from teacher to teacher, making it relatively easy to determine students' strengths and weaknesses on specific topics at any point in time.

Tammy Heflebower

Tammy Heflebower, EdD, is a highly sought-after school leader and consultant with vast experiences in urban, rural, and suburban districts throughout the United States, Australia, Canada, Denmark, Great Britain, and the Netherlands. Dr. Heflebower has served as an award-winning classroom teacher, building leader, district leader, regional professional development director, and national and international trainer. She has also been an adjunct professor of curriculum, instruction, and assessment at several universities, and a prominent member and leader of numerous statewide and national educational organizations. Dr. Heflebower was the vice president and then senior scholar at Marzano Research and continues to work as an author and associate with Marzano Resources and Solution Tree. In addition, she is the CEO of her own company, !nspire Inc: Education and Business Solutions, specializing in powerful presentation and facilitation techniques, writing about them, and sharing them worldwide.

Dr. Heflebower is the author of *Crafting Your Message: Tips and Tricks for Educators to Deliver Perfect Presentations* (2019). She is lead author of the award-winning and best-selling book *A School Leader's Guide to Standards-Based Grading*, lead author of the award finalist *A Teacher's Guide to Standards-Based Learning*, coauthor of *Collaborative Teams That Transform Schools: The Next Step in PLCs* and *Teaching & Assessing 21st Century Skills*, and contributing author to over a dozen other books and publications, many of which have been translated into multiple languages and referenced internationally.

Dr. Heflebower holds a bachelor of arts from Hastings College, where she was honored as Outstanding Young Alumna and her team was inducted into the athletic hall of fame. She has a master of arts from the University of Nebraska Omaha, and her educational administrative endorsement and doctorate from the University of Nebraska–Lincoln.

To learn more about Dr. Heflebower's work, visit www.inspirementor.com or follow @tammyhef on Twitter.

To book Tammy Heflebower for professional development, contact pd@Solution Tree.com.

In this chapter, Dr. Heflebower focuses on the leader's role in making the transformation from traditional grading to standards-referenced reporting. She discusses the essential components of standards-referenced reporting and details a multiyear plan for developing a standards-referenced reporting system.

Chapter 7

A Multiyear Plan for Standards-Referenced Reporting

Tammy Heflebower

The fourth level of the High Reliability Schools model is standards-referenced reporting. This major initiative entails a change from a traditional grading system to a standards-referenced reporting system. This is no small task. It is a lot like parenting—exciting, challenging, rewarding, frustrating, and extremely gratifying. It is a transformational (second-order) change in education, unlike lesser transactional (first-order) changes that are simply tweaks to existing practices. In a standards-referenced reporting system, clearly articulated proficiency scales clarify the knowledge and skills for prioritized standards. Using such proficiency scales for the basis of reporting provides a clearer and more accurate depiction of how students are progressing in their learning. As a building or district leader, you must be well versed in standards-referenced reporting and all it entails.

Much has been written about the *what*, *why*, and *how* of standards-referenced reporting from a variety of perspectives (Gobble, Onuscheck, Reibel, & Twadell, 2016; Guskey & Bailey, 2001; Heflebower, Hoegh, & Warrick, 2014; Heflebower, Hoegh, Warrick, & Flygare, 2019; Marzano, 2010; O'Connor, 2009; Reeves, 2011; Schimmer, 2016; Wiggins, 1996; Wormeli, 2006). This chapter will

In a standards-referenced reporting system, clearly articulated proficiency scales clarify the knowledge and skills for prioritized standards.

primarily focus on the leader's role in guiding this important work in your school or district.

To make the transformation from traditional grading to standards-referenced reporting, leaders must consider the myriad of calculated processes and products that serve as the foundation for solid execution of the change, including the following.

1. Identifying prioritized standards—those most essential for monitoring and reporting purposes

2. Creating detailed proficiency scales to clarify common understanding for the varying degrees of proficiency

3. Ensuring teachers use proficiency scales for planning instruction, providing students with meaningful feedback, tracking their own learning progress, and creating student-focused learning goals

4. Considering how this work affects exceptional students

5. Monitoring how students are progressing and achieving toward the prioritized standards through the use of quality common classroom assessments

6. Consistently applying standards-referenced reporting practices—including any conversions to traditional percentages from a hundred-point scale or letter grades (A–F)

All these essential components serve as the groundwork for standards-referenced reporting. Without them, your progress will be limited and your efforts may even be counterproductive. For instance, you may change your reporting document and create unnecessary angst in your system, without addressing the imperative foundational work regarding standards prioritization, proficiency scale development, and quality assessment alignment. By so doing, your inconsistencies may be equal to your existing practices.

Ideally, the work in components one, two, four, and six should be done at a district level. It is important that the identified prioritized standards, the use of proficiency scales, and how each school addresses exceptional students are consistent from school to school within a district. If you find yourself in a situation where districtwide work is not in your purview, then certainly begin this work in your own building. Yet, be cautious; you may need to make adjustments later on when your district's focus comes into play. Where most schools vary slightly may be in components three and five. How principals guarantee teachers use prioritized standards, proficiency scales, and common assessments may look a bit different based on structures in place, the grade levels served, and the number of students and staff in the building. What also may fluctuate is how each school monitors student progress. The greater the consistency among schools in a district, the better. All of these essential components are detailed in the multiyear plan this chapter outlines for developing a standards-referenced reporting system.

Leading New Structures, Processes, and Products

Leading this critical work requires having agile school and district structures as well as setting up and guiding new processes and products. The HRS model identifies the processes and products (leading indicators) while the PLC process creates the structure. The HRS level 4 leading indicators for standards-referenced reporting are as follows (Marzano, Warrick, Rains, & DuFour, 2018).

> *The HRS model identifies the processes and products (leading indicators) while the PLC process creates the structure.*

4.1:   The school establishes clear and measurable goals focused on critical needs regarding improving achievement of individual students.

4.2:   The school analyzes, interprets, and uses data to regularly monitor progress toward achievement goals for individual students.

The first leading indicator (4.1) involves clarifying the first two critical PLC questions: (1) What do we want students to learn? and (2) How will we know if students are learning? (DuFour, DuFour, Eaker, Many, & Mattos, 2016; Marzano, Heflebower, Hoegh, Warrick, & Grift, 2016). This is the curriculum and assessment side of the work. Leading indicator 4.2 necessitates tracking, correlating, and monitoring student achievement. This indicator addresses PLC critical questions three (How will we respond when students don't learn?) and four (How will we extend learning for students who are already proficient?; DuFour et al., 2016).

The multiyear plan this chapter outlines merges this work (HRS model) with the structures for *doing* the work (PLC process). (See *Collaborative Teams That Transform Schools* [Marzano et al., 2016].) Changing from a traditional grading system to a standards-referenced system will test the strength of your collaborative teams. You see, when complicated and philosophical topics like giving and grading homework or reliably scoring common assessment items (to name a few) become the topic of discussion, strong teams will push one another's thinking and work collaboratively to problem solve.

> The multiyear plan this chapter outlines merges this work (HRS model) with the structures for doing the work (PLC process).

They will draw on their strength as a team, use their team norms effectively, and work through issues of dissension. Weaker teams tend to make the issues personal; team members may shut down or get so angry the team is debilitated. This not only stalls the work, but creates a negative climate among teammates.

Crafting a Multiyear Plan

Leading the shift to a standards-referenced reporting system involves thoughtfully crafting a multiyear plan as well as a corresponding time line for all phases of implementation. Figure 7.1 (page 196) is an example of a multiyear plan that describes the phases for each year. It is important to note that your school or district may move faster or slower than the plan suggests, accelerating or decelerating any of the phases. If in doubt, go slower rather than faster. Remember, changing grading practices is a mammoth change and it may feel overwhelming at times.

Note how leading indicator 4.1 is embedded in the first two years of the implementation plan in figure 7.1. These careful processes of clarifying the most prioritized standards and then linking those standards with specificity to proficiency scales are the first and most important steps. Next, work toward aligning your classroom assessments with the proficiency scales. Every single teacher does not need to complete this arduous process. In fact, as Heflebower

> Remember, changing grading practices is a mammoth change and it may feel overwhelming at times.

et al. (2014) suggest in *A School Leader's Guide to Standards-Based Grading*, use a carefully selected subgroup of teachers to draft the prioritized standards, proficiency scales, and aligned assessments.

Year One

Some of the essential actions in year one are referenced in chapter 5 (page 129), which focuses on developing a guaranteed and viable curriculum. It is advisable to complete such curriculum and assessment work during a naturally occurring standards-revision cycle. The reason is simple: you will need to review and revise existing state or provincial standards and assessments within the time line your state or province requires. Completing this initial work in tandem makes great sense and will also guard against signifying monumental school or district changes at that point in time. There will be plenty of changes to your system with the shift to standards-referenced reporting. The curriculum and assessment part of the work is already-necessary curriculum revision and assessment development. There is no need to cause angst among your staff by announcing a big grading change within the first year. In fact, doing so might actually hijack your efforts and cause some negativity without the opportunity and direction necessary for clarity. If you cannot or will not wait for a naturally occurring standards-revision cycle, then begin the work on a school-by-school basis and not districtwide.

Identify Prioritized Standards

Begin by identifying (or clarifying) prioritized standards. In other words, determine which standards are the *most* essential ones—those teachers must ensure all students attain. It is on these standards teachers will reteach and reassess students, as well as report results in a standards-referenced reporting document (report card). Bring a selected group of teachers—often called a *design team*—together to begin this work. A good size for this team is between forty and fifty members—no matter the size of the district. Obviously, if you are a very small district, you may involve most teachers or every teacher. The suggested group size is representative, yet manageable. The team will begin the plan, yet you, as leader, will build in processes for feedback from teachers not directly involved with the design team. During this process, content-area expert teachers will review existing standards, use a vetting process to determine the prioritized standards, and conduct horizontal and vertical alignment. Additionally, there are some combined prioritized standards, also known as *measurement topics*, available

Determine which standards are the most essential ones—those teachers must ensure all students attain.

Year One: Curriculum, Assessment, and Communication	Year Two: Capacity Building	Year Three: Implementation	Year Four and Beyond: Implementation and Continuation
• Identify prioritized standards. • Clarify terminology. • Create (or revise) proficiency scales. • Obtain feedback and refine the prioritized standards and proficiency scales. • Align quality classroom assessments. (Note: Some systems move this into implementation at year two.) • Draft an initial implementation and communication plan. Consider sharing the draft plan with key leaders.	• Include teachers of exceptional students for adjusting proficiency scales for special education students, English learners, and gifted and talented students. • Assemble a guiding team. • Communicate the initial implementation and communication plan with key leaders (teachers on design teams, building leaders, district leaders). • Enlist "scouts" to learn and explore other schools' and districts' systems. • Decide on the rollout (for example, by grade: K–2, 3–5, 6–8, 9–12). Will this be in phases and stages or all at once?	• Announce implementation and share written implementation plans with all staff. • Implement proficiency scales in predetermined grade levels and phases. • Implement common classroom assessments in predetermined grade levels and phases. • Organize learning opportunities for all staff. • Share belief statements. • Involve parents. • Implement new reporting for established grades and phases.	• Train new staff. • Provide refreshers for existing staff. • Train new parents. • Train new board of education members. • Implement proficiency scales in additional grade levels and phases. • Implement common classroom assessments in next determined reporting levels and phases. • Implement new reporting for next established reporting and phases. • Conduct focus groups with students and parents.

• Decide electronic reporting methods with your technology staff.	• Examine existing grading practices and beliefs. • Establish core beliefs with lead teachers and leadership teams. • Enlist consultants. • Begin to educate the board of education about the nature of the work and the time line. • Allow teachers to use proficiency scales with students. Gather empirical evidence and make any necessary modifications. • Begin working with technology staff on electronic reporting documents.	• Provide board of education members opportunities to observe, and provide continued updates and information. • Conduct focus groups with students and parents. • Begin tracking correlations among proficiency scales, common assessments, and statewide assessments. • Finalize your technological reporting system.	• Continue tracking and monitoring correlations among proficiency scales, common assessments, and statewide assessments.

Figure 7.1: Sample multiyear plan.

Source: Adapted from Heflebower et al., 2014.

through Marzano Resources (visit www.marzanoresources.com /the-critical-concepts to view a copy). These may assist in expediting this portion of the process. (See also *A School Leader's Guide to Standards-Based Grading* [Heflebower et al., 2014] for more details about defining, outlining, and implementing step-by-step processes, and leading the work of prioritizing standards.) We suggest this work begin at the district level to add clarity and coherence within your system. After initial drafts are completed, disseminate the work within your PLC to obtain feedback and implement it with teams, and, ultimately, in each classroom. If your influence is at the team or building level, then by all means, begin there. Understand, however, that ultimately, for the work to be coherent and comprehensive, it should have district support and direction. It should not matter which classroom or school a student is in; what students learn and what proficiency looks like should be clear and consistent.

Clarify Terminology

Before continuing, it is important as a leader to decide on and clarify the language you will consistently use in your school (or district). You need language for the standards you will continually reference and report about. You may also need terminology for the classroom components that specify learning for students, as well as terminology for assessment components. For instance, you may elect to use the language of *prioritized standards* (Heflebower et al., 2014), *power standards* (Ainsworth, 2003), *learning targets* (Moss & Brookhart, 2009), or *essential learnings* (Wiggins & McTighe, 2005), to name a few. Decide on the terminology you will use, share it, and use it consistently. Do not underestimate this step. If school personnel continually interchange the curriculum and assessment language, teachers, parents, and students may mistakenly perceive changes to the content or processes when there are none.

> It is important as a leader to decide on and clarify the language you will consistently use in your school (or district).

Create (or Revise) Proficiency Scales

After your building or district designs and aligns the prioritized standards (or groups of standards), you will need to embark on creating or revising your proficiency scales. This entails teachers clearly articulating the simpler, complex, and advanced knowledge and skills from the prioritized standards in order of complexity. These proficiency scales are the hub for the remaining steps during year one (obtaining feedback, tracking progress, setting goals, and designing quality classroom assessments). Some states offer guidance in their standards documents (for example, the Georgia Milestones [https://gadoe.org/Pages/Home.aspx], Colorado Academic Standards [https://cde.state.co.us/standardsandinstruction/coloradostandards -academicstandards], and California Common Core [https://cde .ca.gov/re/cc]). Additionally, there are proficiency scales for person-alization available through Marzano Resources. (See also *A School Leader's Guide to Standards-Based Grading* [Heflebower et al., 2014, pp. 26–33] for more details on defining, outlining, and implementing step-by-step processes, and leading this work.)

Obtain Feedback and Refine the Prioritized Standards and Proficiency Scales

After your team drafts prioritized standards and proficiency scales, it is imperative to obtain feedback from teachers who were not members of the original design team. This feedback may lead to a few iterations of these documents over time. You may elect to use multiple feedback loops. The first may occur after your team initially identifies the prioritized standards. This does a couple of things. First, it gets a draft of the work into your building or system. This feedback oppor-tunity demonstrates interest in others' opinions, and may even support buy-in from teachers who didn't serve on the original design team; it gives them voice. This feedback loop also serves as a vetting checkpoint since teachers of the same grade level or content-area courses can share their feedback, thus possibly limiting revisions at a later point. The feedback opportunities are easy to create during col-laborative team meetings and by using electronic means, such as an electronic survey instrument.

The second feedback loop often happens after the design team develops the initial proficiency scales draft. Again, seeking input from teachers in the same content areas or grade levels is key. After each round of feedback, the recommendations and sug-gestions go back to the original design team.

> *Feedback opportunities are easy to create during collaborative team meetings and by using electronic means, such as an electronic survey instrument.*

Ultimately, that team should make decisions about what feedback to include or disregard. The team then notes the modifications in the revised documents, along with the rationale for discounting some of the feedback. This process provides support for the design team's work; even if the team does not fully accept the suggestions, at least the rationale helps those making suggestions feel heard.

Align Quality Classroom Assessments

Following the design team's reviewing and finalizing of the set of prioritized standards and proficiency scales, it is time to align your classroom assessments. You can do this in multiple ways. Some districts ask teachers to use their existing classroom assessments to align prioritized standards and proficiency scales at the building level. Others add an additional layer of interim assessments for the district to administer in order to track student progress throughout the year, and a common set of carefully crafted and aligned assessments. During this phase of implementation, teachers will see direct connections among the prioritized standards, proficiency scales, and classroom assessments. This alignment is essential to a coherent and comprehensive system foundation that supports further efforts toward standards-referenced reporting. See also *A School Leader's Guide to Standards-Based Grading* for more details about defining, outlining, and implementing step-by-step processes for and leading the assessment-alignment work (Heflebower et al., 2014, pp. 43–49).

Draft an Initial Implementation and Communication Plan

Work as a district leadership team to draft both implementation and communication plans. The leadership team may comprise key leaders at both the building and district level—assistant superintendents, directors, coordinators, and principals. You want leaders involved and supporting the drafted implementation and communication plans. Remember, these will be fluid documents—flexible enough to respond to increased or decreased pacing of the components in your multiyear plan. You may find you can complete implementation faster at the secondary level, as teachers focus on one content area, versus many content areas at once like elementary school teachers. You may be able

You want leaders involved and supporting the drafted implementation and communication plans.

to move faster at certain grade levels for various reasons; for example, you may have efforts already underway at certain levels. A draft of the implementation plan helps teachers and leaders see commitment to this work. It also communicates deadlines for work completion.

In addition to the draft implementation plan, compose a preliminary communication plan. Who needs to know what and when? Consider various constituents. Teachers are the first users of the work. Students are next, and parents follow. Decide on the rollout. Will it be in phases and stages (for example, for K–2, 3–5, 6–8, and then 9–12) or all at once? As you draft your communication plan, contemplate the various modes for sharing your message. These may include—but are not limited to—your school or district website, course syllabi, curriculum documents, classroom websites, written feedback documents, links via QR codes, and the like. Find additional support for drafting communication plans in *A School Leader's Guide to Standards-Based Grading* (Heflebower et al., 2014, pp. 88–97) and *A Teacher's Guide to Standards-Based Learning* (Heflebower et al., 2019, pp. 121–127).

Decide Electronic Reporting Methods With Your Technology Staff

Your district technology team needs information. The team needs to fully understand the changes and the upcoming needs in order to be working with external vendors to support existing electronic grading and reporting systems. You don't want to wait to build the understanding with your technology support teams until your teachers are needing electronic gradebooks to function differently. Instead, you want this technology team to be involved in the philosophical changes in order to assist with and anticipate programming or technology support for teachers.

> You don't want to wait to build the understanding with your technology support teams.

Year Two

Year two contains many components. Don't fear—although there seem to be many moving parts, many of them happen simultaneously. In other words, you will likely have teams working on the exceptional learner supports while you are assembling your guiding team for more of a focus on grading issues while you are also adding specificity to the implementation plan regarding the appropriate rollout for your system. None of this occurs in a vacuum; each piece affects the other. You will have to carefully consider your abilities to lead multiple facets and adjust accordingly. For instance, you may elect to completely finish the exceptional learner supports before you begin assembling your guiding team.

You will have to carefully consider your abilities to lead multiple facets and adjust accordingly.

Include Teachers of Exceptional Students

In year two, your district will address proficiency scales in relation to exceptional learners. How do the proficiency scales work for students with special learning needs, English learners, and gifted and talented learners? In most instances, students who struggle cognitively or who are learning English as their secondary or tertiary language will thrive with accommodations to the regular classroom proficiency scales. Address these instructional accommodations on the right side of the proficiency scale—where teachers often delineate sample classroom activities. See figure 7.2 for an example.

You are justified in involving specialists in these discussions because it brings these supporting teachers directly into the work. In some instances, struggling students may require a modified scale— one that *slides up*. This means, for example, that the 2.0 knowledge and skills may become 3.0 expectations, and 3.0 knowledge and skills slide up to the 4.0 level on the proficiency scale. Just as teachers adjust the scale for struggling learners who require modifications based on an individualized education plan (IEP), the opposite may assist gifted and talented learners. For advanced learners, the 4.0 content may become 3.0 content, and the original 3.0 becomes the 2.0 knowledge and skills. It is also important to consider the .5 levels on proficiency scales, as it fosters growth conversations for exceptional learners. Minimally add 2.5 and 3.5 levels for students who may get all of the level 2.0 content and skills, yet not all of the 3.0. As well, add the 3.5 classification for students who obtain all of the 3.0 content and skills, yet not all of the 4.0. For further detailed information and examples of how to adjust scales for exceptional learners, see chapter 5 in *A School Leader's Guide to Standards-Based Grading* (Heflebower et al., 2014) or *A Teacher's Guide to Standards-Based Learning* (Heflebower et al., 2019).

Prioritized standard: The student will apply knowledge of organizational patterns found in informational text.		
Level	**Description**	**Sample Activities (With Instructional Accommodations)**
4.0	In addition to score 3.0 performance, the student demonstrates in-depth inferences and applications that go beyond what was taught.	When the teacher provides the student with a folder containing an informational text (of no more than four paragraphs) cut into paragraphs, the student reads (or listens to) and organizes the text. The student then identifies (from a list of possible structures) the structure the author uses (for example, main idea with supporting detail, sequence, compare and contrast, fact and opinion) and cites specific examples within the text that are characteristic of the identified organizational structure. The student writes (or dictates) an original text that incorporates a self-selected organizational pattern.
3.0	The student will apply knowledge of organizational patterns found in informational text, such as: • Sequence • Cause and effect • Compare and contrast • Fact and opinion • Description • Proposition and support	When the teacher provides the student with a folder containing an informational text (of no more than three paragraphs) cut into paragraphs, the student reads (or listens to) and organizes the text, then identifies (from a list of possible structures) the structure the author uses (for example, main idea with supporting detail, sequence, compare and contrast, fact and opinion). The student classifies short selections of text using a graphic organizer (texts may be read to the student).

Figure 7.2: Sample activities with accommodations.   Continued →

| 2.0 | The student will:

 • Sequence three or more events in informational text

 • Identify the cause and effect in a given text

 • Identify what is being compared and contrasted in a given text

 • Recognize or recall specific vocabulary, such as *sequence, cause, effect, compare, contrast, proposition, description,* and *support* | The student reads (or listens to) a text and highlights signal words within the text that indicate the structure of the text (for example, *first, second,* and *third* signal chronology; because and *as a result of* signal cause and effect; *above, beneath,* and *beside* signal description).

 The student identifies (three) types of texts (for example, biography, article, or story) and the organizational patterns usually associated with those types of texts.

 The student defines specific terms associated with organizational patterns by matching terms from a word bank to provided definitions. |

Source: Heflebower et al., 2019, p. 100.

Assemble a Guiding Coalition, Communicate the Implementation and Communication Plans, Enlist "Scouts" to Explore Other Systems, and Decide on the Rollout

A guiding coalition will help with many facets of the work, including communicating and monitoring the implementation efforts. This team *may* consist of some members of the year one design team, but *should* involve other teachers as well as some leaders, instructional coaches, and district staff. Because this team is a learning and guiding team, members read literature to strengthen their understanding of the work; members of the guiding team may also serve as "scouts" who contact or visit other schools or districts where components of standards-referenced reporting are already in place. This team helps communicate efforts at the building level. It is important to involve key, trusted people in the building or system who possess abilities to sell ideas and who are good listeners.

It is important to involve key, trusted people in the building or system who possess abilities to sell ideas and who are good listeners.

Examine Existing Grading Practices and Beliefs

Instead of assuming existing practices and beliefs about grading, it is important to do a reality check. What are the common practices? How do you know? What evidence is there to support prevailing practices? Are there differences among various grade levels (elementary, middle, and high school)? Acquire this information by asking teachers during collaborative team meetings or through electronic surveys. A great place to start is with the following three topic questions.

> Instead of assuming existing practices and beliefs about grading, it is important to do a reality check.

1. What are our homework practices? Do we give homework? Do we grade it?

2. How do we address behaviors and academic skills with grading? Do we separate them, or are they merged into one omnibus summative grade? How do we deal with late or missing work? Will points be taken off? If so, how many? Will we allow students to submit late or missing assignments?

3. What are our beliefs and practices about reteaching and reassessment?

The answers will allow you to gain a pulse about current practices. You may have more changes to make at various levels. For instance, many elementary school teachers separate behaviors from academics already. This practice is not as prevalent at the secondary level.

Establish Core Beliefs With Lead Teachers and Leadership Teams

By discerning current beliefs and practices, you will better understand where to validate or modify practices. Look for commonalities and agreements. Again, this can be achieved at the collaborative team level first, then in departments, and then throughout the school and district.

Be certain to seek leaders' beliefs as well, perhaps addressing them during a leadership meeting. Display the three topic questions from the previous section on charts around the room. Ask leaders to first consider their own beliefs, placing such beliefs on sticky notes. Divide your

> Be certain to seek leaders' beliefs as well.

leadership team members into smaller teams of three or four. The small leadership teams then rotate to view each chart, discussing their thinking and placing their belief sticky notes on the charts. As small leadership teams rotate to the next chart, they read, reflect on, and add to the statements. At the conclusion, seek areas of agreement. Use these agreements to draft leaders' belief statements about grading practices. Leaders may also elect to use a similar process at the building level. Crafting some initial belief statements will be important when providing guidelines and practices for your system.

Enlist Consultants

Enlisting the support of outside consultants may be very useful. Consider when an outsider can serve as a critical friend and trainer for content. Evaluate your own capacities for knowing, understanding, and delivering the various components involved in a comprehensive standards-referenced reporting system. Some schools or districts bring in consultants to lead the year-one work; others use their existing capacity to lead the work. Either can work very well. Sometimes consultants are great support in leading your guiding team, leadership teams, teacher leaders, and collaborative teacher teams. Consultants may also be involved in each year of your implementation plan.

Consider when you need support and enlist that support from those who have strong content and process skills.

Consider when you need support and enlist that support from those who have strong content and process skills.

Educate the Board of Education About the Work and Time Line

Keeping your board of education abreast of this transformational work is important. What will your board need to know and understand? Consider providing board members with articles, research, and information to support your work. They do not need to know all of the minutiae, yet they may find a regular report about implementation efforts useful. In some cases, sharing pictures of teachers involved

Keeping your board of education abreast of this transformational work is important.

in the work or having teachers and students share how proficiency scales support learning can be really rewarding and informative. Some districts have a standing agenda item for board meetings to keep members informed about implementation.

Over time, grading issues (sometimes from disgruntled parents or staff) will reach board members. Front-load them to inform board members so they can thoughtfully articulate the processes and products related to standards-referenced reporting endeavors.

Allow Teachers to Use Proficiency Scales With Students, Gather Evidence, and Make Modifications

Next, encourage teachers to use the team-created proficiency scales with students. Use proficiency scales to draft a unit instructional plan (Heflebower et al., 2019; Marzano, 2017). Begin with simpler content and processes teachers use early in the unit, working through to the more complex learning targets and even extending the learning for some students. Reflect on the scales in collaborative teams. Provide students with feedback about their levels on the proficiency scales and help them set goals based on feedback and next learning steps. What worked well? Are there modifications you may suggest? What do you notice about student ownership, conversations, and achievement? Obtain feedback from collaborative teams about commendations and recommendations for proficiency scale refinement and use. Seek and use this empirical evidence by reconvening your original design team for a half day so team members can reflect on the scales after teams use them with students.

Work With Your Technology Staff on Electronic Reporting Documents

By now, you and your technology staff have decided which technology reporting methods will best support your work. Be certain to include technology staff early on in the processes (year one) and be confident they understand the rationale behind how grades are calculated and entered. You want technology to support your practices, not the other way around. Often schools and districts simply make modifications to their existing student information and management systems. Other times, they select new ones. In either case, remember to plan for any needed refinements and train the users accordingly. Consider piloting these modifications in a few grades before a systemic rollout, which allows opportunities to correct any issues and results in a smoother comprehensive enactment later.

Year Three

In year three, you begin deep implementation of the standards-referenced reporting system. Be certain to keep feeding pertinent information into the system, including updates with your board of education.

Announce Implementation and Share Written Implementation Plans

You've probably heard the quote by Tim Pawlenty (n.d.), "Hope is not a plan." With transformational change, you must not simply *hope* your staff implement the plan as you intend—you must ensure they do.

> With transformational change, you must not simply hope *your staff implement the plan as you intend—you must ensure they do.*

You cannot, nor would you want to, rely on informal networks or "grapevines" to share the details of your implementation plan. You are better off sharing even a draft of the plan than sharing nothing at all. Remember, without information, people will naturally fill in the blanks themselves. Do not allow your work to be derailed by misinformation.

Implement Proficiency Scales in Predetermined Grade Levels and Phases

In accordance with your plan, have teachers implement proficiency scales in predetermined grade levels. Be certain you provide teachers with the *what*, *why*, and *how* of proficiency scales during the initial implementation. A consultant may be a great support to your teachers. You may elect to begin implementation in a large group, via webinars or through well-executed collaborative team meetings. Ensure you provide multiple opportunities for learning about proficiency scales and provide examples of how teams may begin using them, and then monitor their use. Collaborative team agendas may be a means of evidence of implementation, yet make sure site leaders are monitoring the implementation in their buildings. On collaborative team agendas, you will see an agenda item listed to read, discuss, and implement proficiency scales. In fact, it will likely be a standing agenda item for quite some time. Provide your teams with strategies and structures for easily sharing evidence with leadership.

Implement Common Classroom Assessments in Predetermined Grade Levels and Phases

Coinciding with the implementation of proficiency scales is the use of aligned classroom assessments. Depending on your plan, this may be in tandem with the scales, or you may elect to have a semester of proficiency scale implementation followed the next semester with the aligned, matching classroom assessments. Either approach is appropriate. Simply monitor staff members' workload and needs. Some staff will want assessments available at the same time as the scales, while others may want to try the scales first, then move toward the assessments. At any rate, set a soft deadline for teachers to carry out the assessments and then expect, monitor, provide support for, and seek evidence of the assessments. Remember, "What gets monitored gets done" (DuFour & Eaker, 1998, p. 107). If leaders fail to follow the expectations of building-level implementation, the message sent to staff is that this work is not essential, and other expectations will fill their agendas instead.

Organize Learning Opportunities for All Staff

Learning opportunities need thoughtful consideration. You should differentiate training for novice and experienced educators. You also may want some training specific for leaders and instructional coaches, classroom teachers, specialists, and teachers of exceptional learners. And don't forget parents; plan a training for them as well. As you consider learning opportunities, be mindful of various formats, which might include full-day sessions or minisessions (lasting an hour or so), and arrange book studies and podcasts. Using your PLC structure may also be an effective and efficient means for disseminating information and conducting training sessions. Consider working with your leadership team to plan professional development opportunities. Table 7.1 (page 210) highlights various modes of professional development with the corresponding impact, immediacy, time and effort, and interactivity. In other words, it helps you consider the type of training mode to use and also identifies the characteristics of each.

Table 7.1: Modes of Professional Development and Characteristics

	Impact	Immediacy	Time and Effort	Interactivity
Face to Face	High	Variable	High	High
Book Study	Moderate	Limited	Moderate	Moderate
Podcasts and Webinars	Moderate	Variable	Low	Moderate
Printed Materials for Team Conversations	Limited	Variable	Low	Limited
Conferences	High	Variable	High	High

Source: Adapted from Heflebower et al., 2014.

The key to planning and providing learning opportunities is to consider your educators' needs.

See *A School Leader's Guide to Standards-Based Grading* (Heflebower et al., 2014) for additional information and ideas. The key to planning and providing learning opportunities is to consider your educators' needs. What will they need and when? What professional development mode is most efficient and effective? What will you consider for new hires every year? What will you do for boosters?

Share Belief Statements

Disseminate the belief statements your team drafted during year two, but first determine if you will simply distribute them, or do you also want input? Will you want buildings to engage in a similar process, but use a draft set of beliefs? Will collaborative teams use the belief statements as the centerpiece to construct their actions? You may want to reference these belief statements on your district or school website. Or, you may want teachers to post them. Whatever you decide, you need to be sure they are not only dispersed but also *lived*. How will these beliefs guide staff practices?

Involve Parents

As mentioned in the section about providing learning opportunities, ensure you include parents. They likely need some specific information. When is it best to provide this information? What structures already exist to disseminate it? Consider open houses, websites, and parent-teacher organization meetings, as well as school advisory group meetings. Begin sharing information with parents using existing structures. Consider keeping standards-based learning a standing agenda item during any parent meetings, as needed. Use smaller structures to serve small groups of parents first; then move to involve larger groups. Some districts add podcasts and links to other resources on their school or district websites. Also, soliciting a few supportive parents to help train others may work well. Consider referencing this process during student-led and parent conferencing. See *A Teacher's Guide to Standards-Based Learning* (Heflebower et al., 2019, pp. 124–128) for more ideas.

Implement New Reporting for Established Grades and Phases

Report cards change with the shift to standards-referenced reporting. You are done piloting, and you've reviewed and decided on the best technology option for your school or district. Continue to train teachers on the software necessary for the change. Ensure you have tutorials at the beginning of the year and during the times you expect teachers to configure and report grades.

Bring students into the discussion. Spend the time necessary for students to understand how reporting will be similar to and different from grading in the past. If you are beginning implementation with primarily elementary families, they may not have a lot of past learning to unlearn. Yet, when students clearly understand what their grades represent, ways they impact them, opportunities for reassessment, and the like, parents will be far more at ease in making the transition. Consider informing parents early on about the changes they will see in grading processes. You may pair this with the parents' training previously discussed, or make this a separate information-sharing opportunity.

Report cards change with the shift to standards-referenced reporting.

Provide Board of Education Members Opportunities to Observe, and Provide Continued Updates and Information

As mentioned in year two, board of education training is essential. At this point, consider having board members visit buildings to see how teachers are using proficiency scales with students. Or have students, teachers, or parents share positive changes about the implementation thus far. Board of education members could also obtain information about how collaborative team structures are augmenting and supporting the implementation efforts. This information might be in team minutes or short video clips showing teams engaged in meaningful discussions about execution of the implementation. Also remember to proactively train any new board of education members. Encourage them to share the information at their own local or regional conferences.

Conduct Focus Groups With Students and Parents

Focus groups are a useful way to gauge more qualitative information from constituent groups like students and parents. Using a specific protocol for conducting effective focus groups (see Krueger, 1994) will help you formulate effective questions, code the responses, and extract a meaningful pulse of how standards-referenced reporting is permeating the beliefs and practices of various stakeholders. You may also consider this idea for teachers as well, although you will likely have other means of obtaining staff feedback. For example, you may use Google surveys, principal leadership team meetings, suggestion boxes, or discussions and minutes from collaborative team meetings.

Track Correlations Among Proficiency Scales, Common Assessments, and Statewide Assessments

Put systems in place to track student achievement data. Not only will this help you see your efforts with student achievement measures come to fruition, but it will also provide support and information for any areas of concern. Many districts and schools (such as Clark-Pleasant Community School Corporation, Indiana; Charlotte Public Schools, Michigan; City of St. Charles School District, Missouri; and Aurora Public Schools, Colorado), for example, are finding significant correlations between how students are performing to proficiency within the classroom and their proficiency on external statewide and national exams (personal communication, June 15, 2017). Ultimately, that is the goal. Student learning should improve with all students minimally proficient. More students, from various subgroups, should demonstrate proficiency on the prioritized standards.

Put systems in place to track student achievement data.

Finalize Your Technological Reporting System

As your technology staff members better understand the philosophy and needs of a standards-based learning environment, they will want to compare and contrast existing reporting systems with such needs. This may mean minor tweaks need to be completed within an existing system—for example, changing defaults within an existing program to not always figure the mean score for determining a grade, or allowing teachers to omit or modify weights of assignments and assessments to better reflect the learning journey. It may mean more of a complete overhaul if the existing system is outdated. It may mean reviewing other options and resources better aligned to the new system needs. At any rate, your technology staff are a critical factor in supporting the implementation and successful rollout. The technology should support the intended practice, not dictate old processes of figuring grades or impede the efforts of teachers calculating grades differently.

> *The technology should support the intended practice, not dictate old processes of figuring grades or impede the efforts of teachers calculating grades differently.*

Year Four

During year four, you are still deep in the implementation and making needed modifications. During this year, you should also monitor the earlier phases while implementing later phases of your plan.

Train New Staff, Parents, and Board of Education Members and Provide Refreshers for Existing Staff

As mentioned in year three, remember to provide training and support to new staff. Be mindful that leading this work is imperative, so leaders new to you or to their role need strong knowledge of the rationale and details of implementing a standards-referenced reporting system. New teaching staff will need specific training and support as well. It will also be important to provide refreshers for existing staff. Although implementation is well underway, staff will face struggles and have new questions, and they will need support and answers. They will also have ideas leaders can foster. Continue to use multiple methods and modalities for training staff. Continue to inform new parents to your district or school. You may consider web videos, information dissemination at parent orientations, and the like. Also, if you have new board members elected to your school board, take the time to personally bring them up to the level of understanding of existing members. Any lack of understanding among various constituents may cause hiccups in your implementation.

Implement Proficiency Scales in Additional Grade Levels and Phases

After initial implementation of proficiency scales at certain grade levels, you are now ready to move into the next phases with new grade levels (or courses). As you do so, recall all your efforts for training and support in the earlier phases and infuse them into these newer phases. As part of the new phases of implementation, add in the quality classroom assessments. Then move into the new reporting for the next established grades, all the while learning from past efforts and enhancing your data tracking. Conduct focus groups with students and parents. Continue tracking and monitoring correlations among proficiency scales, common assessments, and statewide assessments.

Any lack of understanding among various constituents may cause hiccups in your implementation.

Year Five and Beyond

Year five is a continuation of previous implementation efforts and includes all of the facets of training, feedback, support, and problem solving. Some districts elect to implement this work in phases over many years. For instance, they may begin with phase one at grades K–2, and then add grades 3–5. The following year they may add middle school grades 6–8, and then phase in grades 9–10, and finally grades 11–12. Others complete implementation more quickly and move toward monitoring and maintenance. Whatever your preference, remember, this transformational change will continue to need support. Nourish your staff, parents, and students, and provide outreach for students, even once they are in college, the work world, or the military. Monitor their preparation. Plan for next steps and the needs of your school or district. Don't forget to pat yourself on the back. This has been difficult, arduous work!

Plan for next steps and the needs of your school or district.

Reflecting On the Work

As you work to implement standards-referenced reporting, you may find it helpful to self-reflect periodically. The scale in figure 7.3

may assist you in recognizing where you are in the process, and where you may decide to go next. As you recall, the first leading indicator (4.1) involves clarifying the first two critical questions of a PLC: (1) What do we want students to learn? and (2) How will we know if students are learning? (DuFour et al., 2016). This is the curriculum and assessment side of the work.

Sustaining	Applying	Developing	Beginning	Not Implementing
The school continually cultivates information through quick data sources to monitor and establish clear and measurable goals and focus on critical needs regarding improving achievement of individual students. And the school takes proper actions to intervene when quick data indicate a potential problem.	The school has protocols and practices in place to establish clear and measurable goals and focus on critical needs regarding improving achievement of individual students. And the school can produce lagging indicators to show the desired effects of these actions.	The school has protocols and practices in place to establish clear and measurable goals and focus on critical needs regarding improving achievement of individual students.	Although incomplete, the school is in the beginning stages of drafting protocols and practices to establish clear and measurable goals and focus on critical needs regarding improving achievement of individual students.	The school has not attempted to establish clear and measurable goals and focus on critical needs regarding improving achievement of individual students.

Source: Adapted from Marzano et al., 2018.

Figure 7.3: Reflection scale for leading indicator 4.1.

Leading indicator 4.2 encompasses the tracking, correlating, and monitoring of student achievement. This work connects to the third and fourth PLC critical questions: (3) How will we respond when students don't learn? and (4) How will we address learning for students who are already proficient? (DuFour et al., 2016). The following self- and system-reflection scale (figure 7.4) may be helpful as you contemplate your efforts moving forward with indicator 4.2.

Sustaining	Applying	Developing	Beginning	Not Implementing
The school continually cultivates information through quick data sources to monitor the analysis and use of data to regularly monitor progress toward achievement goals for individual students. The school takes proper actions to intervene when quick data indicate a potential problem.	The school has protocols and practices in place to ensure the analysis and use of data to regularly monitor progress toward achievement goals for individual students. The school analyzes, interprets, and uses data to produce lagging indicators.	The school has protocols and practices in place to ensure the analysis and use of data to regularly monitor progress toward achievement goals for individual students.	Although incomplete, the school is in the beginning stages of drafting protocols and practices to ensure the analysis and use of data to regularly monitor progress toward achievement goals for individual students.	The school has not attempted to ensure the analysis and use of data to regularly monitor progress toward achievement goals for individual students.

Source: Adapted from Marzano et al., 2018.

Figure 7.4: Reflection scale for leading indicator 4.2.

Such reflective scales help you step back and evaluate your progress toward applying and sustaining levels of practice.

Conclusion

As you consider the necessary components of this colossal change to standards-referenced reporting, remember to celebrate the small successes and products from each year of implementation. Your new system is better for students!

To better serve students of the future, we must reflect on and improve the grading practices of our past.

Leading a shift to standards-referenced reporting is moving your entire system toward increased reliability and value. To better serve students of the future, we must reflect on and improve the grading practices of our past.

References and Resources

Ainsworth, L. (2003). *Power standards: Identifying the standards that matter the most.* Boston: Houghton Mifflin Harcourt.

Ames, C. (1992). Classrooms: Goals, structures, and student motivation. *Journal of Educational Psychology, 84*(3), 261–271.

Bangert-Drowns, R. L., Kulik, C.-L. C., Kulik, J. A., & Morgan, M. (1991). The instructional effects of feedback in test-like events. *Review of Educational Research, 61*(2), 213–238.

Biggs, J. (1998). Assessment and classroom learning: A role for summative assessment? *Assessment in Education, 5*(1), 103–110.

Brookhart, S. M. (2017). *How to give effective feedback to your students* (2nd ed.). Alexandria, VA: Association for Supervision and Curriculum Development.

Butler, D. L., & Winne, P. H. (1995). Feedback and self-regulated learning: A theoretical synthesis. *Review of Educational Research, 65*(3), 245–281.

Chapman, C., & Vagle, N. (2011). *Motivating students: 25 strategies to light the fire of engagement.* Bloomington, IN: Solution Tree Press.

DuFour, R., DuFour, R., & Eaker, R. (2008). *Revisiting Professional Learning Communities at Work: New insights for improving schools.* Bloomington, IN: Solution Tree Press.

DuFour, R., DuFour, R., Eaker, R., Many, T. W., & Mattos, M. (2016). *Learning by doing: A handbook for Professional Learning Communities at Work* (3rd ed.). Bloomington, IN: Solution Tree Press.

DuFour, R., & Eaker, R. (1998). *Professional Learning Communities at Work: Best practices for enhancing student achievement.* Bloomington, IN: Solution Tree Press.

Gareis, C. R., & Grant, L. W. (2008). *Teacher-made assessments: How to connect curriculum, instruction, and student learning.* Larchmont, NY: Eye on Education.

Gobble, T., Onuscheck, M., Reibel, A. R., & Twadell, E. (2016). *Proficiency-based assessment: Process, not product.* Bloomington, IN: Solution Tree Press.

Guskey, T. R., & Bailey, J. M. (2001). *Developing grading and reporting systems for student learning.* Thousand Oaks, CA: Corwin Press.

Hattie, J., & Timperley, H. (2007). The power of feedback. *Review of Educational Research, 77*(1), 81–112.

Heflebower, T., Hoegh, J. K., & Warrick, P. B. (2014). *A school leader's guide to standards-based grading.* Bloomington, IN: Marzano Resources.

Heflebower, T., Hoegh, J. K., & Warrick, P. B. (2017). Get it right the first time! *Phi Delta Kappan, 98*(6), 58–62.

Heflebower, T., Hoegh, J. K., Warrick, P. B., & Flygare, J. (2019). *A teacher's guide to standards-based learning.* Bloomington, IN: Marzano Resources.

Heritage, M. (2008). *Learning progressions: Supporting instruction and formative assessment.* Washington, DC: Council of Chief State School Officers.

Hoerr, T. R. (2014). Principal connection/goals that matter. *Educational Leadership*, *72*(1), 83–84.

Krueger, R. A. (1994). *Focus groups: A practical guide for applied research* (2nd ed.). Thousand Oaks, CA: SAGE.

Marzano, R. J. (2006). *Classroom assessment and grading that work*. Alexandria, VA: Association for Supervision and Curriculum Development.

Marzano, R. J. (2010). *Formative assessment and standards-based grading*. Bloomington, IN: Marzano Resources.

Marzano, R. J. (2017). *The new art and science of teaching*. Bloomington, IN: Solution Tree Press.

Marzano, R. J., Heflebower, T., Hoegh, J. K., Warrick, P. B., & Grift, G. (2016). *Collaborative teams that transform schools: The next step in PLCs*. Bloomington, IN: Marzano Resources.

Marzano, R. J., Warrick, P. B., Rains, C. L., & DuFour, R. (2018). *Leading a high reliability school*. Bloomington, IN: Solution Tree Press.

Marzano, R. J., Warrick, P. B., & Simms, J. A. (2014). *A handbook for high reliability schools: The next step in school reform*. Bloomington, IN: Marzano Resources.

Marzano Resources. (n.d.). *Critical concepts*. Accessed at www.marzanoresources.com /customizing-critical-concepts-scales-pdf on November 20, 2019.

Moss, C. M., & Brookhart, S. M. (2009). *Advancing formative assessment in every classroom: A guide for instructional leaders*. Alexandria, VA: Association for Supervision and Curriculum Development.

O'Connor, K. (2009). *How to grade for learning, K–12* (3rd ed.). Thousand Oaks, CA: Corwin Press.

Pawlenty, T. (n.d.). *Quotehd—Pawlenty*. Accessed at www.quotehd.com/quotes/tim-pawlenty -quote-hope-is-not-a-plan on November 1, 2019.

Reeves, D. (2011). What makes a good leader? *ASCD Express*, *7*(6). Accessed at http://www .ascd.org/ascd-express/vol7/706-toc.aspx on November 1, 2019.

Schimmer, T. (2016). *Grading from the inside out: Bringing accuracy to student assessment through a standards-based mindset*. Bloomington, IN: Solution Tree Press.

Scriffiny, P. L. (2008). Seven reasons for standards-based grading. *Educational Leadership*, *66*(2), 70–74.

Turkay, S. (2014). *Setting goals: Who, why, how?* Accessed at https://academia.edu/10363659 /Setting_goals_who_why_how on August 28, 2019.

Wiggins, G. (1996). Honesty and fairness: Toward better grading and reporting. In T. R. Guskey (Ed.), *Communicating student learning: 1996 ASCD yearbook* (pp. 141–177). Alexandria, VA: Association for Supervision and Curriculum Development.

Wiggins, G., & McTighe, J. (2005). *Understanding by design* (2nd ed.). Alexandria, VA: Association for Supervision and Curriculum Development.

Wormeli, R. (2006). *Fair isn't always equal: Assessing and grading in the differentiated classroom*. Portland, ME: Stenhouse.

Eric Twadell

Eric Twadell, PhD, is superintendent of the Adlai E. Stevenson High School District in Lincolnshire, Illinois. He is a former social studies teacher, curriculum director, and assistant superintendent for leadership and organizational development. As a dedicated professional learning community (PLC) practitioner, he has worked with state departments of education and schools and districts across the United States to achieve school improvement and reform.

Dr. Twadell is a coauthor of *Leading by Design, Pathways to Proficiency, Proficiency-Based Assessment*, and *Proficiency-Based Instruction*, and a contributor to *Proficiency-Based Grading in the Content Areas*, as well as two other anthologies. He is the author of several professional articles.

Dr. Twadell earned a master's degree in curriculum and instruction and a doctorate in educational leadership and policy studies from Loyola University Chicago.

To learn more about Dr. Twadell's work, visit the Leading by Design website (www.erictwadell.squarespace.com) or follow @ELT247365 on Twitter.

To book Eric Twadell for professional development, contact pd@SolutionTree.com.

In this chapter, Dr. Twadell shares the elements of Adlai E. Stevenson High School's effective standards-based grading and reporting system. The United States Department of Education describes Stevenson as one of the most recognized and celebrated schools in America. The high school is repeatedly named one of America's top high schools and is recognized as the "birthplace" of the PLC at Work process. Dr. Twadell shares not only what the standards-based grading and reporting system at Adlai E. Stevenson looks like but also the underlying philosophy of how the district assesses and reports student progress.

Chapter 8

Grading and Reporting for Learning in a PLC

Eric Twadell

If those who advocate for the creation of PLCs have tried to make any one thing absolutely clear, it is that in schools that function as PLCs, the first and foremost priority—the fundamental purpose, the reason for existence, or as Richard DuFour used to say, the *sine qua non*—is *learning*. It stands to reason, then, as we restructure and reculture schools as PLCs, there should be no stone left unturned as we critically examine all procedures and practices to determine if, in fact, they are consistent with this fundamental purpose. If we take an honest and brutal look at our current reality, it quickly becomes obvious that traditional grading practices in most schools are entirely inconsistent and incompatible with learning as the fundamental purpose.

> Traditional grading practices in most schools are entirely inconsistent and incompatible with learning as the fundamental purpose.

At Adlai E. Stevenson High School, our efforts to reform grading practices began in 2007; however, we doubled down on our work in February 2010 when Robert J. Marzano gave a keynote presentation to our seven Consortium 125 school districts on the need to rethink and redesign traditional grading and reporting practices. In the question-and-answer session after his keynote, a participant asked Marzano, regarding grading, "Everything seems to be working just fine. Why do we need to change our practices?" Marzano's answer was as hard hitting as it was spot-on: "The answer is quite simple. At this point, grades are so imprecise that they are nearly meaningless."

Marzano's response caused quite the stir among our faculty, who are celebrated for teaching and leading in the birthplace of the PLC at Work movement. Richard DuFour served as principal and then superintendent. "Did Marzano really just say that our grades are nearly meaningless? How can that be? We spend hours upon hours grading student work. Did he just say that I am doing it wrong?" The questions went on and on. However, as teachers began to examine their work critically through the lens of learning as our fundamental purpose, it became clear we could no longer defend and protect that status quo of our traditional grading practices.

What a Grade Should Represent

At Stevenson High School and in our consortium elementary and middle schools, we began our journey of reforming traditional grading practices in the early 2000s. One of the first conversations our leadership team had involved a discussion of the following indicators of what a grade might represent, knowing that a single grade certainly couldn't represent all of these things. The question we asked our department chairs and teacher team leaders was, "Of the following indicators, which two, in your mind, are the most important in determining what a final grade should represent?"

- Comparison with other students

- Effort

- Achievement of a standard

- Participation

- Improvement

- Behavior

- Promptness

It didn't take long for the team to come to a conclusion. Since then, I have asked the same question to tens of thousands of teachers and leaders in various settings. The answer is always the same. Teachers and leaders always determine that in the end, when a grade goes home, it should represent *improvement* and *achievement of a standard*. In fact, I have never asked a group this question and had members come to a different conclusion. It's not that effort, behavior, participation, and so on are unimportant; rather, when teachers and leaders identify the most important indicators, *improvement* and *achievement* always rise to the top.

> When a grade goes home, it should represent improvement and achievement of a standard.

Common Grading Mistakes

If we can agree that in the end, grades should represent the actual learning and achievement of students on standards and learning targets and whether or not they are growing and improving, then we can begin to critically examine some of the most common grading mistakes we make every day in our schools. While certainly not exhaustive, the following is a list of some of the mistakes we make using traditional grading and reporting practices.

- The percentage system
- Points
- Zeros
- Averages
- Weighting
- Grades as reward and punishment

The following sections explore these mistakes.

The Percentage System

One of the most ubiquitous elements of traditional grading is also one of the most illogical. In most schools, teachers use a percentage system. Grades are calculated by a pre-established range, typically 90 to 100 percent = A, 80 to 89 percent = B, 70 to 79 percent = C, 60 to 69 percent = D, and 0 to 59 percent = F. What is fascinating about this percentage system is how little sense it makes in the real world, and yet we are so committed to it in education. Does it really make sense that 50 percent is failure? If a baseball player were to hit a single 50 percent of the time, he would be in the hall of fame; actually, they might even name the hall of fame after him! If a doctor performs surgeries and only 90 percent of the time the patients survive, I seriously doubt he or she would be a doctor for very long. If 75 percent of the time we drive a car we get into a crash, most of us would be biking or walking everywhere we go. And yet, we still use and treat the percentage system as grading gospel. However, beyond "This is the way we have always done it," does it make sense that 50 percent is *always* failing and 90 percent is *always* excellent?

If grades should reflect student achievement and improvement, we need to move beyond a percentage system that establishes an arbitrary range for grades including 11 percentage points for an A; 9 percentage points for a B, a C, and a D; and 60 percentage points for an F. The justification for using this system cannot be, "Well, this is the system we have been using for more than one hundred years." Doing what we have always done will get us what we have always gotten. There are a lot of really, really smart educators out there; there is no doubt we can design and implement a grading system that is built on learning as our fundamental purpose and that actually reflects improvement and achievement.

> *If grades should reflect student achievement and improvement, we need to move beyond a percentage system that establishes an arbitrary range for grades.*

Points

If we had to choose a video game that best represents our traditional grading and reporting practices, there is none better than *Pacman* or *Ms. Pacman*. As a child of the '80s, I can remember endless hours playing and maneuvering *Pacman* and *Ms. Pacman* all the while avoiding the ghosts and collecting as many dots as I could. Interestingly, if we are willing to think about it, traditional grading works in a similar way. Students spend lots and lots of time doing homework and completing quizzes and tests all in an effort to earn as many points as possible. Students know intuitively, if not explicitly, that the more points they earn, the higher their overall grade will be at the end of the game—I mean class. I very much doubt teachers state at the beginning of the school year that the goal of their class is for students to chase and collect as many points as they possibly can. In fact, I believe most teachers feel strongly that grades should be a reflection of a student's learning and achievement.

Zeros

If there was ever a grading and reporting practice more inconsistent with the principles of a school culture focused on learning than the zero, I would be fascinated to hear about it. The use of the zero in grading and reporting is a nonsensical practice for educators claiming they are interested in creating and sustaining their school as a PLC.

The most significant problem with the zero is that it lets students and teachers off the hook. Once the teacher assigns a zero and reports it in the gradebook, the message to the student is *the learning is done and the opportunity to demonstrate understanding and mastery is over*. I seriously doubt any student would continue to extend him- or herself and do homework if the zero communicates that the opportunity for learning is over. Similarly, if the fundamental premise of a PLC is to do whatever it takes to ensure high levels of learning for all students, it makes no sense for a teacher to give students a zero and put a stop to student learning. The zero becomes an easy out for teachers not going above and beyond on behalf of students to ensure learning and growth.

Far more often than not, the teacher assigns a zero when a student does not turn in an assignment or complete an aspect of required work. As such, the zero, entered as a grade, is a reflection of a student's behavior—the behavior being not turning in required work. If grades are a reflection of student achievement and improvement, then the use of the zero doesn't really make sense. This is not to say that we shouldn't report on the student's behavior; we should. However, grades that reflect a student's behavior should be reported separately from grades that reflect a student's learning.

One of the most common refrains I hear in passionate defense of the zero is, "We must teach these students to be responsible." While I would completely agree that an important aspect of our responsibility as teachers is to help students learn to be responsible, letting students ignore their responsibilities is not an effective way to teach them to be responsible. That simply does not make sense. Every April 15, there is a learning target the Internal Revenue Service expects us all

If grades are a reflection of student achievement and improvement, then the use of the zero doesn't really make sense.

to master. If for some reason we do not pay our taxes by that deadline, the response is never, ever, "Well, then don't turn in your taxes; we are just going to give you a zero." Similarly, if a teacher were to miss the Monday 8:00 a.m. deadline to turn in his or her grades and eligibility reports, I seriously doubt the response from his or her supervisor would be, "OK, no problem, you don't have to turn in your grades. We will just give you a zero for grading and reporting this week." Author Douglas Reeves (2000) says it best in "Standards Are Not Enough: Essential Transformations for School Success": "The consequence for a student who fails to do the work should not be a low grade, but rather an opportunity—indeed, the requirement—to resubmit the work" (p. 11). Teaching students to be responsible will never happen if we allow them to abdicate their responsibilities.

Averages

If we really believe grades should represent achievement and improvement, then there is no more damaging grading practice than averaging—in other words, adding up the total number of points a student has collected and dividing that number by the total number of points possible. Consider the grades Carol received in her sixth-grade English class (see figure 8.1).

Carol clearly started off the term struggling. She was only collecting approximately half of the points possible to acquire 4/10, 5/10, and so on. However, as she moved through the middle part of the unit, Carol started to understand the material a little bit more and began to earn and collect more points. Following a series of interventions and the teacher's help and support, Carol began to develop a much clearer understanding of the learning targets for the class and even ended the unit with an A on the end-of-unit test.

	Homework Assignments				Homework Assignments				Homework Assignments				
Student	1	2	3	Quiz	4	5	6	Quiz	7	8	9	Quiz	Test
Carol	4/10	5/10	5/10	12/20	6/10	5/10	7/10	14/20	7/10	8/10	9/10	17/20	92/100

Figure 8.1: Grades in a sixth-grade English class example.

Consider, however, how this all combines into a final unit grade when we rely on an average to determine Carol's overall score. When we add up her scores on the nine homework assignments, three quizzes, and one test, Carol earned 191 of 250 total possible points. When we use an average to calculate her grade, Carol receives a 76 percent; in other words, she gets a C. Ironically, of the thirteen different events recorded in the gradebook, Carol only received a score in the 70 percent range twice! This regression to the mean certainly doesn't represent Carol's learning over time and throughout the unit. In fact, the 76 percent she received as a final score doesn't represent a single grade Carol ever received throughout the unit; it is merely a result of a calculated numerical average.

Statisticians would remind us that the average is only one way to measure and determine a central tendency. While the average is useful to measure many things, it does not help paint an accurate picture of student learning and understanding, and in no way does an averaging of scores produce a grade to help show how a student may have improved in his or her learning over time.

> While the average is useful to measure many things, it does not help paint an accurate picture of student learning and understanding.

Weighting

Although an obvious grading mistake (just as using the average or percentage system is), weighting grades can also be damaging if we are trying to ensure grades reflect learning. As we explored our own grading mistakes at Stevenson, a teacher reflected on a test he had given in class, noting in retrospect how silly and obvious the weighting mistake should have been. By way of example, consider the following.

- The teacher gave a fifty-point test weighted to one hundred points.
- The last question on the test was a multiple-choice question worth four points.
- There was a total of three hundred points available for the six-week grading period (ten homework assignments worth ten points each, a quiz worth fifty points, a project worth fifty points, and the test).

A student pointed out to the teacher the high-stakes nature of that last question. Although only one of many questions on the test, because of the way it was weighted on the test, and how the test was weighted in the grading period, that one question was worth 3 percent (2.66 percent, to be exact) of the overall grade. If a student missed that one question, the highest grade he or she could receive for the grading period was 97 percent. If there had been four questions worth four points each and the student had missed those questions but gotten everything else right on the test, a perfect score on every homework assignment, and a perfect score on the project and quiz, the highest grade he or she could have received for the term was 88 percent!

A similar weighting mistake is apparent when we categorize different types of student work across a grading term. For example, let's say when calculating a grade for a quarter or semester, we count homework as 40 percent of the final grade, quizzes and tests as 40 percent of the final grade, and participation as 20 percent of the final grade. Consider the following example of a typical gradebook in a traditional grading system (see figure 8.2).

When examining the various elements in the gradebook, we can see the interesting effect weighting certain categories differently can have on the overall final grade. Clearly, participation would end up having the most significant effect on the final grade. The teacher assumed that since the tests were summative assessments and counted for more points than any other element, they would have the biggest impact on the student's grade. However, when we look closely at all of the grades in the gradebook, we can see that following participation, the element that has the most significant impact on the final grade is the very first homework assignment. What was that first assignment? Requiring parents to sign the course syllabus at the beginning of the year! That first homework assignment, a fairly meaningless one at that, counted as a larger percentage of the overall grade than the fifty-six-point test, the forty-point test, and every quiz and homework assignment during the grading period.

Grades as Reward and Punishment

One of the more discouraging grading practices often present in elementary schools is the *red-light classroom management plan*. The basic premise for this plan is students start off their day with a green

	Homework		Quizzes and Tests			Participation	
Assignment	Points Possible	Percentage of Grade	Quizzes and Tests	Points Possible	Percentage of Grade	Points Possible	Percentage of Grade
Homework 1	15	15	Quiz 1	10	2.6	100	20
Homework 2	10	10	Quiz 2	7	1.8		
Homework 3	10	10	Quiz 3	10	2.6		
Homework 4	5	5	Test 1	40	10.4		
			Quiz 4	10	2.6		
			Quiz 5	15	3.9		
			Quiz 6	6	1.6		
			Test 2	56	14.5		
Totals	40	40		154	40	100	20

Figure 8.2: Gradebook example.

light, and if or when their behavior strays from expected class norms, their chart will reflect a yellow light, and maybe even a red light if the misbehavior continues. In many cases, teachers up the ante by threatening to and then actually taking points off students' grades if the behavior is particularly egregious and upsetting to the teacher. Beyond the obvious violations of the Family Educational Rights and Privacy Act (FERPA) laws, we do significant damage to students when we publicize and share their class charts of individual behavior scores and grades. In some middle schools and high schools, the practice is even more brutal. Teachers often wield grades as a weapon, using them as a tool for trying to maintain control of the classroom by reducing students' grades or eliminating them from the gradebook when they misbehave in class. While there is no doubt it is important to hold students responsible for their behavior, there are many, many alternatives to conflating grades as a reflection of achievement and improvement with grading for punishment and misbehavior.

While there is no doubt it is important to hold students responsible for their behavior, there are many, many alternatives to conflating grades as a reflection of achievement and improvement with grading for punishment and misbehavior.

The other side of the same coin, however, is using grades as reward. If, ideally, grades reflect improvement and achievement, then we must be willing to question the time-honored practice of giving extra credit. For example, a phenomenon occurs every December 1 in many northern U.S. states: loads of extra-credit points are doled out to students when they provide their teachers with . . . boxes of tissues. If you're a student of parents with a wholesale club membership—jackpot! So the message we end up sending to students is simple: "Come to the football game on Friday night, clean off the whiteboard, or bring in tissues and you don't have to understand the periodic table or the causes of World War I. You'll get extra credit and all will be OK." To anyone even remotely familiar with the basic principles of PLCs, this is obviously a silly grading practice whose time has come and gone.

In *The Learning Leader*, Douglas Reeves (2006) states, "Simply put, letter grades do not reflect student achievement in an astounding number of cases. . . . When providing students with feedback . . . [it] must take place within boundaries of fairness, mathematical accuracy, and effectiveness" (p. 113). As an educator, if you don't agree that grades should be fair, accurate, and effective, then we probably need to sit down for a longer conversation than what this chapter can accomplish. Ultimately, we must acknowledge that traditional grading and reporting practices do not reflect learning—our fundamental purpose—which in a PLC must be the basis of all decision making.

Standards-Based Grading and Reporting Practices

If we are going to move beyond traditional grading and reporting practices, we must be mindful of the research. There can be little doubt that researcher and author Robert J. Marzano and his colleagues are on the cutting edge of educational research and reform. In their work on researching high reliability schools, Robert J. Marzano, Philip B. Warrick, Cameron L. Rains, and Richard DuFour (2018) find that schools can leverage significant change in grading and reporting when two leading indicators of the HRS model are in place:

> 4.1 The school establishes clear and measurable goals focused on critical needs regarding improving achievement of individual students.

> 4.2 The school analyzes, interprets, and uses data to regularly monitor progress toward achievement goals for individual students. (p. 32)

While it is certainly possible to try to implement these two leading indicators in schools still using traditional grading practices, making the transition to standards-based grading and reporting ensures a school will do so successfully. First, educators must get clear on *why* the change is needed and then develop a common understanding of the essential elements necessary for the shift.

Getting Clear on *Why*

While the traditional percentage system's use of points, zeros, averages, and weighting and weaponization of grades as reward and punishment are both reasons to stop outdated grading and reporting practices, they are not the reasons to move into standards-based grading and reporting. Standards-based grading and reporting is an essential practice for districts and schools looking to make the transition to PLCs. The practice does the following.

1. Promotes student self-reliance and efficacy

2. Transforms the gradebook into a reflection of learning

3. Focuses conversations between teachers and students on learning

4. Increases collaboration among teams

Understanding Essential Elements

One of the first and most important steps in the shift to standards-based grading and reporting is to develop a clear schoolwide common language regarding the essential elements of the curriculum. Across the United States, there is tremendous variation in how educators understand, discuss, and implement the various elements of a curricular hierarchy. Listening to educators talk about curriculum, you will hear that we often utilize many terms synonymously—*essential standards, essential targets, learning targets, learning progressions,* and so on. While the task of developing a common curricular language for an entire country would be out of reach, at the very least, schools and districts answering the four critical questions of a PLC must develop a clear and common understanding of the essential elements of curriculum. In Stevenson's consortium, we spent considerable time developing and simplifying a language to support our shift to standards-based grading and reporting.

As we began the process of answering the first critical question of a PLC—What do we want all students to learn? (DuFour, DuFour, Eaker, Many, & Mattos, 2016)—we realized we needed to use the same curricular language. After considerable dialogue and debate in professional development sessions and in our collaborative teams, we developed a curricular hierarchy to define and clarify the essential language we would use in all our work (see table 8.1).

Table 8.1: Hierarchy of Essential Curricular Language

Curriculum Level	Definition
Standard	The enduring transferable skills of a course or grade level
Objective	The way a student demonstrates understanding of a standard
Target	The scaled learning progression of a standard
Success Criteria	The content and skills needed to meet and exceed proficiency on a learning target

There is nothing particularly innovative about this curricular hierarchy; what is important and notable is we developed a consortiumwide agreement and common language. Far too many districts and schools use a tangled web of language to describe their curricular work, making meaningful reform and improvement efforts unnecessarily complicated and frustrating.

We answer the first question of a PLC by identifying the *essential* standards—the most important and enduring skills we want students to know and be able to do at a specified grade level or in a particular course. We define *objectives* as the way a student demonstrates his or her understanding of the standard. However, the absolutely most essential element of a standards-based grading and reporting system is the *learning target*—the scaled learning progression of a standard. While different experts may call learning targets different names, everyone seems to agree on their importance. Coauthors Connie M. Moss and Susan M. Brookhart (2012) summarize the importance of learning targets perfectly:

> *The absolutely most essential element of a standards-based grading and reporting system is the* learning target—*the scaled learning progression of a standard.*

> Learning targets are student-friendly descriptions—via words, pictures, actions, or some combination of the three—of what you intend students to learn or accomplish in a given lesson. When shared meaningfully, they become actual targets that students can see and direct their efforts toward. (p. 9)

In a truly standards-based teaching and learning culture, the learning target becomes the essential ingredient and foundation for instructional design and delivery, and the way we assess students (our grading and reporting practices). For learning targets to be effective tools in each of these areas, they must be clear, measurable, scalable, and assessable.

Learning Targets Must Be Clear

For learning targets to be effective, educators should write them in a way students can easily understand. Consider the following seventh-grade mathematics learning target from a school district in the midwestern United States:

> *Describe simple and complex situations in which oppo-site quantities combine to make 0. For example, a hydrogen atom has zero charge because its two constit-uents are oppositely charged.*

While there is no doubt this learning target represents good math-ematical practices, a typical student would not look at this target and understand what the teacher expects him or her to know and be able to do. Additionally, as a general rule, if a learning target needs to include a "for example . . ." element to help students understand what teachers expect of them, the target is probably vague at best and confusing at worst. In the spirit of clarity preceding competency, the following learning target might provide students with a simpler and clearer expectation:

> *I can effectively analyze functions using differ-ent representations.*

In learning targets, as in life it is important to follow the KISS (Keep It Simple, Silly) principle.

Learning Targets Must Be Measurable

The structure and language of learning targets must be measur-able. It makes no sense to write a learning target to reflect a learning progression for students if teachers cannot measure it. While "writing clearly" or "actively listening" might reflect elements of an overall standard, overly general language does not help produce clear and concise learning targets useful to students. If the learning target does not contain language the teacher can measure with the support of success criteria (content and skills), the learning target is of little to no value.

The structure and language of learning targets must be measurable.

Learning Targets Must Be Scalable

It is not enough for the teacher to simply write a learning target on the board and expect it will all become clear to students. Learning is not analogous to a light switch—you cannot flip it on or off. Learning occurs more slowly and deliberately along a gradation. Learning is more like a dimmer switch—there is a gradual development of understanding and skills over time. As such, we need to ensure that, in addition to the clear articulation of what achieving proficiency on the learning target looks like, we also specify what the exceeding, approaching, and basic levels of the target represent.

The sample scaled target in figure 8.3, used in world languages classes, reflects the gradation or levels of mastery on the standard.

Standard	Exceeding Expectations	Meeting Expectations	Approaching Expectations	Still Developing
2a. I can engage in conversation.	I can independently maintain a conversation using above-level communication strategies and language control.	I can independently maintain a conversation using level-appropriate communication strategies and language control.	I can independently maintain a conversation using level- and non-level-appropriate communication strategies and language control.	I can independently maintain a conversation using non-level-appropriate communication strategies and language control.

Figure 8.3: Scaled learning target for world languages classes example.

When writing proficiency-based learning targets, it is important to follow these three simple rules.

1. **Don't be negative:** Learning targets should focus on a positive representation and description of what a learning progression looks like.

2. **Don't use numbers:** The goal is to provide a clear description of the learning and achievement progression. Suggesting a student is proficient on a task if he or she can do it five of ten times or eight of ten times doesn't provide the clarity and prescriptive feedback to help a student use the target as a learning tool.

3. **Don't change the verb:** It is important to understand that scaled learning targets are not scaffolded learning progressions. Writing good learning targets means describing the same skill at different levels of proficiency. Scaffolding various standards and objectives together does not help a student become proficient on a specific learning target.

For students, having a scaled learning target is a critical element in their ability to reflect on and assess their own learning. Without a scaled target, it is difficult for students to see a progression of learning; they are often left with the sense that either they "get it" or they don't.

Learning Targets Must Be Assessable

For a scaled learning target to have value for students, there must be multiple opportunities for them to assess their own learning, and teachers must provide students with feedback on their learning progression. A well-written target will provide both students and teachers a clear picture of what the evidence of learning should look like.

Reflection, Feedback, and Assessment

In a PLC, the second essential question educators must ask *and* answer is, "How will we know if students are learning?" (DuFour et al., 2016). Educators in traditional school cultures answer this question by developing summative quizzes and end-of-unit or end-of-course tests to determine a student's grade. However, one of the many problems with these traditional quizzes and tests is they don't provide teachers (or students) with valuable information about the actual learning of students. A quiz grade of 16/20 on fractions or a test grade of 78/100 on World War II doesn't communicate clearly on which targets the student has exceeded expectations, has met expectations, or is still working toward proficiency. Quizzes and tests that only provide evaluative feedback, numeric indicators, and percentage scores don't help students learn. We can and should do better!

> *One of the many problems with these traditional quizzes and tests is they don't provide teachers (or students) with valuable information about the actual learning of students.*

Feedback and Reflection

Ideally, in a standards-based grading and reporting culture, feedback, reflection, and assessment are all synonymous. When teachers provide students with feedback, that feedback must align with the learning target and also must be positive, prescriptive, and co-constructed.

Positive Feedback

When working with students, frame feedback, first and foremost, on what the students *can do*—not on what the students can't do. Very few of us enjoy the experience of being told what we are bad at. Telling students to "try harder" or that they "lack clarity" or "didn't provide enough details" does not reflect affirming statements. The most useful feedback supports students in the learning process and is framed in a positive and proficiency-based way, rather than in a negative and deficiency-based way.

Prescriptive Feedback

The feedback teachers provide must help students *reflect* on the specific content and skills they are working on, and also how to improve their learning. For example, telling students to "write a clear thesis statement" really isn't helpful, given if students know how to write clear thesis statements, they do so in the first place. Giving students very clear ideas about how to write or improve thesis statements gives them *actionable* feedback they can respond to in a forward-facing manner.

Co-Constructed Feedback

The feedback students receive is not a one-way interaction. Learning is a social experience; reflection and feedback should be an engaging experience students have with their peers and their teacher. For example, in a standards-based classroom, students' sharing their ideas and practicing their skills with other students and their teacher is a daily experience. The gasoline that fuels the engine of the learning cycle is metacognition. Metacognition is not a natural skill; we must nurture and develop it in students. The purpose of co-constructed feedback is to give students the opportunity not to determine if they are right or wrong, but to examine their thinking processes and develop their ability to reflect on and improve their own learning. Figure 8.4 (page 238) shows a learning target with examples of types of feedback.

Figure 8.5 (page 238) presents a reflection and feedback tool that provides students the opportunity to reflect on a scaled learning target with their teacher and classmates in a way that is positive, prescriptive, and co-constructed.

Learning Target	Negative and Evaluative Feedback	Positive Feedback	Positive and Prescriptive Feedback	Positive, Prescriptive, and Co-Constructed Feedback
I can independently maintain a conversation using level-appropriate communication strategies and language control.	Student does not engage in conversations effectively due to limited content knowledge. Student also needs to work on active listening skills.	Engaging in conversations effectively requires proper active listening skills and flexible knowledge of the required content.	The more you listen and react to others' ideas using relevant facts and details, the better your engagement in conversations will be.	The more you listen and react to others' ideas using relevant facts and details, the better your engagement in conversations will be. If a classmate were to say [this], what details from the reading could you add?

Figure 8.4: Learning target on engaging in conversation example.

Standard 2: Interpersonal Speaking Feedback Sheet

Standard	Exceeding Expectations	Meeting Expectations	Approaching Expectations	Still Developing
Engaging in conversation	I can independently maintain a conversation using above-level communication strategies and language control.	I can independently maintain a conversation using level-appropriate communication strategies and language control.	I can independently maintain a conversation using level- and non-level-appropriate communication strategies and language control.	I can independently maintain a conversation using non-level-appropriate communication strategies and language control.

	Success Criteria		Feedback: Provide evidence and specific examples from your work.
Communication Strategies	**Interaction** (two-way)	• Active and equal participation • Advances conversation	What comments did you make based on your partner's ideas? What questions did you ask? Were your questions open-ended? Was the conversation balanced?
	Elaboration (one-sided)	• Details and examples • Relevant connections	What were some details, examples, or personal connections that you made? Did you include any connecting words that allowed you to expand your ideas? What were they?
Language Control	**Word Choice**	• Relevance • Accuracy • Variety	What relevant words did you use? Did you use a variety of words? Were any words misused?
	Structures	• Relevance • Accuracy • Variety	What structures, tenses, or moods did you use to communicate your ideas? Were they varied? Did you recognize errors after listening?
	Delivery	• Pronunciation • Fluency	Were you hesitating at all? Did you mispronounce any words? What were they?

Figure 8.5: Sample student reflection and feedback tool.

Source: Adlai E. Stevenson High School Spanish II Collaborative Team. Reprinted with permission.

Assessments

The problem with most assessment cycles is they are linear and time bound. Most assessment cycles occur in one-, two-, or three-week units of study and follow a predictable pattern; educators provide instruction, give homework, assess students with quizzes, provide more instruction, assign more homework, and then give a test (see figure 8.6).

Instruction → Homework → Instruction → Quiz →
Instruction → Homework → Test

Figure 8.6: Traditional learning and assessment cycle.

Steve Heller, an outstanding English teacher at Stevenson, has the very best description of assessment for educators looking to implement effective strategies to support standards-based grading and reporting: "Assessment should always be done in the service of something else. Assessment should be a beginning—not an end" (personal communication, September 13, 2013). He perfectly describes the role of assessment in standards-based grading and in a PLC culture. *Assessment must have a purpose.*

Assessment must have a purpose.

When creating assessments to support standards-based grading and reporting, educators must consider what exactly they will be using the assessment results for. What is the purpose of the assessment? The following questions can guide your thinking about how to design meaningful and purposeful assessment experiences for students.

- Do our questions gather evidence of proficiency?
- Do the assessment's components collect evidence on the full range of the scalable learning target?
- Is there enough evidence to determine proficiency?
- How much time will students need to work on the assessment?
- Does the assessment produce evidence of students' perceptions, thinking patterns, and mental maps?
- Does the assessment allow the student and teacher to measure growth?

In a standards-based grading and reporting culture, all aspects of the teaching-learning cycle can produce evidence of student learning and understanding. Identifying a student's level of proficiency doesn't need to be reserved for a single test; educators can provide feedback, support students' learning, and evaluate students as they complete class warm-ups, in-class activities, exit slips, and every other piece of evidence students produce.

Most traditional testing experiences feel like "gotcha" moments to students. In real life, we are not introduced to an idea or skill, given a few opportunities to practice, and then tested on it. Imagine how many more car accidents there would be if we were told how to drive, watched a short video about driving, went out to drive once or twice, and then took a driving test. There would be significantly more accidents and none of us would pass driving exams.

Assessment experiences in the classroom should be similar to students' experiences outside the classroom. For example, if a student is in a play, he or she is not given the script and then expected to perform the next day. Typically, there are many rehearsals, some dress rehearsals, and then two or three performances. Likewise, coaches don't just roll a basketball out on the floor and expect players to play and win games. Teams have many practices, some scrimmages, and then multiple games. Assessment should work the same way. We should have assessments that *deliver* information to students, help *develop* student understanding, and then *determine* student proficiency (see table 8.2, page 242).

> *Most traditional testing experiences feel like "gotcha" moments to students.*

If educators want to implement standards-referenced grading and reporting with efficacy and fidelity, then they must rethink and redesign traditional tests. Traditional tests simply do not produce the right kind of evidence to provide students with meaningful feedback or to allow teachers to make a professional interpretation of students' proficiency level. The three Ds (delivery, develop, and determine) assessment framework provides both teachers and students with multiple opportunities to create new knowledge and skills, reflect on and receive feedback on proficiency-based assessment experiences, and then evaluate a student's mastery of a proficiency-based learning target.

Table 8.2: The Three Ds of Assessment Design

Deliver	Develop	Determine
Prepare for the standard.	Experience the standard.	Evaluate student proficiency on the standard.
Assessments are not scored or graded. They are used to: • Develop prerequisite skills • Create foundational knowledge • Generate feedback	Assessments are scored and may not be graded. They are used to: • Experience and explore proficiency • Mimic the proficiency experience • Promote self- and teacher awareness, reflection, and appraisal skills	Assessments are graded. They are used to: • Determine proficiency • Judge a mastery experience • Create an accurate self-perspective

Source: Adapted from Reibel, 2018; Twadell, Onuscheck, Reibel, & Gobble, 2019, p. 42.

Scores for Evidence of Student Learning

The shift to standards-referenced grading and reporting is less a shift in scoring and grading practices and more a shift in how we provide feedback to students and assess their learning. While it's simple to stop the former, it's more difficult to start the latter. As a result, teachers in schools making this shift often ask, "If we are no longer using points and the percentage system, how do we score student work and assessments?" For many teachers, this is a turning point. Once they resolve the dissonance between current practice and scoring evidence in a standards-based grading system, the insights become clearer and clearer.

The shift to standards-referenced grading and reporting is less a shift in scoring and grading practices and more a shift in how we provide feedback to students and assess their learning.

The reality is, scoring students' homework, quizzes, and tests is no more or less complicated once teachers commit to no longer using points aligned to the percentage system, to using scaled learning targets as the foundation for feedback to students, and to engaging in conversations with students about their learning. Consider the following example from a middle school Spanish teacher involving a simple assignment in which students must identify a symbol for a food item and use proper grammar to write a complete sentence description of the food. Figure 8.7 represents how teachers grade this assignment in a traditional point and percentage system.

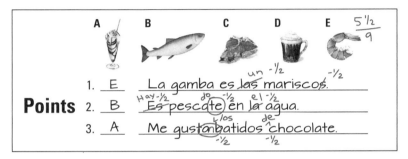

Source: Adlai E Stevenson High School Spanish II Team, 2019. Reprinted with permission.
Figure 8.7: Spanish class assignment with traditional grading example.

The student used improper grammar on a number of occasions and ended up with a final score of 5.5 of 9 points—and a percentage score of 61 percent—nearly failing. Keeping in mind the many obvious problems discussed earlier with traditional grading and reporting, it is clear the student knows *some* Spanish, so the student is not a failure (or even close to being one).

Standards-referenced grading and reporting provides students with a more accurate reflection of where they are in their learning. Note in the following example (see figure 8.8, page 244) the teacher provides an indicator of where the student is currently scoring on a scaled learning target and prescriptive feedback on where he or she needs to focus effort in the future. Scoring learning events in this way is a far more accurate reflection of the student's current stage of learning.

Similarly, in the following examples from a high school physics class (see figures 8.9 and 8.10), you can see the same problem with traditional points-based scoring, and how the teacher scores the item in a standards-referenced grading and reporting system.

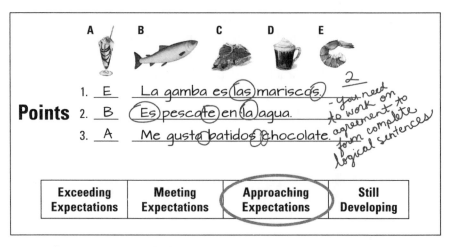

Source: Adlai E Stevenson High School Spanish II Team, 2019.

Figure 8.8: Spanish class assignment using standards-referenced grading example.

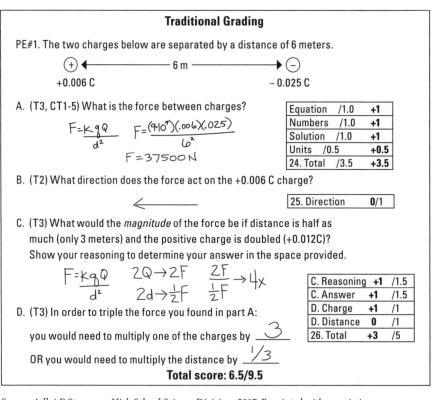

Source: Adlai E Stevenson High School Science Division, 2017. Reprinted with permission.

Figure 8.9: High school physics example of grading in a points-based system.

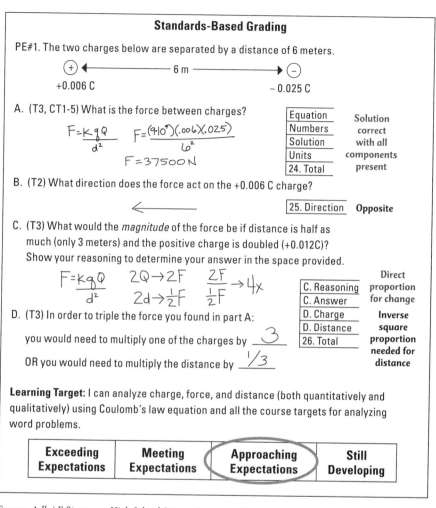

Source: Adlai E Stevenson High School Science Division, 2017. Reprinted with permission.

Figure 8.10: High school physics example of scoring in a standards-referenced system.

Grade Calculation

In a standards-based system, a calibrated professional interpretation of student-produced evidence in relationship to a clearly communicated and understood proficiency expectation should determine all student learning (growth and aptitude). In other words, teachers regularly working in their collaborative teams should examine student work and make a team decision on the criteria and evidence a student needs to produce for each indicator.

Teachers regularly working in their collaborative teams should examine student work and make a team decision on the criteria and evidence a student needs to produce for each indicator.

Clearly, in a standards-based grading and reporting system, the gradebook takes on a new look and feel. Because they no longer simply tally up points students earn on homework, quizzes, and tests, teachers have the opportunity to format the gradebook in a more meaningful way that focuses on student learning. The elements of an effective gradebook include—but are not limited to—the following.

- The gradebook should communicate performance on learning targets.
- Achievement data should be separate from academic behaviors.
- Develop events should be separate from determine events.
- The gradebook organization should show growth, re-performance (retakes), and recent evidence.

Figure 8.11 shows the elements of an effective gradebook based on the Common Core Writing standard, "Write arguments to support claims with clear reasons and relevant evidence" (W.6.1; National Governors Association Center for Best Practices & Council of Chief State School Officers [NGA & CCSSO], 2010).

Once a school makes the commitment to focus scoring of student learning events on the proficiency-based learning target, the next question that naturally emerges is, "OK, well, I can't just have a bunch of 2s, 3s, and 4s in the gradebook. . . . How do I calculate a grade?" While there are any number of ways to roll up the target scores into an overall grade, it is important to avoid repeating the same mistakes often made in a traditional grading and reporting system. For example, while it would be easy to average all the scores together, in the end teachers would not get an accurate measurement of student learning.

It is important to keep in mind the following considerations when determining a student's letter grade from a standards-referenced gradebook.

1. The grade must reflect the student's full body of work.
2. When calculating a final grade, factor the central tendency of evidence *and* the most recent evidence of student learning.

Standard: Write arguments to support claims with clear reasons and relevant evidence.

Event	Learning Target—Making Claim	Learning Target—Clear Reasoning	Learning Target—Clarify Relationships	Learning Target—Utilize Appropriate Transitions	Learning Target—Maintain Formal Style
Determining Event	ME	ME	EE	EE	ME
Developing Event	ME	AE	AE	AE	AE
Developing Event	ME	ME	EE	EE	EE
Developing Event	AE	ME	EE	EE	EE
Developing Event	AE	AE	ME	EE	ME
Deliver Event	AE	AE	ME	ME	ME

Student Name

Figure 8.11: Effective standards-referenced reporting in a gradebook example.

EE = exceeding expectations, ME = meeting expectations, AE = approaching expectations, SD = still developing
Source for standard: NGA & CCSSO, 2010.

While there may be a number of different ways that a grade can be calculated based on the preceding considerations, the matrix in table 8.3 (page 248) is one example of how we have moved away from the averaging of scores and utilized a bimodal matrix to help teachers determine a final letter grade.

1. Review each learning target and note the event scores. For example, in figure 8.11 (page 247), the student earned a meeting expectations (ME), ME, exceeding expectations (EE), EE, approaching expectations (AE), and EE in relationship clarification.

2. Use the bimodal matrix in table 8.3 to determine an overall score for each learning target. For example, for relationship clarification in figure 8.12, the student's bimodal scores are EE-ME, which results in an overall score of exceeding expectations (Reminder: The mode is the most frequently occurring score. So, the first number represents the most frequent score on a learning target and the second score represents the second-most-frequent score on that learning target.)

3. Follow the same steps for the other learning targets.

Table 8.3: Bimodal Matrix Example

Exceeding Expectations	Meeting Expectations	Approaching Expectations	Still Developing
EE-ME	AE-EE	AE-ME	SD-EE
EE-AE	ME-AE	AE-SD	SD-ME
ME-EE	EE-SD	ME-SD	SD-AE

Once the teacher determines the final indicators for each learning target, it is fairly easy to determine a final letter grade, if needed. Simply identify a rubric that prescribes how many targets a student must achieve proficiency on to earn an A, B, C, D, or F. For example, teachers and teams at Stevenson High School use the following rubric (see figure 8.13, page 250).

If we were to apply this rubric to the gradebook in figure 8.12, it is clear because Carolyn met or exceeded proficiency in each of the learning targets, she earned a letter grade of A.

Standard: Write arguments to support claims with clear reasons and relevant evidence.

Student Name	Learning Target—Making Claim	Learning Target—Clear Reasoning	Learning Target—Clarify Relationships	Learning Target—Utilize Appropriate Transitions	Learning Target—Maintain Formal Style
Deliver Event	AE	AE	ME	ME	ME
Developing Event	AE	AE	ME	EE	ME
Developing Event	AE	ME	EE	EE	EE
Developing Event	ME	ME	EE	EE	EE
Developing Event	ME	AE	AE	AE	AE
Determining Event	ME	ME	EE	EE	ME
	Meeting Expectations	Meeting Expectations	Exceeding Expectations	Exceeding Expectations	Exceeding Expectations

EE = exceeding expectations, ME = meeting expectations, AE = approaching expectations, SD = still developing

Source for standard: NGA & CCSSO, 2010.

Figure 8.12: Effective standards-referenced reporting in a gradebook with bimodal scores example.

A	Score of meeting or exceeding expectations for each of the five learning targets
B	Score of approaching for any learning target, with a meeting or exceeding in all remaining learning targets
C	Score of approaching for two or more learning targets (no score of still developing)
D	Score of still developing for a learning target and at least one score of approaching or above
F	Score of still developing in three or more learning targets

Source: Adlai E. Stevenson High School, 2019. Reprinted with permission.

Figure 8.13: Final letter grade rubric.

A question teachers frequently ask early in the standards-referenced grading and reporting process is, "Once we have identified the indicators for the various events, why don't we just average all of the approaching expectations and meeting expectations and exceeding expectations together?" This is a legitimate question and, in fact, in many cases averaging is the default setting for electronic and online grading systems. However, the problem with averaging in a standards-referenced grading and reporting system is the same as it is in a traditional grading system. It is only one way to compute a central tendency, and it does not provide an accurate picture of the student's current state of learning. For example, if the temperature is 90 degrees for two days and then 50 degrees for two days, it would be widely inaccurate to suggest that it felt like 70 degrees for four days. Similarly, if a student was struggling to learn a new skill and scored three still developing, but then, through hard work and support from the teacher, the student scored three exceeding expectations, it would be inaccurate to suggest the average of approaching expectations is an accurate reflection of the student's improvement and achievement—the two indicators a grade should represent.

Implications for Interventions

In PLCs, there is a relentless effort to ensure all students are learning. Staff answer the third critical question of a PLC—How will we respond when students don't learn? (DuFour et al., 2016)—more clearly and with more specificity if the school has also transitioned to standards-referenced grading and reporting.

In a traditional grading and reporting system, it would be common for a student to receive a mathematics quiz or a test back from the teacher with a grade of D+ or 68 percent. If the teacher then assigned the student to an intervention, and the intervention teacher asked, "What do you need help with?" the student's typical response might be, "I don't know . . . math." To the frustration of both the student and the intervention teacher, the grade of D+ or 68 percent doesn't really provide any clear direction on what the student needs to do to improve.

Because the learning target is the foundation of a standards-referenced grading and reporting system, interventions focus more on the actual needs of students. While a grade of 68 percent is not particularly helpful to an intervention specialist, it would be helpful to have clarity regarding the specific targets the student needs help with to achieve proficiency. Rather than a D+, in a standards-referenced system, an intervention teacher receives information on the specific targets the student needs help and support with (see figure 8.14).

> *Because the learning target is the foundation of a standards-referenced grading and reporting system, interventions focus more on the actual needs of students.*

Tony	I can give an example of a linear equation with one variable that has one solution, infinitely many solutions, and no solutions.	Student at 2.0 on the rubric
	I can apply the Pythagorean theorem to find the distance between two points in a coordinate system.	Student at 2.0 on the rubric
	I can describe the effect of dilations, translations, rotations, and reflections on two-dimensional figures using coordinates.	Student at 1.0 on the rubric

Figure 8.14: Information for intervention in a standards-referenced system example.

With specific information on what the student needs help and support with, teachers can respond meaningfully to students when they are not learning.

Conclusion

If we were to somehow try to calculate the amount of time that is spent in the hard work of grading and reporting, we would quickly realize the sheer magnitude of time teachers spend in this important work. At the same time, however, if we were to closely examine the actual grading and reporting practices, we would soon find that, in many cases, the missing ingredient in these traditional practices is a *focus on learning.*

We would be naïve to think that the shift to a standards-based grading and reporting system is an easy one. In fact, we have seen many of these transitions flounder and eventually fail when the initiative is rushed and implemented within an arbitrary time frame ("We will be doing standards-based grading in two years!"). In the end, similar to the other aspects of PLC work, what we are ultimately talking about is not simply structural change to our grading and reporting practices, but a cultural change in the way we think about, talk about, and implement our grading practices. If in a PLC culture everything that we do is based on learning as our fundamental purpose, then it must follow that grading and reporting must reflect learning. The following email exchange from a student at Adlai E. Stevenson High School and a mathematics teacher perfectly illustrates that cultural change that standards-based grading can have within a school and change that comes in the way that we talk about student achievement and improvement.

> *We would be naïve to think that the shift to a standards-based grading and reporting system is an easy one.*

In Their Own Words

While there is an immense amount of research on the benefits of standards-referenced grading and reporting, sometimes the best *why* for moving forward with a new initiative is when we can see the positive effects on students. In the second year of our transition to standards-referenced grading and reporting at Stevenson, a teacher and a former student exchanged the following email correspondence (edited only for emphasis and to protect anonymity).

Student: I've actually kept it at an A this whole year, Mr. Smith! I'm actually smart! Look! You should be so proud of me right now. Yours truly, Sam.

Teacher: Sam, I absolutely am very, very proud of you! I know how hard you work and how committed you are to do your best! Well done and keep it up! Mr. Smith. PS, Have you shared your excitement with your teacher? I am sure she would appreciate it!

Student: I have multiple times hahaha :) I really like the way Mrs. Jones teaches, like she makes it easy to understand. I'm pretty sure that's what really helped. Plus, to be quite honest I didn't really work that hard. I thank standards-referenced grading for that! ☺

Teacher: What do you mean by the last statement? Does standards-referenced grading work so well that you feel you are not working hard to improve your learning? Does it mean that the feedback that you get is helpful, so that you don't have to work hard to improve? Do you think you would not have received an A if it was not standards based? If so, why do you think that? I hope you share your thoughts. They are valuable to me!

Student: Standards-referenced grading makes it easier in a sense that it bunches things together compared to our normal grading. Like you know we have three sections: creating new functions, reasoning, and equivalence. It's easy for me as a student to see what I'm struggling with using these three "buckets," as Mrs. Jones would say. In normal grading, I would have to worry about one little unit. Plus, when it comes down to the final, it really points out what you need to work on, which in my case is creating new functions. So it's almost as if you're working twice as hard because the units are all bunched together—it's not all separated. Plus, we have formative assessments and summative assessments, which are basically quizzes and tests, but the formatives don't really count for a grade. They also allow you to know what type of problems you struggle with, or you might have the right idea of how to approach a problem, but don't know how to execute it correctly. *It allows the teacher to swoop in and guide you to the correct answer.* As far as standards-referenced grading is concerned, it should be required in all classes. I personally love it. (personal communication, January 8, 2015)

References and Resources

DuFour, R., DuFour, R., Eaker, R., Many, T. W., & Mattos, M. (2016). *Learning by doing: A handbook for Professional Learning Communities at Work* (3rd ed.). Bloomington, IN: Solution Tree Press.

Marzano, R. J., Warrick, P. B., Rains, C. L., & DuFour, R. (2018). *Leading a high reliability school.* Bloomington, IN: Solution Tree Press.

Moss, C. M., & Brookhart, S. M. (2012). *Learning targets: Helping students aim for understanding in today's lesson.* Alexandria, VA: Association for Supervision and Curriculum Development.

National Governors Association Center for Best Practices & Council of Chief State School Officers. (2010). *Common Core State Standards for English language arts and literacy in history/social studies, science, and technical subjects.* Washington, DC: Authors. Accessed at www.corestandards.org/assets/CCSSI_ELA%20Standards.pdf on June 26, 2019.

Reeves, D. (2000). Standards are not enough: Essential transformations for school success. *NASSP Bulletin, 84*(620), 5–19.

Reeves, D. (2006). *The learning leader: How to focus school improvement for better results.* Alexandria, VA: Association for Supervision and Curriculum Development.

Reibel, A. (2018, May). Three purposes of assessment: Deliver, develop, determine. *The Assessor, 5,* 14–15.

Twadell, E., Onuscheck, M., Reibel, A. R., & Gobble, T. (2019). *Proficiency-based instruction: Rethinking lesson design and delivery.* Bloomington, IN: Solution Tree Press.

LEVEL 5:

Competency-Based Education

Clearly, leading indicators such as a guaranteed and viable curriculum, standards-referenced reporting, and effective teaching imply that students should become highly successful learners of specific competencies. There must be clarity regarding what students should know and be able to do, and the dispositions they should possess. Further, in a high-performing PLC, teams focus on the question, What would this competency look like *in student work* if students were successful? In short, success within the HRS model and the PLC framework can only occur when the specificity reflective of competency-based education is deeply ingrained in both the district or school's structure and its culture.

Successfully capturing the full potential of competency-based education requires confronting the question, Which competencies are essential for students in the 21st century and beyond? It also requires confronting the question, How will we ensure all students meet these competencies before they graduate? Addressing this last question requires a sea change in school organization, schedule design, and student support.

Mike Ruyle

Mike Ruyle, EdD, has served in the roles of classroom teacher, athletic coach, school principal, alternative program director, university professor, and school consultant. He led schools in Montana and California through the implementation of personalized, competency-based protocols and is a recognized authority in the areas of assessment practice, mindfulness in classrooms, trauma-informed schools, culturally responsive pedagogy, and healing- and resiliency-centered education. He has facilitated professional development in schools, districts, state agencies, and universities both nationally and internationally.

Dr. Ruyle is author of *Leading the Evolution: How to Make Personalized Competency-Based Education a Reality*, as well as a coauthor of *The New Art and Science of Classroom Assessment* and a contributor to *Cultivating Mindfulness in the Classroom*. He earned bachelors of arts in history and English from the University of San Francisco, plus master's and doctoral degrees in educational leadership from Montana State University.

To learn more about Dr. Ruyle's work, visit the Marzano Resources website (www.marzanoresources.com) or follow @MikeRuyle on Twitter.

To book Mike Ruyle for professional development, contact pd@SolutionTree.com.

In this chapter, Dr. Ruyle describes the High Reliability Schools (HRS) perspective on personalized, competency-based education (PCBE), and provides a solid theoretical and research base for transitioning to the model. He asserts that this is the necessary next step for all K–12 educators to embrace as schools evolve into the future.

Chapter 9

Personalized, Competency-Based Education

Mike Ruyle

In his best-selling book *Drive*, author Daniel H. Pink (2009) asserts there are three foundational factors in human motivation: (1) autonomy, (2) mastery, and (3) purpose. In terms of schooling, these elements speak specifically to personalized, competency-based education (PCBE), which occupies level 5 of the HRS model—the apex of the pyramid that all schools must strive to reach as education continues to evolve into the future. At the local school level, PCBE entails transforming culture and schedules to accommodate how students progress through various curricula and content areas. Level 5 takes the *time* component of schooling out of the equation and allows learners to accelerate through content areas based on their demonstrated mastery of skill and knowledge. On a larger, systemwide scale, evolving educational schemes to a personalized, competency-based model will require a fundamental paradigm shift in how we do business in schools, and presents a revolutionary change in mindset for educators at all levels, from classroom teachers, building leaders, and district leaders to the colleges that conduct teacher certification programs.

This paradigm shift is important for a number of reasons, not the least of which is how we prepare students for the world of tomorrow. Our commitment as educators must be to ensure each student can find and fulfill his or her greatest potential. Young adults emerging from the traditional school system are being asked to function within and contribute to an increasingly globalized society and workforce. It is essential, that they are able to demonstrate full mastery of the skills, knowledge, and competencies educators identify as critical for their subsequent success. Thus, there is a critical need to evolve our educational systems into more relevant and innovative models that can keep pace with a rapidly changing world. PCBE epitomizes what can happen when a school replaces a system that matriculates students based on time with one that responds to students personally based on demonstrated competence in specific content areas.

PCBE serves to shift the main responsibility of teachers away from simply addressing curriculum, instruction, and assessment—from teaching *at* learners—to monitoring student progress toward academic goals, diagnosing academic strengths and weaknesses, and facilitating the learning process for every student to achieve at high levels. In other words, *a teacher's job is not just to teach kids, but rather to help kids learn.* It is from this critical perspective that all of the elements and strategies Robert J. Marzano (2017) identifies in his seminal work *The New Art and Science of Teaching* reach their fullest potential. The tools in a teacher's proverbial tool kit become more powerful when the focus is on student learning as opposed to teaching content to an entire class.

The important point to make is that level 5 is where HRS, PLC, and *The New Art and Science of Teaching* come together and can take teacher expertise and professionalism to a whole new level. Being able to shift their frame of reference, change their instructional focus, and then effectively dedicate time to deliberately practice appropriate instructional strategies to help enhance the learning experience for each student is very hard work for teachers to consider and implement. But it is in this hard work that the tremendous power of collaboration via PLC can be best realized.

Using an example from the medical field, at the Mayo Clinic, the clinical model of practicing medicine has been the accepted protocol for generations. In this setting, a doctor does not awaken at the start of the day with an explicit plan he or she will use on patients during his or her shift. Rather, the doctor will evaluate each person he or she encounters and adjust according to the distinct needs of each individual. The doctor is keenly aware of health goals and uses data from a variety of assessments to generate a treatment plan. Doctors at Mayo also collaborate closely and constantly with colleagues to validate their findings and brainstorm ideas for best practices moving forward. The doctor then proceeds with presenting and implementing the treatment plan, using a variety of skills, knowledge, and tools at his or her disposal, monitoring according to the distinct needs of each individual the effect the plan has on a patient, and adjusting as needed. Every decision is based on data and made with the individual's specific needs in mind.

Likewise, in a PCBE system, a teacher does not awaken in the morning with an explicit curriculum plan he or she will use on all students over the course of the school day. Lesson planning needs to be flexible and easily adjustable. In this scenario, teachers are keenly aware of desired learning outcomes to which every student will be held to achieving at proficiency or above and use data from a variety of assessments to evaluate the learners in their classroom. In addition, teachers confer regularly with colleagues in collaborative teams to analyze assessment data and brainstorm ideas to help them monitor student progress. They then use all the tools, knowledge, and skills at their disposal to help drive their instruction and facilitate the learning process. Every decision is based on data and with the individual's specific needs in mind. A teacher from a PCBE high school in California speaks to this reality when she says:

> In traditional classes, I would make lesson plans to try to keep kids on task and address curriculum. The focus was on the content and my lesson. In PCBE classes, I try to understand where kids are in their learning and figure out how to help them. Sometimes I use direct instruction, sometimes I use flexible grouping, and sometimes I create individualized lessons. But in PCBE classes, I really get to know the students better and the focus is always on their learning. This is so much better. It was hard to get the school here, but I really love coming in to work every day now. (personal communication, March 6, 2014)

The Evolutionary Triad

Once schools take the step of shifting toward full implementation of the PCBE system, profoundly positive psychological constructs become apparent that affect students, teachers, and building and district leaders. Research indicates in effective PCBE schools, leaders display certain behaviors to grow and sustain the model, which leads to increased levels of teachers' academic optimism as well as higher levels of student engagement (Ruyle, 2019). This assertion can be best illustrated by the *evolutionary triad*.

The evolutionary triad (see figure 9.1) is a powerful visual that connects the leaders, students, and teachers in the PCBE system within the overarching theme of social justice. For a school to move forward and successfully evolve toward the PCBE model, *all three components*—leaders, teachers, and students—are equally important and must necessarily be actively engaged in facilitating the shift. If any of the stakeholders are underdeveloped or unsupported, the triad will collapse. For example, if a school has exceptional leaders and outstanding students engaged in their learning, but the teachers are not on board with transforming the model, ultimate school change simply will not happen. Likewise, if students and teachers are seeking real evolution but the leaders are weak or lack vision, substantive change will fail to take hold as well. Successful schools of the future need leaders who are eager to provide commitment, guidance, and resources, as well as teachers who continually evolve their professional practice into something beyond what they were exposed to, and students who are capable of assuming the mantle of ownership over their own learning and education. What the shift to PCBE can look like for the three major stakeholders of students, teachers, and leaders is described in more detail in the following sections.

> For a school to move forward and successfully evolve toward the PCBE model, all three components—leaders, teachers, and students—are equally important and must necessarily be actively engaged in facilitating the shift.

PCBE and Students

Conventional structures, policies, and procedures often imbue traditional schools with a culture that makes truly implementing personalized approaches to learning and instruction difficult. The impact of this phenomenon can be profound. Educators Lannie Kanevsky and Tacey Keighley (2003) describe a powerful study that reveals a number of high school students identified as gifted in elementary school were classified as underachieving in later grades. This led to the assertion that associates *schooling* with boredom and *learning* with

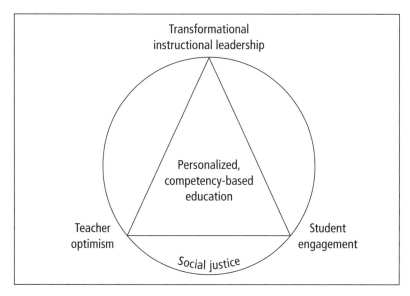

Source: Ruyle et al. 2019, p. 7.

Figure 9.1: The evolutionary triad.

engagement. Although educators are intuitively aware of this reality, Pink (2009) addresses the staidness of tradition-bound organizations:

> As the world economy demands more nonroutine, creative, conceptual abilities—too many schools are moving in the wrong direction. They're redoubling their efforts on routines, right answers, and standardization. . . . We're bribing students into compliance instead of challenging them into engagement. (p. 185)

One of the most exciting benefits corresponding to the adoption of PCBE paradigms, however, is academic and behavioral data as well as interview protocols measuring these models tend to facilitate an increase in individual student engagement and motivation (DeLorenzo, Battino, Schreiber, & Gaddy-Carrio, 2009; Priest, Rudenstine, Weisstein, & Gerwin, 2012; Ruyle, 2019). In other words, for the learners, PCBE entails a dramatic culture shift that allows for and encourages higher levels of student engagement as well as *student agency*—students assuming active ownership of their own learning and educational progress. As two high school students from a freshly developed PCBE program in Montana said:

> In the normal high school, I was just in the middle of a big herd of people, and we were moved along like cows. In PCBE, I get to choose my own path and move that way. It's so much more interesting and motivating, and I want to be done early so I can move on with life. And now I will be done early with a higher skill level! (personal communication, March 28, 2014)

> I need more personal time to learn things—not lots, but enough to help me get into it. Then I can go on and do it quickly, and sometimes I help others. I'm not like a cow in a herd here. Here, it's not just "Shut up and listen, shut up and do this." It's more of "How can I help you to really master this learning goal?" (personal communication, March 28, 2014)

This increase in student engagement seems to correlate with corresponding increases in student academic achievement. Educational researchers Chen-Lin C. Kulik, James A. Kulik, and Robert L. Bangert-Drowns's (1990) analysis of over one hundred previous studies of mastery learning uncovered positive effects for high-achieving students and even greater positive effects for low-achieving students. While it is true that higher academic achievement does not always correlate directly with higher levels of engagement (some students may garner good grades purely as a result of sheer compliance to teacher rules), the design of PCBE systems specifically helps all learners engage with content at their current capability levels. In other words, the personalized component allows teachers to meet and challenge each student at his or her appropriate level of skill.

The design of PCBE systems specifically helps all learners engage with content at their current capability levels.

PCBE and Teachers

For teachers, the shift from a traditional, teacher-centered environment to a true learner-centered school can be daunting. But teachers working in effective PCBE systems clearly state that the model seems to have a tremendous impact on the engagement level of their students, which has a corresponding effect on their own level of teacher optimism (Ruyle, 2019). A vast body of research focuses on a variety of factors that demonstrate strong statistical relationships with student achievement. Especially significant for PCBE schools is the research of educational researchers Wayne K. Hoy, C. John Tarter, and Anita Woolfolk Hoy from The Ohio State University (2006a), who identify three specific characteristics of teaching staffs—(1) collective efficacy, (2) faculty trust, and (3) academic emphasis —that show a strong positive correlation with student achievement. The researchers eventually combined these three traits to form the construct of *academic optimism* (Hoy et al., 2006a). An assessment tool, the School Academic Optimism Survey (SAOS), measures this construct. (Visit www .waynekhoy.com/school-ao for further information on the SAOS.)

For teachers, the shift from a traditional, teacher-centered environment to a true learner-centered school can be daunting.

It is encouraging to note, in schools that fully adopt the PCBE model, teachers exhibit higher academic optimism scores on the SAOS than they did when their schools were operating under more traditional paradigms. Teachers also tend to display higher academic optimism scores than their colleagues in traditional school settings. In simple terms, teachers in PCBE systems tend to be happier, more confident, and more optimistic about their jobs, which has a strong correlation with subsequent student achievement (Hoy & Miskel, 2005; Hoy et al., 2006a, 2006b; Ruyle, 2019). This reinforces the critically important teacher optimism–student engagement connection, which forms the bottom line of the evolutionary triad; happier, more optimistic teachers lead to more engaged and successful students, and vice versa. As educational thought leaders Fred Bramante and Rose Colby (2012) state, "The good news for educators is that a 21st century, anytime, anyplace, anyhow, any pace, student-centered, move-on-when-ready model will rekindle the idealism that inspired most educators to enter the profession in the first place" (p. 62). A teacher from a prominent PCBE school in Maine echoes this assertion:

I am focused on finding things, how to engage individual kids. It's like the coaching process in sports: I need to evaluate where kids are in terms of skills and knowledge, and then figure out how I can get them excited to keep moving. . . . I have to really use all my skills and be able to shift according to kids' needs. It's all about connections. It's not about me, it's about them, and I need to always think about that so that

I can be better and more effective. (personal communication, October 5, 2018)

In addition, PLCs are a crucial element for increasing the academic optimism of teachers using the PCBE model. By building the individual capacity of teachers to learn a new system and helping them to see improved educational practices personally, professional teamwork can ultimately increase the effectiveness of the overall teaching staff and add to feelings that the content they teach matters (academic emphasis); that they are, as an entire staff, truly able to meet the needs of all learners (collective efficacy); and that students and parents are on the same page with them (faculty trust). Thus, collaborative efforts to learn, embrace, and implement PCBE principles can positively reinforce academic optimism for teachers. Having teacher teams effectively collaborate via the PLC process in this work has the potential to shift culture and send a clear message that PCBE is *our* system, it is necessary to move in this direction, and we will work together to maintain a laser focus on successful implementation of the model.

> PLCs are a crucial element for increasing the academic optimism of teachers using the PCBE model.

The discovery that a PCBE system leads to increased and pervasive levels of teacher academic optimism is important and compelling. While no single educational model will cure all the ills of modern society, we can now educate our learners in a way that works better for them and for teachers. A constant refrain of teachers using this model is, "I cannot go back to teaching the old way anymore. If I were ever to move to another place, I'd need to find a school that uses competency-based education, or I'd get into a new line of work."

PCBE and Leaders

The PCBE model represents a dramatic departure from the tired, anachronistic conventional school system and points to a pedagogy in which classroom teachers treat learners as cocreators of their own knowledge. This entails teachers and students operating in a new and evolved system with little or no previous frame of reference or deep knowledge of what a different model looks like. So, it is critical for leaders to demonstrate and coach teachers on an evolved way of operating in classrooms. As such, leaders must truly model a different way to do their own jobs and work alongside teachers as all staff learn how to operate in a different instructional framework. Leaders must provide the vision, energy, and expertise to bring the paradigm shift to reality. As a high school teacher from California states:

Leaders must provide the vision, energy, and expertise to bring the paradigm shift to reality.

> I love how my principal is so available for us. He challenges us all the time, which can be exhausting, but he seems to show up in my room just when I need it. It's not one of those situations where the principal tells us to do something, then disappears or is busy. This guy is here, available, and takes the heat so we don't always have to. (as cited in Ruyle, 2019, p. 44)

Instructional leadership strategies and mentoring qualities for helping all staff shift to new learning habits are key for leaders. This is due to the change in the teacher's role from the purveyor of information and assessment in a teacher-centered classroom to a facilitator of learning and growth in a more personalized, student-centered classroom. The researcher Philip Hallinger (2012) states, "Instructional leadership has recently been reincarnated as a global phenomenon in the form of 'leadership for learning'" (p. 1). In terms of leading the evolution to a PCBE model, the most effective leadership approach is *transformational instructional leadership*. There is solid research behind this specific construct. Coauthors Robert J. Marzano, Timothy Waters, and Brian A. McNulty (2005) indicate the skillful leader is someone who develops people by combining elements of instructional leadership with transformational qualities. The skillful leader provides individualized support and intellectual stimulation and cultivates a climate where all teachers are held accountable while also experiencing consistent success. In addition, Hallinger (2012) advocates integrating transformational and instructional theoretical approaches and cites supporting research from *Education Week* senior contributing writer Catherine Gewertz (2003) and the Virginia Department of Education (2004), among others. Hallinger (2012) further describes how leadership for learning has become a new paradigm for 21st century school leadership due to "global interests in educational reform and school-level accountability" (p. 2).

Evolving schools into the PCBE system requires more than just holding workshops and book studies or hiring consultants. Necessary changes may include schools' revising their approaches to scheduling, identifying learning objectives, assessing, and engaging students (DeLorenzo et al., 2009; Littky, 2004; Marzano, 2007; Marzano, Norford, Finn, & Finn, 2017; National Education Commission on Time and Learning, 2000; Priest et al., 2012). Schools with a successfully implemented PCBE model undergo a fundamental paradigm shift in the organizational structure that affects leaders, teachers, students, and parents. The full implications of implementing PCBE are huge; schools are no longer confined to being the guardians of information slowly disseminated through books and worksheets in classrooms during 180-day school years. The PCBE model includes a number of elements, such as the following.

Evolving schools into the PCBE system requires more than just holding workshops and book studies or hiring consultants.

- Learning goals for each standard that continuously measure individual progress toward proficiency

- Varied learning structures (self-directed, one-to-one, large group, small group, field study, mentoring)

- Teacher assessment and student self-assessment on progress toward learning goals

- Common use of a variety of assessment practices (obtrusive, unobtrusive, student generated)

- Immediate intervention based on assessment data

- Assignment to learning groups based on proficiency level, rather than age-grade distinctions

School leaders who have the greatest impact on student learning dedicate as much attention to the daily realities of instructional leadership as they do to the loftier concepts of transformational leadership.

Great teachers are essential in schools, but PCBE systems need great principals and superintendents to lead and develop them. Simply put, school leaders who have the greatest impact on student learning dedicate as much attention to the daily realities of instructional leadership as they do to the loftier concepts of transformational leadership. These types of leaders evolve both hearts and practice as they inspire stakeholders and nurture a culture of learning and collaboration in a new educational paradigm. The effort will be great, but the rewards (in the form of student achievement) will be even greater.

PCBE in the HRS Model

We now address the three leading indicators for HRS level 5 and what they mean on a more practical level.

Leading Indicator 5.1

> 5.1:   Students move on to the next level of the curriculum for any subject area only after they have demonstrated competence at the previous level.

This leading indicator speaks to the personal mastery component of PCBE—the foundation of the entire system. Educational researcher Thomas R. Guskey (2008) asserts, "When compared to students from traditionally taught classes, students in mastery learning classes have been shown to learn better, reach higher levels of achievement, and develop greater confidence in their ability to learn and in themselves as learners" (p. 194). Schools adopting PCBE paradigms accomplish this by clearly articulating what proficiency looks like in every content area and encouraging students to play an active role in their learning process. For example, students could work with teachers to create learning projects high in rigor and personal relevance. In this case, they are no longer addressing abstract learning objectives or completing assignments simply for the sake of plowing through the classroom curriculum. Rather, students are using their individual knowledge, culture, and personal experience to create individual learning plans that facilitate the comprehension and mastery of the crucial skills necessary to move to the next learning goals. This equates to students taking control of their own learning by asking probing questions to expand their learning and applying previously mastered material to new learning objectives, which is linked to increased student achievement and motivation. As two middle school students explain:

> The goals and scales—that's where it's at when we take the time to really get them. I understand my classes better, and then I can do better on the test. It feels *great* knowing how I will do on a test. And if I mess up, I fix it, and can still move on. I like this so much better, so I'm a lot more motivated. Most all the kids like it better. They can get ahead, and they

have a choice on what to read, and on what to do. It motivates me to move and get done more quickly. It can be harder
sometimes to have independence, but I do learn things better. I just have to work harder at it, which is probably a good
thing. (personal communication, October 29, 2018)

Teachers help kids more here—it's not just about getting
assignments and worksheets and stuff out to kids. Teaching is
more personalized for each kid. I can tell if I understand things
or not, and I know when I'm ready to demonstrate it. I love that
and I do better. (personal communication, October 29, 2018)

Lagging indicators (evidence showing students can move to the
next level of the curriculum in any subject area after demonstrating
competence at the previous level) include the following.

- There are clearly communicated and specific learning goals
  with provided exemplars so students understand what competence in each essential element looks like.

- Clear criteria are established for each essential element with
  minimum scores that demonstrate competence.

- Students can explain the learning goal and they have the
  opportunity to demonstrate competence or proficiency in a
  variety of ways.

- A system is in place that tracks each student's status on the
  essential elements for each subject area at the student's current level.

- There is continual monitoring of student status and progress
  for each essential element in each subject area.

- When students reach criterion scores for the essential elements at a particular level in a subject area, they immediately
  start working on the elements at the next level.

For teachers, the initial stages in the shift to PCBE require a significant amount of curriculum work that includes identifying priority
standards, describing what mastery of those standards looks like, and
creating ways for students to demonstrate their understanding. While
there are many ways to accomplish this foundational work, having
teacher teams collaborate in a PLC is clearly the optimal method. But

curriculum work is never truly done. Each year, teacher teams should review assessment data (both state and local), make decisions regarding alignment and assessment rigor, and continue to revise and improve proficiency scales. As this work moves forward, it continually sends the message that the school has an academic focus and students demonstrate proficiency on identified content that matters.

While there are many ways to accomplish this foundational work, having teacher teams collaborate in a PLC is clearly the optimal method.

Leading Indicator 5.2

5.2: The school schedule accommodates students moving at a pace appropriate to their situation and needs.

This leading indicator can be challenging for schools to implement, as it entails removing time requirements for students to move through levels of knowledge and adjusting traditional reporting systems. This speaks to reorganizing the entire structural foundation of traditional schools. As educators, we know children do not learn in the same way and at the same pace. But in the standard traditional education system, leaders expect teachers to cover material or address standards based on predetermined pacing guides that do not account for student learning. By definition, in this outdated system, teachers move forward in the curriculum *knowing students are being left behind*. In addition, some students are held back because they are bound by the teacher's established pace of learning, which he or she designs to meet the needs of the whole group.

In the PCBE model, however, there is an inherent agreement among students, teachers, and parents that begins with establishing and communicating clear, non-negotiable learning goals. There is, essentially, a promise from teachers to students—these are the things you will master before you leave this class, and I, as your teacher, will not stop working with you until you get there. In addition, since learning for every student is the ultimate goal, teachers should challenge and move advanced-level learners at an accelerated pace most appropriate for them. This commitment to each student builds a level of trust between teachers and

There is, essentially, a promise from teachers to students—these are the things you will master before you leave this class, and I, as your teacher, will not stop working with you until you get there.

students, as well as parents, that can be difficult to achieve in a traditional model.

This second leading indicator is what teachers continually mention when taking surveys about their higher levels of academic optimism in a PCBE system. When we allow students to learn at a challenging yet appropriate pace, they can all experience success. When all students are making progress and achieving their goals, it builds teachers' understanding that their efforts are having an impact on every student, which increases their own sense of collective efficacy. As a high school teacher from Florida expresses:

> I'm always trying to find ways to engage kids with the content. Our school is so much different than it used to be. The sleepers don't exist anymore. I can't say that all students are engaged, but it's getting better and better every year. And that's exciting. It makes me more optimistic about what I do and how successful our kids can be. (personal communication, March 28, 2014)

Lagging indicators (evidence showing the school schedule accommodates students moving at a pace appropriate to their situation and needs) include the following.

- Multiple venues are available simultaneously for students to learn and demonstrate competency in the essential elements for each level of each subject area.

- Online competency-based instruction and assessment are available in the essential elements for each level of each subject area.

- There is constant monitoring of the time it takes for students to move through the various levels of the curriculum for each subject area at each level.

The great challenge for school leaders regarding this leading indicator is how to build a schedule that allows for personalization in a standardized system.

The great challenge for school leaders regarding this leading indicator is how to build a schedule that allows for personalization in a standardized system. A couple of questions are important for school leaders to consider.

1. Once students have demonstrated mastery of content in a specific field, do they go deeper into the content or accelerate through the curriculum?

2. If they can accelerate (or they fall behind), does it entail a schedule change, or can the existing class schedule meet their needs?

Schools can address these questions in a number of ways. One large high school in California created a culture in which students are expected to work at the teacher's pace or faster on all learning goals. The school designed the schedule so three content-area teachers all teach similar levels at the same time and constantly practice flexible grouping strategies. This way, the teachers can meet learners' needs as they progress through the curriculum.

Leading Indicator 5.3

5.3: The school affords students who have demonstrated competency levels greater than those articulated in the system immediate opportunities to begin work on advanced content or career paths of interest.

The concept of *student voice and choice* is at the heart of this leading indicator. It is important to note that improving academic capacity and improving student engagement are issues for *all* learners. Noted gifted education expert Joseph S. Renzulli (2008) asserts that the traditional educational model has produced flatline academic growth among the most able and gifted learners. Educators often tend to confuse compliance with engagement. Teachers may hold back high-achieving students and not encourage them to stretch their learning to the highest levels; instead, teachers bind these students to the predetermined pace established for the class. Rigor, relevance, and differentiation are common refrains of educators. Yet traditional school models do not commonly create environments in which teachers expect and support gifted and advanced learners to perform at their highest levels (Renzulli, 1978, 2008). As one high school freshman identified as gifted by a large comprehensive school in Montana shares:

This is not as easy as people think. It's actually harder, but I'm doing better in school now than I ever have. It all makes more sense to me, and I feel good when I see myself moving and getting things done. We are getting a better education here. All the other kids are getting cheated. Too bad for them! (personal communication, April 14, 2015)

Lagging indicators (evidence showing teachers afford students who demonstrate competency levels greater than those articulated in the system immediate opportunities to begin work on advanced content and career paths of interest) may include the following.

- Students who demonstrate the highest level of competence in a given subject area receive opportunities for even more advanced study in that subject area.

- Students who demonstrate competence adequate for high school graduation begin and receive credit for college work.

- Students who demonstrate competence adequate for high school graduation begin and receive credit for work toward a trade of interest to them.

The great challenge for school leaders regarding this leading indicator is how to build relationships with community and college partners that allow students to engage with different future paths while still in school. Does meeting this challenge entail changing the student schedule, or can teachers meet their needs using the existing class schedule? One year-round high school in California follows a protocol in which students are expected to master the content in their required courses early in their senior year, and then the counseling staff guide students to either attend college courses at the local university or junior college, engage in internships, or work in jobs the school helps them find. The school's mindset is for students to begin engaging in the next steps of their adult life with critical support from the school staff as they take their first steps into the real world.

> The great challenge for school leaders regarding this leading indicator is how to build relationships with community and college partners that allow students to engage with different future paths while still in school.

Horizontal articulation and vertical articulation of educational goals are important components of this leading indicator. It is also especially critical for leaders to communicate proficiency scales with clear academic goals and learning progressions across the entire school so this information is in the hands of students at the beginning of the school year.

Conclusion

Implementing substantive educational reform is difficult and draining work. The shift to a PCBE model is a monumental change that requires a fundamental paradigm shift; this change demands leaders examine and implement paradigms that transform the expectations and roles of principals, teachers, students, and parents. Effective, transformational leadership based on social justice and moral courage is an absolute requirement to implement such dramatic change. Many programs attempt to implement the competency-based system and fail, simply due to the difficulty of clearly understanding a direction and committing to the energy necessary to lead such change.

> The shift to a PCBE model is a monumental change that requires a fundamental paradigm shift.

When implemented correctly, the PCBE model actually gives learners an advantage over students who endure the traditional system, as authentic learning and increased student achievement are subsequent, inherent results of increased engagement. Educational consultants and coaches Sonia Caus Gleason and Nancy Gerzon (2013) make the case that effective schoolwide implementation and use of personalized learning are essential to the pursuit of greater educational equity. The PCBE model addresses the needs of each student, removes many of the time constraints common in more traditional models, and allows each student to accelerate through the curriculum as he or she demonstrates proficiency on identified learning goals. PCBE epitomizes a complete transformation of what public education looks like, and has the potential to help all schools realize unprecedented levels of success for all students.

References and Resources

Bramante, F., & Colby, R. (2012). *Off the clock: Moving education from time to competency.* Thousand Oaks, CA: Corwin Press.

DeLorenzo, R. A., Battino, W. J., Schreiber, R. M., & Gaddy-Carrio, B. (2009). *Delivering on the promise: The education revolution.* Bloomington, IN: Solution Tree Press.

Gewertz, C. (2003). N.Y.C. chancellor aims to bolster instructional leadership. *Education Week, 22*(16), 7.

Gleason, S. C., & Gerzon, N. (2013). *Growing into equity: Professional learning and personalization in high-achieving schools.* Thousand Oaks, CA: Corwin Press.

Guskey, T. R. (1997). *Implementing mastery learning* (2nd ed.). Belmont, CA: Wadsworth.

Guskey, T. R. (2007). Closing achievement gaps: Revisiting Benjamin S. Bloom's "Learning for Mastery." *Journal of Advanced Academics, 19*(1), 8–31.

Guskey, T. R. (2008). Mastery learning. In T. L. Good (Ed.), *21st century education: A reference handbook* (Vol. 1, pp. 194–202). Thousand Oaks, CA: SAGE.

Guskey, T. R. (2010). Lessons of mastery learning. *Educational Leadership, 68*(2), 52–57.

Guskey, T. R., & Bailey, J. M. (2001). *Developing grading and reporting systems for student learning.* Thousand Oaks, CA: Corwin Press.

Hallinger, P. (2012). *School leadership that makes a difference: Lessons from 30 years of international research.* Accessed at www.utsbasilicata.it/attachments/article/810/03a _Leadership_21st_century_schools[1].pdf on January 19, 2018.

Hallinger, P., & Murphy, J. (1985). Assessing the instructional management behavior of principals. *Elementary School Journal, 86*(2), 217–247.

Hoy, W. K. (2002). Faculty trust: A key to student achievement. *Journal of School Public Relations, 23*(2), 88–103.

Hoy, W. K., & Miskel, C. (2005). *Educational administration: Theory, research, and practice* (7th ed.). Boston: McGraw-Hill.

Hoy, W. K., Tarter, C. J., & Hoy, A. W. (2006a). Academic optimism of schools: A force for student achievement. *American Educational Research Journal, 43*(3), 425–446. doi: 10.3102/00028312043003425

Hoy, W. K., Tarter, C. J., & Hoy, A. W. (2006b). Academic optimism of schools: A second-order confirmatory factor analysis. In W. K. Hoy & C. Miskel (Eds.), *Contemporary issues in educational policy and school outcomes* (pp. 135–156). Greenwich, CT: Information Age.

Kanevsky, L., & Keighley, T. (2003). To produce or not to produce? Understanding boredom and the honor in underachievement. *Roeper Review, 26*(1), 20–28.

Kulik, C-L. C., Kulik, J. A., & Bangert-Drowns, R. L. (1990). Effectiveness of mastery learning programs: A meta-analysis. *Review of Educational Research, 60*(2), 265–299.

Littky, D. (2004). *The big picture: Education is everyone's business.* Alexandria, VA: Association for Supervision and Curriculum Development.

Martin, A. J., & Liem, G. A. D. (2010). Academic personal bests (PBs), engagement, and achievement: A cross-lagged panel analysis. *Learning and Individual Differences, 20*(3), 265–270.

Marzano, R. J. (2007). *The art and science of teaching: A comprehensive framework for effective instruction.* Alexandria, VA: Association for Supervision and Curriculum Development.

Marzano, R. J. (2017). *The new art and science of teaching.* Bloomington, IN: Solution Tree Press.

Marzano, R. J., Norford, J. S., Finn, M., & Finn, D., III. (2017). *A handbook for personalized competency-based education.* Bloomington, IN: Marzano Resources.

Marzano, R. J., Warrick, P. B., & Simms, J. A. (2014). *A handbook for high reliability schools: The next step in school reform.* Bloomington, IN: Marzano Resources.

Marzano, R. J., Waters, T., & McNulty, B. A. (2005). *School leadership that works: From research to results*. Alexandria, VA: Association for Supervision and Curriculum Development.

National Education Commission on Time and Learning. (2000). *Prisoners of time: Too much to teach, not enough time to teach it*. Peterborough, NH: Crystal Springs Books.

Pink, D. H. (2009). *Drive: The surprising truth about what motivates us*. New York: Penguin.

Priest, N., Rudenstine, A., Weisstein, E., & Gerwin, C. (2012). *Making mastery work: A close-up view of competency education*. Quincy, MA: Nellie Mae Education Foundation.

Renzulli, J. S. (1978). What makes giftedness? Reexamining a definition. *Phi Delta Kappan, 60*(3), 180–184, 261.

Renzulli, J. S. (2008). Engagement is the answer. *Education Week, 27*(43), 30–31.

Ruyle, M., O'Neil, T., Iberlin, J., Evans, & Midles, R. (2019). *Leading the evolution: How to make personalized competency-based education a reality*. Bloomington, IN: Marzano Resources.

Virginia Department of Education. (2004). *Virginia drive to strengthen school leadership wins additional funding from the Wallace Foundation: Effective leadership is key to raising student achievement* [Press release]. Accessed at www.doe.virginia.gov/VDOE /NewHome/pressreleases/2004/apr26.html on June 12, 2018.

Mike Mattos

Mike Mattos is an internationally recognized author, presenter, and practitioner who specializes in uniting teachers, administrators, and support staff to transform schools by implementing response to intervention (RTI) and professional learning communities (PLCs). Mattos cocreated the RTI at Work model, which builds on the foundation of the PLC at Work process by using team structures and a focus on learning, collaboration, and results to drive successful outcomes.

He is former principal of Marjorie Veeh Elementary School and Pioneer Middle School in California. At both schools, Mattos helped create powerful PLCs, improving learning for all students. In 2004, Marjorie Veeh, which has a large population of youth at risk, won the California Distinguished School and National Title I Achieving School awards.

To learn more about Mattos's work, follow @mikemattos65 on Twitter.

To book Mike Mattos for professional development, contact pd@SolutionTree.com.

In this chapter, Mike Mattos explores the skills and behaviors students need for college and career readiness, shows how PLCs support the acquisition of these skills, and digs deeper into each of the level 5 HRS indicators, considering how a PLC school would interpret and implement these outcomes.

Chapter 10

Preparation for Tomorrow: A Competency-Based Focus and PLCs

Mike Mattos

The previous chapters of this book focus on how the PLC at Work process is the best way to effectively implement the proven indicators of the HRS model. Yet becoming a PLC—or a certified HRS—is not the goal, but the means to a much more important end. The fundamental purpose of school is to ensure all students acquire the essential academic skills, knowledge, and behaviors they need to become self-sufficient adults and responsible citizens. This higher goal drives the work of a PLC and guides each HRS level. A school staff can work collaboratively and embrace HRS practices, but unless students are learning the skills necessary for their future success, the school has failed to achieve its primary mission. Harvard University professor David N. Perkins (2014) captures this point with a simple, straightforward question: Is what a student is learning likely to matter in the life of the learner and to his or her future?

> A school staff can work collaboratively and embrace HRS practices, but unless students are learning the skills necessary for their future success, the school has failed to achieve its primary mission.

Historically, teachers have been in the perfect position to answer this question. Unlike people in most careers, educators begin their professional apprenticeship in kindergarten (Lortie, 1975). Teachers successfully navigate the traditional educational system, first learning the skills and dispositions they need to succeed in school, and then mastering the content knowledge and specialized training necessary to become professional educators. Who would be better prepared to guide students through the labyrinth of school than those who have already mastered the maze? Yet today's educators face a challenging dilemma; they must prepare students to succeed in the 21st century, while they experienced school—and were prepared to succeed—in the previous century. Due to rapid advances in technology, our world has changed radically and permanently, as have the academic skills and behaviors required for future success.

> Due to rapid advances in technology, our world has changed radically and permanently, as have the academic skills and behaviors required for future success.

Preparing Students for Yesterday

What academic skills and behaviors did students need to prepare for the 20th century? Because most Americans worked on farms or in factories, fewer than 20 percent of all jobs required even a high school diploma (Hagenbaugh, 2002). Consequently, the required academic skills and behaviors for labor-intensive jobs represented three foundational learning outcomes.

1. **Basic academic skills:**

    + *Reading*—The ability to decode and comprehend text

    + *Writing*—Spelling, penmanship, and the basic grammar required to write notes and letters

    + *Mathematics*—Addition, subtraction, multiplication, division, fractions, decimals, and percentages

    + *English*—The ability to speak and communicate in the English language

2. **Content knowledge:** Basic knowledge in history, geography, and science

3. **Social behaviors:**

    + Follow directions and stay on task.

+ Use appropriate language.

+ Respect property and materials.

+ Attend school regularly and be on time.

These foundational learning outcomes—which historically composed much of the curriculum in the primary grades of elementary school—represented *all* the academic competencies most students needed to become self-sufficient adults and responsible citizens in the 19th and 20th centuries.

Because a grammar-school education was sufficient for most students, secondary schools were established as selective institutions, "catering to the relatively few students who had the interest and the means to attend school after the primary grades" (Rumberger, 2011, p. 21). As Harvard University president Charles Eliot advocated to Congress in 1893:

> The main function (of high school) is to prepare for the duties of life that small proportion of all the children in the country—a proportion small in number, but very important to the welfare of the nation—who show themselves able to profit by an education prolonged to the eighteenth year, and whose parents are able to support them while they remain in school so long. (as cited in Dorn, 1996, p. 36)

Translated frankly, high school was for white boys from wealthy families. Most women and minorities were not allowed a formal education at that time, and very few families could afford to have their adolescent sons not work. This philosophy became reality, as only 14 percent of children fourteen to seventeen years old attended high school at the beginning of the 20th century (Rumberger, 2011). While the percentage of America's youth attending high school increased dramatically throughout the 20th century, the expectation remained that not all students would need a high school diploma, and even fewer would need postsecondary training. Those fortunate enough to attend secondary school competed to secure admittance to college. Educational practices designed to rank student achievement were developed, such as the hundred-point scale and grading on a curve. Lower-achieving students were encouraged—or forced—to drop out, leaving the highest-achieving students best prepared for the academic rigors of top universities.

This traditional K–12 school system is not only the system most educators experienced as students; they became part of the "proportion small in number" that actually excelled and earned postsecondary degrees. If most of today's students planned to make a living off the land or on an assembly line, replicating this system would make sense. But considering that less than 2 percent of the United States' workforce directly farms (Hagenbaugh, 2002), and less than 10 percent works in factories (U.S. Department of Agriculture, n.d.), educators are now preparing students for a markedly different future.

Educators are now preparing students for a markedly different future.

Preparing Students for Tomorrow

Are the foundational skills, content knowledge, and social behaviors of the 20th century still important and relevant for 21st century students? Of course. Students still must learn how to decode and comprehend text, apply number sense, write effectively, have basic content knowledge, and display appropriate social behaviors.

These outcomes are still essential, but also woefully insufficient to academically prepare students for their adult lives. In the 21st century, robotics and machinery provide most of the labor in agriculture and industry, so technology, innovation, and service jobs drive the economy. These careers predominantly require higher levels of education. A Georgetown University study estimates that by 2020, 65 percent of all jobs in the United States will require postsecondary education and training beyond high school (Carnevale, Smith, & Strohl, 2013). The study also projects occupations that typically require a master's degree for entry to grow the fastest, followed by occupations that require associate's degrees and doctorates or professional degrees (Bureau of Labor Statistics, 2013). In 2018, nine of ten new jobs in the United States went to people with a college degree, a finding that shows the American economy's growing reliance on a trained workforce (Goldstein, 2018).

While there remains a demand for jobs requiring vocational training, technological advances are also impacting these careers. An ACT (2006) study examining mathematics and reading skills required for electricians, construction workers, upholsterers, and plumbers concludes these skills match the skills necessary to do well in first-year college courses. Additionally, wages for careers that require higher levels of education and training will outpace wages for other jobs, with the average college graduate earning 77 percent more than the typical high school graduate (Bureau of Labor Statistics, 2013). So not only will the elementary school–level foundational learning be insufficient to prepare students for most careers, but also a high school diploma will not be enough. As the American Diploma Project (2004) states:

> No longer do students planning to work after high school need a different and less rigorous curriculum than those planning to go to college. In fact, nearly all students will require some postsecondary education, including on-the-job training, after completing high school. Therefore, a college and workplace readiness curriculum should be a graduation requirement, not an option, for all high school students. (pp. 8–9)

Or as the Cohen professor of holocaust and genocide studies at Keene State College James Waller (1998) states more candidly, a high school diploma has become a ticket to nowhere. When students graduate from high school, their diplomas must represent more than time served and credits earned. Instead, their diplomas must certify these students mastered the skills and behaviors required to continue to learn throughout their adult lives.

Diplomas must certify these students mastered the skills and behaviors required to continue to learn throughout their adult lives.

Developing Skills and Behaviors for College and Career Readiness

If all students must leave the K–12 system college and career ready, then what specific academic skills and behaviors are likely to matter in the future? According to the RAND study *The 21st Century at Work: Forces Shaping the Future Workforce and Workplace in the United States*:

> Rapid technological change and increased international competition place the spotlight on the skills and preparation of the workforce, particularly the ability to adapt to changing technologies and shifting product demand. Shifts in the

nature of business organizations and the growing importance of knowledge-based work also favor strong non-routine cognitive skills, such as abstract reasoning, problem solving, communication, and collaboration. Within this context, education and training become a continuous process throughout the life course involving training and retraining that continues well past initial entry into the labor market. . . . We can expect a shift away from more permanent, lifetime jobs toward less permanent, even nonstandard employment relationships. (Karoly & Panis, 2004, p. xiv)

This means in addition to traditional foundational skills, students must—first and foremost—develop higher-level-thinking skills. In the 21st century world, there is no longer a competitive advantage in knowing more than the person next to you because knowledge is a commodity available to all with the swipe of a finger. Now, adults must be able to ask great questions, critically analyze information, form independent opinions, collaborate, and communicate effectively. These are the skills essential for both career and citizenship (Wagner & Dintersmith, 2016). University of Oregon professor David T. Conley (2007) recommends the critical higher-level-thinking skills for college and career readiness in figure 10.1.

Students must—first and foremost—develop higher-level-thinking skills.

These critical thinking skills should be transdisciplinary—and not only taught in one subject, course, or specific year in school. Transdisciplinary skills create impact across disciplines and are relevant for students in life beyond school (Stuart, Heckmann, Mattos, & Buffum, 2018). This greater focus on thinking skills does not mean content knowledge in specific subjects is unimportant. Being able to think critically about a topic or solve a problem in a particular domain demands sufficient background knowledge. And an important aspect of creativity is making connections across domains of knowledge—something impossible to do unless the person knows enough in different domains to make such a connection (Jerald, 2009).

Content knowledge taught in isolation and primarily at a comprehension level is not enough to properly prepare students for the academic demands of postsecondary education and the global economy.

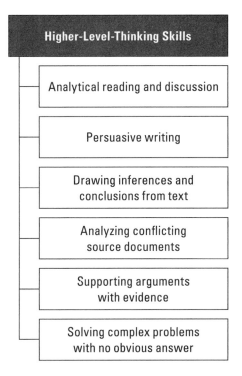

Source: Conley, 2007.

Figure 10.1: Critical higher-level-thinking skills for college and career readiness.

The point is, content knowledge taught in isolation and primarily at a comprehension level is not enough to properly prepare students for the academic demands of postsecondary education and the global economy.

Academic Behaviors

In addition to traditional social behaviors that focus primarily on demonstrating respectful and safe conduct, there are academic behaviors critical to developing a successful learner (see figure 10.2, page 284).

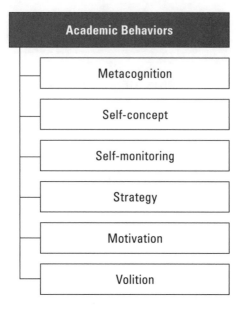

Source: Jerald, 2009.

Figure 10.2: Academic behaviors critical to developing a successful learner.

Academic behaviors are transdisciplinary skills built on foundational learning and taught across the curriculum and grade levels.

These behaviors are essential to a student's ability to develop self-efficacy, take responsibility for his or her learning, and become a true lifelong learner. Like higher-level-thinking skills, academic behaviors are transdisciplinary skills built on foundational learning and taught across the curriculum and grade levels.

- **Metacognition:** Knowledge and beliefs about thinking
- **Self-concept:** A student's belief in his or her abilities
- **Self-monitoring:** The ability to plan and prepare for learning
- **Strategy:** Techniques for organization and memorization of knowledge
- **Motivation:** The ability to initiate and maintain interest in tasks
- **Volition:** The efforts and techniques needed to stay motivated and engaged in learning

Students who transition to postsecondary education without these behaviors often struggle, not because they lack the academic ability, but because they do not consistently demonstrate the organizational skills or self-discipline to succeed. Academic behaviors are equally important in the 21st century workplace. Due to an ever-increasing competitive global economy, successful businesses have moved from a costly, hierarchical leadership structure characterized by layers of management to a more "flattened" organizational structure in which employees are expected to take much greater responsibility for managing their work (Jerald, 2009). While educators acknowledge that many students struggle because they lack these academic behaviors, most teachers do not explicitly or systematically teach them. Instead, traditional schools often expect students to learn academic behaviors at home, or they think that students should intrinsically possess them.

Collaboration

Although the 21st century workplace requires employees to take greater personal responsibility, this does not mean these employees will work in isolation. Quite the contrary; the result of a flattened work structure is a greater reliance on project-based teams to achieve organization goals. And due to advances in technology (including social media), the concept of a team is not limited to proximity or locale. As author Thomas L. Friedman (2005) writes in his book *The World Is Flat*, "Suddenly more people from more different places could collaborate with more other people on more different kinds of work and share more different kinds of knowledge than ever before" (p. 194).

It would be difficult to design an environment more misaligned to adult and student collaboration than the 20th century classroom. Traditionally, students would sit in rows, most staring at the backs of their classmates around them. For most instruction, teachers would expect students to sit silently, with little interaction with the teacher or one another. Likewise, educators worked mostly in the isolation of their own classrooms. It is extremely difficult to prepare students for a collaborative workplace in an educational system where profes-

It would be difficult to design an environment more misaligned to adult and student collaboration than the 20th century classroom.

sionals work in isolation and each student works in the solitary confinement of his or her own assigned classroom desk.

Working collaboratively requires transdisciplinary academic skills and behaviors. The ability to collectively problem solve, analyze, infer, and persuade is different from applying the same higher-level-thinking skills independently. At the same time, successful collaboration depends on each individual displaying appropriate behaviors. Teachers must explicitly teach and students must practice these behaviors to properly prepare to work in a team environment.

Lifelong Learning

In the 20th century, it was common for adults to retire from their original profession entered in adulthood—in many cases, retiring from the same company. In the 21st century workplace, students will have not a job or a career, but jobs and careers. According to *The New American Workplace* (O'Toole & Lawler, 2006), the increasing speed of technology change, growing sophistication of foreign competitors, export of manufacturing jobs, and downsizing of the workforce (due to pressure to increase profits) amount to an almost perfect storm, creating an ever-increasing need for workers to update their skills regularly and often to develop entirely new skills. Earning a post-secondary degree or certificate will mark not the end of a student's learning, but merely a prerequisite to join a profession.

Subsequent learning may require students to earn additional formal degrees and certificates or engage in self-guided study. This means students must leave the K–12 system with the ability to direct their own learning. As coauthors Michael Fullan and Maria Langworthy (2014) note, the goal is not only to master content knowledge; it is to master the learning process. Learning to learn requires students to define their own learning goals and success criteria; monitor their own learning; critically examine their own work; incorporate feedback from peers, teachers, and parents; and use all of this information to deepen their awareness of how to function in the learning process.

This means students must leave the K–12 system with the ability to direct their own learning.

While many schools and districts declare in their mission statement the goal to develop lifelong learners, very few have clearly defined the specific skills and behaviors their students must master to actually achieve this outcome. In *Personalized Learning in a Professional Learning Community at Work: Student Agency Through the Four Critical Questions* (Stuart et al., 2018), my coauthors and I advocate the key to creating true lifelong learners is through designing curriculum that allows students to personalize their learning and develop student agency.

Stuart et al. (2018) define personalization in two ways.

1. **Learning progressions:** Students should progress through essential disciplinary outcomes by accelerating and decelerating their rate of learning based on their learning needs.

2. **Learning pathways:** Schools should provide the opportunity for students to pursue their interests and passions.

These two outcomes are the driving indicators at level 5 of the HRS model.

To lead their own learning, students must also develop *student agency*—a student's ability to take specific and purposeful action to impact his or her level of success (Stuart et al., 2018). Young people with high levels of agency do not respond passively to their circumstances; they tend to seek meaning and act with purpose to achieve the conditions they desire in their own and others' lives. Developing student agency may be as important as the skills teachers measure with standardized testing (Ferguson, 2015).

Facing a Daunting Task

So, the defining characteristics of the 21st century workplace are as follows.

- A premium on higher-level-thinking skills and postsecondary achievement

- Self-regulated working conditions

- Collaboration

- Continuous learning and adaptation

Figure 10.3 (page 288) shows a diagram of essential academic skills, knowledge, and behaviors all students must master to be college and career ready.

Transdisciplinary Skills

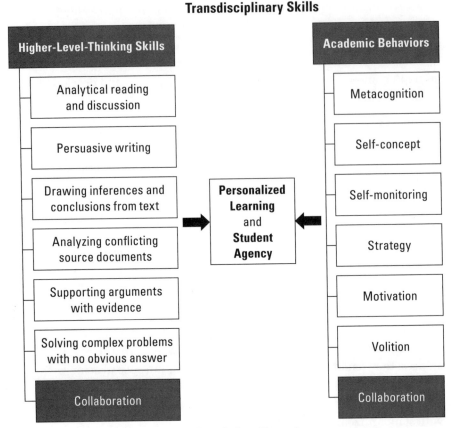

Foundational Learning:
Basic Academic Skills, Content Knowledge, and Social Behaviors

Source for skills and behaviors: Conley, 2007; Jerald, 2009.

Figure 10.3: The essential academic skills, knowledge, and behaviors all students must master to be college and career ready.

This graphic (see figure 10.3) is intended to be not *the* definitive list of 21st century skills and behaviors students must master for future success, but rather a research-based beginning point to guide discussion on the ultimate goal of educators striving to implement PLC and HRS practices. Focusing on these learning outcomes will impact how a school organizes collaborative teams, plans instruction, prioritizes curriculum, and assesses students to ensure they leave the K–12 system college and career ready.

While these expectations are rigorous, they are probably not new to most educators. Teaching higher-level-thinking skills has been prevalent for decades, from the introduction of Bloom's taxonomy (Bloom, 1956) to Webb's Depth of Knowledge (Webb, 2012). Almost every high school has college preparatory and advanced placement coursework to prepare students for university study. I remember in the 1990s, my wife—a fellow classroom teacher at the time—attended a cooperative learning conference and applied many of the structures and strategies in her classroom. As a teacher, I received a supplemental authorization to teach gifted and talented students. The curriculum and instructional practices focused primarily on providing students voice and choice in their learning, along with interdisciplinary and collaborative projects focused on solving problems and applying what they learned to real-life situations. Allowing some students to accelerate through the curriculum at a faster rate, and potentially graduate early, is not uncommon. And many schools have created schoolwide processes to teach and reinforce essential behaviors, utilizing research-based recommendations such as positive behavioral interventions and supports (PBIS), or programs such as Character Counts (https://character counts.org).

The problem is that most schools have not systematically and purposefully provided these expectations and opportunities to *all* students. Instead, these rigorous learning outcomes have been offered almost exclusively to the students deemed most capable—which disproportionately have been students from more affluent homes—or have been provided randomly based on the personal discretion of administrators and teachers. The challenge for 21st century educators is that every student needs to master these skills and behaviors to have a realistic chance to succeed as an adult. Undoubtedly, achieving this goal will require educators to abandon the ranking and tracking policies they successfully navigated when they were students, and instead work collaboratively to rethink their instruction, curriculum, assessment, and intervention practices.

> *The challenge for 21st century educators is that every student needs to master these skills and behaviors to have a realistic chance to succeed as an adult.*

Preparing Students for Tomorrow Instead of Yesterday

How does a school ensure every student masters the rigorous skills, knowledge, and behaviors needed to be college and career ready? The following elements must be in place.

1. **A collaborative culture:** Students can't learn the 21st century transdisciplinary skills in an individual teacher's classroom, a specific subject, or a single school year. Instead, mastery requires a highly collaborative culture, a concept captured in the second big idea of the PLC at Work process (DuFour, DuFour, Eaker, Many, & Mattos, 2016), and level 1 of the HRS model—a safe, supportive, and collaborative culture (Marzano, Warrick, Rains, & DuFour, 2018). This collaboration requires more than traditional grade-level or subject-specific team meetings. Interdisciplinary and vertical collaboration is needed to teach skills and behaviors across the curriculum and from year to year.

2. **Effective teaching:** In addition to working collaboratively, educators must apply effective teaching in every classroom—level 2 of the HRS model (Marzano et al., 2018). Effective instruction requires an expectation for all teachers to use practices proven to have the greatest impact on student learning, while simultaneously infusing their own style and offering differentiated instruction for individual student needs. The key to achieving this outcome lies in identifying and leveraging the right practices—the best practices for the kind of instruction all students must receive, regardless of what teachers they are assigned for core instruction (Gregory, Kaufeldt, & Mattos, 2016).

   Based on his synthesis of over eight hundred meta-analyses of the factors that most positively impact student learning, renowned researcher John Hattie (2009) asserts a school can improve student learning using the following four best collective practices.

   a. Teachers must work collaboratively rather than in isolation.

   b. Teachers must agree on the essential learning all students must acquire.

   c. Teachers must agree on how students will demonstrate their learning.

   d. Teachers must assess their individual and collective effectiveness based on evidence of student learning.

Teacher teams—working in a PLC—best achieve these most effective teaching practices when focusing their collaboration on the four critical questions of the PLC at Work process (DuFour et al., 2016).

    a. What do we want students to learn?

    b. How do we know if students are learning?

    c. How will we respond when students don't learn?

    d. How do we extend learning for students who are already proficient?

A continuous, collaborative focus on these four critical questions also provides teachers with job-embedded staff development to improve their individual and collective practices (DuFour et al., 2016). If the 21st century workplace requires employees to continuously learn and update their skills, professional educators working in the 21st century must do the same.

3. **A guaranteed and viable curriculum focused on the learning likely to matter in the life and future of the learner:** Many schools have started to implement the highly effective practices the PLC process and HRS model advocate. But when determining what all students must learn—level 3 of the HRS model—they mistakenly focus mostly on traditional foundational learning outcomes and content knowledge. The pressure of teaching to high-stakes standardized tests exasperates this problem; these tests are primarily in a multiple-choice format that cannot effectively measure the higher-level-thinking skills and personalized goals of 21st century learning. These schools are implementing highly effective teaching practices, but teachers are not teaching students the learning-progressive outcomes critical to their future (Stuart et al., 2018). A school system dedicated to ensuring every student is college and career ready must focus on the transdisciplinary skills and behaviors required to achieve this outcome.

4. **Assessment practices that monitor each student's progress on every guaranteed learning outcome:** Because the goal is to ensure all students master the essential skills, knowledge, and behaviors required for future success, monitoring each

student's learning in relation to these outcomes is also required. In place of traditional grading practices (the accumulation of points, grading on a curve, and using averages), learning-progressive schools should adopt standards-referenced grading practices—the focus of level 4 of the HRS model. The PLC literature captures this same approach by monitoring student learning by name and by need (DuFour et al., 2016), kid by kid, skill by skill (Eaker & Keating, 2015), and by student and by standard (Buffum, Mattos, & Malone, 2018).

5. **Student ownership of his or her own learning:** The first four levels of the HRS model are educator driven—the adults on campus work collaboratively to determine what students must learn, how to best teach these standards, and how to best assess students. Likewise, the PLC process has educators—the adults on campus—work collaboratively to answer the four critical questions about student learning. But if the ultimate goal is to ensure every student becomes a lifelong learner, there must be a systematic progression from teacher-driven instruction to student-driven learning. This transition is how a school creates true lifelong learners. Achieving this outcome requires students to develop student agency skills and teachers to give students opportunities to guide their own learning through personalized pathways and progressions. These outcomes are the primary focus of HRS level 5: competency-based education (Marzano et al., 2018).

Once a school truly commits to preparing every student to be college and career ready, this mission frames the work of a PLC and connects all five levels of the HRS model.

It is important to note, once a school truly commits to preparing every student to be college and career ready, this mission frames the work of a PLC and connects all five levels of the HRS model. These outcomes provide context and purpose to the work, and leaders must continuously reference and reconsider them when implementing PLC practices and HRS indicators. Likewise, many schools trying to implement personalized learning have not built the collaborative structures, instructional practices, guaranteed curriculum, and assessment practices necessary for success. The last step—level 5—is not created in isolation, but instead is built using the PLC process and the foundation of the four previous HRS levels.

Digging Deeper Into Level 5

Level 5 of the HRS model has three leading indicators (Marzano et al., 2018).

5.1: Students move on to the next level of the curriculum for any subject area only after they have demonstrated competency at the previous level.

5.2: The school schedule accommodates students moving at a pace appropriate to their situation and needs.

5.3: The school affords students who have demonstrated competency levels greater than those articulated in the system immediate opportunities to begin work on advanced content or career paths of interest.

Let's dig deeper into each of these indicators, and consider how a PLC would interpret and implement these outcomes.

Leading Indicator 5.1

This indicator directly relates to the fourth critical question of a PLC: How will we extend learning for students who are already proficient? (DuFour et al., 2016). Answering this question is also the entry point to the essential college- and career-readiness goal of personalized learning. As mentioned earlier, one way to provide students with personalized learning opportunities is through the creation of learning progressions, which allow students to progress through essential learning outcomes by accelerating and decelerating their rate of learning based on their learning needs. Achieving this outcome begins with teacher teams answering the first and second PLC critical questions.

1. What do we want students to learn? (HRS level 3; DuFour et al., 2016; Marzano et al., 2018)

2. How will we know if students are learning? (HRS level 4; DuFour et al., 2016; Marzano et al., 2018)

In the PLC at Work process, collaborative teacher teams are formed based on shared essential curriculum. Most commonly, these are grade-level teams at the elementary level, and subject- or course-specific teams at the secondary level. These teams take lead responsibility for the following.

1. Identifying the absolutely essential academic content standards all students must master for their grade level or course

2. Teaching the team-identified essential learning outcomes

3. Gathering evidence of learning for each student on the essential standards, and using these data to reflect on the effectiveness of their individual and collective teaching

4. Leading interventions when students struggle on the essential standards, and extending learning when students achieve mastery

If students are to progress through the essential curriculum at differing rates, there must also be vertical collaboration and articulation across disciplinary teams. This means in addition to disciplinary teams, the school should form logical vertical and transdisciplinary teams to identify the essential cross-disciplinary and multiyear skills and behaviors all students must master for future success. These teams could take many different forms, based on the size of the school, student needs, and the school's level of competency in the PLC process. As *Personalized Learning in a PLC at Work* (Stuart et al., 2018) recommends, transdisciplinary team structures include the following.

> *If students are to progress through the essential curriculum at differing rates, there must also be vertical collaboration and articulation across disciplinary teams.*

- **Vertical teams:** Vertical teams consist of team members spanning multiple grade levels, and they focus on identifying skills and behaviors taught over years of schooling. For example, drawing inferences and conclusions is a higher-level-thinking skill taught not in a single grade, but rather across multiple years. Determining a common vocabulary, a progression of specific rigor expectations, proficiency-scaled common assessments, and targeted interventions and extensions drives the work of these teams.

- **Interdisciplinary teams:** Like vertical teams, these teams identify essential skills stretching across subjects. For example, educators can teach *argumentation*, an essential skill, across disciplines. These teams also determine a common vocabulary, a progression of specific rigor expectations, proficiency-scaled common assessments, and targeted interventions and extensions.

- **Task force:** A task force convenes for a specific transdisciplinary topic, such as determining essential schoolwide academic and social behaviors. For example, some schools have successfully created a school task force made up of cross-grade or cross-disciplinary team members to study essential academic behaviors. This team identifies these skills, determines a common vocabulary, identifies specific rigor expectations, develops assessments to monitor student progress, and leads interventions and extensions.

- **Full faculty:** Faculty meetings can engage the entire staff in applying the four critical questions of a PLC to transdisciplinary skills and behaviors.

As transdisciplinary teams identify essential skills and behaviors, it is important to share these learning outcomes with disciplinary teams so teachers can use their course-specific content as a vehicle to teach essential transdisciplinary skills and behaviors. To this end, it is likely for faculty members to be members of both disciplinary and transdisciplinary teams.

This is a critical point. In a PLC, each teacher team is *not* "a PLC." Instead, the entire organization is the PLC. So, if a school is implementing PLC practices, the entire school is a PLC. If a district commits to the process, the entire district

It is likely for faculty members to be members of both disciplinary and transdisciplinary teams.

is the PLC. This also means the entire PLC takes collective responsibility for each student's success. This collective approach is critical to achieving indicator 5.1 and the HRS learning progressions. It is likely some students will master grade-level essential curriculum before the end of the school year. These students demonstrated competency at the previous level and are now ready to move to the next level of curriculum. It is unrealistic to expect an individual teacher, instructing only his or her assigned students for the entire school year, to differentiate instruction to effectively teach many levels at once. Likewise, it is unlikely a grade-level or course-specific team can achieve this just by sharing students with other team members. Instead, the staff must create a collaborative, collective culture in which students can be regrouped flexibly—most likely across grades—to provide systematic opportunities to extend and accelerate student learning. This outcome is difficult to achieve if each teacher team views itself as an independent PLC, responsible only for the students assigned to that team. Many PLC schools are successfully answering the four critical questions *within* each teacher team, but are not answering these questions across the entire PLC. The HRS leading and lagging indicators, especially at levels 4 and 5, help drive a PLC toward these system-wide outcomes.

Finally, as teacher teams identify essential standards, define learning progressions, and create proficiency scales, they must also set benchmarks and time lines for student progress. While students can move through the curriculum at their own pace, schools ultimately have students for a finite amount of time—for most students, this is thirteen years in a K–12 system. If a student's learning pace slows to a point where it is unlikely he or she will be college and career ready by the end of grade 12, then he or she is more likely on track to become a high school dropout. Creating benchmarks along the way will help educators know if a student needs additional time and support to increase his or her rate of learning—one of the goals of indicator 5.2.

> *Finally, as teacher teams identify essential standards, define learning progressions, and create proficiency scales, they must also set benchmarks and time lines for student progress.*

Leading Indicator 5.2

HRS leading indicator 5.2 states that the school schedule accommodates students moving at a pace appropriate to their situation and needs (Marzano et al., 2018). It is both a proven fact and a universal truth in education that all students do not learn the same way or at the same speed (Bloom, 1968; Buffum, Mattos, & Weber, 2012a; Guskey & Pigott, 1988). If we condensed these two universal truths into a simple formula to ensure student learning, the equation would look like this:

$$\text{Targeted Instruction} + \text{Time} = \text{Learning}$$

If a school makes both teaching and time variables in this equation and targets them to meet each student's individual learning and developmental needs, the school can help struggling students master essential curriculum and, at the same time, provide acceleration and extension opportunities for students who have reached benchmark learning goals. A PLC captures this need through the third and fourth critical questions (DuFour et al., 2016).

3. How will we respond when students don't learn?

4. How will we extend learning for students who are already proficient?

The key word in each PLC question is the pronoun *we*. Expecting each individual teacher to differentiate instruction in his or her own classroom—primarily through the use of in-classroom flexible groupings to meet individual student needs—has proven insufficient at best. Hattie's (2009) meta-analysis of flexible in-class regrouping finds an effectiveness impact of 0.18 effect size, which is hardly better than the 0.10 effect size of students not attending school at all. Instead, schools must create a schoolwide, systematic process to provide students with additional time and support to reteach and extend learning.

When creating such a system, it is absolutely critical for staff to keep their focus on the fundamental purpose of school—to ensure all students leave the K–12 system college and career ready. At many schools, staff could interpret the statement *the school schedule accommodates students moving at a pace appropriate to their situation and needs* to justify the continued use of tracking or ability-grouping students. Few practices in education have a more detrimental impact on youth at risk. As presidential professor emeritus in educational equity at the University of California, Los Angeles, Jeannie Oakes (2005) finds in her landmark study:

> *When creating such a system, it is absolutely critical for staff to keep their focus on the fundamental purpose of school—to ensure all students leave the K–12 system college and career ready.*

The deep structure of tracking remains uncannily robust. Most middle and high schools still sort students into classes at different levels based on judgments of students' "ability." This sorting continues to disadvantage those in lower-track classes. Such students have less access to high-status knowledge, fewer opportunities to engage in stimulating learning activities, and classroom relationships less likely to foster engagement with teachers, peers, and learning. (p. xi)

Hattie (2009) finds ability grouping to have minimal effects on student learning (producing just a 0.12 standard deviation increase), but at the same time, it can have profoundly negative effects on equity, as students perceived to have the lowest ability are most often minorities, English learners, and students from poverty.

To address this concern, an effective and equitable system of interventions and extensions must achieve four outcomes (Stuart et al., 2018).

1. **Students must have access to essential curriculum as part of their instruction:** This chapter began by clearly defining the skills, knowledge, and behaviors all students need to be college and career ready. A student cannot learn these skills if he or she is in tracks of learning that do not address this level of rigor. This means in a PLC, there should not be a less-rigorous, remedial track of learning for students educators deem less capable. The one exception might be for students who are profoundly disabled; educators might individualize their curricular goals based on each student's cognitive needs and independence level.

2. **Schools must embed flexible time within the school day:** Because all students do not learn the same way or at the same speed, flexible time provides students support in learning the essential skills, knowledge, and behaviors required for future success. Likewise, teachers can use flexible time to extend and accelerate learning when students master the current core essential curriculum.

   Targeting this time to meet individual student needs will require timely assessment information. The lifeblood of the PLC process is the use of team-created common formative assessments. When these assessments align to the learning progressions and proficiency scales of team-identified essential standards, they provide the information needed to target students for interventions and extensions.

3. **Schools must provide intensive remediation:** Undoubtedly, some students fall behind on an essential learning progression, thus entering the next school year lacking the needed prerequisite skills, knowledge, and behaviors to learn new essential curriculum. Consequently, the school should design the

schedule so those students can receive intensive remediation to catch up on these prior skills and behaviors without missing new essential curriculum.

This is absolutely critical. Indicator 5.1 states students move on to the next level of the curriculum for any subject area only after they demonstrate competency at the previous level. However, schools should not use this outcome to justify retention. The research on retention shows it does not promote higher levels of learning, close achievement gaps, or increase an at-risk student's odds of future success. The most comprehensive meta-analysis on retention finds being retained one year almost doubles a student's likelihood of dropping out, while being retained twice almost guarantees it (Hattie, 2009).

4. **Some students will require all three preceding outcomes:** To learn at high levels, some students will need the following.

   a. Access to new essential curriculum

   b. Interventions to learn this curriculum

   c. Intensive remediation on prior skills

Creating a school schedule that achieves all three outcomes provides a multitiered system of supports (MTSS), also commonly referred to as *response to intervention (RTI)*. A meta-analysis on RTI finds an exceptional average impact rate of 1.27 standard deviation growth in a single school year (Hattie, n.d.). To put this in perspective, a 1.0 standard deviation increase is typically associated with advancing student achievement by two to three grade levels in a single school year (Hattie, 2009).

For examples of schools that have successfully scheduled these levels of support, a helpful resource is the AllThingsPLC website (www .allthingsplc.info). This site lists hundreds of schools as model PLCs.

Leading Indicator 5.3

This indicator—the school affords students who have demonstrated competency levels greater than those articulated in the system immediate opportunities to begin work on advanced content or career paths of interest (Marzano et al., 2018)—captures the ultimate goal of education: ensuring students personalize their own learning and become lifelong learners. As stressed throughout this chapter, this goal must be offered not to only the most gifted students, but instead to *all* students who will someday need to earn a living in the global economy. We cannot achieve equity if some students are denied access to these rigorous expectations.

> *We cannot achieve equity if some students are denied access to these rigorous expectations.*

To frame the same point through the language of the indicator, advanced content and opportunities to explore career paths should be part of the system's articulated goals. These outcomes should include learning progressions and proficiency scales, with the ability for some students to extend their learning beyond proficiency. All students should have access.

As previously mentioned, the key to creating true lifelong learners is through designing a curriculum that allows students to personalize their learning and develop student agency. Schools can teach these outcomes by engaging students in answering the four critical questions revised to reflect the students' perspective (Stuart et al., 2018).

1. What do I want to know, understand, and be able to do?

2. How will I demonstrate I have learned?

3. What will I do when I am not learning?

4. What will I do when I am already proficient?

Due to a lack of foundational knowledge and prior experience, students are at first ill-prepared to guide their own learning. So much like teaching a young adult how to drive, personalized learning must be a systematic process of gradual release. To this end, it is advisable to release the questions to students in reverse order (Stuart et al., 2018).

> *Personalized learning must be a systematic process of gradual release.*

4. **What will I do when I am already proficient?** This question represents extending learning when students master essential curriculum. These students know the essential content and skills, which is a prerequisite to applying what they know to personalized areas of interest, having a greater depth of application, and applying what they know between disciplines. Beginning in the earliest grades, teacher teams can create opportunities for students to have a voice and choice in how to extend their learning.

Following are four practical ways to provide additional challenge to students who master essential disciplinary learning outcomes.

   a. *Voice and choice*—Provide students with freedom to more deeply explore an area of interest within the current content.

   b. *Depth and complexity*—Provide students the option to explore more complex concepts within the existing content.

   c. *Interdisciplinary connections*—Allow students to explore a concept or idea across multiple disciplines.

   d. *Real-world connections*—Provide students with a real-world context for the learning of the existing content.

3. **What will I do when I am not learning?** As students begin to accept responsibility for their learning, educators must teach them how to self-advocate when they need additional time and support to learn essential disciplinary and transdisciplinary skills or extend learning. However, student agency should not place students in a "sink or swim" environment, but instead teach students how to seek help if they begin to struggle.

4. **How will I demonstrate I have learned?** For the next steps in gradual release, students have choice and voice in how they demonstrate their learning of teacher team–determined essential learning outcomes. Teaching students how to do this requires students understand the learning targets and assessment criteria, and self-monitor their learning on all needed skills to reach the ultimate learning goal of answering critical question one.

1. **What do I want to know, understand, and be able to do?** The ultimate goal of HRS indicator 5.3, personalized learning and student agency, is for students to answer this question. Because teachers release the previous three questions first, students have already been "drivers" who have practiced how to apply personal choice to extended learning outcomes, advocate for help when they get stuck, break down learning outcomes into specific learning targets, and assess and monitor their progress. Equally important, the teachers must ensure students master

the essential prerequisite disciplinary and transdisciplinary content and skills first to independently drive their learning.

When educators engage students in their own learning, they are leveraging our profession's most effective teaching practices. As Hattie (2009) states:

> The biggest effects on student learning occur when teachers become learners of their own teaching, and when students become their own teachers. When students become their own teachers they exhibit the self-regulatory attributes that seem most desirable for learners (self-monitoring, self-evaluation, self-assessment, self-teaching). (p. 22)

Undoubtedly, some students will need additional time and support to achieve these outcomes. Personalized learning and student agency do not abdicate educators from taking responsibility for student learning. This is why a school must create flexible time—indicator 5.2—to provide students systematic support to move at a pace appropriate to their situation and needs.

Conclusion

To properly prepare students for a rapidly changing world, educators must shift their focus from producing learned graduates to producing graduates who continue to learn. While most educators attended schools designed to prepare them for the 20th century, this does not exclude them from learning and practicing the skills necessary to succeed in the 21st century. Teachers should work collaboratively, apply higher-level-thinking skills to their craft, display academic behaviors of motivation and volition, and model lifelong learning. That is the very purpose of a PLC—to collaboratively study and apply high reliability practices to improve student learning. By becoming the students we want our students to become, we can better prepare them for their future. Or as writer, poet, musician, and artist Rabindranath Tagore (n.d.) advises, "Don't limit a child to your own learning, for he was born in another time."

References and Resources

ACT. (2006). *Ready for college and ready for work: Same or different?* Iowa City, IA: Author.

American Diploma Project. (2004). *Ready or not: Creating a high school diploma that counts.* Washington, DC: Achieve. Accessed at www.achieve.org/files/ReadyorNot.pdf on March 5, 2014.

Bloom, B. S. (Ed.). (1956). *Taxonomy of educational objectives: The classification of educational goals; Handbook I: Cognitive domain*. New York: McKay.

Bloom, B. S. (1968). Learning for mastery. *Evaluation Comment, 1*(2), 1–12. (ERIC Document Reproduction Service No. ED053419)

Buffum, A., Mattos, M., & Malone, J. (2018). *Taking action: A handbook for RTI at Work*. Bloomington, IN: Solution Tree Press.

Buffum, A., Mattos, M., & Weber, C. (2012a). *Pyramid response to intervention: Four essential guiding principles* [Video]. Bloomington, IN: Solution Tree Press.

Buffum, A., Mattos, M., & Weber, C. (2012b). *Simplifying response to intervention: Four essential guiding principles*. Bloomington, IN: Solution Tree Press.

Bureau of Labor Statistics. (2013). *Education and training outlook for occupations, 2011–22*. Washington, DC: U.S. Department of Labor. Accessed at www.bls.gov/emp/ep_edtrain _outlook.pdf on April 7, 2014.

Carnevale, A. P., Smith, N., & Strohl, J. (2013). *Recovery: Job growth and education requirements through 2020* [PowerPoint slides]. Washington, DC: Georgetown University Center on Education and the Workforce.

Conant, J. B. (1959). *The American high school today: A first report to interested citizens*. New York: McGraw-Hill.

Conley, D. T. (2007, March). *Redefining college readiness*. Eugene, OR: Educational Policy Improvement Center.

Dorn, S. (1996). *Creating the dropout: An institutional and social history of school failure*. Westport, CT: Praeger.

DuFour, R., DuFour, R., Eaker, R., Many, T. W., & Mattos, M. (2016). *Learning by doing: A handbook for Professional Learning Communities at Work* (3rd ed.). Bloomington, IN: Solution Tree Press.

Eaker, R., & Keating, J. (2015). *Kid by kid, skill by skill: Teaching in a Professional Learning Community at Work*. Bloomington, IN: Solution Tree Press.

Ferguson, R. F. (2015, October). *The influence of teaching beyond standardized test scores: Engagement, mindsets, and agency*. Boston: Harvard University.

Friedman, T. L. (2005). *The world is flat: A brief history of the twenty-first century*. New York: Farrar, Straus and Giroux.

Fullan, M., & Langworthy, M. (2014, January). *A rich seam: How new pedagogies find deep learning*. London: Pearson. Accessed at https://michaelfullan.ca/wp-content/uploads/2014 /01/3897.Rich_Seam_web.pdf on September 4, 2019.

Goldstein, S. (2018). Nine out of 10 new jobs are going to those with a college degree. *MarketWatch*. Accessed at www.marketwatch.com/story/nine-out-of-10-new-jobs-are -going-to-those-with-a-college-degree-2018-06-04 on September 15, 2019.

Gregory, G., Kaufeldt, M., & Mattos, M. (2016). *Best practices at tier 1: Daily differentiation for effective instruction, secondary*. Bloomington, IN: Solution Tree Press.

Guskey, T. R., & Pigott, T. D. (1988). Research on group-based mastery learning programs: A meta-analysis. *Journal of Educational Research, 81*(4), 197–216.

Hagenbaugh, B. (2002, December 12). U.S. manufacturing jobs fading away fast. *USA Today.* Accessed at www.usatoday.com/money/economy/2002-12-12-manufacture_x.htm on July 8, 2011.

Hattie, J. (n.d.). *Hattie ranking: 252 influences and effect sizes related to student achievement.* Accessed at https://visible-learning.org/hattie-ranking-influences-effect-sizes-learning -achievement on March 22, 2019.

Hattie, J. (2009). *Visible learning: A synthesis of over 800 meta-analyses relating to achievement.* New York: Routledge.

Hattie, J. (2012). *Visible learning for teachers: Maximizing impact on learning.* New York: Routledge.

Jerald, C. D. (2009, July). *Defining a 21st century education.* Alexandria, VA: Center for Public Education.

Karoly, L. A., & Panis, C. (2004). *The 21st century at work: Forces shaping the future workforce and workplace in the United States.* Santa Monica, CA: RAND.

Lortie, D. C. (1975). *Schoolteacher: A sociological study.* Chicago: University of Chicago Press.

Marzano, R. J., Warrick, P. B., Rains, C. L., & DuFour, R. (2018). *Leading a high reliability school.* Bloomington, IN: Solution Tree Press.

Oakes, J. (2005). *Keeping track: How schools structure inequality* (2nd ed.). New Haven, CT: Yale University Press.

O'Toole, J., & Lawler, E. E., III. (2006). *The new American workplace.* New York: Palgrave Macmillan.

Perkins, D. N. (2014). *Future wise: Educating our children for a changing world.* San Francisco: Jossey-Bass.

Rumberger, R. W. (2011). *Dropping out: Why students drop out of high school and what can be done about it.* Cambridge, MA: Harvard University Press.

Stuart, T. S., Heckmann, S., Mattos, M., & Buffum, A. (2018). *Personalized learning in a PLC at Work: Student agency through the four critical questions.* Bloomington, IN: Solution Tree Press.

Tagore, R. (n.d.). *Goodreads.* Accessed at www.goodreads.com/quotes/125590-don-t-limit-a -child-to-your-own-learning-for-she on September 15, 2019.

U.S. Department of Agriculture, Utah State University Extension, & LetterPress Software. (n.d.). *Growing a nation: The story of American agriculture.* Accessed at www.agclassroom .org/gan/classroom/pdf/embed1_seeds.pdf on July 8, 2011.

Wagner, T., & Dintersmith, T. (2016). *Most likely to succeed: Preparing our kids for the innovation era* [Kindle version]. New York: Scribner.

Waller, J. (1998). *Face to face: The changing state of racism across America.* New York: Insight Books.

Webb, N. L. (2012). *Depth of knowledge and content complexity.* Accessed at www.dmac -solutions.net/files/TAG/DOK/TexasKilgoreDec2012slides.pdf on November 11, 2019.

PART II

Professional Learning Communities, High Reliability Organizations, and School Leadership

Becoming a high reliability school within a PLC at Work requires effective leadership. Although both the HRS model and the PLC process are research-based, proven approaches for successful school improvement, they—like other school-improvement initiatives—cannot overcome weak and ineffective leadership.

While the importance of effective leadership is common sense, what constitutes effective leadership in high reliability schools and PLCs requires a deeper understanding than the mere recognition that effective leadership is important. In the two chapters of this part, the authors address the question, What leadership behaviors would one observe if he or she spent a considerable amount of time in a high reliability school that functions as a PLC?

Philip B. Warrick

Philip B. Warrick, EdD, is an author and consultant and has worked globally in the areas of school leadership, instruction, collaborative practices, and grading. He served for fifteen years as an educational leader in two states. He led school-improvement initiatives in Nebraska at Waverly High School and was named Nebraska High School Principal of the Year in 2005. He also led school-improvement efforts as principal at Round Rock High School in Round Rock, Texas, and was invited to participate as an inaugural member in the Texas Principals Visioning Institute in 2010. Dr. Warrick is a coauthor of *Leading a High Reliability School, A Handbook for High Reliability Schools, A Teacher's Guide to Standards-Based Learning, Collaborative Teams That Transform Schools,* and *A School Leader's Guide to Standards-Based Grading.*

Dr. Warrick earned a bachelor of science from Chadron State College and master's and doctoral degrees from the University of Nebraska–Lincoln.

To learn more about Dr. Warrick's work, follow @pbwarrick on Twitter.

To book Philip B. Warrick for professional development, contact pd@Solution Tree.com.

In this chapter, Dr. Warrick provides a description of school leadership through the lens of the HRS model. He makes the case that leadership from an HRS perspective requires a fundamental shift from viewing effective leadership as the acquisition of a series of personal traits and skills to having a laser-like focus on specific actions with specific outcomes. The effective leader knows what to do to produce specific results across the five levels of the HRS model, and continually collects and analyzes data to those ends, making changes and corrections as the data indicate. He also highlights the use of some high reliability leadership tools.

Chapter 11

High Reliability Leadership

Philip B. Warrick

Three personal and professional beliefs influence my ongoing work in developing high reliability schools and high reliability leadership in schools.

1. Schools are the single most important organizations required to sustain a democracy.

2. The linchpin for a successful school is highly effective leadership.

3. Leadership in schools is more about action than position.

Additionally, two guiding principles continue to drive the development of high reliability leadership. First is practicing the *art of possibility*, which means thinking about what a school can accomplish if it stays focused on the right work, monitors the effectiveness of that work, and strategically sustains the work over time. In their book *The Art of Possibility*, authors Rosamund Stone Zander and Benjamin Zander (2000) address the concept of framing *possibility*:

> It is about restructuring meanings, creating visions, and establishing environments where possibility is spoken—where the buoyant force of possibility overcomes the pull of the downward spiral. The steps to the practice of framing possibility are:
>
> 1. Make a new distinction in the realm of possibility: one that is a powerful substitute for the current framework of meaning that is generating the downward spiral.

308 PLCs AT WORK AND HIGH RELIABILITY SCHOOLS

2. Enter the territory. Embody the new distinction in such a way that it becomes the framework for life around you.

3. Keep distinguishing what is "on the track" and what is "off the track" of your framework for possibility. (p. 163)

The second guiding principle is thinking as a *legacy builder* by considering what the school will be when it is passed on to the educators, students, parents, and community that inherit it in the future. In *Leadership 101*, leadership expert and author John C. Maxwell (2002) identifies five characteristics of leaders who leave a legacy. These leaders do the following.

1. Lead the organization with a long view.

2. Create a leadership culture.

3. Pay the price today to ensure success tomorrow.

4. Value team leadership over individual leadership.

5. Walk away from the organization with integrity.

> The value of the HRS framework and high reliability leadership is they empower leaders to lead their schools with the art of possibility and operate as legacy builders in the process.

While working with many school leaders, both new and experienced, it has become clear to me that the value of the HRS framework and high reliability leadership is they empower leaders to lead their schools with the art of possibility and operate as legacy builders in the process. It is an honor to include a few short testimonials from several high reliability leaders to start this chapter:

> When I first heard about the HRS process, it seemed like a logical, comprehensive process of ensuring best practices were in place, clearly communicated to staff, and regularly revisited for clarity and revision. Putting HRS levels 1–3 into place helped me as campus leader focus on staff collaboration and it also increased teacher leadership and agency. The HRS process is not just a checklist, but it is a road map to campus improvement by building teacher efficacy and resulting in increased student engagement and success.
>
> —Kathy Cawthron, principal, Berkman Elementary Arts Integration Academy, Round Rock, Texas (personal communication, March 11, 2019)

The HRS framework is exceptional for the perpetual development of leadership capacity among all staff when consistency in the instructional process is being shaped by like subject areas or collaborative teams. It supports in-depth analysis and the progression of learning that is necessary but not solely relying on one individual to create and/or implement.

—Mark Roberts, principal, Hall High School, Little Rock, Arkansas (personal communication, March 10, 2019)

The HRS framework is an essential tool for me as a building leader. Our school has been committed to examining and improving processes through the filter of the HRS framework for two years. For us, HRS is not one more thing we are doing, but the guiding framework through which we examine our practices. We are committed to growing our craft and improving student outcomes through the research-based leading indicators that make up the framework.

—Joe Gordy, principal, Graham High School, Graham, Texas (personal communication, March 8, 2019)

The HRS model provides a streamlined, focused, and powerful approach to school improvement and professional development. The surveys provide authentic feedback on where we are as a school with respect to the leading indicators at each level, and the development of and attention to the lagging indicators leads us to targeted work designed to build on our strengths and shore up our weaknesses. However, perhaps the most important element of the overall HRS process is the fact that no certification level can be achieved without the collaboration, buy-in, and ownership of the pieces and processes from the whole staff, which results in the strengthening of teacher leadership, the deep development of teacher efficacy, and the institutionalizing of a common language of improvement and instruction.

—Bill Barnes, principal, Charlotte High School, Charlotte, Michigan (personal communication, March 18, 2019)

This chapter will explain the concept of high reliability leadership, explore the tools and processes for high reliability leadership, and examine the concept of leader accountability using a reflective scale.

The Concept of High Reliability Leadership

The vast body of literature on leadership addresses two aspects of leadership. The first aspect deals with the development of personal characteristics of leaders and how leaders interact with the people they lead—in essence, a leader's ability to understand his or her strengths and talents and leverage those to successfully interact with people and empower them to action. There is no doubt this first aspect is important, and there is a great deal of quality literature about it.

The second aspect of leadership involves the integrity of leadership. This second aspect is required to engage in high reliability leadership. In *Legacy: What the All Blacks Can Teach Us About the Business of Life*, best-selling author James Kerr (2013) addresses and defines the integrity aspect of leadership:

> Integrity comes from the Latin word *integritas* or integer. It means being whole and undivided. It is the ethical "accuracy of our actions."
>
> Integrity means that our thoughts and words and deeds are "as one," a chiropractic alignment in which our core values, purpose, beliefs, and behaviors all flow in the same direction. It's useful to think of integrity not as morality, as many people do, but as *workability*. It is not about being pure or noble—it's about getting stuff done. Though the end result is trust, belief and respect, these are merely the by-products of the fact that when we say something will happen it actually does happen.
>
> This means that others can count on us to deliver. And, most importantly, that we can count on ourselves. (pp. 126–127)

Kerr (2013) additionally offers, "If integrity is a central leadership tool and everyone in a team does exactly what they say they will do, clarity, certainty, productivity, and momentum are the results" (p. 128). This second aspect of leadership is as important—if not more important—to the success of an organization as the first. In *Good to Great and the Social Sectors*, researcher and author Jim Collins (2005) states:

> Every institution has its unique set of irrational and difficult
> constraints, yet some make a leap while others facing the
> same environmental challenges do not. This is perhaps the
> single most important point in all of Good to Great. Greatness
> is not a function of circumstance. Greatness, it turns out, is
> largely a matter of conscious choice and discipline. (p. 31)

The ability to make the conscious choice about what an organization will do and to be disciplined enough to remain focused on that work requires integrity. North Highland Worldwide Consulting (2014) includes organizational integrity in its description of high reliability organizations. The group identifies five aspects of practice for high reliability organizations. These organizations do the following:

- Organize its [sic] efforts to increase the amount and quality of attention to failure and data analysis

- Engage every member and level of the organization in the problem-resolution and prevention process

- Increase alertness to detail so all people can detect subtle differences in context by examining data and looking for predictions

- Focus on what the organization needs to do to reach the performance target on a continuous basis

- Act as a "mindful" organization; thinking and learning constantly by empowering individuals to interact continuously with others in the organization as they develop in their roles (North Highland Worldwide Consulting, 2014, p. 3)

Schools with high integrity offer high reliability for delivering on their missions to engender learning for all students. This requires integrity in leadership, which is about keeping a school focused on the right work to enhance the chances of achieving and sustaining success.

High reliability leadership is developing this capacity to focus on the right work and the discipline to sustain that work over time to deliver a highly reliable opportunity for learning.

In the era of accountability, the U.S. government and most other governing bodies expect schools to be high reliability organizations.

Schools are charged with creating safe environments, implementing systems that improve teaching and learning, increasing and maintaining high graduation rates, and preparing students in college and career readiness. In *Leading a High Reliability School*, leadership experts Robert J. Marzano, Philip B. Warrick, Cameron L. Rains, and Richard DuFour (2018) state:

> This pressure has grown with the Every Student Succeeds Act (ESSA), which, according to the U.S. Department of Education (2017), "requires—for the first time—that all students in America be taught to high academic standards that will prepare them to succeed in college and careers." Ensuring that *all* students learn at high levels requires schools and their staff to take a high reliability perspective. (p. 28)

School leaders face the challenge of accounting for the unique needs of their schools while still working to achieve district and state or provincial goals and outcomes. In an attempt to meet this challenge, many schools have fallen into several common standards-era ruts of practice, such as the following.

- Chasing scores for individual standards across different content areas and different grade levels—effectively playing whack-a-mole with standards year after year

- Relying on "magic fix" programs to rescue the school from low scores in a specific content area or grade level

- Implementing new initiatives every year, which drives the staff into *initiative fatigue*, stretching resources to the point of unsustainability as staff find it hard to commit to anything

There is a better option! School leaders can effectively serve their schools by understanding and practicing high reliability leadership. Marzano and colleagues (2018) explain the perspective of high reliability leadership: "At its core, a high reliability perspective involves monitoring the relationship between actions an organization takes to enhance its effectiveness and the extent to which these actions do, in fact, produce the desired effects" (p. 28). High reliability leadership focuses on creating operating systems that work coherently to target the endgame of student learning. In *Schools*

There is a better option! School leaders can effectively serve their schools by understanding and practicing high reliability leadership.

That Learn, coauthors Peter Senge, Nelda Cambron-McCabe, Timothy Lucas, Bryan Smith, Janis Dutton, and Art Kleiner (2012) state:

> The discipline of systems thinking provides a different way of looking at problems and goals—not as isolated events but as components of larger but less visible structures that affect each other. To understand a system is to understand those interrelationships and how they recur and change over time. (p. 124)

To sustain such a system, high reliability leaders have several tools in their toolbox.

High Reliability Leadership Tools

High reliability leaders use three systems-based tools: (1) leading indicators, (2) lagging indicators, and (3) quick data. When used correctly, these tools guide leadership decisions in short- and long-term strategic planning and inform leaders about the health and effectiveness of their systems over time.

Leading indicators identify critical aspects of operation that leadership should focus on to enhance the school's ability to educate all students. The leading indicators in the HRS model keep leaders focused on the right work. *Lagging indicators* are concrete artifacts of practice and data that show the presence and effect of the leading indicators. Lagging indicators are the evidence that leading indicators are successfully in place in a school's operation. As researchers and coauthors Robert J. Marzano, Philip B. Warrick, and Julia A. Simms (2014) explain:

> In order to know what to work on and to measure their success at each level, school leaders need ways to assess their school's current status, gauge their progress through each level, and confirm successful achievement of each level. Leading and lagging indicators are useful to these ends. (p. 4)

At first glance, the term *lagging* might have a negative connotation of being *less than*. However, from a high reliability perspective, *lagging* actually is more accurately thought of as *the evidence trailing behind*. Consider the following metaphor to illustrate the relationship of leading and lagging indicators.

If a person looks into the night sky to view a shooting star, he or she doesn't actually see the star, but rather knows it is there because he or she can observe the tail as it shoots across the sky. The star is the leading indicator; we know it is there because the tail is the lagging indicator or evidence that tells us so. This is the same relationship we see in the HRS process. (To view all of the leading indicators in the HRS model, see tables I.3 to I.7 [pages 18, 19, 21, 23, and 24] in the introduction.)

Quick data are the third tool of high reliability leadership. *Quick data* bring the aspect of data-driven leadership into the process by creating an information loop for school leaders to efficiently and effectively monitor the health of the school's leading indicators. This is a vital aspect of high reliability leadership; it allows leaders to identify and fix errors in the school's operation before those errors can become systemwide failures.

These three HRS tools—leading indicators, lagging indicators, and quick data—cultivate the integrity aspect of school leadership. These tools help identify, monitor, and sustain the right work on which schools should focus. Used correctly, these tools of high reliability leadership can help leaders maximize the school's opportunities for success. In fact, the success of the school as a whole becomes less dependent on the actions of a sole dynamic leader and more dependent on the integrity of the school's operating systems. In clarifying the concept of high reliability leadership, Marzano and colleagues (2018) state:

> *These three HRS tools—leading indicators, lagging indicators, and quick data—cultivate the integrity aspect of school leadership.*

> This approach minimizes the importance of a school leader's personal characteristics and maximizes critical, data-informed actions a leader takes. Effective leadership is not a function of having a specific personality type or a certain demeanor; it is a function of informed action aimed at continuous improvement. (p. 24)

This approach to leadership can greatly reduce the backsliding and starting over that occurs in schools due to a change in a formal leadership position such as the principal. It can also help transition a new principal into a school through the sharing of lagging indicators and quick data during the transition.

School leaders can use leading indicators, lagging indicators, and quick data in conjunction with another leadership concept known as the sigmoid curve, which represents the process of high reliability leadership.

The Process of High Reliability Leadership

The *sigmoid curve* is an S-shaped curve laid on its side to model stages in a life cycle. Initiatives or systems put in place by schools move through the three life cycle stages of the sigmoid curve shown in figure 11.1. The website Manage Train Learn (n.d.; http://manage trainlearn.com) addresses the concept of the sigmoid curve as it applies to organizational leadership:

> The challenge to those who live through natural life cycles is how to create new life from existing life rather than to go down with the existing cycle and having to start from scratch again.
>
> So what is the solution to beating the inevitability of the life cycle? It lies in managing change and the art of timing. And one of the most helpful models in doing this is the sigmoid curve.

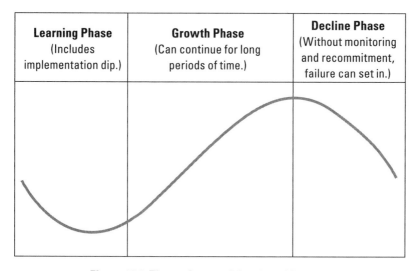

Learning Phase (Includes implementation dip.)	Growth Phase (Can continue for long periods of time.)	Decline Phase (Without monitoring and recommitment, failure can set in.)

Figure 11.1: Three phases of the sigmoid curve.

The sigmoid curve employs the following three phases in a life cycle to help guide leaders.

- **The learning phase** is the initial section of the curve and shows a dip in performance before starting to rise. This corresponds to an initial period of learning when a new practice or initiative is developing and may not show signs of early success. This dip in the curve is known as an *implementation dip* and is common with new initiatives in organizations. It occurs because the school is in the beginning stages of implementing its new instructional practice model, and it takes time for teachers to learn, understand, and develop consistent and successful practices.

- **The growth phase** is when the initiative is growing and there are perceptible evidence and results as an outcome of the growth and maturation of the initiative. The growth phase can continue for long periods of time, producing successful results if managed properly.

- **The decline phase** is when the curve starts to fall, indicating the initiative has grown and matured but is in need of attention or repair. If the initiative is not tended to properly, it will start to die, which can cause an organization to completely start over in developing the initiative. In order to avoid the decline phase and maintain a growth curve, leaders need to periodically revisit, revise, and recommit to the initiative.

High reliability leaders can correlate the sigmoid curve concept in conjunction with leading indicators, lagging indicators, and quick data. Additionally, leadership scales are available for each of the twenty-five leading indicators in the HRS model. Figure 11.2 shows a generic version of a high reliability leadership scale. The leadership scales provide guides for using these tools in a level of progression for establishing and sustaining a leading indicator. You can match leadership scales to all the specific leading indicators, which appear in the introduction to this book (page 1) and in the book *Leading a High Reliability School* (Marzano et al., 2018).

Not Implementing	The school does not have the leading indicator in place.
Beginning	The school is in the beginning, yet incomplete, stages of implementing the leading indicator.
Developing	The school has taken specific actions to implement the leading indicator schoolwide.
Applying	The school has taken specific actions to implement the leading indicator schoolwide and identified lagging indicators to show the desired effects of these actions.
Sustaining	The school cultivates information through quick data sources to monitor the leading indicator and takes proper actions to intervene when quick data indicate a potential problem.

Source: Adapted from Marzano et al., 2018.

Figure 11.2: Generic high reliability leadership scale.

Used together, the sigmoid curve and high reliability leadership scales can guide school leaders in their thinking and understanding of the HRS model. The sigmoid curve represents the life cycle of a leading indicator, while the levels of the scales correlate leadership actions to implement and sustain the leading indicator.

Let's examine some scenarios that demonstrate the process of high reliability leadership in conjunction with the sigmoid curve and the high reliability leadership scale. The focus for the scenarios is leading indicator 2.1: *The school communicates a clear vision as to how teachers should address instruction.*

> Used together, the sigmoid curve and high reliability leadership scales can guide school leaders in their thinking and understanding of the HRS model.

Implementing High Reliability Leadership

Assume leading indicator 2.1 is not present in a school. The first step a leader should take is to initiate strategic planning for the school to develop strategies that establish the leading indicator as part of its operation. These initial actions correlate to the learning phase of the sigmoid curve and the move from *not implementing* to *beginning* on the high reliability leadership scale. During the learning phase, school leaders are in the strategic planning and early implementation of a particular initiative or program. To establish this leading indicator, the school begins to implement a common instructional practice model (or framework). The eventual goal is for all teachers to consistently use the elements of the school's common instructional practice model. To monitor the implementation of this initiative, school leaders identify specific lagging indicators (evidence) that will determine the extent the leading indicator is becoming part of the school's operation. For example, school leaders might identify two lagging indicators: (1) a schoolwide document in place that clearly articulates the school's instructional practice model and (2) classroom walkthrough observation data that indicate 90 percent of teachers are using the instructional practice model 90 percent of the time. In this manner, the leading and lagging indicators begin to work together to monitor the status and growth of the implementation.

Early in the implementation of the instructional practice model, the school will be in the learning phase of the sigmoid curve. The shape of the sigmoid curve during the learning phase indicates a dip in initial performance (see figure 11.1, page 315). This dip in the curve—the implementation dip—is normal during the implementation of new initiatives. However, too often school leaders see an initial dip in performance and make the mistake of abandoning the initiative or—worse yet—adding other initiatives to "fix" the situation. If this is the way leaders react, the cliché of the initiative as "just another new thing" begins to become a reality in a school. This can result in initiative fatigue and damage the integrity of leadership. Conversely, high reliability leaders understand this phase of the sigmoid curve during early implementation and strategically focus on continuing to build teacher capacity and agency within the instructional practice model to allow teachers an opportunity to understand it and get comfortable using it in their professional practice.

The growth phase of the sigmoid curve correlates with developing and applying the high reliability leadership scale levels. By maintaining the collective organizational focus on implementing a common instructional practice model for leading indicator 2.1, the school moves into the growth phase. During this phase, the curve begins to climb and successful implementation is becoming more noticeable as leaders see the extent the lagging indicators show up in the school's operation. Early in the growth curve, the lagging indicators may show the instructional practice model not yet fully in place schoolwide. However, by having the lagging indicators, school leaders can begin to gauge the level of success and make strategic decisions for the continued development of the instructional practice model schoolwide. For example, achieving the first lagging indicator (having a schoolwide document for the instructional practice model) would indicate initial success and early growth in this leading indicator. As the instructional practice model becomes more systemic and embedded schoolwide, the second lagging indicator becomes evident, as school administrators and teachers continue to use the language and concepts of the school's instructional practice model in individual planning, the work of their collaborative teams, and ultimately, their daily classroom practice. In this scenario, school administrators are looking closely at the second lagging indicator and notice that walk-through observation data show 90 percent of the teachers are using specific aspects of the instructional practice model 90 percent of the time. At this point, the school has reached the applying level on the high reliability leadership scale and is firmly operating in the growth phase of the sigmoid curve. Now leadership focus must turn to sustaining the leading indicator over time.

Sustaining High Reliability Leadership

The use of quick data is the defining characteristic in the sustaining level of the high reliability leadership scale. The use of quick data correlates with the junction of the growth and decline phases of the sigmoid curve. Quick data enable school leaders to monitor the school's lagging indicators in order to successfully sustain the leading indicators. Marzano and colleagues (2014) identify three sources of quick data leaders can use effectively for this purpose: (1) quick conversations, (2) quick observations, and (3) easy-to-collect quantitative data.

In the sigmoid curve, the growth phase is the desired state of operation. The shape of the curve indicates an organization can continue to cultivate success and experience growth. In fact, the growth phase can be the longest stage in terms of time and continually cultivating successful results for an organization. For high reliability leaders, this is where some of the most important work occurs, as the sustaining level of the high reliability leadership scale represents (see figure 11.2, page 317). Leaders must monitor a school's leading indicators while in the growth phase so they can recognize early signs of a potential decline phase. This monitoring provides a vital information loop through the use of quick data. Once quick data indicate errors are beginning to occur, high reliability leaders address the issues and make necessary interventions and adaptations. This leadership action allows the school to avoid the decline phase and actually create a new growth phase curve for the leading indicator. Figure 11.3 shows the concept of quick data in correlation to the growth and decline phases of the sigmoid curve. In figure 11.3, point *A* in the growth curve represents when quick data began to indicate issues of concern in the implementation of the leading indicator. Point *B* represents leaders successfully addressing the issues before they could become systemwide failures. In so doing, they extended the growth phase.

In the sigmoid curve, the growth phase is the desired state of operation.

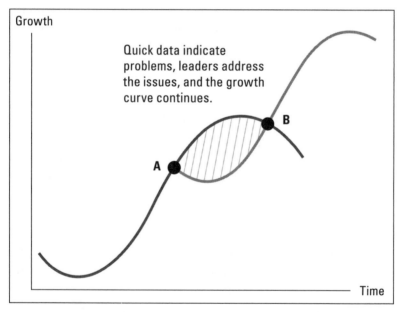

Source: Adapted from Handy, 1994.

Figure 11.3: Quick data correlating to the growth and decline phases of the sigmoid curve.

A key aspect of quick data monitoring is that it should not be a function of only school administrators. In fact, quick data are more efficiently and effectively gathered and better serve the school if all members of a staff are included periodically in the quick data process.

Marzano and colleagues (2014) use the example of a FOD (foreign object debris) walk aboard an aircraft carrier to demonstrate this point, noting:

> During a FOD walk, personnel on the aircraft carrier walk along the deck shoulder to shoulder, picking up anything that they find. . . . FOD walks require all members of a ship's crew to work together to identify and resolve potential problems. (p. 7)

Quick data can involve the entire staff in the monitoring process—in essence, FOD walks become part of the school's high reliability operation systems.

In the scenario of a school implementing leading indicator 2.1, the school communicates a clear vision of how teachers address instruction. Once the school leader clearly quantifies the two lagging indicators—(1) a document is in place that clearly articulates the school's instructional practice model and (2) 90 percent of teachers use elements of the instructional practice model 90 percent of the time—these lagging indicators can form the basis for quick data monitoring. For this purpose, school leaders might engage collaborative team leaders or content department chairs in the use of quick observations and discussions with their colleagues to note specific elements of the instructional practice model they see teachers use in classrooms and discuss in meetings. Likewise, school administrators decide to periodically ask random teachers what specific elements of the model they are using and how they are using them. Additionally, an administrative assistant can track professional development leave requests compared to specific elements in the school's instructional practice model. The quick data from these three sources allow school leaders to efficiently monitor the status of leading indicator 2.1 and react accordingly in a timely manner.

Examining quick data will reveal one of two situations: (1) there are problems beginning to occur with the implementation of the instructional practice model schoolwide, or (2) the school's instructional practice model is healthy and being implemented schoolwide. Each of these findings is valuable and should inform leaders to react accordingly. Considering the first situation, let's assume the quick data indicate new teachers are not using specific elements of the instructional practice model and are unaware of what some of the elements within the model actually mean. By knowing this in a timely manner, school leaders can address the problem and continue to sustain the leading indicator in the school's operation with some intervention strategies to build the capacity of new teachers. However, if school leaders remain unaware of these problems, they could continue to grow with new teachers coming in each year. In that case, the decline phase of the sigmoid curve will begin for leading indicator 2.1 and will require much more effort in the future to get the instructional practice model re-established as part of the school's operation.

Leaders' reactions to quick data should also include celebrations and recognitions of success. In general, schools tend not to celebrate or at least not to celebrate substantial aspects of their operations. Quick data can provide the opportunity for celebration of doing the right work. Communications consultant and author Judith E. Glaser (2015) addresses the power of celebration as a leadership action: "Great leaders identify, measure, recognize, and reward meaningful efforts and achievements—and celebrate often with the people involved. Creating a feeling of celebration helps meet people's needs for inclusion, innovation, appreciation, and collaboration."

Likewise, Rob Hopkins and Chris Johnstone (2014) express the need for celebration:

> Without food, we wither away. Food is nourishment. We also have needs for psychological nourishment or psycho-spiritual nourishment, emotional nourishment. I see celebration as one of those things that nourishes us psychologically, emotionally, spiritually. I was thinking about this also in terms of how important celebration is in keeping us going.
>
> One of the thought blocks that people bump into sometimes is the voice that says "well what's the point of doing this?" What celebration does is it gives us an answer to that. I think of it as helping shifting us from a going nowhere story where we feel we're making no progress and have no direction to what I think of as a going somewhere story, where we feel that we're on the way somewhere because we're celebrating and marking important steps along the way.

When quick data indicate success in sustaining a leading indicator schoolwide, high reliability leaders should share these data with staff and seize these opportunities for celebration to build resilience in the staff for sustaining the systems of operation. Considering the example of a school implementing leading indicator 2.1, if quick data indicate schoolwide implementation, school leaders might celebrate by identifying and sharing some of the effective practices they are observing in classrooms. This could include using pictures of instructional practice from different classrooms and having collaborative teams (or individual teachers) talk about how they are using different elements in their practice and their student results. Celebration can also involve more covert methods, such as writing personal notes to individual teachers (or teams) to recognize their proficiency or growth in using a specific aspect of the instructional practice model.

School leaders might celebrate by identifying and sharing some of the effective practices they are observing in classrooms.

The leadership act of celebration establishes a currency for accomplishment within a school, and what gets celebrated often gets replicated.

Strategic Planning and High Reliability Leadership

The HRS model and the specific high reliability leadership tools can naturally drive long- and short-term strategic planning.

For long-term planning, the five levels of the HRS model are organized in a hierarchy that provides a focused perspective for school leaders as they consider and plan for what comes next in their school's development (Marzano et al., 2014).

The HRS model and the specific high reliability leadership tools can naturally drive long- and short-term strategic planning.

- **Level 5:** Competency-based education
- **Level 4:** Standards-referenced reporting
- **Level 3:** Guaranteed and viable curriculum
- **Level 2:** Effective teaching in every classroom
- **Level 1:** Safe, supportive, and collaborative culture

The five levels of the HRS model give leaders a clear picture of what their school's journey will focus on during a multiyear period. Each level is constructed to support and mesh with the prior and subsequent levels, thus ensuring tight alignment of initiatives over time. The five levels can also keep school leaders focused on purposeful, interdependent initiatives clearly dedicated to student learning. Using the HRS model for long-term planning also helps schools avoid the trap of chasing every new initiative. By charting a course of improvement across the different levels of the HRS model, school leaders establish a covenant to pursue real and lasting school improvement rather than engage in isolated, independent initiatives. The discipline to stay focused long term can also reduce backsliding and starting over when a new principal joins a school. Using the HRS model, the school has already identified future focus areas. This allows a new principal to honor the school's previous work so staff can continue to build on initiatives and systems they are sustaining within their current levels of the HRS model.

Specific leading indicators drive short-term strategic planning within the individual levels of the HRS model. The first three levels of the HRS model—(1) safe, supportive, and collaborative culture; (2) effective teaching in every classroom; and (3) guaranteed and viable curriculum—are critical for all schools to accomplish to operate with a high level of organizational integrity.

Schools should work on the first three levels simultaneously to some degree; however, school leaders should prioritize and attain all of the leading indicators in a lower level (1–3) before prioritizing all of the leading indicators in levels above (4–5). Often, schools will work on some of the leading indicators in the levels above in conjunction, with the bulk of their work focused on attaining and sustaining the leading indicators in a lower level (1–3) of the model. For example, a school working on HRS level 1 will primarily focus on attaining and sustaining the eight level 1 leading indicators.

School leaders should prioritize and attain all of the leading indicators in a lower level (1–3) before prioritizing all of the leading indicators in levels above (4–5).

1.1   The faculty and staff perceive the school environment as safe, supportive, and orderly.

1.2   Students, parents, and community members perceive the school environment as safe, supportive, and orderly.

1.3 Teachers have formal roles in the decision-making process regarding school initiatives.

1.4 Collaborative teams regularly interact to address common issues regarding curriculum, assessment, instruction, and the achievement of all students.

1.5 Teachers and staff have formal ways to provide input regarding the optimal functioning of the school.

1.6 Students, parents, and community members have formal ways to provide input regarding the optimal functioning of the school.

1.7 The principal acknowledges the success of the whole school as well as individuals within the school.

1.8 The principal manages its fiscal, operational, and technological resources in a way that directly supports teachers.

At the same time, the school might also begin to work on developing a model of instructional practice (leading indicator 2.1) and implement a strategy such as instructional rounds (leading indicator 2.6).

Lagging indicators and quick data provide a quality snapshot about what is working well and being sustained in the school's operation as well as present opportunities to enhance a school's operation without making wholesale changes that may be unnecessary. Consider the previous scenario of a school that successfully implemented a schoolwide instructional practice model. The school had two lagging indicators: (1) a document is in place that clearly articulates the school's instructional practice model, and (2) 90 percent of teachers use elements of the instructional practice model 90 percent of the time. Additionally, the school had quick data indicating teachers were continuing to use the instructional practice schoolwide. This type of information would be critically valuable to a new principal and help him or her avoid unknowingly dismantling a system that was already working schoolwide. In fact, there would be wisdom in using this information as a way to acknowledge the school's previous good work.

Conclusion

High reliability leadership equals integrity in leadership. It involves focusing on the right work and monitoring the effectiveness of school initiatives to accomplish the right work. Used correctly, the tools of high reliability leadership—leading indicators, lagging indicators, and quick data—work together in the high reliability leadership process to help school leaders implement, monitor, and sustain the right work within each of the five levels of the HRS model.

High reliability leadership equals integrity in leadership.

Kerr (2013) says, "True leaders are stewards of the future. They take responsibility for adding to the legacy" (p. 171). The concept of high reliability leadership helps school leaders operate as legacy builders and is appropriate for all schools—from turnaround schools to those experiencing high levels of success.

References and Resources

Collins, J. (2001). *Good to great: Why some companies make the leap—and other don't.* New York: HarperBusiness.

Collins, J. (2005). *Good to great and the social sectors: Why business thinking is not the answer—A monograph to accompany good to great.* New York: HarperCollins.

DuFour, R., & Marzano, R. J. (2011). *Leaders of learning: How district, school, and classroom leaders improve student achievement.* Bloomington, IN: Solution Tree Press.

Glaser, J. E. (2015, December 9). A celebration cocktail each executive should know how to mix! *HuffPost.* Accessed at https://huffpost.com/entry/a-celebration-cocktail-ea _b_8766102 on June 20, 2019.

Handy, C. (1994). *The empty raincoat: Making sense of the future.* London: Hutchinson.

Hopkins, R., & Johnstone, C. (2014, July 16). "Without celebration, we wither away." *Resilience.* Accessed at https://resilience.org/?type=Filter+by&s=WITHOUT+CELEBRATION %2C+WE+WITHER+AWAY on June 20, 2019.

Kerr, J. (2013). *Legacy: What the All Blacks can teach us about the business of life.* London: Constable.

Manage Train Learn. (n.d.). *Management models: The sigmoid curve.* Accessed at www.manage trainlearn.com/page/the-sigmoid-curve on January 15, 2019.

Marzano, R. J., Warrick, P. B., Rains, C. L., & DuFour, R. (2018). *Leading a High Reliability School.* Bloomington, IN: Solution Tree Press.

Marzano, R. J., Warrick, P. B., & Simms, J. A. (2014). *A handbook for High Reliability Schools: The next step in school reform.* Bloomington, IN: Marzano Resources.

Maxwell, J. C. (2002). *Leadership 101.* Nashville, TN: Nelson.

North Highland Worldwide Consulting. (2014). *Principles of high reliability organizations* [White paper]. Atlanta, GA: Author. Accessed at https://northhighland.com/-/media /Files/NH/White%20Papers/WP_Principles_Of_High_Reliability_Orgs.pdf on August 14, 2019.

Senge, P. M., Cambron-McCabe, N., Lucas, T., Smith, B., Dutton, J., & Kleiner, A. (2012). *Schools that learn: A fifth discipline fieldbook for educators, parents, and everyone who cares about education* (Rev. ed.). New York: Crown Business.

U.S. Department of Education. (2017). *Every Student Succeeds Act (ESSA)*. Accessed at www .ed.gov/essa?src=rn%20Retrieved%20August%203,%202017 on June 20, 2019.

Zander, R. S., & Zander, B. (2000). *The art of possibility*. Boston: Harvard Business School Press.

Timothy D. Kanold

Timothy D. Kanold, PhD, served as both head of the mathematics department and district superintendent of Adlai Stevenson High School District 125, a model professional learning community. In addition to his practical experience with the PLC at Work process, Dr. Kanold is an award-winning educator and accomplished author and consultant. His book *The Five Disciplines of PLC Leaders* captures his ideas regarding effective leadership within the structure and culture of a PLC. He is also the author of *HEART! Fully Forming Your Professional Life as a Teacher and Leader* and editor of the *Beyond the Common Core: Mathematics in a PLC at Work* series.

To learn more about Dr. Kanold's work, follow him on @tkanold on Twitter.

To book Timothy D. Kanold for professional development, contact pd@Solution Tree.com.

In this chapter, Dr. Kanold addresses the issue of effective leadership within a PLC. He reviews the three big ideas of a PLC and provides five coherence-building actions leaders can emphasize in their daily efforts to make these big ideas a constant focus: (1) lead a common understanding of PLC language, (2) lead a simultaneously loose and tight culture, (3) build collaborative teacher team efficacy, (4) frequently monitor teacher team actions and results, and (5) lead the systematic schoolwide response for students in need of additional time and support.

Chapter 12

Leadership in a PLC: Coherence and Culture

Timothy D. Kanold

"Well, Dr. Kanold, we have our final report for you."

After a bit of hesitation, the leader of the National Blue Ribbon Schools Program award committee said, "There is fear your school district will no longer continue to grow and improve—that entropy will set in with a new superintendent."

The current school district superintendent was Richard DuFour, the architect of the PLC at Work process, along with his colleague Robert Eaker. But DuFour was leaving the district, where he birthed the PLC at Work movement, to lead the movement on a national level.

DuFour had served as both principal and superintendent of the district. He had become a relentless thought leader on creating coherence in our daily routines through the ideals of PLCs and led the district culture of collective adult efficacy built on shared wisdom around results. He did so with passion for the work and humility of self. And now this could suddenly disappear with a new superintendent on board.

So who was the new superintendent? *It was me.*

DuFour once told me, "Think of the culture of your school as a garden. Inattention inevitably results in weeds, which are certain to flourish if the garden is left unattended. A strong culture of continuous improvement needs constant attention and nurturing" (personal communication, April 23, 2016). I spent the previous seventeen school seasons as a leader at Adlai Stevenson High School District 125. Moving forward as superintendent, I wanted our PLC culture of continuous change and improvement to honor his challenge: *a strong culture of continuous improvement needs constant attention and nurturing.*

Would we have clarity regarding the coherence required to preserve our collaborative culture without the leadership of the man who started it all? The answer is yes, but not without relentless attention to the weeds in our cultural garden that were sure to creep in. DuFour had left us with a sustainable culture to survive the ebb and flow of the educators who would move in and out of our district. It was a garden firmly rooted in the three big ideas of a PLC.

> *DuFour had left us with a sustainable culture to survive the ebb and flow. . . . It was a garden firmly rooted in the three big ideas of a PLC.*

Three Big Ideas

DuFour's leadership provides deep insight into how a school principal or superintendent should *think and act.* As principal, he taught other leaders to relentlessly monitor the engagement and energy of those they lead toward the collective fulfillment of faculty and staff commitments for optimal student learning and growth.

> *For your PLC leadership to be successful, the collective efficacy of every teacher and staff member needs to be as important as the self-efficacy and learning culture you expect for your students.*

For your PLC leadership to be successful, the collective efficacy of every teacher and staff member needs to be as *important* as the self-efficacy and learning culture you expect for your students. This means you daily weed the garden of your school culture to ensure the following three big ideas thrive (DuFour, DuFour, Eaker, Many, & Mattos, 2016).

1. **A focus on learning:** The fundamental purpose of the school is to ensure all students learn at high levels (grade level or higher).

2. **A collaborative culture and collective responsibility:** Educators work collaboratively and take collective responsibility for the success of each student.

3. **A results orientation:** To assess their effectiveness in helping all students learn, educators in a PLC focus on results—or evidence of student learning.

A Focus on Learning, A Collaborative Culture and Collective Responsibility, and A Results Orientation

Education is a social sector profession. Researcher and author Jim Collins (2005) reminds us that the outcomes of business and social sector professions are a bit different:

> The confusion between inputs and outputs stems from one of the primary differences between business and social sector professions. In business, money is both an input (a resource for achieving greatness) and output (a measure of greatness). In the social sectors, money is only an input, and not a measure of greatness. (p. 5)

In the business sector, money goes into the organization to produce more money. The output of the work is profit. In social sector professions like education, money goes into the organization, but the output is different. It is not more money; in the case of education, it is smart and competent students. Student learning and character development measure educational success. We measure our change *effectiveness* via actual evidence of student learning.

As learning organization and leadership experts Fred Kofman and Peter M. Senge (1995) conclude, "The rationale for any strategy for building a learning organization revolves around the premise that such organizations will produce dramatically improved results" (p. 43). When measuring your success as a leader, whether or not each collaborative teacher team in your school positively impacts student learning is much tougher to determine than your leadership efforts, which measure how much money the school made during a quarter. Your leadership success rests in the hands of your teachers and their students, and in your ability to coordinate teacher learning toward a predetermined level of student achievement for each grade level or course. That can be a very challenging leadership reality.

As a school principal, DuFour always asked the question, "So what?" *What* will be the dramatically improved results, the evidence of student learning, if we take this action, endorse this new program, add this technology, provide this intervention, and so on? If we did not connect our leadership actions to actual measurable student results, DuFour would reject any proposal, and require resubmission with a "So what?" prediction of improved student performance expectations linked to specific student learning standards. He wanted more than action. He wanted to know that our actions were connected to predicted results.

> In order to make these three big ideas a constant and intentional focus, leaders can emphasize five coherence-building actions in their daily efforts.

In order to make these three big ideas a constant and intentional focus, leaders can emphasize five coherence-building actions in their daily efforts, which I address in the following section.

Coherence-Building Leadership Actions

Leaders often question their ability to sustain meaningful change. They fear their school is regressing as other schools and districts continue to move forward and improve. They might also fear their leadership voice no longer matters. As the leader of a PLC, you can overcome this fear by evaluating your daily efforts on the following five PLC leadership actions that focus on the three big ideas and build coherence into your school culture.

1. Lead a common understanding of PLC language.

2. Lead a simultaneously loose and tight culture.

3. Build collaborative teacher team efficacy.

4. Frequently monitor teacher team actions and results.

5. Lead the systematic schoolwide response for students in need of additional time and support.

Figure 12.1 (page 334) provides an evaluation tool you can use to self-reflect on these leadership actions and improve your leadership.

When you decide to lead the PLC process in your school, you will quickly understand that your leadership actions will prevent stagnation and the natural drift to mediocre school performance. You understand your leadership skills should reflect the meaning behind each of the three words *professional, learning,* and *community* for everyone you lead. Your leadership work begins, then, with the first leadership action: lead a common understanding

> Your leadership actions will prevent stagnation and the natural drift to mediocre school performance.

of PLC language so there is a fundamental and coherent agreement about exactly *what* the PLC process is and *why* it is so important.

Action One: Lead a Common Understanding of PLC Language

Quoting former administrator and educational author Mike Schmoker (2004), PLC at Work leader Rebecca DuFour often emphasizes to school administrators that "clarity precedes competence" (p. 85). As a PLC principal, this clarity begins with providing faculty and staff with a common understanding of PLC language and a solid understanding of the *why* and *how* of the PLC life.

PLC leaders seek clarity on the actual definition of a PLC and reinforce this clarity every school year. PLC is a process, not a single-year event. According to the website AllThingsPLC (n.d.a):

> [A] professional learning community [is] an ongoing process in which educators work collaboratively in recurring cycles of collective inquiry and action research to achieve better results for the students they serve. Professional learning communities operate under the assumption the key to improved learning for students is continuous job-embedded learning for educators.

Breaking this definition down into six characteristics helps clarify the PLC components.

1. Educators work collaboratively—isolation is obsolete!

2. In recurring cycles—before, during, and after each unit of study throughout the year, and forever

3. Of collective inquiry and action research—teams ask, "What does the research say about best practices? Do you think our collective strategies will work? Let's try together!"

4. To achieve better results—by looking at evidence of learning based on collective effort and action

5. For the students they serve—keeping the primary focus on student learning

6. Because the key to improved learning for students is continuous job-embedded learning for educators—building collective teacher efficacy and academic competence in the service of student learning is our pursuit

PLC Leadership Actions	Description of Level 1	Requirements of the Indicator Are Not Present	Limited Requirements of This Indicator Are Present	Substantially Meets the Requirements of the Indicator	Fully Achieves the Requirements of the Indicator	Description of Level 4
Lead a common understanding of PLC language.	There is vague clarity on the what and why of the PLC culture. There is little evidence of teacher team transparency and a wide variance in daily rigor, routines, and practices of teachers.	1	2	3	4	There is a clear and coherent response from every faculty member regarding the definition of the PLC process and why it is so important to pursue every year. Teachers work to limit the wide variance in their practice.
Lead a simultaneously loose and tight culture.	The school culture is built on extremes. The principal leads by "do as I say" top-down decision making or by "do what you want" bottom-up decision making.	1	2	3	4	Teacher team risk taking is not random and serves the shared vision for instruction, assessment, and intervention in the school. The school culture reveals clarity on loose-tight actions.

	1	2	3	4
Build collaborative teacher team efficacy.	Teachers continue to work in isolation and demonstrate no awareness of the four critical questions of a PLC.			Every teacher improves his or her personal academic knowledge and growth through the collective teacher efficacy of his or her collaborative team and by answering the four PLC critical questions during every unit throughout the school year.
Frequently monitor teacher team actions and results.	Few teams and teachers share and know overall student performance results for their grade level or course. Teacher teams do not use those results to impact their daily routines, work, planning, or actions.			Every teacher provides evidence to the principal regarding student performance results and his or her response to those results. The principal provides timely feedback on the data analysis and results.
Lead the systematic schoolwide response for students in need of additional time and support.	Intervention is up to individual teachers and seems random, and if teachers provide it, the intervention is too late to impact current student learning progress.			Every team implements a required intervention response to student learning that is timely, targeted (to the student and standard), fluid and flexible, and systemic, and produces evidence of success.

Figure 12.1: Principal leadership actions in a PLC culture evaluation tool.

Visit go.SolutionTree.com/PLCbooks for a free reproducible version of this figure.

As this definition suggests, the PLC process starts with the creation of an effective collaborative culture that you nurture, expect, defend, monitor, and lead, which ultimately builds adult learning capacity (academic and relational competence) in the service of one

The PLC process starts with the creation of an effective collaborative culture that you nurture, expect, defend, monitor, and lead.

very singular purpose: to impact student learning. A PLC consists of *professionals* working in service of *learning* in a *community* of collaborative grade-level or course-based teams working toward a common goal of learning for all. Your progress toward this goal is how your superintendent should ultimately measure your site leadership success.

Action Two: Lead a Simultaneously Loose and Tight Culture

DuFour first introduced the phrase *loose-tight school culture* to the Adlai Stevenson staff in the late 1980s, after reading the book *In Search of Excellence: Lessons From America's Best-Run Companies* (Peters & Waterman, 1982). A *tight* culture ("Do as I say" with top-down decision making) and a *loose* culture ("Do what you want" with bottom-up decision making) are seemingly contradictory. Is it possible to create a both loose and tight culture as a school leader? According to AllThingsPLC (n.d.b):

> In a culture that is simultaneously loose and tight . . . leaders encourage autonomy and creativity (loose) within well-defined parameters and priorities that must be honored (tight). This environment of empowerment and discipline helps build distributed leadership and mutual accountability.

By 2002, researchers Abraham Sagie, Nurit Zaidman, Yair Amichai-Hamburger, Dov Te'eni, and David G. Schwartz verified the positive impact loose-tight leadership has on school processes by enhancing decision making and actual task performance as well as motivation-related variables such as goal commitment, self-efficacy, and leader-follower mutual trust. As the leader of a PLC, you must be both directive and facilitative; you must be tight when guiding the *what* and *why*, and loose when allowing teacher teams to decide *how* within established high-quality parameters. These parameters create a culture of defined autonomy. Authors Robert J. Marzano and Timothy Waters (2009) note "the superintendent expects building principals and all other administrators in the district to lead within the boundaries defined by the district goals" (p. 8). As the PLC leader in your school, you become a boundary defender. Your school vision and goals define the most critical boundaries in the common work of each grade-level, department, or teacher team. These boundaries are tight and non-negotiable.

Further, Marzano and Waters (2009) indicate that defined autonomy boundaries lower variance and increase the reliability of adult actions to improve student achievement. That is exactly the goal of a PLC: high reliability and low variance in the academic knowledge regarding the quality of teaching, learning, and assessing the routines of every teacher and staff member in the school.

As the PLC leader in your school, you become a boundary defender.

How do you know what to be tight about and loose about? As a PLC leader, you are tight about the components of your shared vision for the PLC culture (DuFour et al., 2016), and then you turn the vision into action by being loose with how those responsible for the implementation accomplish *those* vision components. Vision helps you to achieve clarity on what you are supposed to be changing *toward*. It should pull all adult actions forward. When well articulated and understood, your shared vision for instruction, assessment, and intervention places loose-tight boundaries on the risk-taking efforts you approve and provides the direction for change to make good judgments and decisions each day.

Every risk-taking action cannot be random. Rick DuFour would often ask me, "Tim, I do not want to know your opinion about what we should do. Do you have any research to support the best actions we can take in order to improve student learning?" He expected our collaborative actions to be interdependent with the vision, but it had to be an *informed* vision. The PLC leadership lesson for me was this: a well-understood and operational vision built on the three big ideas of a PLC provides the boundaries for judging the quality of daily decision making.

In a healthy school culture, those you lead take risks because they have become part of a culture that calls them to meet the moral and professional obligation to honor the school or department vision for their daily practice. From the moment new teachers join your staff, you teach them with great clarity your school's coherent vision for effective instruction, assessment, and intervention, and help them learn how to collectively experiment with strategies that honor the vision. Your school's vision, then, becomes a coherence builder. There is no randomness, no chaos—only focused risk taking.

Aaron Hansen, a teacher and author who was named Nevada's 2009 Innovative Educator of the Year, offers this advice about how to achieve magnified impact in any team and cut through the noise of widely variant professional judgments:

> When members of a team truly commit to the process of working with each other in the pursuit of a worthy cause that they really care about, they make a trade. They trade in the immediate gratification of being able to make all their own decisions for faith in the team's collective power to make a bigger difference. The sense of freedom comes as teams actually achieve goals [outcomes] they couldn't have reached on their own. In my mind, that's the essence of true autonomy—when you give up some immediate freedom in order to get something that means more. (personal communication, July 12, 2016)

Ultimately, however, common understanding and loose-tight leadership are not enough for sustainable change. PLC leaders also build collaborative teacher team efficacy.

Action Three: Build Collaborative Teacher Team Efficacy

Early in my teaching career, I had a vague awareness of my own isolation and lack of academic knowledge development as a teacher of mathematics. In my first job, I was the only mathematics teacher in the school, and the principal left me alone to work in isolation. After a few years on the job, I realized I did not know enough about the content and pedagogy of my field to be a teacher who could maximize student learning. The reality of my first teaching experience provides a contrast to the reality I would later experience in a high-impact PLC.

Research at the start of Adlai Stevenson's PLC transformation shows collaborative and shared teacher actions were a primary school culture factor most commonly associated with improving student performance in schools (Georgiades, Fuentes, & Snyder, 1983). All staff worked to improve teacher self-efficacy through collaborative grade-level and course-based teams. Further research from Stanford

University professor emeritus Albert Bandura (1997) confirms this focus as best practice with his view of collective teacher efficacy as "the groups' shared belief in the conjoint capabilities to organize and execute the courses of action required to produce given levels of attainment" (p. 411).

At Adlai Stevenson, staff discovered that the best opportunities to improve our academic competence occurred in the following ways.

- In a social and collaborative setting rather than in isolation

- In an ongoing and sustained way, rather than in an infrequent and transitory way

- Embedded in the job, rather than external (occurring in the context of the real work of the school and classroom rather than in off-site workshops or courses)

- With a focus on results (that is, evidence of improved student learning) rather than on activities or perceptions

With systematic alignment with school and district goals, rather than random efforts, DuFour closely studied subsequent research, which repeatedly concludes teacher isolation has adverse consequences for students, teachers, and any effort to improve schools (see DuFour, DuFour, & Eaker, 2008, pp. 172–177). When educators share a sense of collaborative efficacy, their beliefs that reflect high expectations for student success characterize the school culture. The focus of the work of teacher teams becomes student learning and the development of teacher learning as well.

PLC leaders convey a message about the importance of collaboration. Teaching well is a complex activity learned through knowledge sharing, coaching, and field-based experience. Everything from making your choices for team leaders and monitoring how well team members interact (Do they undermine or build on one another's self-efficacy?) to building time for teacher team collaboration into the regular (contractual) school day conveys a message about the importance of continuous and ongoing learning. Finding ways to make more effective use of the time available and seeking ways to enhance time available—as part of the teachers' workday—becomes an essential part of your leadership responsibilities. Collaboration, then, is a continuous job-embedded learning process.

PLC leaders convey a message about the importance of collaboration.

In a PLC, teams work collaboratively to answer the four critical questions of a PLC (DuFour et al., 2016).

1. What do we want students to learn?

2. How will we know if students are learning?

3. How will we respond when students don't learn?

4. How will we extend learning for students who are already proficient?

The teams answer these questions in a cycle of continuous improvement of frequently monitoring actions and results (see the following section on action four for more details). Teams build an agenda for each meeting around these four critical questions. These four critical questions provide a lens of coherence for your leadership and for your team expectations. The opportunity gaps and inequities that transpire when teams do not reach complete agreement on the level of rigor critical questions one and two expect cause the student learning experience to be widely variant based on the random assignment of a teacher. This teacher practice noise causes greater gaps in student learning.

In addition, the PLC process—and the effort teacher teams make when working together on issues to impact student learning—serves a greater good in your school culture. Teachers become more transparent in their work. What had previously been private decision making moves into a public sphere, not for shaming or to feed egos, but for learning and growing *together*.

To be effective, teacher collaboration must be in the context of an ongoing examination of the results of their collaborative work. Sabina Neugebauer, Megan Hopkins, and James Spillane (2019) point out, "Social interactions firmly anchored in instructional and assessment practice can move your teachers beyond contrived collegiality to a culture that can influence a teacher's self-efficacy" (p. 14). This is where leadership action four comes into play, as school leaders and teacher teams frequently monitor team actions and results.

Action Four: Frequently Monitor Teacher Team Actions and Results

Rick and I would often discuss the question, Why do some teachers, teacher teams, schools, or districts become great (in terms of student achievement and teacher self-efficacy and competence) and some do not? There are many factors, but we were in complete agreement about the impact of the principal as a coherence and culture builder in the school, based on a willingness to monitor and provide formative feedback about teacher team actions.

As the school leader, how do you help teachers feel valued and important? How do you monitor the work of the teams, provide feedback on the quality of their work, hold members accountable to one another, address conflicts as needed, and excessively celebrate successes?

For DuFour, the answer resides in how leaders monitor and provide constant feedback to grade-level and course-based collaborative teams on concrete actions. Teacher team actions should provide answers to the four critical questions of a PLC.

As principal, then, you should expect each teacher team to routinely provide evidence that members have developed teacher efficacy and academic competence by developing the teacher team actions figure 12.2 (page 342) describes. In what I reference as *differentiation* for your teams, you may expect one grade-level or course-based team to focus its work on a partial set of these ten teacher team actions, while asking another team to focus on other actions, based on the team's areas of strength or areas that need improvement.

As a leader of a PLC culture, you expect every member of your faculty and staff to act as a professional. Professionals understand the outcomes of their work with great clarity (see actions 8, 9, and 10 in figure 12.2, page 342). Helping those closest to the action, your teachers, to learn how to reflect on student learning evidence and respond to results in a healthy and meaningful way is what distinguishes high levels of sustainable and effective change initiatives in your school culture, or not.

> *As a leader of a PLC culture, you expect every member of your faculty and staff to act as a professional.*

Risk taking by your faculty begins with the hope that their risks will result in improved learning for students in each classroom of your school. As a PLC principal, you expect your faculty to connect any initiative to predicted results for improved student learning. As evidence of student learning becomes available during and at the end of every unit in the curriculum, as a leader, you look back and ask, "How did we do? Did we hit those predicted targets for student learning?"

Directions: Provide evidence of your teams' current engagement in each of the following actions.

1. Obtaining a complete understanding of the essential learning standards for each unit of study

2. Agreeing on research-affirmed lesson design elements for each unit of study

3. Teaching episodes together—becoming transparent and open in learning to improve practice, discovering strategies, and teaching routines through lesson study

4. Developing common unit assessments and calibrating scoring of those assessments

5. Using student self-assessment, reflection, and action on assessment errors during and at the end of a unit of study

6. Implementing meaningful interventions by collaborating with principal support as needed

7. Implementing meaningful and timely feedback loops with the principal on the teams' daily routines to improve practice

8. Engaging in teacher team self-assessment, reflection, and action on student learning during and at the end of each unit of study

9. Setting student achievement long-term (three-year) and short-term (one-year) stretch goals based on recent student performance

10. Participating in achievement and celebration routines regarding student performance goal progress

Figure 12.2: PLC collaborative teacher team actions for collective teacher efficacy.

*Visit **go.SolutionTree.com/PLCbooks** for a free reproducible version of this figure.*

Monitoring and providing formative feedback regarding weekly, monthly, and yearly student learning targets becomes your relentless pursuit and is important to the cycle of improved student achievement in your school. Failure to notice student learning results on a frequent basis can be embarrassing. A failure to monitor student learning results, act as a broker of resources for teacher teams struggling to move student learning forward, and provide celebrations for small wins along the way can cause student learning results to leave you and your teacher teams surprised, defeated, and dismayed.

You can model monitoring formative feedback by expecting every teacher team to complete and submit to you (electronically or on paper) a simple feedback form with a reflective response about the most recent data the team has reviewed regarding student performance. On the form, teacher teams can declare evidence of student strength, standards in need of improvement, and a brief plan to help students improve—each week or month. For this feedback form to be effective, you should review it within twenty-four hours, celebrate the team's successes, and provide feedback to help the team improve. Then, follow up to determine if the teacher team took action on your feedback.

This monitoring-and-feedback process provides hints about the nature of your public celebrations as well. As your teacher teams reach unprecedented levels of student performance, you not only monitor their effort privately but also celebrate the results publicly. And as principal, realize it is not just about the student learning results. When you connect teacher actions to actual evidence of student learning, you become a *bridge-building* principal. At the end of your bridge-building leadership career, you can look back and know that the answer to the question, "Did our change efforts matter?" is a resounding *yes!*

If your monitoring process reveals students have not yet learned what they are meant to learn, then as PLC leader, take action five, leading the systematic schoolwide response for students in need of additional time and support.

Action Five: Lead the Systematic Schoolwide Response for Students in Need of Additional Time and Support

"Get these students out of my class!" These were the first words spoken to me three days after my arrival as an administrator at Adlai Stevenson (six years before the birth of what is now the PLC process). This is when I realized our unfortunate cultural response to intervention: if a student had gaps in learning, then we would place him or her either into a lower-level course or with a teacher in a grade-level classroom filled with lower-performing students. As DuFour and colleagues (2016) note, selecting and sorting students is never an intervention option. The third critical question asks your team and school to develop a robust response when students do not learn the expected standards for each grade level or course.

Imagine a bar that is held high in the air. The bar represents the essential learning standards for each grade level or course. As the leader of your school's culture, what happens when a student, based on the time normally allotted for daily instruction, cannot make it over the bar? At Adlai Stevenson, we wanted to provide students access to the curriculum by providing a "box of support" to stand on, as needed, so students could reach the bar.

DuFour was adamant about every adult in our school culture understanding the essential learning standards are immovable. We will close any gaps. We will not lower the bar for some of our students. But *time for learning* could be variable. Some students might need more time than others. Adlai Stevenson's five guidelines for student intervention emerged out of this cultural mindset. You should use the following five criteria when judging the quality of your teacher teams' intervention programs.

1. **Systematic and required**—Support for a struggling student is required, meaning if any student is at academic risk in a grade level or course, he or she must receive the additional support.

2. **Targeted**—Support targets each student based on his or her standard proficiency level for the essential learning standard.

3. **Fluid and flexible**—Support is not locked in forever; as soon as a student demonstrates understanding or proficiency on the standards, he or she is removed from the support.

4. **Just in time**—The intervention program provides feedback in growing student learning, so all interventions focus on essential learning standards the student is currently learning or has recently encountered in previous units of study.

5. **Proven to show evidence of student learning**—The support is effective and actually improves student learning on the targeted essential learning standards.

As principal, you are the leader of the schoolwide response to intervention to support struggling students. This part of your school culture is a great place to exercise loose-tight leadership. Be tight about the five criteria for intervention, while loose about how the teacher teams might achieve the necessary interventions to close gaps in student learning through the use of additional time.

As principal, you are the leader of the schoolwide response to intervention to support struggling students.

A Message for District Superintendents

Although part III of this book focuses on districtwide leadership in high reliability organizations, I would like to include a brief message for superintendents here. Effective superintendents of PLCs work with school principals to identify the essential skills and vital behaviors necessary for leading the PLC process to become part of the school culture. As a superintendent examines the monthly training of building principals on the coherence aspects of the PLC process, he or she will need to consider whether or not principal and administrator professional development impacts the culture of continuous change described in this chapter.

In *Learning by Doing: A Handbook for Professional Learning Communities at Work*, DuFour and colleagues (2016) describe several essential questions superintendents should ask to monitor the right work of principals and administrative team leaders (see figure 12.3).

To assess principal commitment to districtwide PLC implementation, ask:

1. "How do we know if we have a common language about the PLC process throughout the district?"

2. "How do we know if all educators throughout the district know what must be tight in our organization and in each school?"

3. "How do we know if educators are organized into collaborative teams (not merely groups) working interdependently on the right work, and building their collective teacher efficacy?"

4. "How do we know if the principal is closely monitoring each student's learning in every school on a frequent (weekly and monthly) unit-by-unit, just-in-time basis?"

5. "How do we know if every teacher and teacher team is using student assessment results to inform and improve their self-efficacy and professional practice?"

6. "How do we know if every student who experiences difficulty in acquiring essential knowledge and skills will receive additional time and support for learning in a timely, directive, and systemic way?"

Source: Adapted from DuFour et al., 2016.

**Figure 12.3: Assessing principal commitment
to districtwide PLC implementation.**

*Visit **go.SolutionTree.com/PLCbooks** for a free reproducible version of this figure.*

The question, How do we know? in each of the questions in figure 12.3 speaks to the superintendent's expectations and leadership accountability. Yet, PLC leadership is so much more than just knowing (although that is a great place to start). Superintendent leadership begins with the How do you know? question, but expects constant formative feedback about the quality of that knowing and then expects action on that feedback. Thus, superintendents lead this reflect, refine, and act pattern of behavior year after year.

Conclusion

The PLC process works because school leaders, along with faculty and staff, weed their cultural garden and fall in love with their work once again. Together, they find hope. They experience the full engagement and energy that calls them to the PLC commitments necessary for meaningful and relevant teaching and student learning.

> The PLC process works because school leaders, along with faculty and staff, weed their cultural garden and fall in love with their work once again.

They experience optimal growth in an inspirational change environment in which the needs of the faculty and staff are as *important* as the needs of their students to be successful.

DuFour, in his final message to a group of 1,800 educators in August 2016, stated, "I don't know how much longer I can be on this journey with you, but I know you are the greatest generation of American educators and know that you can meet these expectations. I wish you Godspeed." And, the educators in turn remembered, once again, that their teaching career, supported by your leadership, is making a difference.

References and Resources

AllThingsPLC. (n.d.a). *About PLCs*. Accessed at www.allthingsplc.info/about on May 1, 2019.

AllThingsPLC. (n.d.b). *Frequently asked questions: What constitutes a simultaneous loose and tight culture*. Accessed at www.allthingsplc.info/frequently-asked-questions/page,3/term on August 4, 2019.

Bandura, A. (1997). *Self-efficacy: The exercise of control*. New York: Freeman.

Collins, J. (2005). *Good to great and the social sectors: Why business thinking is not the answer—A monograph to accompany good to great*. New York: HarperCollins.

DuFour, R., DuFour, R., & Eaker, R. (2008). *Revisiting Professional Learning Communities at Work: New insights for improving schools*. Bloomington, IN: Solution Tree Press.

DuFour, R., DuFour, R., Eaker, R., Many, T. W., & Mattos, M. (2016). *Learning by doing: A handbook for Professional Learning Communities at Work* (3rd ed.). Bloomington, IN: Solution Tree Press.

Gallup. (2014). *State of America's schools: The path to winning again in education.* Washington, DC: Author. Accessed at www.gallup.com/services/178709/state-america-schools -report.aspx on May 1, 2016.

Georgiades, W., Fuentes, E., & Snyder, K. (1983). *A meta-analysis of productive school cultures.* Houston: University of Texas.

Kahneman, D., Rosenfield, A. M., Gandhi, L., & Blaser, T. (2016, October). Noise: How to overcome the high, hidden cost of inconsistent decision making. *Harvard Business Review, 94*(10), 38–46. Accessed at https://hbr.org/2016/10/noise on October 1, 2016.

Kofman, F., & Senge, P. M. (1995). Communities of commitment: The heart of learning organizations. In C. Sarita & J. Renesch (Eds.), *Learning organizations: Developing cultures for tomorrow's workplace* (pp. 15–43). Portland, OR: Productivity Press.

Marzano, R. J., & Waters, T. (2009). *District leadership that works: Striking the right balance.* Bloomington, IN: Solution Tree Press.

Neugebauer, S., Hopkins, M., & Spillane, J. (2019). Social sources of teacher self-efficacy: The potency of teacher interactions and proximity to instruction. *Teachers College Record, 121*(4), 1–32.

Peters, T. J., & Waterman, R. H., Jr. (1982). *In search of excellence: Lessons from America's best-run companies.* New York: Warner Books.

Sagie, A., Zaidman, N., Amichai-Hamburger, Y., Te'eni, D., & Schwartz, D. G. (2002). An empirical assessment of the loose-tight leadership model: Quantitative and qualitative analyses. *Journal of Organizational Behavior, 23*(3), 303–320.

Schmoker, M. (2004). Learning communities at the crossroads: Toward the best schools we've ever had. *Phi Delta Kappan, 86*(1), 84–88.

PART III

Professional Learning Communities, High Reliability Schools, and District Leadership

The late 1970s and early 1980s saw an increased emphasis on improving the knowledge base regarding effective teaching practices as a means for improving student achievement. This emphasis on improving individual classrooms reaped many benefits relating to effective teaching practices, and also raised the question, If the practices within individual classrooms affect student achievement, what about practices at the school level? As a result of addressing this question, the 1990s brought an intense interest in effective schools research. With decades of consistent research findings relating to effective schooling practices, the obvious question emerged, If classroom behaviors matter, and if school practices matter, does districtwide leadership matter? The answer is *yes. It matters a lot!*

While district-level leadership does not replace the importance of effective classroom- and school-level practice, it does play a critical role in maximizing the impact of school-improvement initiatives such as the HRS model and the PLC at Work framework. District leadership that allows for a certain measure of school autonomy (within defined common districtwide practices) enhances and accelerates the effects of the concepts and practices that form the foundation of these two approaches to school improvement.

Cameron L. Rains

Cameron L. Rains, EdD, is director of school improvement for Solution Tree, where he works with schools, districts, and state education agencies to ensure all students are learning at high levels. Previously, Dr. Rains was a teacher, an instructional coach, and an administrator in multiple capacities. Most recently, he served as the assistant superintendent for Clark-Pleasant Community School Corporation in Indiana, where the schools and district were recognized as certified High Reliability Schools.

Dr. Rains is passionate about teacher, school, and district leadership and applying research findings in the school environment. He has coauthored many articles and books, including *Leading a High Reliability School* (2018) and *Stronger Together: Answering the Questions of Collaborative Leadership* (2018).

He earned a bachelor of science degree in elementary education and a master of science degree in educational leadership from Indiana University. He also holds an educational specialist degree and doctorate in educational leadership from Ball State University.

To learn more about Dr. Rains's work, follow @CameronRains on Twitter.

To book Cameron L. Rains for professional development, contact pd@Solution Tree.com.

In this chapter, Dr. Rains describes how district leaders use the HRS model as the driving force for improvement within each school and classroom. He also introduces the concept of *defined autonomy* (all schools in a system operate within a set of non-negotiable principles and actions, but also have great latitude as to how these principles and actions manifest in individual buildings).

Chapter 13

Leadership in High Reliability School Districts

Cameron L. Rains

The research on district leadership is clear. District leadership matters and has a measurable impact on student learning (Marzano & Waters, 2009; Waters & Marzano, 2006). While this seems like common sense, educators have not always accepted that district leadership makes any difference at all. It was not until 2006 when researchers J. Timothy Waters and Robert J. Marzano completed the first meta-analysis of district leadership that the impact of district leadership began to become very clear. Waters and Marzano's (2006) findings from investigating twenty-seven research studies quantify the district leadership impact on student achievement as a correlation of 0.24. As the authors point out, this means a superintendent performing at the 50th percentile in a district where students are performing at the 50th percentile can raise student achievement to the 59.5th percentile simply by increasing his or her performance by one standard deviation to the 84th percentile. This is not trivial when you consider the positive impact it could have on every student in the district.

Supporting and Serving Schools

Simply having district leaders does not ensure effective district leadership. The focus of district leadership must be on those things that make a difference for students. Beginning with the right frame of reference is important. While it is true district leadership impacts student learning, the impact is indirect. Nothing district leaders do alone can guarantee all students learn at high levels. To achieve this mission, there must be a strong partnership with staff of each school. Only through a coordinated team effort can leaders ensure all students get what they need and all students learn at high levels. This frame of reference leads to an understanding—the most important role district leaders can fulfill is supporting and serving schools so each school staff can serve their students.

The focus of district leadership must be on those things that make a difference for students.

Serving schools as a district leadership team can be tricky work. Operating in isolation—in silos—at the district office will not assist in generating high levels of learning for all students. School districts are made up of many interrelated parts and departments. What occurs in one area impacts other areas. Because of this, district leaders need to work together as a collaborative team to address the challenges surrounding high levels of learning for all students. At the school level, leaders must consider many complexities—from the current student performance level and ongoing large-scale initiatives, to the school culture, and barriers to learning faced by students. All of these dynamics impact the capacity for change in a school and the steps leaders should take. Multiply these variables by the number of schools in a district and you begin to understand why an effective district leader's work is so challenging. Knowing all of this, it stands to reason there is no cookie-cutter approach to engaging in becoming an HRS district. Leaders must consider all variables and develop the best plan for addressing crucial HRS leading indicators on a school-by-school basis. District leaders can serve schools by setting up district-level conditions more likely to lead to schools becoming highly reliable.

Leading Toward a High Reliability District

District leadership in HRS districts, at a minimum, requires attention to the first three hierarchical levels of the HRS framework and work at all five levels for districts where schools are working toward standards-referenced reporting (level 4) or competency-based education (level 5). These levels have been the focus of the previous chapters in this book (Marzano, Warrick, Rains, & DuFour, 2018).

- **Level 5:** Competency-based education
- **Level 4:** Standards-referenced reporting
- **Level 3:** Guaranteed and viable curriculum
- **Level 2:** Effective teaching in every classroom
- **Level 1:** Safe, supportive, and collaborative culture

District leaders should consider how best to support each school's staff through each of the five levels. There are specific non-negotiables leaders must set up at each level (ideally districtwide) to maximize the likelihood of success. While leaders should explicitly address each leading indicator at the school level and districtwide as part of district-level conversations, it would be difficult to set up district-level non-negotiables for every leading indicator and still allow staff sufficient autonomy at the school level. As a result of this need for autonomy, a smaller number of districtwide non-negotiables is preferable. In each of the following sections, we'll examine recommended district non-negotiables. Before digging into those, however, it is important to heed some cautionary advice.

> *There are specific non-negotiables leaders must set up at each level (ideally districtwide) to maximize the likelihood of success.*

When district leadership is effective, the focus is on giving schools *defined autonomy* (Marzano & Waters, 2009; Waters & Marzano, 2006). This term refers to district leaders setting up very clear parameters for schools to work under and then getting out of the school staff's way to innovate, problem solve, and move forward. The PLC at Work process advances this thinking as well. The architects of PLC at Work refer to each of these schools as having a "culture that is simultaneously loose and tight" (DuFour, DuFour, Eaker, Many, & Mattos, 2016, p. 13). Identifying the parameters schools should operate under is not only important but also an effective way of doing business at the district level, according to Marzano and Waters (2009). It is possible to take things too far, or to tighten things up to the point where building staff no longer feel any autonomy or ability to try new things, form unique plans for their students, and collectively commit to their plans rather than complying with district-level demands. Maintaining a balance and ensuring everyone understands each and every staff member is on the same big district team is crucial.

The non-negotiables this chapter discusses should *not* be on a list leaders roll out to staff all at once; rather, non-negotiables should represent key areas of investment leaders will address districtwide over time. The non-negotiables represent relevant key leading indicators and require district leadership. While there is no exact "right" time line for putting these non-negotiables in place, it is safe to say, at minimum, it will take several years to do well. The time, effort, and energy associated with tackling all the pertinent district-level leading indicators, and the magnitude of change and leadership required to navigate that change, are simply too much for a district to tackle all at once. As author Mike Schmoker (2019) states, "Countless leadership studies point to the power of devoting our precious time and energy to a tiny set of priorities" (pp. 25–26). Choosing the right things to focus on and gradually taking them on is crucial. The metric for success should be that school leaders and staff members understand the reasoning and rationale for tightening things up in the leading indicator areas at the district level, and most staff perceive that they still have enough autonomy to do great work at the building level.

District Leadership in HRS Level 1: Safe, Supportive, and Collaborative Culture

Ensuring that school environments are safe, supportive, and collaborative is a crucial first step. If students or staff do not feel safe at school, high levels of student learning will never occur (Marzano, Scott, Boogren, & Newcomb, 2017; Sulkowski & Lazarus, 2017). While it is impossible for leaders to ensure this at the district level, it is important that they set it as a minimum expectation for all schools. District leaders do play a supportive role. They can assist with gathering evidence in this area, meet with school guiding coalitions to discuss evidence about safety in the school, and share action steps other schools in the district take to ensure safety. Table 13.1 highlights the recommended district-level focus for HRS level 1.

Operate as a PLC

The most crucial step at level 1 is for each school to operate as a PLC. And when districts engage in the work to become highly reliable, the district should operate as a PLC as well. This includes forming district-level collaborative teams. One of the most crucial

Table 13.1: HRS Level 1 District-Level Non-Negotiables

Non-Negotiable	Required District-Level Action	Intended Outcome
We will have safe and supportive school environments.	Constantly gather information (surveys, quick conversations, quick observations, and artifacts) that informs the guiding coalition or school leadership team about current status.	Students, parents, staff, and the community perceive the school as safe and supportive.
We will operate as a PLC.	Ensure every staff member is part of a collaborative team, each collaborative team has time to do its work, and the right work is defined.	Each school will emerge as a high-functioning PLC, and each staff member will serve an integral role on a collaborative team with the goal of ensuring high levels of learning for all students.
Teachers have a strong voice in making decisions regarding the optimal functioning of the school and regarding school-improvement initiatives.	Ensure processes and structures are in place for all staff to provide input and feedback. Ensure some teachers are involved in making decisions as part of the school-improvement team.	The best ideas regarding the optimal functioning of the school rise to the top and are implemented, and staff believe in, support, and implement school-improvement initiatives.

district-organized collaborative teams includes building principals and district staff who have responsibilities for curriculum, instruction, and assessment. Building principals have a very difficult job. Through collaboration with a high-performing team, leaders produce more organized work, generate better ideas, and learn lessons as a whole, which in turn increases the capacity of all individual team members.

In addition to participating as a member of district-level collaborative teams, district leaders also need to help schools find time for collaboration. While individual schools can take on this task alone, it is far easier when an entire district addresses the issue of time for collaborative teams. There are typically more resources available at the district level than at the school level, and leaders

Through collaboration with a high-performing team, leaders produce more organized work, generate better ideas, and learn lessons as a whole, which in turn increases the capacity of all individual team members.

can make broader decisions. Whether the district implements a late start, an early release, common time within the school day (beyond the typical teacher preparation period), or any other strategy, district leaders must ensure all school-level collaborative teams have the time they need to do their important work.

District leaders need to work on ensuring all schools and staff embrace the three big ideas of a PLC, and collaborative teams answer the four critical questions of a PLC (DuFour et al., 2016). The following three big ideas of a PLC help schools and districts establish their culture (DuFour et al., 2016).

1. A focus on learning

2. A collaborative culture and collective responsibility

3. A results orientation

When districts do not fully embrace these big ideas, they will likely stifle the PLC process. As the authors of *Leading a High Reliability School* state, "The extent to which educators consider and embrace these ideas has a significant impact on that process's outcomes in a district or school" (Marzano et al., 2018, p. 3).

> District leaders need to work on ensuring all schools and staff embrace the three big ideas of a PLC.

The four critical questions of a PLC that serve as the focus for collaborative teams are as follows (DuFour et al., 2016).

1. What do we want students to learn?

2. How will we know if students are learning?

3. How will we respond when students don't learn?

4. How will we extend learning for students who are already proficient?

In *Collaborative Teams That Transform Schools*, coauthors Robert J. Marzano, Tammy Heflebower, Jan K. Hoegh, Philip B. Warrick, and Gavin Grift (2016) add the following two questions.

5. How will we increase our instructional competence?

6. How will we coordinate our efforts as a school?

Simply organizing staff into collaborative teams is not enough. Engaging them in the right work during their precious time together is crucial to improving outcomes for students. These six critical questions should serve as the guideposts for collaborative teamwork. We'll address some of the more specific work required to fully address these questions in the upcoming sections on HRS levels 2, 3, and 4.

Provide Opportunities for Teacher Input and Voice in Decision Making

The last non-negotiable district leaders must address at level 1 is ensuring teachers have a strong voice in the decision making regarding the optimal functioning of the school, and ensuring teachers are part of making decisions regarding school-improvement initiatives. One way leaders can do this well is to ensure each school has multiple avenues for staff to provide input, with follow-up from the building leadership team. Examples of these input opportunities include the following.

- To the grade-level or department chair to share at his or her meeting
- To a union representative to share at a formal meeting with administrators
- To the principal or other school leaders directly
- To any school-improvement team member
- To committee members to share at their committee meetings
- On quarterly staff input surveys

District leaders should set some minimum expectations regarding the input avenues. It is crucial enough to the school cultures to warrant leaders' focus and attention to get this right.

District leaders should also guarantee that teachers represent a significant portion of each school-improvement team, and that formal structures are in place to ensure team members make decisions together. When all staff understand a school's vision, they come together to carry out that vision across a school. Research indicates this is important for the school to be successful (Hitt & Tucker, 2016; Louis, Leithwood, Wahlstrom, & Anderson, 2010). Making sure staff have a strong voice in the school-improvement process to carry out the vision ensures more commitment to the plan; so, staff are more likely to implement the

When all staff understand a school's vision, they come together to carry out that vision across a school.

plan and it is less likely to sit on a shelf and gather dust (Elmore, 2004). District leaders should also ensure the district vision and each school's vision align and are cohesive.

District Leadership in HRS Level 2: Effective Teaching in Every Classroom

Ensuring effective teaching in every classroom is an enormous task. It is quite possible that in this pursuit, the journey is as important as the destination because the work is really never finished. How leaders choose to pursue effective teaching matters immensely in terms of whether or not they can possibly ever achieve the goal. There are several important components at this level. The leading indicators that inform non-negotiables at the district level appear in table 13.2.

How leaders choose to pursue effective teaching matters immensely in terms of whether or not they can possibly ever achieve the goal.

Table 13.2: HRS Level 2 District-Level Non-Negotiables

Non-Negotiable	Required District-Level Action	Intended Outcome
Each school will have a defined model of instruction, and staff will set instructional growth goals within the model.	Establish processes to allow individual schools or the entire district to come to consensus regarding what high-quality teaching is (with a good degree of specificity), and ensure all staff set growth goals around high-quality teaching.	All staff have a common understanding and language regarding high-quality teaching. They know what high-quality teaching is (what it looks like and sounds like) and get better each day, week, and year as a result of working toward growth goals.
Teacher evaluations outline pedagogical strengths and weaknesses based on multiple data sources.	Establish a districtwide evaluation process with a primary focus on helping teachers grow.	The evaluation process helps teachers become better at their craft.
Teachers have opportunities to observe and discuss effective teaching.	Assist in providing multiple opportunities for staff to see and discuss effective teaching, and set minimum expectations regarding participation.	Staff become better as a result of watching and discussing effective teaching.

Have a Defined Model of Instruction

The most crucial aspect of HRS level 2 at both the school and district levels is to identify or develop a high-quality model of instruction. When an entire district engages in the work of becoming highly reliable, it is often most beneficial to have districtwide conversations to reach consensus on a districtwide model of instruction. While this is not the only effective approach, there are some big advantages to having a common districtwide instructional model in place, including the ability to have quality conversations about instruction across the entire district, organize districtwide professional development on the common model, increase efficiency dealing with one model (rather than multiple models for different schools), and create synergy, which is only possible when an entire district engages in common work. Another option is for each school to lead the process of establishing its own model of instruction. Building staff might attain a higher commitment level associated with the autonomy of making their own decisions. The biggest disadvantage with this option is that it becomes increasingly more difficult for districts to support schools when many instructional models exist. As a result, most districts do not require each school develop its own model for instruction.

Leaders have many choices when implementing a districtwide model of instruction. First, schools and districts can choose to utilize an existing instructional model. Examples of such models include *The New Art and Science of Teaching* (Marzano, 2017) and *The Framework for Teaching* (Danielson, 2014). An advantage of this approach is leaders avoid much of the heavy lifting regarding researching effective teaching, identifying key elements, categorizing the elements, and developing the skill progressions for each element. If a leader chooses this route, the initial task is to ensure staff have a deep understanding of the instructional model. For example, if a school utilizes *The New Art and Science of Teaching* as its instructional model, all staff must understand the three categories, ten design areas, and forty-three elements within the model (Marzano, 2017). Table 13.3 (page 360) shows a visual depiction of the model that includes the three categories, ten design areas, and forty-three elements.

Leaders have many choices when implementing a districtwide model of instruction.

A disadvantage of this approach is staff might not have a high level of commitment during implementation of the model. School-level leaders must build and develop commitment over time, as staff become more familiar with the model.

Another option for schools and districts is to develop their own model of instruction from scratch. In this approach, staff would discuss elements of effective teaching, research the most important aspects, and come to consensus regarding which elements to include in the model. Once this work is complete, teams develop a skill progression (or rubric) for each element showing the various levels of possible teacher performance. Figure 13.1 (page 362) shows a sample skill progression for the element, chunking content. This particular example uses the element from the set of forty-three elements in *The New Art and Science of Teaching* (Marzano, 2017); the figure is in the upcoming book *Reflecting On, Observing, and Coaching Teaching* (Marzano, Rains, & Warrick, in press).

Table 13.3: *The New Art and Science of Teaching* Model Visual Representation

Feedback	Content	Context
Providing and Communicating Clear Learning Goals 1. Providing scales and rubrics 2. Tracking student progress 3. Celebrating success **Using Assessments** 4. Using informal assessments of the whole class 5. Using formal assessments of individual students	**Conducting Direct Instruction Lessons** 6. Chunking content 7. Processing content 8. Recording and representing content **Conducting Practicing and Deepening Lessons** 9. Using structured practice sessions 10. Examining similarities and differences 11. Examining errors in reasoning **Conducting Knowledge Application Lessons** 12. Engaging students in cognitively complex tasks 13. Providing resources and guidance 14. Generating and defending claims	**Using Engagement Strategies** 23. Noticing and reacting when students are not engaged 24. Increasing response rates 25. Using physical movement 26. Maintaining a lively pace 27. Demonstrating intensity and enthusiasm 28. Presenting unusual information 29. Using friendly controversy 30. Using academic games 31. Providing opportunities for students to talk about themselves 32. Motivating and inspiring students **Implementing Rules and Procedures** 33. Establishing rules and procedures 34. Organizing the physical layout of the classroom 35. Demonstrating withitness

	Using Strategies That Appear in All Types of Lessons 15. Previewing strategies 16. Highlighting critical information 17. Reviewing content 18. Revising knowledge 19. Reflecting on learning 20. Assigning purposeful homework 21. Elaborating on information 22. Organizing students to interact	36. Acknowledging adherence to rules and procedures 37. Acknowledging lack of adherence to rules and procedures **Building Relationships** 38. Using verbal and nonverbal behaviors that indicate affection for students 39. Understanding students' backgrounds and interests 40. Displaying objectivity and control **Communicating High Expectations** 41. Demonstrating value and respect for reluctant learners 42. Asking in-depth questions of reluctant learners 43. Probing incorrect answers with reluctant learners

Source: Marzano, 2017, p. 8.

This example (figure 13.1, page 362) defines the various levels of teacher performance well. Level 0 indicates the element was called for, but not used. Level 1, beginning, indicates the teacher used chunking, but there were parts missing. Level 2, developing, indicates the teacher is doing his or her part in utilizing the strategies associated with chunking, but the student evidence shows those strategies are not present. Level 3, applying, indicates the teacher is effectively delivering the strategies associated with chunking and monitoring students, and the student evidence shows this is apparent with most students (over 50 percent). Level 4, innovating, indicates the teacher is effectively delivering the strategies and monitoring student evidence, and the student evidence shows this is evident with almost all students. The student evidence for level 3 and 4 performance and the teacher evidence for level 2 performance is very clear and straightforward.

As figure 13.1 (page 362) shows, there must be specificity in the elements in a school's instructional model. This allows staff to accurately self-reflect on their current level of performance, set meaningful

Design area 3: When content is new, how will I design and deliver direct instruction lessons that help students understand which parts are important and how the parts fit together?

Element 6 planning question: How will I chunk the new content into short, digestible bites?

Level 2 (Developing): Teacher Evidence	Level 3 (Applying) or 4 (Innovating): Student Evidence
I use preassessment data to plan chunks.	Students actively engage in processing content between chunks.
I present new content in larger or smaller chunks based on students' initial understanding of new content.	Students can explain why the teacher stops at specific points during a presentation of new content.
I group students to process the chunks taught.	Students appear to understand the content in each chunk.
When I present new declarative knowledge, I ensure the chunks comprise concepts and details that logically go together.	
When I present new procedural knowledge, I ensure the chunks comprise process steps.	

	How Am I Doing?				
	4 **Innovating**	**3** **Applying**	**2** **Developing**	**1** **Beginning**	**0** **Not Using**
Chunking Content	I engage in all behaviors at the applying level. In addition, I identify students for whom the chunking process is not helping them understand the content. I design alternate activities and strategies to meet their specific needs, leading to almost all students understanding the new content.	I engage in activities to chunk content when presenting new information without significant errors or omissions, and the chunking process is helping the majority of students understand the new content.	I engage in activities to chunk content when presenting new information without significant errors or omissions. Evidence for this level of performance includes: 1. Grouping students to process the chunks 2. Varying the length of each chunk based on students' initial understanding	I engage in activities to chunk content when presenting new information but with errors or omissions—for example, not breaking the new content into small enough chunks so students can easily process it or breaking up content into chunks that are too small.	I do not engage in activities to chunk new content when presenting new information. In situations when I should use the element, I do not use it.

Figure 13.1: Skill progression for chunking content example.

Source: Marzano et al., in press.

goals, and monitor their progress over time. This helps avoid the elements within the model becoming dichotomous in the minds of teachers. If the model only highlights what teachers should do and shouldn't do, they will not develop expertise. Teaching is complex and the elements within an instructional model cannot be narrowed to a checklist. In order to get better each day, teachers must understand and utilize a skill progression. Obviously, developing a model of instruction with this level of specificity is not an easy task. The biggest disadvantages of this approach are the time it takes to develop, the expertise required to lead the development, and the difficulty of accessing the best and most current research regarding effective teaching.

Teaching is complex and the elements within an instructional model cannot be narrowed to a checklist.

Developing and utilizing an effective model of instruction is the most important component of HRS level 2. The success of (or lack of) ensuring effective teaching in every classroom first hinges on a high-quality model of instruction. While this is ongoing, the additional work at level 2 can begin.

Use Teacher Evaluation That Outlines Strengths and Opportunities

There are at least two purposes for teacher evaluation: (1) to measure teacher effectiveness and (2) to help teachers develop. In an HRS district, the primary purpose of teacher evaluation is to help teachers develop. Unfortunately, with the push that began with the U.S. Race to the Top initiative, many states, districts, and schools emphasize measuring teachers as evidenced by what Matthew P. Steinberg and Matthew A. Kraft (2017) cite as the three main components of the new evaluation era: (1) utilizing multiple measures, (2) incorporating multiple rating categories, and (3) providing incentives and professional development that are tied to a teacher's categorical rating. The emphasis on these items highlights the focus on measuring teachers. Teacher evaluation systems that help teachers grow require honest appraisals of teacher performance, but with the primary purpose of helping them reflect, set goals, form plans to improve, and receive feedback along the way. When the stakes around teacher evaluations are high (ability to continue on the job, pay linked to ratings, and so on), teachers are less likely to be open and honest, and less likely to take risks and try new strategies with students. District leaders can support schools and teachers by ensuring their evaluation system focuses primarily on teacher development.

District leaders can support schools and teachers by ensuring their evaluation system focuses primarily on teacher development.

Provide Teachers Opportunities to Observe and Discuss Effective Teaching

The final non-negotiable at the district level for HRS level 2 is to ensure teachers have opportunities to see and discuss effective teaching. There are many ways to achieve this, including—but not limited to—staff members participating in the following.

- Engaging in instructional rounds with three to five other teachers

- Watching videotaped lessons of exemplary teaching and discussing them with colleagues

- Videotaping oneself, rating the video, and discussing it with an instructional coach, administrator, or colleague

- Engaging in lesson study with the collaborative team

District leaders should set expectations for this work, but buildings and teacher teams should have the freedom to engage in the practices more frequently. For example, district leaders might set the expectation for every teacher to participate in observing and discussing effective teaching at least five times per semester through a format of their choosing. Staff can always do more, but the minimum expectation is clear to every staff member in the district.

The expectation in an HRS district is for all staff members to get better each day, week, month, and year. District leaders should make the promise to every prospective employee that if he or she chooses to work in their district, he or she will become better at the craft. The non-negotiables in this level help districts achieve this.

The expectation in an HRS district is for all staff members to get better each day, week, month, and year.

District Leadership in HRS Level 3: Guaranteed and Viable Curriculum

Once a safe, supportive, and collaborative culture is in place throughout a district, and staff take important steps to achieve effective teaching in every classroom, districts should focus on the work of ensuring a guaranteed and viable curriculum. The phrase *guaranteed and viable curriculum* (Marzano, 2003) represents the notion that the curriculum should give teachers the time they need to teach it, and *all* students, no matter the teacher to whom they are assigned, have access to the same high-quality curriculum. Taking on this work at the district level requires specific actions relating to the leading indicators within the HRS framework. Table 13.4 shows the recommended non-negotiables (or items that should be tight across a district).

Table 13.4: HRS Level 3 District-Level Non-Negotiables

Non-Negotiable	Required District-Level Action	Intended Outcome
Ensure curriculum and assessments adhere to state and district standards.	Put processes in place for staff to monitor curriculum and assessments, and adjust as standards change.	All curriculum and assessments tightly align to state and district standards.
Ensure teachers can adequately address the curriculum in the time available.	Put a process in place to continually monitor the viability of the curriculum by asking teachers to rate or provide feedback regarding viability.	Teachers report they have the time needed to teach essential content.
Develop district-level goals, ensure each school sets clear and measurable goals focused on improving overall student achievement, and monitor progress toward those goals.	Develop clear districtwide goals, and establish expectations regarding schoolwide goals for student achievement that align to district goals. Communicate the expectations to all school staff. Periodically monitor the progress of each school toward its goals.	Appropriate school- and district-level goals are in place and the district monitors these goals.
Ensure processes are in place to guarantee all students have access to extra time and help when needed.	Develop and share expectations for school schedules that allow all students to receive extra time and help when needed.	All students receive intervention when needed through extra time and extra help within the school day.

Ensure Curriculum and Assessments Adhere to State and District Standards

Leaders might take ensuring curriculum and assessments align to state and district standards for granted in this day and age, but with standards, materials, and assessments ever changing, it is important to have solid processes in place at the district level to maintain alignment. There are many ways to do this, but perhaps the most powerful is to have teacher teams constantly align their learning outcomes, materials, and assessments to standards, then compare and share resources across the district. Carving out time at the district level for this work is crucial, or it is easy for it to fall by the wayside. This should become an annual process—an intentional focus on alignment becomes the way the district does business.

> *Carving out time at the district level for this work is crucial, or it is easy for it to fall by the wayside.*

A natural first step is to identify priority standards. In high-functioning collaborative teams within a PLC, team members would have already identified priority standards. The district-level task is then to help teams across the district responsible for teaching the same courses come to consensus regarding the priority standards. This creates a districtwide guaranteed curriculum, rather than only one in each individual team or school. Many districts form curriculum committees, with representatives from each school, to accomplish this work. If collaborative teams within a district have not chosen the essential content, they could consider the following five criteria. The first three come from consultant and author Larry Ainsworth (2003), and the last two come from Marzano et al. (2016).

1. **Endurance:** The standard contains knowledge and skills that will last beyond a class period or single course.

2. **Leverage:** The standard contains knowledge and skills that cross over into many domains of learning.

3. **Readiness:** The standard contains knowledge and skills important to subsequent content or courses.

4. **Teacher judgment:** Teachers, as content-area experts, deem the content critical.

5. **Assessment connectedness:** Students have access to the content teachers will assess.

When district leaders use a continual process to align curriculum, instruction, and assessment to state standards and to identify priority standards, they are well prepared to address changes in standards, materials, and external assessments without missing a beat.

District leaders also need to confirm the implemented guaranteed and viable curriculum aligns to state and district assessment outcomes.

One efficient and effective way to do this is to compile the number of priority standards students are proficient on and correlate those numbers with state exam results. Figure 13.2 and figure 13.3 (page 370) from *Leading a High Reliability School* (Marzano et al., 2018) show this type of correlation for Clark-Pleasant Community School Corporation in Indiana. Taking this step lets district leaders see if what they are focusing on is paying dividends on state assessments when students are proficient with the content. District leaders should take this step and do the heavy lifting in this area for each school.

> District leaders also need to confirm the implemented guaranteed and viable curriculum aligns to state and district assessment outcomes.

Ensure Teachers Can Adequately Address the Curriculum in the Time Available

It is critical for district leaders to focus on the curriculum and ensure it is viable. To measure the viability of the curriculum, ask teachers whether or not they have enough time to address the essential standards (or priority standards) in the time they have available. Develop a continual process to gauge teachers' perceptions of this viability, such as the following Likert scale.

> It is critical for district leaders to focus on the curriculum and ensure it is viable.

4. I have all the time I need to address the priority standards with my students.

5. I usually have the time I need to address the priority standards with my students.

6. I sometimes have the time I need to address the priority standards with my students.

1. I rarely have the time I need to address the priority standards with my students.

Using this type of scale, keep mean scores at or above 3. If scores dip below a 3, it is a sign that teachers do not perceive the curriculum as viable. When this is the case, some trimming of priority standards is likely necessary.

Number of Priority Standards With Which Students Reached Proficiency	Third-Grade Language Arts Pass Percentage	Third-Grade Mathematics Pass Percentage	Fourth-Grade Language Arts Pass Percentage	Fourth-Grade Mathematics Pass Percentage
0	0	0	0	0
1	11.1	0	12.5	0
2	14.3	0	25	0
3	23.1	0	57.1	0
4	45	0	20	9.1
5	77.8	23.1	40	0
6	70.6	20.7	52	20
7	62.2	41.7	65.2	33.3
8	75	51.7	73.1	16.7
9	94.4	75.9	66.7	48.3
10	96.8	48.3	88.4	42.9
11	98.3	80	81.5	58.3
12	98.3	84.1	94.9	56
13		95.6		72.7
14				82.1
15				96
16				97.4
Correlation	0.95	0.95	0.94	0.96

Note: All correlations significant at 0.01.
Source: Marzano et al., 2018, p. 178.

Figure 13.2: Percentage of students who passed the 2015 state test who had reached proficiency on priority standards.

Number of Priority Standards With Which Students Reached Proficiency	Third-Grade Language Arts Pass Percentage	Third-Grade Mathematics Pass Percentage	Fourth-Grade Language Arts Pass Percentage	Fourth-Grade Mathematics Pass Percentage	Fifth-Grade Language Arts Pass Percentage	Fifth-Grade Mathematics Pass Percentage
0	24	0	4.4	0	5.9	0
1	25	7.7	12	7.7	13.6	0
2	29.4	0	43.8	0	22.2	13.3
3	60	16.7	56.5	12.5	27	15
4	54.2	18.8	37.5	6.7	35.1	34.8
5	61.9	31.6	64.7	29.2	50	38.1
6	72	17.7	66.7	21.1	74.4	39.1
7	88.9	69	65.6	36	88.9	56.5
8	87.5	54.6	75	40	84.2	68.8
9	82.4	53.3	79.5	56.7	92.7	60
10	95.6	78.4	78	61.8	95.3	70
11	92.9	88.5	97.1	60.6		73.7
12	98.8	97.9		85.3		72.2
13				95.4		87.5
14				100		82.6
15						100
16						100
17						100
18						100
Correlation	0.95	0.95	0.93	0.96	0.98	0.98

Note: All correlations significant at 0.01.
Source: Marzano et al., 2018, p. 179.

Figure 13.3: Percentage of students who passed the 2016 state test who had reached proficiency on priority standards.

Develop and Monitor District-Level Goals

Setting meaningful goals for overall student achievement and monitoring progress toward the goals is another important task for district leaders. In their book *Learning by Doing: A Handbook for Professional Learning Communities at Work*, DuFour et al. (2016) make the case that good district goals are typically broader in nature, as this allows schools to set goals that align to them and collaborative teams to set goals that align to the school goals.

Establishing alignment within the system is important because it helps every district staff member move in the same direction. Good district goals align to the mission of the district. School goals then align to the district goals, and team goals should be SMART goals. According to coauthors Anne E. Conzemius and Jan O'Neill (2014), SMART goals are:

> *Setting meaningful goals for overall student achievement and monitoring progress toward the goals is another important task for district leaders.*

- **S**trategic and specific
- **M**easurable
- **A**ttainable
- **R**esults oriented
- **T**ime bound

See *Learning by Doing* (DuFour et al., 2016) for additional information and many example templates related to team-based SMART goals. Figure 13.4 (page 372) illustrates the flow of a good districtwide goal.

This example (see figure 13.4, page 372) illustrates the flow of a student achievement goal when the focus is on a guaranteed and viable curriculum (HRS level 3). Districts and schools can also set goals in a similar fashion for students' sense of safety and support at school (HRS level 1) as well as for staff collaboration (HRS level 1), effective teaching in every classroom (HRS level 2), and so on. Once leaders set district goals, an important district leaders' task is to support those goals.

Setting district goals is not a difficult process as long as the districtwide mission and vision is clear. Monitoring and supporting

District goal: All students will reach proficiency
on state and district assessments.

School goal: We will increase our rate of students passing both
the English and mathematics state exams from 72 percent
last year to 79 percent.

Fourth-grade collaborative team SMART goal: Eighty-one percent of our
students will pass our state exam in mathematics (up from 77 percent last
year) and 80 percent will pass the state exam in English language arts
(up from 76 percent last year) this school year.

Figure 13.4: The flow of district, school, and collaborative team goals.

goals can be more challenging. District leaders should set clear expectations for schools to submit their goals. There are several purposes for this. First, district leaders need to ensure the school goals align to district goals. When they do not, discussions between school leadership teams and district leaders must clear up confusion and misconceptions and get the building goals into alignment. The second, and perhaps more important, purpose is so district leaders can understand what schools are working on so they know how best to support school leadership teams, and they can, in turn, support teachers and collaborative teams.

Setting district goals is not a difficult process as long as the districtwide mission and vision is clear.

As an example, the school goal in figure 13.4 states the school will increase its rate of students passing both the English language arts and mathematics state exams from 72 percent last year to 79 percent. Achieving this goal requires the school to make some changes in practice. If the school staff take the exact same approach they took in previous years and do not focus on doing some things even better than before, it is likely their results will be similar to previous years, and they will not improve. Assuming improvements will be made and change will occur, district staff are well positioned to hear a school's plan of attack, ask clarifying questions to help the school staff solidify their plans, and support the school with valuable resources such as time, professional development or funding for professional development, connections with other schools or staff members who have implemented similar strategies, or materials to assist in their progress. *Supporter of schools* is a crucial role for district leaders.

Monitoring the work of schools requires a delicate balance. As mentioned previously in this chapter, empowering school leadership teams to operate with defined autonomy or tight and loose leadership is crucial. When this is done well, schools welcome district staff monitoring because they understand the monitoring comes from a place of support; everyone is on the same big team working for the betterment of students. Perhaps the best way to monitor progress is to set a time to periodically check in with building leadership teams to hear how their action plans are progressing and whether their team- and school-level data indicate they are on track to reach their goals. When they get off track, district leaders should assume some responsibility (rather than point fingers), and do everything they can to help the school adjust to meet its goals.

Ensure All Students Have Access to Extra Time and Help

Another important district-level focus for HRS level 3 is to ensure all students in all district schools have access to extra time and extra help within the school day when they need it. District leaders do not have responsibility for building schedules to ensure extra time and extra help for students who need it, but they are responsible for setting the expectation for school leaders to build this extra time into their schedules. Many students cannot come before school, stay after school, or get tutoring on their own. If a district is serious about all students learning at high levels, it will ensure time becomes more of a variable so learning can become a constant. RTI experts and coauthors Austin Buffum, Mike Mattos, and Chris Weber (2012) provide a simple formula for success: "Targeted Instruction + Time = Learning" (p. 8). This means if schools deliver high-quality instruction geared toward the needs of each learner, and teachers have enough time, learning will occur for all students.

> *If a district is serious about all students learning at high levels, it will ensure time becomes more of a variable so learning can become a constant.*

While the formula is simple, pulling it off in schools can be more challenging. Buffum et al. (2012) add, "Very few schools have designed the instructional day to provide every student differentiated instruction and flexible time to learn" (p. 8). However, to fully commit to HRS level 3, this must change. One of the most efficient ways to get started is for schools to build schedules that include extra time for students to learn priority (or essential) standards. This often comes in the form of zero periods—scheduled periods for intervention and enrichment or acceleration rather than an additional course—at the middle school and high school levels, and is often built into each grade-level schedule at the elementary level. District leaders simply need to review building schedules and continually discuss the importance of time as a variable rather than a constant.

District Leadership in HRS Level 4: Standards-Referenced Reporting

Thus far, this chapter has discussed the work all districts must engage in to function effectively at HRS levels 1, 2, and 3. Further, it is not typically controversial work. All schools working to become highly reliable will spend time and effort on levels 1, 2, and 3, but work at level 4 requires a shift from a whole-school perspective to an individual student perspective. Levels 4 and 5 are optional for schools, and they typically represent second-order change. *Second-order change* is a break from the past because this type of change requires new learning and new direction (Levy, 1986). District leaders should be mindful that embarking on second-order changes will lead to declining perceptions of culture, order, opportunities for input, and communication due to the impact the magnitude of the change has on human beings. It simply comes with the territory. District leaders can help mitigate this by working hard at HRS level 1 to shore up the perceptions in those areas prior to beginning a second-order change initiative.

District leaders should be mindful that embarking on second-order changes will lead to declining perceptions of culture, order, opportunities for input, and communication due to the impact the magnitude of the change has on human beings.

Developing proficiency scales that align to priority standards and reporting individual students' status and growth are concepts most schools have not spent a lot of time on. These concepts do, however, have enormous potential to positively impact student achievement. Table 13.5 shows the HRS level 4 district non-negotiables.

Table 13.5: HRS Level 4 District-Level Non-Negotiables

Non-Negotiable	Required District-Level Action	Intended Outcome
Develop proficiency scales (learning progressions) for the critical content.	Discuss and determine the process for putting proficiency scales in place, form a plan, and implement the plan.	All students know their level of performance and next steps to improve on all priority standards. Students set goals, form plans, and monitor their own progress.
Report both status and growth on the report card using proficiency scales.	Work with student information system vendors to ensure report cards reflect each student's status and growth on proficiency scales.	Reporting mechanisms align to priority standards and teachers communicate to students, parents, and the community each student's status and how much growth he or she has achieved during the reporting period.

Develop Proficiency Scales

Proficiency scales can help students identify and pinpoint their current performance level with content so that they know the next steps in their learning progression. This allows them to set more meaningful goals and more authentically monitor their progress toward their goals. Figure 13.5 (page 376) shows an example of a fourth-grade proficiency scale.

There are at least three options for districts that want to begin the process of developing proficiency scales, or progressions of knowledge and skill, for the identified priority standards that are part of their guaranteed and viable curriculum.

1. Purchase proficiency scales to modify and use.

2. Create proficiency scales from scratch.

3. Implement a hybrid approach of purchasing some and building some from scratch.

Score 4.0	The student will:
	• Research a solution that addresses a cause of weathering and erosion (for example, investigate the rate of erosion by a local stream, determine how human activity impacts this rate, and implement a solution that reduces the effect of human activity, such as planting vegetation by the stream bank or maintaining a designated trail through the area).
	Score 3.5 — In addition to score 3.0 performance, partial success at score 4.0 content
Score 3.0	The student will:
	• Identify factors that contribute to weathering and erosion (for example, explain how weathering and erosion are caused by water, ice, wind, and vegetation, and identify factors that increase the effect and rate of weathering and erosion).
	Score 2.5 — No major errors or omissions regarding score 2.0 content, and partial success at score 3.0 content
Score 2.0	The student will recognize or recall specific vocabulary (for example, *erosion, sediment, water, weathering,* and *wind*) and perform basic processes such as:
	• Explain the difference between weathering and erosion (weathering breaks down rocks and minerals into smaller pieces, whereas erosion moves the smaller pieces from place to place).
	• Identify causes of weathering (for example, precipitation, ice, wind, acid rain, water, and vegetation).
	• Identify causes of erosion (for example, wind, water, gravity, snow, and ice).
	• Compare the effects of weathering and erosion over time (for example, a river may not seem to be causing erosion when observed daily but can carve out canyons over long spans of time).
	• Explain how erosion causes deposition of weathered sediments.
	Score 1.5 — Partial success at score 2.0 content, and major errors or omissions regarding score 3.0 content
Score 1.0	With help, partial success at score 2.0 content and score 3.0 content
	Score 0.5 — With help, partial success at score 2.0 content but not at score 3.0 content
Score 0.0	Even with help, no success

Source: Marzano et al., 2018, p. 138.

Figure 13.5: Proficiency scale for a grade 4 unit on weathering and erosion.

There are pros and cons to each approach. District leaders should carefully weigh the options.

The biggest advantage of purchasing proficiency scales is the time savings associated with having a model and initial thoughts already developed, and knowing that the proficiency scales have already been vetted by a third party. The state of Maine sells its proficiency scales. Marzano Resources has developed a core set of Critical Concept Proficiency Scales (Simms, 2016). Many school districts have developed their own proficiency scales and might be willing to share or sell them to other districts. When taking this approach, district leaders should ensure that teams of teachers from across the district get together to make modifications and changes to make the proficiency scales their own. The biggest disadvantage of this approach is that some level of commitment to the scales could be lost since they are delivered to staff instead of developed by them.

The biggest advantage to having staff create proficiency scales from scratch is that, in the end, staff members are invested in what they created. In addition, when staff get together across schools to discuss and debate the progression of knowledge required for each priority standard, they create a lot of content expertise and clarity. The biggest disadvantage of this approach is that it does take a lot of time, expertise in facilitating, effort, and energy.

The advantages to a hybrid approach are it allows school districts to see some exemplar proficiency scales to model theirs after, and this approach might help teams along who might have initially struggled to develop quality learning progressions on their own. This approach might also be good in districts where funding is tight. The disadvantage of this approach is that it is a challenge to maintain coherence when some proficiency scales are purchased and others are staff developed.

District leaders need to take the lead in proficiency scale development. This is an immense task that would not make sense for each school to take on individually if the entire district were working to become highly reliable in this area. District leaders have the ability to pull multiple stakeholders together from all schools to ensure the highest-quality end product and should take the lead in doing so.

District leaders need to take the lead in proficiency scale development.

Use Report Cards That Indicate Individual Student Status and Growth

Reporting status and growth on student report cards often requires district leaders to work with their student information system vendors to make changes. District leaders must complete this work, as it would be difficult for each school to communicate its needs to these vendors. In addition, school leaders around the world have seen this as a constant area of challenge and often consternation. While it seems easy to adjust report cards to indicate current status or performance level as well as growth over time, these changes often require major alterations within a district's student information system. The reality is, many of those systems were not built on the notion that both status and growth are important. Figure 13.6 represents the type of report card districts utilize to illustrate individual student status and growth.

Language Arts		
Reading:		
Word Recognition and Vocabulary	2.5	
Reading for Main Idea	1.5	
Literary Analysis	2.0	
Writing:		
Language Conventions	3.5	
Organization and Focus	2.5	
Research and Technology	1.0	
Evaluation and Revision	2.5	
Writing Applications	3.0	
Listening and Speaking:		
Comprehension	3.0	
Organization and Delivery	3.0	
Analysis and Evaluation of Oral Media	2.5	
Speaking Applications	2.5	
Life Skills:		
Participation	4.0	
Work Completion	3.5	
Behavior	3.5	
Working in Groups	3.0	
Average for Language Arts	2.46	

Mathematics		
Number Systems	3.5	
Estimation	3.0	
Addition/Subtraction	2.5	
Multiplication/Division	2.5	
Ratio/Proportion/Percent	1.0	
Life Skills:		
Participation	4.0	
Work Completion	2.0	
Behavior	3.5	
Working in Groups	2.0	
Average for Mathematics	2.50	
Science		
Matter and Energy	2.0	
Forces of Nature	2.5	
Diversity of Life	1.5	
Human Identity	3.5	
Interdependence of Life	1.5	
Life Skills:		
Participation	3.0	
Work Completion	1.5	
Behavior	2.5	
Working in Groups	1.0	
Average for Science	2.20	
Social Studies		
The Influence of Culture	3.5	
Current Events	3.0	
Personal Responsibility	4.0	
Government Representation	3.5	
Human and Civil Rights	1.5	
Life Skills:		
Participation	3.5	
Work Completion	3.5	

Figure 13.6: Sample report card for fourth grade.

The black bars represent a student's starting point with the content. The gray bars represent the student's growth over time. Districts can also choose to maintain letter grades with this type of report card; they average the final scores for each subject using a conversion scale like the following.

A = 3.00 to 4.00

B = 2.50 to 2.99

C = 2.00 to 2.49

D = 1.00 to 1.99

F = Below 1.00

Leading the change with proficiency scales and report cards is important work for district leaders.

District Leadership in HRS Level 5: Competency-Based Education

In many districts, moving to competency-based education could seem like a radical idea. In competency-based education systems, students advance based on their demonstrated mastery of the learning objectives for the course whenever that occurs, rather than with a cohort at the end of the school year. Having students matriculate based on their competency at each level (rather than with their age group of peers) is an enormous shift and clearly second-order change almost everywhere. District leaders engage in some important work if or when a decision is made to move in this direction. It is recommended that district leaders discuss the possibilities, concerns, and possible challenges with stakeholder groups prior to a decision being made to move to a competency-based approach. In the best-case scenario, a large majority of stakeholders would agree that it would be good for the students in the district to move to a competency-based approach and would help plan and support the change. Table 13.6 represents the recommended nonnegotiables for HRS level 5.

In many districts, moving to competency-based education could seem like a radical idea.

Table 13.6: HRS Level 5 District-Level Non-Negotiables

Non-Negotiable	Required District-Level Action	Intended Outcome
Students move to the next level of curriculum when they demonstrate competence at the previous level.	Ensure time is a variable. Put processes in place to develop systems and schedules that allow students to progress at their own pace.	Tailored daily work challenges all students toward their unique learning needs.
Students have access to advanced content or career paths of interest once they demonstrate competence at all levels.	Ensure advanced content and career paths of interest are available to students in all schools.	Once students learn all the required content, career paths of interest and advanced content continue to challenge them.

Ensure Student Movement in the System

District leaders should stand ready to assist building leaders in developing schedules that allow students to advance to the next level of content as soon as they demonstrate proficiency with current content. Schedules that work well are highlighted in chapters 9 and 10 of this book (pages 257 and 277). Since such schedules are not traditional, helping school leaders problem solve and find creative ways to make the schedules work is crucial. In addition, district leaders will need to assist by appropriately staffing schools in the districtwide competency-based system. In many states, teaching content at different levels requires different licenses. Ensuring that teachers with proper licensure are available and working in schools moving to competency-based systems is also important work for district leaders.

Provide Student Access to Advanced Content and Career Paths

At some point, students learn all the traditional material teachers expect them to in the preK–12 curriculum. When they do, students need to have a place to go next. One of the best solutions is for the school district to prepare advanced courses, often for college credit. Another option is to get students involved in a career path, where they can continue to learn, hone their skills, and prepare for life after schooling.

Conclusion

District leadership is immensely important—especially in a district seeking to operate from a high reliability perspective. District leaders and district leadership teams should focus on the leading indicators that best fit within their scope of influence. While it is true the work is complex (due to the multiple variables that influence each school), it is also extremely rewarding to know that every student in the district feels the impact of a district leader or leadership team.

District leaders and district leadership teams should focus on the leading indicators that best fit within their scope of influence.

Every student deserves to have all of his or her needs met, and every student deserves to learn at high levels. In an HRS district, these are basic student rights. A PLC foundation and the HRS model at the district level are the mechanisms that help leaders to achieve their mission and ensure delivery on these student rights.

References and Resources

Ainsworth, L. (2003). *Power standards: Identifying the standards that matter the most.* Boston: Houghton Mifflin Harcourt.

Buffum, A., Mattos, M., & Weber, C. (2012). *Simplifying response to intervention: Four essential guiding principles.* Bloomington, IN: Solution Tree Press.

Conzemius, A. E., & O'Neill, J. (2014). *The handbook for SMART school teams: Revitalizing best practices for collaboration* (2nd ed.). Bloomington, IN: Solution Tree Press.

Danielson, C. (2014). *The framework for teaching evaluation instrument, 2013 edition: The newest rubric enhancing the links to the Common Core State Standards, with clarity of language for ease of use and scoring.* Chicago: Author.

DuFour, R., DuFour, R., Eaker, R., Many, T. W., & Mattos, M. (2016). *Learning by doing: A handbook for Professional Learning Communities at Work* (3rd ed.). Bloomington, IN: Solution Tree Press.

DuFour, R., & Marzano, R. J. (2011). *Leaders of learning: How district, school, and classroom leaders improve student achievement.* Bloomington, IN: Solution Tree Press.

Elmore, R. F. (2004). *School reform from the inside out: Policy, practice, and performance.* Cambridge, MA: Harvard Education Press.

Hitt, D. H., & Tucker, P. D. (2016). Systematic review of key leader practices found to influence student achievement: A unified framework. *Review of Educational Research, 86*(2), 531–569.

Levy, A. (1986). Second-order planned change: Definition and conceptualization. *Organisational Dynamics, 15*(1), 5–17, 19–23.

Louis, K. S., Leithwood, K., Wahlstrom, K. L., & Anderson, S. E. (2010, July). *Investigating the links to improved student learning: Final report of research findings.* St. Paul: University of Minnesota, Center for Applied Research and Educational Improvement. Accessed at www.wallacefoundation.org/knowledge-center/Documents/Investigating -the-Links-to-Improved-Student-Learning.pdf on October 11, 2017.

Marzano, R. J. (2003). *What works in schools: Translating research into action.* Alexandria, VA: Association for Supervision and Curriculum Development.

Marzano, R. J. (2017). *The new art and science of teaching.* Bloomington, IN: Solution Tree Press.

Marzano, R. J., Heflebower, T., Hoegh, J. K., Warrick, P. B., & Grift, G. (2016). *Collaborative teams that transform schools: The next step in PLCs.* Bloomington, IN: Marzano Resources.

Marzano, R. J., Rains, C. L., & Warrick, P. B. (in press). *Reflecting on, observing, and coaching teaching.* Bloomington, IN: Solution Tree Press.

Marzano, R. J., Scott, D., Boogren, T. H., & Newcomb, M. L. (2017). *Motivating and inspiring students: Strategies to awaken the learner.* Bloomington, IN: Marzano Resources.

Marzano, R. J., Warrick, P. B., Rains, C. L., & DuFour, R. (2018). *Leading a high reliability School.* Bloomington, IN: Solution Tree Press.

Marzano, R. J., & Waters, T. (2009). *District leadership that works: Striking the right balance.* Bloomington, IN: Solution Tree Press.

Schmoker, M. (2019). Embracing the power of less. *Educational Leadership, 76*(6), 24–29.

Simms, J. A. (2016). *The critical concepts (draft version 2.0).* Centennial, CO: Marzano Resources. Accessed at https://1ddlxtt2jowkvs672myo6z14-wpengine.netdna-ssl.com /wp-content/uploads/2016/02/criticalconcepts-2-18-16.pdf on September 5, 2019.

Steinberg, M. P., & Kraft, M. A. (2017). The sensitivity of teacher performance ratings to the design of teacher evaluation systems. *Educational Researcher, 46*(7), 378–396.

Sulkowski, M. L., & Lazarus, P. J. (2017). *Creating safe and supportive schools and fostering students' mental health.* New York: Routledge.

Waters, T., & Marzano, R. J. (2006, September). *School district leadership that works: The effect of superintendent leadership on student achievement—A working paper.* Denver, CO: McREL.

Marc Johnson

Marc Johnson, MEd, an educator for more than forty years, is codirector of the Central Valley Educational Leadership Institute at California State University, Fresno. He taught in a K–8 district for sixteen years, served as junior high vice principal, and later served as superintendent and principal. He is the former superintendent of Sanger Unified School District in California, having first served as assistant superintendent for human resources and associate superintendent.

Under Johnson's leadership, Sanger became a districtwide professional learning community (PLC). Twenty Sanger schools have been recognized as California State Distinguished Schools and eighteen schools as Title I Academic Achieving Schools, and three schools have been named National Blue Ribbon Schools. Two K–8 schools and the middle school have been named Schools to Watch (all three twice), making Sanger only the second district in the United States to have every middle school on this list. Johnson was named the American Association of School Administrators' 2011 National Superintendent of the Year and is the author of *How to Coach Leadership in a PLC*.

To book Marc Johnson for professional development, contact pd@SolutionTree.com.

In this chapter, Johnson offers his insights into districtwide leadership within the PLC context through his journey of transformation as superintendent of Sanger Unified School District, a district the California Department of Education identified as a Program Improvement (PI) district.

Chapter 14

Leadership in a High-Performing PLC

Marc Johnson

When preparing their children for the start of the school year, parents often worry about which classrooms they will land in. It's impossible to take away all parents' worries; however, they shouldn't have to worry about whether or not their children will learn what they need to learn in a course or grade level. What if parents were assured that the result would be spectacular regardless of classroom or teacher because *learning* is the guaranteed outcome—not for some, but for all—in a district? In my mind, this desire really defines what an HRS district is: a place where the focus, structures, and actions of adults provide every student with the support he or she needs to be successful. This place can become a reality in a district that functions as a PLC.

Thankfully, district leaders now have greater clarity regarding the focus, structures, and actions that make schools highly reliable. Coauthors Robert J. Marzano, Philip B. Warrick, Cameron L. Rains, and Richard DuFour (2018) share, "Although the HRS model is designed as a school-level framework . . . it can become even more powerful when an entire school district decides to embark on becoming highly reliable," adding, "If district leadership sets its sights on all of its schools operating as high reliability organizations, then it should adhere to the general principles of the PLC process" (Marzano et al.,

2018, p. 169). While reform efforts are anchored at the school-site level, *all* schools should be on a journey of improvement, so it makes sense that it should be a shared journey—a districtwide journey.

While reform efforts are anchored at the school-site level, all schools should be on a journey of improvement, so it makes sense that it should be a shared journey—a districtwide journey.

Developing Clarity About the Role of District Leaders

Time and again, Richard DuFour, architect of the PLC at Work process (along with Robert Eaker), would remind school leaders of consultant and author Mike Schmoker's (2004) important words, "Clarity precedes competence!" (p. 85). To help develop clarity about the role of district leadership, we must ask, "Does district leadership involvement in developing PLCs to become HRS districts actually make a difference?"

DuFour partnered with authors, researchers, and leadership experts Michael Fullan and Robert J. Marzano to investigate both the impact and importance of district leadership. DuFour and Fullan (2013) find:

> District leaders maintained a commitment to and focus on building the individual and collective capacity of educators throughout the district. . . . The district provided educators with the ongoing clarity and support to help them succeed at what they were being asked to do. In short, they worked to ensure that every school was functioning as a PLC. (p. 6)

DuFour and Marzano (2011) find:

> Leadership from the central office matters—both in terms of raising student achievement and in terms of creating the conditions for adult learning that lead to higher levels of student achievement. Without effective leadership from the central office, the PLC process will not become deeply embedded in schools throughout a district. (p. 45)

In both findings, the district leadership role is actually essential for successful implementation of the PLC process in every school; these leaders provide the structure and focus needed to raise student achievement. To lead this shift successfully, be aware that district leaders, especially superintendents, must address the culture of your organization. Changing culture can be challenging. As DuFour and Fullan (2013) note:

> Unlike structural change that can be mandated, cultural change requires altering long-held assumptions, beliefs, expectations, and habits that represent the norm for people in the organization. These deeply held but typically unexamined assumptions help people make sense of their world. More simply put, culture is just "the way we do things around here." Systematic implementation of the PLC process requires changing the way things have typically been done at all levels. (p. 2)

They go on to describe the need to develop a sense of *"systemness— the degree to which people identify and are committed to an entity larger than themselves"* (DuFour & Fullan, 2013, p. 18), which exists when everyone not only understands the work of a PLC but also contributes as a member of the PLC. DuFour and Fullan (2013) further describe some of the challenges and issues leaders must address to change the culture:

- Establishing coherence and clarity regarding purpose and priorities throughout the organization

- Building shared knowledge about the rationale for change

- Engaging in meaningful two-way dialogue throughout the change process

- Identifying the specific steps that must be taken immediately to make progress toward long-term aspirational goals

- Creating a culture that is simultaneously loose and tight

- Building collective capacity around the agenda of improving student achievement

- Demonstrating reciprocal accountability by providing the resources and support to help people succeed at what they are being asked to do

- Establishing ongoing feedback loops that help people assess the impact of their efforts and make adjustments accordingly

- Ensuring transparency of results, and using results to inform and improve practice

- Creating a collaborative culture in which people take collective responsibility for the success of the initiative
- Establishing trust
- Developing lots of leaders
- Fostering self-efficacy
- Maintaining focus and limiting initiatives
- Managing resistance
- Sustaining the improvement process—even when key leaders have left the organization
- Celebrating small wins (p. 19)

As a leader, knowing the challenges and issues is not enough, however. Leaders must take action, and *how* they take action is critical.

> Leaders must take action, and how they take action is critical.

Leading by example is how to work through the change process; this is also the best way to clarify focus and expectations (DuFour, DuFour, Eaker, Many, & Mattos, 2016). In *Learning by Doing*, DuFour et al. (2016) note:

> In every instance of effective systemwide implementation of the PLC process we have witnessed, central office leaders visibly modeled the commitment to learning for all students, collaboration, collective inquiry, and the results orientation they expected to see in other educators throughout the district. They created structures and processes to help principals and teachers function as collaborative teams. They celebrated progress and confronted individuals whose actions did not reflect the district's priorities. (p. 239)

The district leader's role involves shifting the organizational culture, and the shift begins with departing from a culture of autonomy and isolation and working toward a culture of collaboration, the foundation of both the PLC process (DuFour et al., 2016) and the HRS model (Marzano, Warrick, & Simms, 2014). It is also necessary for district leaders to model for others the expectations and behaviors necessary to change outcomes.

Others have added their thinking to the conversation regarding the role of district leadership to transform whole systems to high-functioning PLCs that generate highly reliable outcomes in all schools.

DuFour and Marzano (2011) describe the following five points of concentration or focus for district leaders.

1. Effective district leaders both direct and empower others.

2. Effective district leaders create a common language.

3. Effective district leaders monitor the PLC process in each school as they develop principals' leadership capacity.

4. Effective superintendents limit initiatives.

5. Effective superintendents communicate priorities effectively.

The last two reference the superintendent, who is a critical member of the district leadership team and who must be knowledgeable as well as actively and visibly engaged in leading this work. In *How to Launch PLCs in Your District*, author W. Richard Smith (2015) says district leaders should focus their efforts in four main areas to support successful implementation of PLC systems and structures:

1. Developing a district guiding coalition and common language

2. Empowering site leadership through staff development and training

3. Monitoring to sustain momentum

4. Ensuring sustainability through ongoing commitment and implementation (p. 11)

Again we see similarities between the recommendations: the needs to have a common language, to monitor the process along the way to support implementation and gauge where additional capacity building may be needed, and finally, to build staff knowledge and skills and support staff as they lead the work at the site level. Having looked at the recommendations of the experts regarding the role of district leadership in initiating and supporting the implementation and development of the PLC process districtwide, you might find it helpful to hear of one district's journey of implementation and the role district leadership played in the process. In this chapter, I share the PLC journey of Sanger Unified School District, where I served as superintendent.

Taking a Pathway to Improvement

Sanger is located in the heart of the Central Valley of California, east of Fresno. The district has a student enrollment of over eleven thousand students, who mirror the demographics of the region—high poverty, high minority, and high English learner, with an overall low parent education level. In the summer of 2004, the state superintendent of schools notified the district it was among the first group of ninety-eight districts in California designated a Program Improvement (PI) district for failing to meet the annual yearly progress (AYP) requirements under the federal No Child Left Behind Act (NCLB) for multiple years. Six of the district's schools already had PI status at various levels, defined by the number of consecutive years (some as many as six years). Those sites had failed to generate the needed achievement gains, and now the entire district was labeled as underperforming primarily due to its failure to generate adequate achievement gains with English learners.

The entire district leadership team was new to both its roles and the district. With a new leadership team in place, Sanger's PI status could have posed an insurmountable challenge. Instead, it served as a motivator for the leaders to seek a pathway to improvement and make a commitment to becoming a district where every school—no matter its status in the existing accountability system—became a place where all students learn at high levels—and *all* really means *all*! That desire led me (as superintendent), along with the assistant superintendent for curriculum and instruction and two site principals, to travel to Riverside County in Southern California to hear Richard DuFour and Rebecca DuFour deliver a two-day overview of the PLC process. That introduction convinced Sanger's leaders (the superintendent and assistant superintendent) they had found what they had been looking for. They knew the pathway to improvement must be a pathway of districtwide implementation of the PLC process. And so the journey began.

They knew the pathway to improvement must be a pathway of districtwide implementation of the PLC process. And so the journey began.

Starting at the Top

I have worked with many educators who are in charge of implementation of the PLC process in their districts as I prepare to come in and provide a PLC overview for teachers and principals. Some of those I have worked with have the best intentions, truly seeing the value of this work and being committed to this work. Others I have worked with view the effort as just the latest initiative of the curriculum and instruction department or some coordinator's most recent idea for reform because he or she went to a conference or read a book, so they are going through the motions. In those situations, people come to training because they have to (oftentimes in a room filled with teachers only, no principals or district leaders to be found), and they go through the motions as a compliance response. This does not lead to successful implementation in the district or at the site because leaders have not clarified that the PLC journey is the foundational work of the district. For this clarity to exist, the superintendent must be knowledgeable about, committed to, and actually engaged in leading this district work. Leading by proclamation or mandate results in a compliance response. Leading by example helps develop a collaborative culture, the cornerstone of this work and one of the three big ideas of a PLC, along with a focus on learning and a results orientation (DuFour et al., 2016).

Another specific role of the superintendent DuFour and Marzano (2011) suggest is limiting initiatives. When we began our journey at Sanger, it was clear to all that becoming a PLC was the most important work of the district. This belief was tightly held and non-negotiable.

Our other major focus areas actually supported this foundational work: building intervention systems at every site, supporting English learners, and developing a districtwide shared commitment to effective initial instruction. As the superintendent, I clearly and repeatedly communicated these focus areas. School sites, then, had the autonomy to accomplish the work using the strengths of their teams to meet the unique needs of their students. This embracing of a *simultaneously loose and tight* culture is a critical role of district leadership and, in particular, the superintendent.

The superintendent also needs to ensure the board of education not only understands but also supports this ongoing work. The board must understand why the work is essential and *how* students will benefit from the change. Building clarity with your board on the *why* of the improvement effort will make supporting the *what* (the shifts and changes needed to become a PLC) easier in the face of resistance. At Sanger, district leadership not only kept the board informed about the work but also, over time, began a process of establishing board visitations to all the school sites to actually see the work in progress. These visits helped board members develop deeper levels of clarity and understanding.

During a March 2017 visit to Adlai E. Stevenson High School in Lincolnshire, Illinois, where Richard DuFour began this PLC work in the late 1980s, I had the pleasure of meeting an individual who served on the board while DuFour was leading this work. He shared the importance of keeping the board informed, how well DuFour did this, and what a difference it made on their PLC journey.

> A key element of a PLC is building dispersed leadership, which begins at the top.

A key element of a PLC is building dispersed leadership, which begins at the top. District leaders support this by creating district- and site-level guiding coalitions to lead PLC implementation.

Building Guiding Coalitions

The foundational pillars of a PLC are to develop a shared mission, vision, values (collective commitments), and goals (DuFour et al., 2016). The operative word here is *shared*. No matter how much you believe this is the right work, you can't do it alone. Having groups of individuals who not only understand the work but also support and help guide PLC implementation is necessary. Admittedly, we did not formally establish guiding coalitions as we began our journey at Sanger. The four of us who attended the two-day overview with the DuFours had no doubt this structure and focus would transform our district. We also had a group of leaders at our high school who engaged in another learning initiative in Riverside County, California, and they had a growing understanding of PLC work. This small group became the informal district guiding coalition and began to envision a pathway to districtwide implementation. One advantage we had as

> I recommend district leaders establish two guiding coalitions— one district level and the other site level— when embarking on PLC transformation.

we began our journey actually came from the PI label. Because of this designation, we had already built a systemwide understanding of why we needed to do a better job for our students, so we already understood the why. I recommend district leaders establish two guiding coalitions—one district level and the other site level—when embarking on PLC transformation.

District-Level Guiding Coalition

When the Sanger Unified administrative retreat was held before the start of the school year for all administrators, including site principals and vice principals, district office directors and coordinators, and the deputy and assistant superintendent and the superintendent, district leaders gave a brief overview of the PLC process and then gave all principals a copy of the first edition of *Learning by Doing: A Handbook for Professional Learning Communities at Work* (DuFour, DuFour, Eaker, & Many, 2006), instructing them to read the book and begin the journey at their sites. This was not the best implementation strategy, but I was fortunate—our district leadership team included an incredibly talented and pragmatic assistant superintendent for curriculum and instruction. I also knew every principal and at least one teacher leader from every site would be going to Riverside County for two days of PLC training.

The second trip to Riverside helped the district superintendent and assistant superintendent, who were again in attendance, understand the need to formalize developing a guiding coalition at both the district and site levels. Connecting district, site, and teacher team leaders to build clarity about the work helps accelerate the journey toward competence. The district leadership team members realized the need to share a common vision, develop deep understanding of the work, commit to supporting it, and ensure they spoke with one voice. Our district-level guiding coalition included key members of the district leadership team.

Smith (2015) gives some great advice to district leaders regarding how to establish the district-level guiding coalition, including making the highest-ranking district official (in many cases, the superintendent) responsible for PLC implementation and inviting individuals to be members. This district official must intentionally select members who have a focus on ensuring successful implementation. Keep the following points in mind during your selection process:

- Consider those who have the following attributes within the district.
    - Credibility
    - Expertise

- Influence
- Position power

- Avoid inviting those who may see participation as a stepping-stone to getting administrative positions or gaining power.

- Invite those who listen well, give frank and honest observations, and have students' best interest at heart.

- Ensure the prospective members clearly understand the coalition's purpose. (Smith, 2015, p. 14)

The leader must then build the coalition's knowledge, understanding, and capacity by connecting members with resources such as *Learning by Doing* (DuFour et al., 2016) or PLC experts. Smith (2015) adds, "The group's size should allow members to have constructive discussions—too large and the guiding coalition meetings become nothing more than informational gatherings; too small and the coalition may not give a realistic picture of the district's efforts" (p. 14).

Site-Level Guiding Coalition

At Sanger, site principals were members of the district guiding coalition. A critical role for these site leaders was to establish their own site-level guiding coalition. Typically, the site guiding coalition includes the site administration team, the principal and vice principals or the curriculum support provider (a teacher on special assignment in a support role for sites that do not have a vice principal), and all collaborative teacher team leaders. District leaders must make it clear to all principals the importance of selecting guiding coalition leaders rather than allowing their grade-level or subject-specific teams to appoint them. District leaders must also help principals understand they must consider four factors when selecting their guiding coalition teacher leaders:

1. **Their influence with colleagues:** Is this an individual whose credibility with others is so strong that his or her support for an initiative or idea will influence others in that direction?

2. **Their willingness to be a champion of the PLC process:** Is this someone who demonstrates an understanding

and support of the process by modeling commitment to learning, collaboration, and a focus on results?

3. **Their sense of self-efficacy and willingness to persist:** Is this someone who understands that the solutions do not lie anywhere else but with us, who can demonstrate his or her belief that it is the collective actions of the team that will have a positive impact on results, and who will develop solutions when faced with challenges?

4. **The ability to think systematically:** Is this someone who can bring coherence to the team process by helping the team see the connection that teamwork has with improving the school and the district? (DuFour & Marzano, 2011, as cited in Johnson, 2015, p. 27)

The role of the site guiding coalition is critical to move the work forward and to connect the school to the district's work.

At Sanger, we developed our guiding coalitions as we recognized the need. Others recommend initially forming the district guiding coalition to develop a core group of supporters who will then provide essential support in building broader system awareness and buy-in, plus assist in the implementation process (DuFour et al., 2016). Establishing this district guiding coalition and building members' support is a great starting place because, "if you can't persuade a small group of people of the merits of an idea and enlist their help, there is little chance you will persuade the larger group" (DuFour et al., 2016, p. 27). District leaders can then begin to develop a common vocabulary within district- and site-level guiding coalitions.

> *The role of the site guiding coalition is critical to move the work forward and to connect the school to the district's work.*

Developing a Common Language

The need for district leaders to develop a common language and common understanding is critically important to bring clarity to the implementation process. As DuFour and Marzano (2011) note:

Although this sounds relatively simple, many districts settle for the use of jargon without developing a common understanding of *the implications for specific action* behind the terms. *Differentiated instruction, response to intervention, formative assessment,* and *professional learning communities* are just a few examples of terms commonly used in districts who have no clear or consistent understanding of what those terms mean.

Leaders who develop a common language do not settle for a superficial use of key terms. Instead, they drill deeper to ensure that there is understanding behind each term. (p. 34)

Developing a common language is important, but developing clarity on the meaning and, more important, the necessary actions to demonstrate understanding is essential. I have worked with district leaders who believed they had embarked on a PLC journey, but I quickly realized the only thing they had changed was their vocabulary. They called a grade-level or department meeting "collaboration" and the group of people meeting a "team," but their teams showed no evidence of collaboration or that team members had a sense of mutual accountability and interdependence. A common vocabulary is meaningless unless educators understand the actions associated with the vocabulary. There is a reason DuFour, DuFour, Eaker, Many, and Mattos (2016) advocate *learning by doing* and not *learning by labeling*! After all, *actions* create highly reliable outcomes. To aid in the development of common language and the actions needed to "live the language," the assistant superintendent for curriculum and instruction developed a flowchart of the steps taken by collaborative teacher teams to answer the four critical questions: (1) What do we want our students to learn? (2) How will we know they have learned it? (3) How will we respond when they have not learned it? and (4) How will we respond when they have learned it? Everything from *essential standards* to *common formative assessments* and *SMART goals* was on the flowchart, and the tool helped to keep teacher teams focused and aided principals as they worked to deepen the understanding and function of their teacher collaborative teams.

> Developing a common language is important, but developing clarity on the meaning and, more important, the necessary actions to demonstrate understanding is essential.

District leaders should develop and support site principals in many ways in addition to developing a common vocabulary.

Developing and Supporting Site Principals

Research supports the critical role of site leadership in improving student learning outcomes:

> In short, a justifiable conclusion one can glean from the research is that the more skilled the building principal, the more learning can be expected among students. Stated differently, the research now supports what practitioners have known for decades: powerful school leadership on the part of the principal has a positive effect on student achievement. (DuFour & Marzano, 2011, p. 48)

So the role of the principal is clearly to lead learning and to impact student outcomes in a positive way:

> If principals directly influence how teachers can learn together, they will maximize their impact on student learning. Second, although the route to impacting student achievement is one step removed, causally speaking, it must be nonetheless explicit. If principals merely enable teachers to work together and do not help forge the final link to learning, the process will fail. (Fullan, 2014, pp. 65–66)

The role of the principal is clearly to lead learning and to impact student outcomes in a positive way.

Researchers Milbrey McLaughlin and Joan Talbert (2006, as cited in DuFour & Marzano, 2011) also share the importance of the principal's role in their research: "Principals arguably are the most important players affecting the character and consequences of teachers' school-site professional communities. Principals are culture-makers, intentionally or not" (p. 47).

To deliberately impact the culture of their site, principals must understand and be deeply committed to the work they lead. The role of district leadership is to ensure the principals' learning, so district leaders must provide principals with learning opportunities. District leaders must ensure adult learning is an ongoing, job-embedded process at each school site. That support deepens principals' commitment to the work.

Smith (2015) suggests district leaders attend training with principals to send a clear message of their commitment. District leaders can also "directly answer questions, reassure principals of the district's support, and act as a *dipstick* to measure buy-in and site leadership commitment" (Smith, 2015, p. 32).

We took this practice to heart as we implemented the PLC process at Sanger. In addition to our first visit to Riverside County in May 2005, that November we returned with every site principal, at least one teacher leader from every site, bargaining unit leadership including the unit president and vice president, and all cabinet-level district office administrators, including the deputy superintendent for business services, the assistant superintendents for curriculum and instruction and for human resources, and the director of student services. I attended this training as well. At that time, the Riverside County Office of Education was driving the PLC transformation in its region by bringing the DuFours in to train twice a year (fall and spring), and so we made the journey for the next five years. Principals brought different teachers from their schools every time. District leaders led the follow-up by processing conversations at the end of each day of training that engaged the whole district team in reviewing the day's key points of learning.

Attending training with experts is a great way to deepen understanding and commitment, but it is not enough to learn from others about the work. District leaders must also create ways to learn together as they do the work. Principal meetings are a common occurrence in districts; these meetings generally cover the nuts and bolts of operations and expectations. These meetings, with slight modifications, can also serve as strong connections to the PLC work itself. Sanger's assistant superintendent for curriculum and instruction ran the district's

It is not enough to learn from others about the work. District leaders must also create ways to learn together as they do the work.

principal meetings; he made the needed shifts in meeting structure to support principal learning. Rather than occurring at the district office, which had been tradition, principal meetings were moved to the school sites. At each meeting, the host principal would share his or her current focus or problem of practice, and the principals in the meeting would engage in inquiry and provide feedback to the host principal. Often a portion of the meeting time would also involve classroom visitations to see the site's work firsthand. Sanger's principals, seeing the value of site-based learning opportunities, began their own network of collaborative learning and support. Clusters of principals would gather at a host site specifically to walk through classes and observe instructional practice, but more important, to see how effective collaboration and shared commitments to essential student learning were taking place from room to room. Intervention structures, master schedules, and support for English learners all became topics of site-based shared learning opportunities supporting the principals' development as leaders of learning. Schools will not see the student achievement gains they are looking for if district leadership does not support principals' growth.

Just as it is important for district leaders to be present in learning situations with principals, it is equally important for principals to engage in learning with their teachers. Notice that I write *engage*, not just *attend*. I have worked in districts to develop an understanding of the PLC process, and in many cases, a group of well-intended teachers are the only ones from the site in attendance with no one from their site leadership sharing the learning. Sometimes principals are off in a corner of the room answering email, reviewing their master schedule, and so on—they are in the room, but not engaged in learning. This sends a very strong negative message to others regarding the importance of learning. At Sanger, we required principals to attend training with their teachers and to engage with them about the learning during the course of the school day. We later modified our approach, requiring school leadership teams to attend together and then plan together how to share their new knowledge with the rest of the staff, and also how to embed that knowledge into their collaborative teams. We invited the site teams in as cohorts with similar schools who then became a broader collaborative learning network, as site principals and site team leaders interacted with one another. This proved to be a very effective shift in our practice as district leadership invested in capacity building and shared learning.

Another focus of district leaders in a PLC is to implement processes to monitor site and team progress.

Monitoring Progress

District leaders—in fact, leaders at all levels—must develop connections to the work that allow everyone to monitor progress. The old adage "What gets monitored, gets done!" is very true. But monitoring for the sake of monitoring will often only lead to compliance from those being monitored. Effective monitoring generates data about progress on the improvement journey and drives next steps. As we began our PLC journey at Sanger, we believed having some sort of team-generated artifacts would provide principals with information regarding team focus and function. These artifacts also served as a tool for district leadership to monitor principals' engagement and effectiveness in developing a collaborative culture at the site level. We started with a simple district-created agenda each team was expected to complete during meetings. The agenda asked for the following information.

District leaders—in fact, leaders at all levels—must develop connections to the work that allow everyone to monitor progress.

- Date of the meeting
- Team members present
- What do we want students to learn?
- How will we know if students are learning?
- How will we respond when students don't learn?
- How will we extend learning for students who are already proficient?
- Other discussion topics

This agenda structure covers the four critical questions of a PLC that drive the work of collaborative teams, but it does not really demand much of the team in terms of tracking quality outcomes during its collaboration time. This agenda generated compliance responses in many cases: the team met, members talked for a while, and then the team leader wrote something down on the district form and turned it in to his or her principal. When we (district leaders), along with site principals, looked at what teams were generating, we saw that often teams were just having a grade-level meeting and calling it collaboration, which was clear by the number of "other discussion topics," which had little or nothing to do with student learning. It was a start, though, as the agenda provided information that helped drive the clarifying and coaching conversations district leaders needed to have with principals. This, in turn, led to clarifying the conversations principals needed to have with school leadership teams to develop deeper understanding of the four critical questions, which led to a shared commitment to what learning really needed to look like.

It wasn't very long before principals began to push back on the use of the district-created agenda and request we develop a new form. Our response? "If you need a better agenda form, why don't you and your leadership team design the agenda you need to guide the work and serve as a resource for future work! Our only requirement is that you have an agenda that your teams use." Each school began to improve its agenda forms, and as collaborative team function improved, so did the agendas. Principals began to share their latest iterations with one another, which further supported site improvements. Agendas began to include items such as the following.

- Date of the meeting

- Team members present

- Team norms

- SMART goal

- Essential standards and learning targets

- Results from formative assessments in the form of disaggregated data for the grade-level students who did or did not reach proficiency

- Intervention plans

- Strengths and gaps in student learning

- Intervention results

- Data or information requirements for the next meeting

- Notes on what the team learned

A very different level of team response was now occurring! Teams were not filling out a form to be compliant or to meet an expectation; they were documenting student learning outcomes and their own team learning, creating a valuable archive of team learning to refer to in the future.

The agendas were just one artifact teams used to document student learning and team growth. To effectively monitor learning at all levels requires clarity and structure regarding who and what are being monitored. A district monitoring system, according to Smith (2015), looks at numeric data, SMART goals (or goals that are specific and strategic, measurable, attainable, results oriented, and time bound; Conzemius & O'Neill, 2014), programmatic artifacts, and cultural artifacts. At the team level, such information includes data from team-developed common formative assessments. At the site level, the data monitoring must include team formative assessment data, intervention results, English learner fluency and redesignation data, and some summative data as well. District-level data monitoring should include all areas of an effective assessment system, including formative assessment data and district summative data (both locally generated data from district assessments and data from required state summative assessments).

Monitoring SMART goals indicates not only when goals are met but also—and more important—at what level they are met, which is critical. Teams must always have high expectations of their students and of themselves if they are going to see improved learning outcomes. Monitoring SMART goals is an important point of focus on an improvement journey and a measure of reliability.

Programmatic and cultural artifacts are both great resources for measuring team, site, and system growth and needs. These items include a broad spectrum of artifacts, including team meeting agendas and minutes, team norms, rubric ratings, and survey results. The important thing to remember when establishing a monitoring system or protocol is leaders of learning at all levels—the collaborative teacher team leader, site principals, and superintendents—must monitor the things that give them the right data, turn the data into information, and then, most important of all, take action based on what the data and information tell them. Having data is important; responding to the data is essential! Table 14.1 provides clarity regarding what an effective leveled monitoring structure or protocol might look like.

> *Teams must always have high expectations of their students and of themselves if they are going to see improved learning outcomes.*

Table 14.1: Data-Monitoring Protocol

Monitoring Group	Group Being Monitored	Qualities Being Monitored
Grade-level and department teams	Team members	• Common formative assessment data correlated with instructional practices • Reteaching and enrichment data focused on best practices • Achievement of SMART goals
Site guiding coalition	Grade-level and department teams	• Numerical data showing student achievement and learning from common formative assessments and focusing on summative data and achievement of SMART goals • Programmatic artifacts—norms, agendas, minutes, rubric ratings, and the achievement of SMART goals • Cultural artifacts—self-assessment surveys, attendance records, deviations from norms, and specific interpersonal conflicts
District leadership and district guiding coalition	Site guiding coalition	• Numerical data showing student achievement and learning by grade level and department and focusing on summative data and achievement of SMART goals • Programmatic artifacts demonstrating the range of team progress—norms, agendas, minutes, rubric ratings, and the achievement of SMART goals • Cultural artifacts—overall school self-assessment surveys, team participation and buy-in information, and staff's programmatic concerns

Source: Smith, 2015, p. 48.

Monitoring team development and growth requires that you, as a system, first identify and develop clarity and commitment to some descriptors of team development and function and then descriptions of team function at each level. Sanger's assistant superintendent for curriculum and instruction developed what we called our *spectrum of learning*, which identified five stages of team development and team function at each level.

1. **Learning stage:** Teams are learning the basic concepts, vocabulary, and processes of a PLC.

2. **Literal stage:** Staff have developed a basic understanding of the PLC vocabulary and processes. Collaborative teams can move through the process of answering the four critical questions by using notes and a flowchart.

3. **Refinement stage:** The team understands PLC processes and is working to streamline its work and become more proficient in its practices.

4. **Internalized stage:** The team fully grasps the concepts and process of a PLC. The team's practices become an internalized part of what it does as a team.

5. **Refinement stage:** The team now can use the PLC concepts and processes to problem solve, teach others in the organization, and apply team members' understanding to new situations.

As a district, we then incorporated these stages of development into rubrics that described key aspects of our grade-level and subject-matter teams' work and the developmental levels where individuals and teams were currently functioning. Our rubric for PLC developmental reflection and monitoring listed *foundational PLC elements*, which included establishing a collaborative culture, having a guaranteed curriculum, using common assessments, ensuring learning, and enriching learning, and descriptors of team development stages for each element. (For a free reproducible version of the actual rubric, visit **go.SolutionTree.com/PLCbooks**.) Principals used these rubrics to monitor and rate team development. Teams would use them to self-reflect and self-evaluate their own development. Interestingly, when site-level collaborative teams first engaged in the process, we discovered team self-ratings of development were generally always higher than the principal's ratings. As every site continued this process over time, we found the ratings shifted and teams were rating themselves lower than the principal did. Our system leaders at all levels realized the better we got at this work, the more accurately teams, having developed deeper understanding of the work, would reflect on how much more they needed to grow! That's a great place to be since it promotes a growth mentality.

Monitoring work products and team artifacts is helpful and necessary, but so, too, is monitoring the actual work of the teams. I previously discussed the need to develop a common language as a system and why it is especially important staff understand the actions that the vocabulary describes or represents. To develop clarity regarding team actions, our assistant superintendent, Rich Smith, developed a flowchart that outlined the flow of the work and served as a monitoring tool for teams, site leadership, and district leadership. The flowchart in figure 14.1 (page 406) lists team actions for each of the four critical questions.

This flowchart (see figure 14.1, page 406) served as both a monitoring tool and a coaching tool. District leaders have the responsibility to ensure such tools are available and teams utilize them.

Monitoring artifacts and work products is necessary and fairly easy to structure; however, how do district-level leaders, including the superintendent, monitor the understanding and focus of the site leaders guiding the work? That question arose in a conversation I was having with our assistant superintendent one morning early on in our PLC

> Monitoring work products and team artifacts is helpful and necessary, but so, too, is monitoring the actual work of the teams.

journey. District leaders thought principals were leading well. In conversations, they would say the right things, but it wasn't clear how well they really understood what they were expected to lead.

The assistant superintendent at Sanger had an idea to address the issue—a process based on his experiences in a previous district. Two days later, the superintendent and assistant superintendent met again and refined his vision and embarked on a monitoring process known as the *Sanger Summits*. The summits became an annual event early each fall. The format required principals to develop a specific and

1. What do we want students to learn?

- Identify essential standards.
- Understand (unpack) each standard.

2. How will we know if students are learning?

- Develop a common formative assessment.
- Set a SMART goal.
- Deliver the lesson.
- Check for student understanding.
- Appropriately adjust instruction.
- Give a common formative assessment.
- Analyze the data.
- Plan based on common formative assessment results.

3. How will we respond when students don't learn?

- Reteach, individualize, form small groups, deploy for interventions, and so on.
- Reassess learning.

4. How will we extend learning for students who are already proficient?

- Enrich and deepen the learning.
- Produce a product based on the standard.

Source: Adapted from Johnson, 2015, p. 55.

Figure 14.1: Flowchart for answering the four critical questions of a PLC.

focused forty-five-minute summary of their school achievement data for a multiyear period, both overall and disaggregated by subgroups. Principals reported on what they believed was the reason their student achievement data had improved (assuming they had improved) and what their plan was to generate continued improvement in the current year. The principals then summarized the status of their PLC work and team development and function, how their school staff were supporting English learners, and what their school intervention structures looked like. Principals explained how they were working to improve their interventions for struggling students. The Sanger Summits lasted an hour, with the last fifteen minutes reserved for questions. Each day of the summit featured a group of three presenting principals, the superintendent, and all assistant superintendents (of curriculum and instruction, human resources, and business services), who all needed to deeply understand and support student learning. Principals (especially those who had not yet presented) could choose to attend some or all of their peers' summits, both as a support for their colleagues and to learn from them. Also observing were directors, coordinators, and other staff, both certificated and classified, whose job was to support the work at the school sites. It was fascinating to see the audience grow as our process improved. It was not uncommon to see directors of food service, business services, grounds and maintenance, and transportation there to learn about site work and then ponder how their teams could contribute to supporting student learning. We also began to have audience members from other California school districts—and from districts as far away as New York.

Looking back, I think the Sanger Summits process, while intended to help district leaders monitor site development, may have been the most powerful professional learning strategy we implemented for principals as well. During the first year of summits, we discovered principals didn't understand the PLC process deeply, and most of them learned the same thing themselves. District leadership deliberately did not develop a template for the principals' summit presentations—but instead developed just a set of presentation expectations. Principals used a variety of approaches, including overhead slides, science fair–style display boards, and other low-tech approaches, until one principal showed up with full-color bound copies of his PowerPoint presentation. That set a high bar for all future presentations and sent some principals scrambling to up their games. The process caused principals to look deeply at their data and systems. That deep understanding served them well to lead the work.

Over time, the summit process began to appear at the site level as well; for instance, Sanger High School began having a summit process every fall. Each department would present a summit to the entire staff, during which each department's staff reviewed data from the previous year (their strengths and gaps) and plans for improving student learning as a department. After developing the summit process, district leadership realized that we needed to develop a set of leadership expectations to help site principals understand their roles, which site principals received prior to the end of the school year. The summits and principal expectations were powerful monitoring structures that supported developing systemwide clarity regarding our progress on the journey of becoming a PLC.

Cultivating a Collaborative Culture

Cultivating a culture of collaboration is the second big idea of a PLC (DuFour et al., 2016) and part of level 1 (a safe, supportive, and collaborative culture) in the work of becoming an HRS. Too many leaders downplay the need to focus on culture and believe if they bring in a great motivational speaker to start the year and have a collective warm and fuzzy moment, they have done their job and influenced their culture. That warm and fuzzy moment may be a part of the process, but it will not have sufficient long-term impact nor result in lasting cultural change. Marzano clearly supports the importance of a collaborative culture in the work of HRS when he states:

> *That warm and fuzzy moment may be a part of the process, but it will not have sufficient long-term impact nor result in lasting cultural change.*

> A high reliability school does not leave the culture up to chance or happenstance. Rather, leaders in HRS strive to ensure the organization fosters shared beliefs, behaviors and norms relative to at least three areas: (1) Safety, (2) Support, and (3) Collaboration. Although they might also include other areas, these three are essential areas of focus and concern. Of the three, collaboration serves as the keystone. Collaboration fostered by the PLC process works as the engine of Level 1 in the HRS model. (Marzano et al., 2018, p. 37)

So often, organizational culture in education seems to focus on maintaining the comfort and convenience of adults, rather than on improving outcomes for all students. Before becoming a PLC, Sanger's culture could be described as adult focused. I realized one of my main responsibilities as superintendent was to change the culture and focus of the district. Changing a culture is hard; it requires modifying or changing assumptions, habits, and beliefs, and raising expectations—ultimately, changing "the way we do things around here." That change requires a deliberate and ongoing leadership investment. The payoff for that leadership investment in shifting the organization's culture to a collaborative culture and becoming a PLC is large because, as Marzano describes it, "When educators meet and work in high performing collaborative teams, everything else seems to run more smoothly" (Marzano et al., 2018, p. 38).

When I first began to address cultural change, I used the verb *build* to describe the process ("We need to build a collaborative culture"). About five years into the ongoing conversation about cultural change, I realized I was using the wrong verb. Rick DuFour used the verb *cultivate* for a reason in his presentations; it describes a different process than building. When you build something, you have a vision of an outcome. You develop a plan, take action, and *bang*—you are done. It is built. Cultivation, on the other hand, is an ongoing process. A farmer does not walk out into a field and scatter seed and come back in six months to harvest the crop. He preps the field, carefully plants seeds, waters, and nurtures and protects the growing crop. After making the shift from *build* to *cultivate* in my internal conversation, I was surprised to read DuFour's words in his introduction to Marzano et al.'s (2018) book *Leading a High Reliability School*. DuFour says, "The second big idea driving the PLC process is that for a school to help all students learn, it must build a collaborative culture in which members take collective responsibility for all students" (as cited in Marzano et al., 2018, p. 5). I was confused. Do we build or cultivate culture? The answer is actually both. Consider the following example.

My lovely wife Penni grew up on a farm and loves to grow things. She especially likes having a vegetable garden. We moved to a home that did not have an area for a garden, but it did have a long concrete strip along one side of the house. My wife ordered a planter kit online and built a multilevel wooden frame on the concrete. Once she had built the framework, she could begin the cultivation process that requires she tend the garden.

Leaders build a culture by creating the framework needed for staff to function collaboratively. Leaders build knowledge regarding what it means to be a collaborative team, and they ensure teams have adequate time to collaborate. Leaders establish a guaranteed and viable curriculum with priority standards and then develop an assessment system anchored in team-developed common formative assessments that align with instruction of essential standards. Leaders build intervention systems and extension expectations. These actions are the framework of a collaborative culture. When leaders cultivate, they set the conditions and expectations for learning, nurture learning, and "remove the weeds"—or the distractions that might limit learning or effectiveness.

That ongoing cultivation process never ends; it monitors and addresses the habits and behaviors of staff that must change. I have often reminded leaders that the worst behaviors in the culture of any organization define what the organization is willing to tolerate. PLC leaders set the expectations and hold everyone accountable. This requires leaders live the change they hope to see in their organizations. Leaders must constantly message the importance of collaboration to all staff, and leaders must also be role models of collaboration. Actions speak louder than words.

> Leaders build a culture by creating the framework needed for staff to function collaboratively.

If leaders set an expectation for change in the organization, they also have an obligation to ensure staff have the capacity to meet the expectation—leaders must also build organizational capacity.

Building Capacity, Over and Over Again

Leaders expect improvement in outcomes, but they must also invest in building capacity of staff to improve. Building capacity on what is needed to accomplish the most important work, whether it is giving high-quality initial instruction, identifying and unpacking essential standards, or developing and aligning common formative assessments with essential learning, is not a one-time conversation. Building capacity must be a continuous and repeated process of learning.

Admittedly, the most powerful and effective form of professional learning is job-embedded. Team conversations about best practice (as evidenced by student learning data) are a powerful form of job-embedded professional learning. There are times, however, when leaders and staff need to engage in more traditional professional development, such as training to develop initial awareness and understanding. At Sanger, for example, the district superintendent set an expectation to become a PLC as a district. The district leadership began to send groups of principals and teachers to training opportunities. The district sent principals more than once to deepen their understanding and allow them to

> Leaders expect improvement in outcomes, but they must also invest in building capacity of staff to improve.

learn with and guide the learning of their teachers. Even when the district had exposed all staff and teachers to initial learning, the focus on learning and becoming a PLC didn't stop. The district began again refreshing the understanding of those who had already had training and included those who were new to the organization. The superintendent and assistant superintendent developed what they called the *Golden Gate* approach to professional development.

Imagine your job is to paint the Golden Gate Bridge. You begin painting at one end. You paint every day until you have painted your way across the bridge. The day you finish, you pick up your paint bucket, walk back to the starting point, and begin again. Why? Because where you first began painting, there is probably some rust developing. If we, as a district, are going to become a high-functioning collaborative culture, a high-functioning PLC, and an effective HRS, then we must embrace continuous learning. Sometimes this means repeating the same essential foundational learning to keep from getting rusty.

If the leadership responsibilities I have described so far seem overwhelming, the final section that follows will give you cause for celebration.

Celebrating Success to Sustain Momentum

I have spent quite a bit of time backpacking in the Sierra Nevada Mountains near my home. The backcountry is spectacular, but getting there can be a lot of work. The climb is hard, and the pack on your back gets heavy. If, with each step, I continuously looked at the path ahead, the climb still to come, I could easily become overwhelmed. I've realized that every now and then, I need to step off the path, take off my pack, and look back down the path to see how far I have come. That short time of reflection helps me approach the next portion of the climb with a fresh perspective and motivation.

Our journey in schools is similar in many ways; it is discouraging to see only the work yet to be done. Every now and then, in order to renew our energy and focus, we need to remind ourselves of how much work we have already done. Celebrations, when done well and for the right reasons, can provide the same sense of renewal and focus as stopping to reflect on

> Every now and then, in order to renew our energy and focus, we need to remind ourselves of how much work we have already done.

a hike. DuFour et al. (2016) highlight the need for and importance of celebrations:

> When celebrations continually remind people of the purpose and priorities of their organizations, members are more likely to embrace the purpose and work toward agreed-on priorities. Regular public recognition of specific collaborative efforts, accomplished tasks, achieved goals, team learning, continuous improvement, and support for student learning reminds staff of the collective commitments to create a PLC. The word *recognize* comes from the Latin "to know again." Recognition provides opportunities to say, "Let us all be reminded and let us all know again what is important, what we value, and what we are committed to do. Now let's all pay tribute to someone in the organization who is living the commitment. (pp. 221–222)

To be effective, celebrations must be meaningful and purposefully tied to accomplishing the mission and vision. In the introduction to *Leading a High Reliability School*, DuFour (Marzano et al., 2018) provides four guidelines for celebration:

1. **Explicitly state the purpose of celebration:** Continually remind staff members that celebration represents both an important strategy for reinforcing the school or district's shared mission, vision, collective commitments, and goals, and the most powerful tool for sustaining the PLC journey.

2. **Make celebration everyone's responsibility:** Everyone in the organization, not just the administration, has responsibility for recognizing extraordinary commitments. Encourage all staff members to publicly report when they appreciate and admire the work of a colleague.

3. **Establish a clear link between the recognition and the behavior or commitment you are attempting to encourage and reinforce:** Recognition must specifically link to the school's or district's mission, vision, collective commitments, and goals for it to help shape the school culture. The question, What behavior or commitment

have we attempted to encourage with this celebration?
should have a readily apparent answer.

4. **Create opportunities to have many people recognized**:
Celebration can cause disruptions and detriment if people perceive that recognition is reserved for an exclusive
few. Developing a PLC requires creating systems specifically designed not only to provide celebrations but
also to ensure that the celebrations recognize many
winners. (p. 3)

Deliberate, focused, connected, broad-based recognitions keep us
focused on the journey. While some of these celebrations should be
formal, informal focused celebrations should also be part of the process. I regularly ask administrators I mentor and coach, "How often
do you start your meetings by asking who has a win for a student that
you can celebrate?" It is a simple but powerful way to celebrate progress that keeps the conversation centered on our mission. Admittedly,
when I used this simple celebration tool myself, I had to set the stage
by listening to discussions among group members for student-based
wins and then asking the staff member to share the story. That set the
stage for staff to come to the meeting with a win to
celebrate. I have seen the wrong questions lead to
"celebrations" that are not supportive of the mission. One principal I knew would ask, "Do we have
any celebrations before we start?" and his staff
would share if it was a child's birthday or their anniversary, or if they
bought a new car over the weekend—all important to the school family, but not the celebrations that drive the mission.

Deliberate, focused, connected, broad-based recognitions keep us focused on the journey.

Peer-driven recognition can also be a powerful celebration opportunity. One year, our theme was "Be the Light," a reminder that
students must always know they are in the presence of adults who
care about them and believe in them. Building on that theme, our
principals began the Lighthouse Award. At the start of a meeting early
in the year, one principal presented another with a small model of a
lighthouse and told the story of how that principal had helped her
with a tough situation. When she gave the principal the lighthouse
in front of their peers, she said, "Here's the rule: this is yours to keep
until someone in this room is a lighthouse for you, and then you will

tell the story and pass it on." Opportunities like these provide powerful moments for celebration and serve as clear indicators that staff members have climbed another hill on the journey.

Keeping the organization focused, motivated, and committed to the work is essential to sustaining the work. Celebration is a powerful tool to provide that focus, motivation, and commitment and is definitely part of the role of leadership. It's just another way to "tend the garden" and cultivate a collaborative culture.

Conclusion

The journey toward high reliability begins with and must be built on a foundation of becoming a high-functioning PLC. DuFour describes that foundation and process: "In order for the HRS model to drive a school toward excellence, educators in the school must know that the professional learning community process represents the foundation of their efforts" (as cited in Marzano et al., 2018, p. 2). In the introduction to *Leading a High Reliability School*, DuFour continues:

The journey toward high reliability begins with and must be built on a foundation of becoming a high-functioning PLC.

> The PLC process calls for educators to work together collaboratively in recurring cycles of collective inquiry and action research to achieve better results for the students they serve. It operates under the assumption that purposeful, continuous job-embedded learning for educators is the key to improved student learning. (Marzano et al., 2018, p. 2)

Marzano et al. (2018) echo and validate DuFour's comments:

> Rick DuFour's introduction provides the context for schools that seek high reliability status using the PLC process as a foundation. Without a doubt, the PLC process, particularly as articulated by Rick and his colleagues, brings the vision of a true high reliability school within our grasp. (p. 23)

I had the absolute honor of being part of the work that transformed Sanger. It was a journey of becoming that grew out of knowing and doing. Over time, the staff changed as individuals, and as an organization shifted from "doing PLC" to *being a PLC*. We began that journey in the spring of 2005 as one of the ninety-eight lowest-achieving districts in California. In 2006, our district exited PI status—one of the first in the state to do so—and within the next three years, every school in the district had exited PI status as well. Our schools were awarded recognitions: State Distinguished Schools, Title I Achieving Schools, National Blue Ribbon Schools—schools that just a short time earlier had been labeled failures! These schools are now recognized as examples to follow. Coauthors Richard DuFour, Rebecca DuFour, Robert Eaker, and Gayle Karhanek (2010) acknowledge Sanger's transformation and turnaround:

> Clearly, the Sanger mantra—(1) the job of every person in this district is to ensure student learning, (2) hoping things will get better is not a strategy, (3) don't blame the kids, and (4) the best strategy for sustained, substantive improvement is developing our capacity to work as members of a PLC—has benefited the students served by this district. May that mantra become the norm in districts across North America. (p. 162)

If you hope to lead your school or district down a path to high reliability, know the journey begins with, and will continuously build and improve on, becoming a PLC. As the leader of this work, you must build your own knowledge and understanding, build your guiding coalitions, and lead by example. Live the work.

Finally, consider this: don't set a goal of being like Sanger. Set your goal to become better than Sanger in every way, every day. Your students are depending on you. Every child, every day, whatever it takes.

References and Resources

Conzemius, A. E., & O'Neill, J. (2014). *The handbook for SMART school teams: Revitalizing best practices for collaboration* (2nd ed.). Bloomington, IN: Solution Tree Press.

David, J. L., & Talbert, J. (2013). *Turning around a high-poverty district: Learning from Sanger.* San Francisco: Cowell Foundation.

DuFour, R., DuFour, R., Eaker, R., & Karhanek, G. (2010). *Raising the bar and closing the gap: Whatever it takes.* Bloomington, IN: Solution Tree Press.

DuFour, R., DuFour, R., Eaker, R., & Many, T. W. (2006). *Learning by doing: A handbook for Professional Learning Communities at Work* (1st ed.). Bloomington, IN: Solution Tree Press.

DuFour, R., DuFour, R., Eaker, R., & Many, T. W. (2010). *Learning by doing: A handbook for Professional Learning Communities at Work* (2nd ed.). Bloomington, IN: Solution Tree Press.

DuFour, R., DuFour, R., Eaker, R., Many, T. W., & Mattos, M. (2016). *Learning by doing: A handbook for Professional Learning Communities at Work* (3rd ed.). Bloomington, IN: Solution Tree Press.

DuFour, R., & Fullan, M. (2013). *Cultures built to last: Systemic PLCs at Work.* Bloomington, IN: Solution Tree Press.

DuFour, R., & Marzano, R. J. (2011). *Leaders of learning: How district, school, and classroom leaders improve student achievement.* Bloomington, IN: Solution Tree Press.

Elmore, R. F. (2000). *Building a new structure for school leadership* [White paper]. Washington, DC: Shanker Institute.

Elmore, R. F. (2002). *Bridging the gap between standards and achievement: The imperative for professional development in education* [White paper]. Washington, DC: Shanker Institute.

Fullan, M. (2014). *The principal: Three keys to maximizing impact.* San Francisco: Jossey-Bass.

Johnson, M. (2015). *How to coach leadership in a PLC.* Bloomington, IN: Solution Tree Press.

Marzano, R. J., Warrick, P. B., Rains, C. L., & DuFour, R. (2018). *Leading a high reliability school.* Bloomington, IN: Solution Tree Press.

Marzano, R. J., Warrick, P. B., & Simms, J. A. (2014). *A handbook for high reliability schools: The next step in school reform.* Bloomington, IN: Marzano Resources.

McLaughlin, M. W., & Talbert, J. (2006). *Building school-based teacher learning communities: Professional strategies to improve student achievement.* New York: Teachers College Press.

Schmoker, M. (2004). Learning communities at the crossroads: Toward the best schools we've ever had. *Phi Delta Kappan, 86*(1), 84–88.

Smith, W. R. (2015). *How to launch PLCs in your district.* Bloomington, IN: Solution Tree Press.

Index

Learning by Doing, Third Edition
Richard DuFour, Rebecca DuFour, Robert Eaker, Thomas W. Many, and Mike Mattos
The third edition of this comprehensive action guide includes new strategies, tools, and tips for transforming your school or district into a high-performing PLC.
BKF746

A Handbook for High Reliability Schools
Robert J. Marzano, Phil Warrick, and Julia A. Simms
Transform schools into organizations that take proactive steps to ensure student success using a research-based five-level hierarchy and leading and lagging indicators.
BKL020

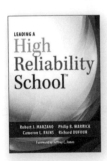

Leading a High Reliability School™
Robert J. Marzano, Philip B. Warrick, Cameron L. Rains, and Richard DuFour
Learn how and why High Reliability Schools use interdependent systems of operation and the PLC at Work® process to establish and maintain school effectiveness.
BKF795

The Leading Edge™ series
The *Leading Edge*™ series unites education authorities from around the globe and asks them to confront the important issues that affect teachers and administrators and impact student success.
BKF180, BKF232, BKF254, BKF278, BKF389, BKF358, BKF399, BKF552, BKF622, BKF659